Child Sexual Abuse within the Family:

Assessment and Treatment

Child Sexual Abuse within the Family:

Assessment and Treatment

The work of the Great Ormond Street Sexual Abuse Team

Edited by

Arnon Bentovim
Anne Elton
Judy Hildebrand
Marianne Tranter
Eileen Vizard

WRIGHT

London   Boston   Singapore   Sydney   Toronto   Wellington

John Wright
is an imprint of Butterworth Scientific

First published 1988

© **Butterworth & Co. (Publishers) Ltd, 1988**

British Library Cataloguing in Publication Data

Bentovim, Arnon
  Child sexual abuse within the family:
  assessment and treatment: the work of the
  Great Ormond Street Sexual Abuse Team.
  1. Child molesting—Great Britain
  I. Title
  362.7'044   HQ72.G7

ISBN 0 7236 0634 X

Photoset by EJS Chemical Composition, Midsomer Norton, Bath

Printed and bound in Great Britain by Page Bros Ltd, Norwich, Norfolk

Preface

This book resulted from experiences gained in setting up and running an assessment and treatment programme to manage cases of 'Child Sexual Abuse within the Family', in the Department of Psychological Medicine at The Hospital for Sick Children, Great Ormond Street, London. The work arose out of a research project on the incidence of sexual abuse in the community carried out in 1980. It was a natural consequence of asking various professionals to fill out questionnaires on cases that they were seeing; they then asked us to assist them in providing therapeutic work for the cases. In this hospital we have been concerned with the management of general cases of child abuse for many years, since the time that Henry Kempe described 'The Battered Child Syndrome' in 1962. In the Department of Psychological Medicine facilities have been developed to help abused children and their families, for example, in the Day Centre. Consultation services have been offered by the hospital to the community in the management of the crisis stages of child abuse, and in helping other agencies to think about the needs of children and the possibilities for treatment of families. Therefore, it seemed a natural development to become involved with the treatment of sexual abuse once we became aware of the extent of the problem.

We are grateful to our colleagues in the Department of Psychological Medicine who facilitated the development of this service, despite their anxieties that it might take over from all other work. In our view child psychiatric teams are uniquely placed to deal with the problem of sexual abuse in the family, since assessment requires skills for interviewing children to make an accurate diagnosis, and also for working with individuals and with families to assess the possibilities for treatment. In addition, skills are needed in working therapeutically with families and with groups of children and parents.

We were fortunate to have working in the department individuals with the appropriate background skills and experience to initiate the project and to learn from the families and from our colleagues in other countries.

The programme was initiated by Arnon Bentovim, Tillman Furniss, Marianne Tranter and Liza Miller, in 1981. Many colleagues have joined us to work for varying periods with the project, including Eileen Vizard, Anne Elton, Judy Hildebrand, Libby Read, Tom Moran, Malcolm Wiseman, Alan Jacobs and Alixe Kent and many trainees in psychiatry, social work and psychology who have worked jointly with us, with children and with their families individually and in groups.

We have also been helped by many visitors who have spent time with us on visits and sabbatical leave, for example, Professor Ken Finkel from Canada and Dr John Leventhal from the USA. John Leventhal has been particularly helpful in reading the penultimate draft of the book and in making many detailed suggestions which have helped us to produce the final draft. Other colleagues, including Professor Jean La Fontaine, Dr David Jones, Dr Marylin Meyer, Mrs Annie Shepherd and Dr Alan McClelland have given us valuable advice on drafts of various chapters. Although the editors have taken responsibility for the various chapters of the book, the work presented represents contributions from many different members of the team in providing a coherent and rich account of our work.

We are grateful to the Joint Research Board of the Hospital for Sick Children and the Institute of Family Therapy, London, who made us grants to enable a research worker (Paula Boston) to carry out a review of a large number of families, to set up a prospective study and follow up a significant number of cases reported in the book. Members of the Academic Department of Child Psychiatry of the Institute of Child Health, Professor Philip Graham and Dr Marjorie Smith, helped facilitate the research and have given valuable advice on matters of statistics and questionnaire design. The Family Studies Fund of the hospital helped support Annemarie van Elburg to carry out the follow-up study, and other colleagues, including Josephine O'Donaghue, Jean La Fontaine, Betty Ann Smith and Esther Delaplane, gave valuable assistance in reading case notes and coding information towards the research. Dr Alan Hume, of the University of London Computer Advisory Centre, gave very considerable assistance with computer programming and program design.

We would also like to express our appreciation to the many secretaries who have supported our work and borne the stress of having to type extensive and often very distressing reports. Julia Claxton played a central organizing role earlier on and Jenny Ashford typed the many drafts of the chapters in this book. Her ability to work with dedication and with tolerance has been one of the most helpful factors in enabling us to complete the work.

In addition we would like to thank colleagues from other agencies, for example, Carolyn Okell-Jones who shared the first Parents Group with us, and the very many professionals, social workers, probation officers, foster parents and residential workers who have been so willing to work cooperatively with us, to complete our questionnaires, to bring families and children to family meetings and groups, and to carry out an enormous amount of devoted work with the children and families.

We would also like to thank the parents and children who have taught us so much about the painful and difficult issues which arise while trying to work with the problem of child sexual abuse in the family. Feedback from them has undoubtedly helped us to develop our treatment programme which will hopefully better meet the needs of our clients.

A. B.
A. E.
J. H.
M. T.
E. V.
June 1987

Contributors

Arnon Bentovim MB BS (Lond.), FRCPsych., DPM (Univ. Lond.)
Consultant Psychiatrist, The Hospital For Sick Children, Great
Ormond Street, and The Tavistock Clinic London. Senior Lecturer
(Hon.), The Institute of Child Health, London.

Paula A. Boston LSW Clinical Social Worker, The American
Embassy, London. Formerly Research Worker, The Hospital for
Sick Children, Great Ormond Street, London.

Anne Elton MA, AAPSW
Principal Psychiatric Social Worker, The Hospital for Sick
Children, Great Ormond Street, London.

Judy Hildebrand CQSW
Director, Institute of Family Therapy, London. Formerly Senior
Psychiatric Social Worker, The Hospital for Sick Children, Great
Ormond Street, London.

Marianne Tranter BSc, CQSW
Psychiatric Social Worker, The Hospital for Sick Children, Great
Ormond Street, London.

Annemarie van Elburg MD
Registrar, 'Vignerdal' Hospital, Maastricht, Holland. Formerly
Clinical Assistant and Research Worker, The Hospital for Sick
Children, Great Ormond Street, London.

Eileen Vizard MRCPsych.
Consultant Child and Adolescent Psychiatrist, Newham Area
Health Authority, Lecturer in Child Psychiatry, The London
Hospital Medical College. Formerly Senior Registrar, The
Hospital for Sick Children, Great Ormond Street, London.

Contents

Chapter 1   Sexual Abuse, Sexuality and Childhood   1
             Arnon Bentovim and Eileen Vizard

Chapter 2   Sexual Abuse—Basic Issues—Characteristics of   16
             Children and Families
             Arnon Bentovim and Paula Boston

Chapter 3   Understanding the Phenomenon of Sexual Abuse—   40
             A Family Systems View of Causation
             Arnon Bentovim

Chapter 4   Recognition and Assessment of Child Sexual Abuse   59
             Eileen Vizard and Marianne Tranter

Chapter 5   Helping Young Children to Describe Experiences   84
             of Child Sexual Abuse—General Issues
             Eileen Vizard and Marianne Tranter

Chapter 6   Helping Children to Describe Experiences of   105
             Child Sexual Abuse—A Guide to Practice
             Eileen Vizard and Marianne Tranter

Chapter 7   The Professional Network and the Management   130
             of Disclosure
             Marianne Tranter and Eileen Vizard

Chapter 8   Assessment of Families for Treatment   153
             Anne Elton

Chapter 9   Treatment Methods and Techniques   182
             Anne Elton

Chapter 10   The Use of Groupwork in Treating Child   205
             Sexual Abuse
             Judy Hildebrand

Chapter 11   Working with Substitute Carers   238
             Anne Elton

Chapter 12   The Results of Treatment   252
             Arnon Bentovim, Annemarie van Elburg and
             Paula Boston

Appendix 1   Transcript of Interview with Sexually Abused   269
             Children
             Marianne Tranter and Eileen Vizard

Appendix 2   An Assessment Interview   280
             Arnon Bentovim

Appendix 3   Treatment Process—Case Study of the   289
             Jones Family
             Arnon Bentovim

Appendix 4   Detailed Group Programmes   300
             Judy Hildebrand

Index   321

Aims of the book

This book aims to describe the treatment of sexual abuse in the family. We consider sexual abuse as a form of child abuse which requires treatment to be carried out in a context of protection of that child. To achieve a proper degree of protection needs an appropriate legal framework.

We will deal with the following issues:

1. The definition of sexual abuse as a phenomenon.
2. Its relationship to sexuality in childhood, and social attitudes to the sexuality of the child.
3. Factors that lead to the occurrence and maintenance of sexual abuse as a phenomenon.
4. The early recognition, assessment and management of sexual abuse.
5. The legal context for the treatment of sexual abuse.
6. The stages of treatment of sexual abuse including family and group work.
7. Ways of working with children who cannot live with their own families and need to be placed in foster and residential care.
8. The results of treatment.

CHAPTER 1

Sexual Abuse, Sexuality and Childhood

Arnon Bentovim and Eileen Vizard

INTRODUCTION AND DEFINITION

Recent interest in sexual abuse as a problem has arisen from the convergence of concerns of two basic groups:[3]

1. The "child abuse" lobby which sees sexual abuse as a major form of abuse whose occurrence needs to be a recognized syndrome, along with physical abuse, neglect, failure-to-thrive syndromes and emotional abuse.[4]
2. The feminist movement which points out that sexual abuse is the most striking example of the exploitation and use of women and children by men.[5] Such views are supported by sociological theorists,[6] who see child abuse as a reflection of societal attitudes and see sexual abuse as a manifestation of social problems reflected in the life of the family, and in attitudes to children.

The best definition that we have of child sexual abuse is that put forward by Schechter and Roberge,[1] advocated by Henry and Ruth Kempe.[2] They define sexual abuse as "the involvement of dependent, developmentally immature children and adolescents in sexual activities they do not truly comprehend and to which they are unable to give informed consent and that violate the sexual taboos of family roles".

Before describing such activities in detail we need to consider:

1. The sexual development of children.
2. 'Normal' sexual activities in childhood.
3. Is it possible for a child to 'consent' to sexual activities with an adult?
4. What are the normal taboos on family roles, relationships and sexual activities?

1

SEXUAL DEVELOPMENT AND THE SEXUAL ACTIVITIES OF CHILDHOOD

Biological Factors

Detailed observation and experimental work with infants has shown that sexual behaviour is present from infancy (*see* the examples below):

1. Genital play and masturbation to the point of orgasm is noted in very young children, as young as six months.[7–9,19]
2. Erections have been observed in the male infant.
3. Vaginal lubrication occurs less certainly in female infants.[10,11]
4. Sexual 'mounting' activities have been described in young children related both to peers and care-takers.[11] Comparisons have been made with the mounting behaviour of young rhesus monkeys as with other forms of sexual play. Such behavioural patterns are explained as being 'innate characteristics' triggered by the normal hormonal activity of childhood.[12]

Gender Identity and Sexual Knowledge

The vast majority of very young children have a well-established sense of gender identity, (i.e., of being male or female) by the age of five years. Direct questioning in one study[13] together with observation of written compositions of sexuality seem to support this observation. When children are asked to distinguish between drawings, photographs or dolls of different gender, they are readily able to do so. They often show a surprising knowledge of the anatomical sexual differences between males and females. Three-year-old children are quoted who knew of the existence of the vagina in women, although they lacked the language to describe such body parts.[14]

So ordinarily children are aware of the anatomical basis for gender identity. They know that penises identify maleness and vaginas femaleness. However, their understanding of the function of genitals is very much more limited.

Children under the age of five would not be expected to know the details of sexual intercourse. By comparison, a quite sophisticated level of understanding about sexuality is often found in older children, around the age of 12. It has been observed[13] that sex education exists on a peer level anyway in schools whatever the formal curriculum content. Parents are often less aware of their children's knowledge, and children often play the game of 'ignorance' so as not to 'disturb' the family.[15]

With the availability of videos with explicit sexual content, it is becoming far more difficult to know what a child should or should not know about sexual matters, for example, intercourse. There is a pressing need for research on the effects on children who see explicit sexual material. It is now known that exposure to video violence may have a deleterious effect on childrens' behaviour.[16] It would be helpful to know if the effects on children of seeing sexual activities are persistent, and if there are long-standing behavioural and interactional effects.

Therefore the assumption that children who show unusual degrees of knowledge must have had inappropriate experiences has to be set against the fact that children may acquire a great deal more information vicariously, and distinct from direct experiences with peers and family members.

EARLY SEXUAL ACTIVITIES

Masturbation and Early Sex Play

Masturbation in infancy is commonplace. We know a great deal more about masturbation and sexual behaviour at puberty (e.g. see Schofield[17]). Elias and Gebhart's study[18] reports on patterns of masturbation from interviews with prepubertal boys and girls. The percentages admitting to masturbation (55 per cent in boys and 30 per cent in girls) were close to those obtained from retrospective studies with adults. Similarly, sex play between peers for both boys and girls was surprisingly common. An interesting finding was that while masturbation starting in childhood was likely to carry on into adolescence in both boys and girls, by contrast, prepubertal sex play with peers usually stopped in girls and often stopped in middle-class boys. Working-class boys continued more active sex play, and were also deemed twice as likely to masturbate as middle-class children, and three times as likely to have attemped intercourse during sex play.

In some ways these findings[18] bear out Kinsey's[19] earlier findings that sexual experimentation in childhood was surpisingly common and sexual activities in adolescence are also very common. Differences between working-class and more middle-class children are difficult to interpret. They may be connected with social class attitudes towards sexuality which reinforce or inhibit certain patterns, including class-based peer group and friendship patterns, lack of privacy in homes, and the consequential lack of privacy in interpersonal physical relationships.

Many studies have looked at so-called 'normal' patterns of sexually explorative behaviour and masturbation, but do not ask questions about, for instance, the persistence of the sort of behaviour which we will later (*see* Chapters 2 and 4) see as early indicators of sexual abuse. Behaviours giving rise to concern include compulsive masturbation in young children, sexualized behaviour, promiscuousness with other children, or an inappropriate sexualized approach to adults. We do not know what percentage of children who have been sexually abused do present with these symptoms, nor do we know about the frequency of such symptomatology in childhood in general, and the exact mechanisms which lead to them. However, Sroufe and Ward's[20] work has shown that sexualized ways of controlling children, for example, touching genitals, kissing in a mouth-to-mouth fashion, can connect with the mother's own sexual abusive experiences.

The So-called 'Latency' Period

The concept of latency was Freud's attempt[21] to explain the fact that sexuality appeared to become latent following the passionate sexual attachments of early childhood. Children appeared to 'turn away' from their parents as sexual objects and became interested in the world of school and the external world. The formulation of sexuality becoming latent emerged from Freud's way of attempting to understand neurotic behaviour. His early analytical work explained emotional illnesses through the effect of trauma and seduction. Sexual seduction by adults was seen as a cause of widespread disturbance. The notion that common emotional illnesses could be 'caused' by seduction, which by implication must also be a common occurrence, was shocking.[23] Freud shifted in his thinking to an increasingly 'intra-psychic' view—of 'conflict' *in the mind*—as causing neurotic behaviour, rather than as a result of trauma. So that instead of sexual 'seduction' being seen as the cause, sexual wishes and drives coming from inside the individual were the danger and had to be dealt with, for example, by repression of the original impulses and replacements with 'actions'. These could include neurotic symptoms (e.g., obsessional rituals) or behavioural problems (e.g., conduct problems).[22] A healthy response could be diversion of sexual wishes to work and learning. Wish fulfilment could occur so that there might be a reversal, from I *want* Daddy to give me the baby he gave Mummy, to Daddy *did* give me the baby like he gave Mummy. So that in this way, trauma becomes wish fulfilment.

There were many other authorities who wanted to see sexuality as 'latent' or even preferably absent. The Christian/Catholic Church propagated notions of childhood innocence. Similarly respectable women, like children, were not supposed to have sexual feelings and both women and children were seen as the 'property' of their male care-takers.

To help explode such myths, it helps to look at how children actually think. In the study by Janus and Bess,[13] 3200 children from a New York sample were studied. Essays and picture drawings were analysed for overt and covert sexual material. Gender identity and topic compositions were given. The overall conclusions of this study were that the latency period is a myth. In this day and age children are exposed to continuing stimulation from sexualized material, both in media and also in the form of often covert discussion with peers at school. What is of interest is how the social skills develop which help a child not to 'show' or 'display' his or her sexuality in an inappropriately open way. Rules of modesty develop in family and social contexts through cues and responses from adults to children when they act inappropriately which create and reinforce boundaries and rules of modesty.

Rosenfeld's[15] observations of the way modesty develops in families support this. He observed that parents stopped walking around in the nude when they *thought* that their children were observing or touching them in an explicit way. The notion that children do *not* observe their parents closely all the time is of course a myth.

When the rule which sees children as being *asexual* is breached by the child *appearing* to observe or to notice, then a new rule emerges—stay dressed in front of the children. The notion of latency is a convenient one to preserve safety of children and maintain boundaries within families. It may be one of the components of the incest taboo.

Puberty and Adolescent Development

Puberty is the stage in physical development when primary and secondary characteristics accelerate in growth under the influence of significant hormonal changes. This occurs in both sexes and results in the prepubescent child becoming the sexually mature adult. While we understand a good deal about the chemistry and physiology of human puberty, there is still a great deal that is unknown and uncertain about sexual and emotional development during puberty.

There is a notion that adolescence is always a time of great turmoil, strife and mood swings. In the Isle of Wight survey,[24] severe depression and disturbance in adolescence was relatively rare, whereas transient feelings of misery and unhappiness, adolescent turmoil, were in fact quite commonplace.

Gagnon and Simon[25] have described the way in which the pre-pubertal child makes the transition from the stage of the relatively secure gender identity of middle childhood to the challenge of puberty, where a final gender identity will be tested out as 'rehearsal' for adult sexual practices. Gagnon and Simon describe 'homo-social sexual behaviour', that is a boy's or girl's 'point scoring' by notching up dates, or sexual experiences, which they then shared within the homosexual peer groups.

Puberty may also be a time when initiation rights of a sexual nature are undertaken, either voluntarily or under duress, in order to register that the adolescent has made a transition into a sexually active phase of life. La Fontaine[26] has said "initiation defines boundaries between members of a group and outsiders, between different statuses and between contrasted ideas . . . . but many rituals serve to reveal further gradations of status to which individuals aspire". A change in sexual status is one of the issues involved in puberty. This may be gradual, as with the practice of fellatio in prepubertal boys in New Guinea[27] which lasts over a number of years until manhood is achieved, or by contrast the initiation may be brief and ostensibly social, as in the (now defunct) practices of debutantes 'coming out'. The term 'coming out' is also used within the Pokot tribe in Western Kenya to refer to the emergence of adolescent girl initiates from the ordeal of public female circumcision.

Adolescent sexual development is therefore variable and there are individual influences in terms of particular growth patterns and physical characteristics, and social class and peer group influences in terms of what is expected in particular contexts. Transient periods of homosexual and heterosexual relating occur before emerging from adolescence into young adulthood with a secure adult identity.

There are individual psychosocial factors which influence sexual development in adolescence. These relate to the specific experiences the individual has had in earlier childhood, and to family influences. These set up a particular pattern of roles and expectations about sexual relationships which influence patterns of adult relating.[28] It is also possible to describe a psychological counterpart to the behaviour and activities of the young person sexually. Laufer and Laufer[29] described the way a dominating image arises around masturbatory activities. This seems to gather together the individual's set of sexual feelings and experiences throughout childhood, and play a part in influencing behaviour and attitudes to partners or to the self. It is here that inappropriate sexual activities with children can influence future development.

CAN A CHILD GIVE CONSENT TO SEXUAL ACTIVITIES WITH ADULTS?

Views about the Sexual Development of Children

There is a wide variety of sexual activities which are described during childhood and adolescence. The adult world has a variety of views about the sexual development of children and adolescents, ranging from:

1. Those who want childhood protected from knowledge about sexuality and experiences of it.
2. Those who want children to be fully informed about sexuality, and to be encouraged to experiment sexually.

The former would include some feminist groups and groups who want to prevent the possibility of contraception and contraceptive advice being available to children without parents' permission. The latter, who want childhood sexuality released, include liberal educationalists who wish to inform and facilitate children's wishes to experiment. It also includes the paedophile lobby who feel that not only should children be actively educated about sexuality, but actively encouraged to find themselves sexually by knowledgeable adults who would introduce them to the world of sexuality. Their motto is "Sex before eight or it is too late".

Sexual Information and Sexual Experiences

Is there any evidence to indicate that one or the other approach is preferable? Will young people have a better approach to sexuality if they learn about it at a later stage in their lives, will their attitudes be more healthy if they have an early experience? What is the ideal age for sexual information to be imparted to children? Should it be around adolescence when girls are beginning to develop and have periods, and boys are maturing sexually? A review by Goldman and Goldman[33] of children's views about their sexual education showed that even in countries where sexual education was given early, children thought they had been given too little information too late. This would appear to support the view that protection of children from sexual knowledge is not helpful and being properly informed enables young people to be more confident about their sexuality.

Is there any evidence that being involved sexually with an adult has a good effect on a young person's later sexual attitudes and activities? The increasing body of research on this topic indicates that although there are individuals who do not feel damaged by sexual contacts by adults, and some who feel their sexuality and sexual relationships are enhanced, the majority do appear to feel damaged.[34] There appears to be a significant distortion of the emotional mental health of the individual, his or her future pattern of sexual activities, and his or her ability to parent. It does appear that if a partner who is knowledgeable and is in a position of authority to a child initiates that child in activities he does not fully understand, it does have ill effects.[30] The child is not in a position to predict or to understand the activities in which he or she is invited to participate. In this situation there can be no proper consent, and even if through activities the child comes to want the contact it is not on a basis of full understanding and knowledge and therefore can be seen as a form of abuse. A current view of a child's rights is that he or she has a right to develop within a framework which enables him or her to take an appropriate role in society. Therefore, he or she needs the opportunity to make sexual relationships appropriate to his or her age and stage of development.

HOW DO ADULTS RATIONALIZE THEIR SEXUAL ACTIVITIES WITH CHILDREN?

Historical Views

Reviews of the incidence of sexual activities between adults and children in a number of countries are now showing just how frequently these occur. How is it that so many adults feel that being sexual with a child is an appropriate way to behave? Are there some general attitudes held towards children, both in terms of their being objects of sexual interest and about sexual activities, which are permissible towards them? De Mause[31] and Aries[32] have shown that originally parents had the right to treat children as objects to be abandoned, killed off and to be beaten, punished and used as sexual objects in any way. Parents had the right to control, shape and model children's behaviour and development. Modes vary from considerable use of force and intrusion into their lives, through a more contemporary mode of socializing, helping and facilitating children's development. Therefore, over the years parents have felt either that it is quite appropriate to shape children's sexual development by repressing it, or by encouraging, or even participating and behaving sexually with the child.

Societal Views

Do current societal views of the way children should be helped to develop entirely subscribe to the notion of facilitating and helping children's development rather than by intruding and controlling children? Current views of the use of children may well unwittingly reinforce the view of the child as property of the parents and therefore an object to be used, despite our avowed respect for childhood.

Finkelhor[3] has pointed to the use of children as 'sexual objects', for example, by giving permission for children to be used in advertising, or in the media, without considering how comfortable the child is with 'public attention', or whether it could have longer-term negative effects.

How should parents and society interpret the notion of 'childrens' rights'? Specifically when can a child be thought to be competent to decide upon how he or she uses his or her body? When is it appropriate to be able to make a decision about the purchase of contraceptives? The official age at which a young person can give consent to a sexual relationship is 16 in the UK. However, there have been moves to approve a younger age of consent in heterosexual or homosexual relationships. The view followed in this book is that when an adult is in a position of authority to a child, then the child by definition is not in a position to be able to exercise true consent, and therefore such activities do constitute a form of abuse of such authority.

ARE THERE TABOOS ON RELATIONSHIPS BETWEEN FAMILY MEMBERS?

The Incest Taboo

A further consideration in looking at relationships between related adults and children is a question of whether there is some form of universal taboo against sexual relationships. Knowledge of the incest taboo comes from anthropological work, and is of importance because it represents a mechanism which ensures that kinship ties are established, and the way rules are established about who may or may not marry. La Fontaine[34] has pointed out that there is great controversy concerning the purpose of the incest taboo and its origins. There are certainly rules in all cultures which specify who may or may not marry, and although there are differences there are no societies which currently sanction intermarriage between the closest of blood relatives. The only society which appeared to permit such marriage was in Pharonic Egypt. There are considerable differences from one society to another, so that marriage between cousins is encouraged in one society as a means of maintaining inherited wealth within the family circle. In another it is forbidden. These are clearly long-established cultural patterns, as are the ways in which children are seen and used. La Fontaine[34] has stated that "childhood ends when marriage occurs whether this is aged 9 or 19 years"· It is therefore extremely difficult to give a list of behaviours or practices which could be seen to apply from one culture to another. Rather, it seems that 'normal' sexuality and therefore 'normal childhood sexuality' can only be judged in relation to one particular society at a time, that is the one under study.

What is Considered Sexually Abusive?

This would include concepts of what is considered sexual abuse, since each culture will have its own accepted practices, some of which might certainly seem to us abusive and deviant, as in the protracted initiation rights mentioned above in New Guinea. However, Korbin[35] has pointed out that despite cultural relativism, it seems that because there are universal notions of children's developmental stages and needs, it *is* possible to recognize situations in every culture where abusive neglect or exploitation of a child's needs can occur. Korbin, for instance, has postulated three levels of child abuse:

Level one—accepted practises in one culture which are perceived as abusive in another, for example, the New Guinea initiation rites.
Level two—idiosyncratic abuse or neglect, perceived as child abuse in any culture, for example, attempted intercourse with an infant in the newborn period.
Level three—societal abuse, that is poverty and malnutrition. This might include child prostitution and pornography.

The definition of sexual abuse therefore extends beyond the incest taboo which is to do with specified forms of sexual relationships between individuals who cannot marry. Incest is seen as a criminal act of varying degrees of severity, but sexual abuse is a far more generalized pattern of sexual activities which arises out of dysfunctional family relationships and attitudes to children.

We know very little about the sociocultural variations of behaviour between adults and children around sexual matters. We know[36,37] about cultural attitudes which are permissive, for example, to peer sexual experimentation, or are punitive towards any form of sexual expression. In a Western culture Rosenfeld[15] has begun to explore the issues by asking parents what they do when a child comes into bed in the night-time, how they respond to a child observing them having sexual intercourse, attitudes towards nakedness, modesty, touching genitals and defining what makes parents dress, rather than go naked around the house.

Such research is in the early phases and illustrates how little we know about sexual forms of contact between adults and children in the community.

HOW FREQUENTLY DOES CHILD–ADULT SEXUAL CONTACT OCCUR?

What is known about the prevalence of sexual activities between adults and children in the community? Are the relatively small number of cases reported to the police or for treatment likely to be representative of the prevalence of sexual abuse in the community in general? When women write of their sexual experiences as children with adults, they indicate many years of secrecy and never having spoken of their trauma to anyone.[39] Every television or radio programme that is broadcast on the subject is followed by floods of 'phone calls to 'help-lines'. The opening of a telephone call line for children was followed by the same rush of wanting to share abusive experiences.

Referrals to Professionals

A study which looked at the pattern in cases presenting to professionals gave an overall incidence of 3 per 1000 children coming to professional notice up to the age of 15.[38,39] Sexual abuse was defined in three ways:

1. Physical abuse with some genital injury.
2. Forms of genital contact.
3. Other forms of sexual activity involving children.

Looking at these findings, three-quarters were abuse within the famility and the family context, a rate of 2 per 1000 children for abuse which involved significant genital contact, and/or intercourse (genital, oral or anal). This incidence was felt to represent a 'tip of the iceberg'. Even this survey of professionals indicated a far higher prevalence than official statistics had revealed.

Population Studies of Prevalence

Series of investigations of populations which were not gathered through professionals[38-42] have indicated the true extent of abuse. Finkelhor[40] found that some 9 per cent of boys and 19 per cent of girls in a college survey had sexual abusive experiences in childhood, 1 per cent with significant genital contact; this is 10 times more cases than those presenting to professionals.

Those abused described a significant feeling of damage, with conflict over their sexual activities and emotional problems resulting. Such effects seemed to be independent of other social and emotional factors. Baker's[41] survey of self-selected teenagers who answered a magazine questionnaire showed that few had disclosed abuse when it occurred. Russell's[40] interview studies also indicated a high level of unreported abusive experiences, as did Baker and Duncan's[42] study of men and women, which was carried out by a national poll. Although this latter study was more representative, interviews were limited to answering a brief questionnaire. Baker and Duncan's survey indicates an overall rate of abuse of 93 per 1000, and incestuous abuse at a rate of 13 in a 1000 of intrafamilial abuse. This represents at least a six-fold increase compared with cases coming to professional notice. Half the respondents described abuse within their own family context, and half abuse by total strangers. This is an interesting observation, since professionals and other surveys in fact describe more individuals abused within their own family circle than by strangers. This may be explained by the fact that of all the cases, 4 per cent reported abuse involving intercourse and 46 per cent genital contact. However, 50 per cent describe experiences, such as being exposed to without contact. This may be so common as not to be reported normally. Abuse within the family and by strangers seems to involve girls in a proportion of 2 to 1, whereas abuse in the family context (i.e., friends, known adults) involves boys (47 per cent) and girls (51 per cent) equally. Under the age of 10, girls are abused in a proportion of 3 to 1, whereas over the age of 11 abuse is reported at the same level for girls and boys. This pattern is reflected in the pattern of referral to an established sexual abuse treatment programme.

Implications of Prevalance Studies

The implications of this study[41] are that as many as 67 000 individuals across the social spectrum will experience incestuous abuse before the age of 15, and that as many as a million will experience some form of sexual abuse by the age of 15—a staggering figure which may have serious mental health implications. Taboos against sexual activities seem far less observed than was thought, and the major taboo seems to have been that of talking of sexual activities. Despite public interest in sexuality as a topic, there is a high degree of secrecy and privacy surrounding sexual activities, and sexual activities which break social roles and rules are even more secret. A father who tells his daughter that all fathers do sexual things with their children but that no one speaks about such things can be confident that the secret will be kept. Proper publicity is essential to inform children that this is not the case! Fortunately, professionals can become aware of the signs of sexual abuse and preconceptions can be explored, for example, vulvo-vaginitis is caused by soiled towels, rather than sexual contact.

References

1. Schechter M.D. and Roberge L. (1976) Sexual exploitation. In: Helfer R.E. and Kempe C.H. (eds.), *Child Abuse and Neglect: the Family and the Community*. Cambridge, Mass.: Ballinger.
2. Kempe R. and Kempe C.H. (1978) *Child Abuse*. London: Fontana/Open Books.
3. Finkelhor D. (1984) *Child Sexual Abuse: New Theory and Research*: New York: Free Press.
4. Kempe C.H. (1979) Recent Developments in the field of child abuse. *Child Abuse and Neglect* 3, ix–xv.
5. Nelson S. (1982) *Incest—Fact and Myth*. Edinburgh: Stamullion.
6. Gil D.G. (1975) Unravelling child abuse. *American Journal of Orthopsychiatry* 45, 346–56.
7. Backwin H. (1973) Erotic feelings in infants and young children. *American Journal of Diseases of Childhood* 126, 53–54.
8. Galenson E. and Roiphe H. (1974) The emergence of genital awareness during the 2nd year of life. In: Friedman R.C., Richard R.M. and R.L. Vande (eds), *Sex Differences in Behaviour*. New York: Wiley.
9. Bancroft J. (1983) Sexual development. In: *Human Sexuality and its Problems*. London: Churchill-Livingstone.
10. Lewis W.C. (1965) Coital movements in the first year of life. *International Journal of Psychoanalysis* 46, 373–374.
11. Langfeldt T. (1981) Sexual development in children. In: Coak M. and Howells K. (eds), *Adult Sexual Interest in Children*. London: Academic.
12. Rutter M. (1980) Psycho-sexual development. In: Rutter M. (ed.), *Developmental Psychiatry*. London: Heinemann.
13. Janus S.S. and Bess B.E. (1976) Latency—fact or fiction?. *American Journal of Psychoanalysis* 36, 339–340.
14. Henshall C. (1983) Investigating Young Children's Concepts of Gender. Presented at the 3rd Margaret Lowenfeld Conference, Cambridge, September 1983.
15. Rosenfeld A.A. et al. (1984) Parental perceptions of children's modesty: a cross sectional survey of ages 2–10 years. *Psychiatry* 47, 351–365.
16. Sims A. and Melville T. (1985) Survey of the opinion of child and adolescent psychiatrists on the viewing of videos by children. *Bulletin of the Royal College of Psychiatrists* 9, 238–240.
17. Schofield M. (1965) *The Sexual Behaviour of Young People*. London: Longmans.
18. Elias J. and Gebhardt P. (1969) Sexuality and sexual learning in childhood. In: Rogers R.S. (ed.), *Sexual Education—Rationale and Reaction*. Cambridge: Cambridge University Press.

19. Kinsey E.J., Pomeroy W.B. and Martin C.E. (1948) *Sexual Behaviour in the Human Male*. Philadephia: Saunders.
20. Sroufe L.A. and Ward M.J. (1980) Seductive behaviours of mothers and toddlers: occurrence, correlates and family origins. *Child Development* **51**, 1222–1229.
21. Freud S. (1905) In: Strachey J. (ed.), *Three Essays on Sexuality— Standard Edition*, Vol. VII. London: Hogarth.
22. Sandler D., Dare C. and Holder A. (1972) Frames of reference in Psychoanalytic Psychology III. A note on the basic assumptions. *British Journal of Medical Psychology* **45**, 143–147.
23. Masson J.M. (1984) *Freud: the Assault on Truth*. London: Faber and Faber.
24. Rutter M. and Graham P. (1973) Adolescent turmoil: fact and fiction. *Journal of Child Psychology and Psychiatry* **17**, 35–36.
25. Gagnon T. and Simon W. (1973) *Sexual Conduct in The Social Sources of Human Sexuality*. Chicago: Archive.
26. La Fontaine J. (1985) *Initiation—Ritual Drama and Secret Knowledge Across the World*. Harmondsworth: Penguin.
27. Stoller R.J. and Heardt G.H. (1985) Theories of male sexuality— a cross-cultural look. *Archives of General Psychiatry* **42.**
28. Scharfe D.E. (1982) *The Sexual Relationship: An Object Relations View of Sex and the Family*. London: Routledge & Kegan Paul.
29. Laufer M. and Laufer M.E. (1984) *Adolescence and Developmental Breakdown: A Psycho-analytic view*. New Haven: Yale University Press.
30. Bentovim A. and Okell Jones C. (1986) Sexual abuse of children; fleeting trauma or lasting disaster. In: Anthony E.J. (ed.), *Year Book of the International Association of Child Psychiatry*. London: Wiley.
31. De Mause L. (ed.) (1976) *The History of Childhood: a Social History of Family Life*. London: New Souvenir.
32. Aries P. (1962) *Centuries of Childhood—the Evaluation of Parent– Child Relationships as a Factor in History*. London: Souvenir Press.
33. Goldman R. and Goldman J. (1982) *Children's Sexual Thinking*. London: Routledge & Kegan Paul.
34. La Fontaine J. (1986) personal communications.
35. Korbin J. (1981) *Child Abuse and Neglect: Cross Cultural Perspectives*. California: University of California Press.
36. Malinowski B. (1929) *The Sexual Life of Savages in North West Melanesia*. New York: Eugenia.
37. Bass E. and Thornton L. (1983) '*I Never Told Anyone*': *Writings by Women Survivers of Child Sexual Abuse*. New York: Harper & Row.

38. Mrazek P., Lynch M. and Bentovim A. (1983) Sexual abuse of children in the United Kingdom. *Child Abuse and Neglect* **7**, 147–154.
39. Finkelhor D. (1979) *Sexually Victimised Children*. New York: Free Press.
40. Russell D.H. (1983) The incidence of and prevalence of intra-familial and extrafamilial sexual abuse of female children. *Child Abuse and Neglect* **7**, 133–146.
41. Baker T. (1983) Child sexual abuse report on a reader survey. *19 (magazine) May 1983*.
42. Baker A.W. and Duncan S.P. (1985) Child sexual abuse: a study of prevalence in Great Britain. *Child Abuse and Neglect* **9**, 457–468.

CHAPTER 2

Sexual Abuse—Basic Issues— Characteristics of Children and Families

Arnon Bentovim and Paula Boston

INTRODUCTION

The plight of sexually abused children has been recognized at a later stage than other forms of abuse. It is interesting to speculate on why professionals have been so late in recognizing sexual abuse when children, young people and adults have described their experiences, and yet have had them dismissed as a fantasy. A review of the historical literature[1-4] indicates that child abuse and sexual abuse were described between 1868 and the 1890s. These observations were an aspect of concern for children, which led to incest being made a criminal act in 1908 in the UK. It was in the face of the concern about the extent of sexual abuse that Freud retracted his views about the role of seduction and trauma theory in the causation of psychiatric illness.[2] Freud's 'retraction' was accepted in scientific circles despite the availability of other information. The pressures to retract for children who are abused on professionals who recognize the problem are often very considerable indeed.

The Nature of Sexual Abuse

The Schecter and Roberge[5] definition of sexual abuse in abusive terms (*see* Chapter 1) covers a wide variety of possible sexually abusive events both inside and outside the family. The nature of the definition thus influences the prevalence of abuse. Sexual abuse includes the classical definition of incest, which is sexual intercourse between individuals in a defined relationship which includes father–daughter, mother–son, grandfather–daughter, brother–sister, and so on. Sexual abuse as an umbrella term also covers a far broader spectrum of activities beyond vaginal intercourse, including digital penetration, fondling, mutual masturbation, anal, oral/genital contact and involvement in pornographic photographs. The individuals involved can go beyond the immediate family to include step-parents, extended family members, and those in the family context, for example, baby-sitters, neighbours, friends, as well as absolute strangers.

The patterns of abuse described are varied. At one end of the spectrum is 'daddy's girl', where there is a long-standing affectionate relationship which progresses by small steps from ordinary loving cuddling and care, to a covert and then far more overt sexual contact until intercourse occurs, often very much later in the relationship. At the other end is the child used in a perverse way, for example, objects being used to penetrate in an abrupt sadistic way, involvement in a group context, or used in prostitution in a sexual ring. Jane, aged 14, described her father's sadistic behaviour when drunk; Ruth aged 15, the way she was 'the jam in the sandwich' between her parents and her mother's lover; Diana, 16, the way her mother brought home men she had picked up in pubs to have intercourse with her.

The Adult's Responsibility Versus a Child's Activity

What characterizes the relationships of the adult to a child is the authority to demand a particular response and to expect compliance. If the demand is a sexual one then this becomes the sexual abuse of that authority. This authority is abused whether the adult is a parent or someone acting in that parents' stead, whether they are step-parents, older siblings, foster parents, baby-sitters, more distant relatives, neighbours, people working with a child whether in a teaching, care-taking or other capacity, or trusted friends of the family. These are all situations where the child is dependent and the adult is given a legal 'right' to make certain demands on the child. Dingwall, Eekelaar, Murray and Parton[6-9] have pointed out that this conferred right also implies that there is a duty to the state to protect the child and to be responsible for his welfare. In this context the sexual use of a child, whatever the justification, is an abuse of dependency and authority when the child does not have the knowledge or choice to take this role. Because of his age and developmental state there cannot be true consent.

A common argument against this view is that children are highly sexualized beings, and often initiate and are very active in such contacts. If one follows the argument of dependency, immaturity and authority, then one has to distinguish between the responsibility of the adult and the activity of the child. Children often *feel* responsible for their activities, but no adult can take a child's activity and a child's sense of responsibility as adequate justification for his or her actions. Finkelhor[10] has also pointed out that the majority of sexual abuse is adult-initiated, even if children later activate their parent as part of a self-maintaining pattern.

The Effects of Sexual Abuse

Sexual abuse is to do with the use of a child for the adult's sexual needs. This is not always explicit, since it is possible for an adult to be able to disguise or confuse the issues to himself in terms of whose needs he is meeting, his own or what he perceives as the child's expectation through perceived activities. Rationalization of behaviour is an inevitable accompaniment of an abusive act, particularly acts carried out without obvious threat or violence and which seem to capitalize on the child's activity. Rationalizations may be 'pseudo-educative', teaching the child the facts of life, thus disguising sexual activities from both the child and from the adult.

Because of the 'hidden' nature of sexual abuse, it can become an activity which a child may want, and indeed from which he or she may derive pleasure. Only at a later stage may the experience feel abusive, for instance when the child realizes that his or her experience, which was not shared by peers, has created expectations which are out of alignment with contemporaries. For example, Nicola, aged 16, became angry with her father in retrospect when her heightened sexuality led her to becoming pregnant. Earlier she had been far less sure that the sexual contact with her father, which she enjoyed, had been an abuse.

Such is the ability to avoid painful realities, and indeed the necessity to do so for all participants in the sexually abusive drama, that the family's rule is *see no evil, hear no evil and speak no evil*.

POPULATION OF CHILDREN REFERRED TO A SEXUAL ABUSE PROJECT

To examine the patterns of sexual abuse among children we carried out a study of 274 families referred to the Sexual Abuse Project at The Hospital for Sick Children, Great Ormond Street between 1980 and the middle of 1986. The information was gathered retrospectively for the first half of the cases by abstracting information from case files. For the second half, information was obtained prospectively by sending out a questionnaire to the referral agencies. We thus had information on 411 abused children and their 362 non-abused siblings.

Patterns of Sexual Abuse

Table 2.1 shows the details of the sexual abuse in 274 families. These categories are not mutually exclusive and a number of children would have had for instance a degree of inappropriate fondling, oral–genital contact and even partial sexual intercourse. The most frequent experience was one of inappropriate fondling of genitals. Clinically the pattern of inappropriate fondling progressing to various forms of genital contact and partial or attempted intercourse was commonly described. It is also very difficult to know whether the pattern described at referral (shown in *Table 2.1*) may be the 'tip of the ice-burg', since during treatment a child may well reveal a more extensive abuse than is first described.

Table 2.1. Details of sexual abuse (274 families)*: as seen by referring agency

Type of abuse	Has possibly occurred	Has probably occurred	No evidence	Not known
Exhibitionism	15 (5%)	21 (8%)	19 (7%)	219 (80%)
Child voyeur to adults (video etc.)	17 (6%)	15 (6%)	25 (9%)	217 (79%)
Inspection of genitals	11 (4%)	18 (6%)	21 (8%)	224 (82%)
Inappropriate fondling	50 (18%)	128 (47%)	—	96 (35%)
Adult masturbation	20 (7%)	60 (22%)	10 (4%)	184 (67%)
Oral–genital contact (adult to child)	13 (5%)	25 (9%)	16 (6%)	220 (60%)
Oral–genital contact (child to adult)	13 (5%)	30 (11%)	13 (5%)	218 (79%)
Partial sexual intercourse	23 (8%)	56 (20%)	18 (7%)	177 (75%)
Full sexual intercourse	14 (5%)	48 (17%)	21 (8%)	191 (70%)
Anal intercourse	18 (7%)	31 (11%)	21 (8%)	204 (24%)
Other	8 (3%)	16 (6%)	18 (6%)	232 (85%)

* Each case could contain any number of sexual abuse categories. This information is by a case rather than an individual child basis.
Percentages given are for all cases within *each* category.

CHARACTERISTICS OF THE POPULATION

The Proportion of Females and Males

Table 2.2 shows the sex of the children, divided into victims and siblings. There is a very considerable excess of girl victims over boy

Table 2.2. Sex of children (from 274 families)

Victims	No.	%
Victims		
Females	317	77
Males	94	23
Total	411	100
Non-victims		
Females	151	43
Males	202	57
Total	362*	100

* Includes 9 children, sex not known.

victims and a reverse trend among siblings. These figures are borne out in various epidemiological studies, for example, Baker and Duncan's observations that a preponderance of girls report having been abused in their families over boys. The proportion of boys who were abused (23 per cent) does, of course, represent a very considerable number of abused children. Cases where boys had been victimized usually occurred within families where a girl had already been victimized. It was usual to find a girl as the only child victimized in a family; it was far less common for a boy to be the only child abused. Boys who were abused tended to be subjected to the more serious forms of abuse, e.g. intercourse.

The Number of Victims in Each Family

Table 2.3 shows the number of victims in each family at intake. Sixty-five per-cent of families have one victim only, and there were a considerable number of families where there were two or more victims, even as high as five or six victims in some families. These figures are probably an underestimate since this information was obtained from referral agencies and does not represent those cases

Table 2.3. Number of victims abused per family and by sex

No. of victims per family	Male/female	All female victims	All male victims	Total and %
1	—	153	26	179 (65%)
2	24	36	4	64 (23%)
3	11	10	1	22 (8%)
4	7	—	—	7 (3%)
5	2	—	—	2 (1%)
Total	44 (16%)	199 (73%)	31 (11%)	274 (100%)

who reveal later than other children in the family have been abused. We have found it important to assess all children in a family where one child has been abused, as so often a particular child takes on the role of drawing attention to the abuse and it is important to be aware of the high likelihood of multiple victims in the family.

Ages of Onset

The age of onset was evenly distributed in the age-groups 3–5, 6–8, 9–11, 12–14, and least for children under 3 years and over 15 years. It is important to note that abuse began very early (<3 years) in 6 per cent of our population (*Table 2.4*). Although there has been a supposition that only adolescent children are likely to be abused, it is now becoming clear that abuse occurs across the age-groups. Our clinical experience, like that of others,[11-13] has shown a startling increase in referrals of children up to the age of 10, and indeed the figures show that almost 40 per cent of abuse is initiated under the age of 10.

Table 2.4.   Age of onset of sexual abuse (from 274 families)

Age (yr)	Raw	%	Percentage of known cases (excluding 'Not known' category)
<3	14	6	5
3–5	66	16·5	23
6–8	70	17	24
9–11	66	16·5	23
12–14	64	16	22
15–16	10	2	3
Not known	121	29	—
Total	411	100	100

Duration of Abuse

Table 2.5 indicates that 44 per cent of the known cases were abused for less than 12 months and that over half of the known cases were abused for a year or more. Abuse could continue for as long as five years or more, but again there does appear to be a change in comparison with the first series of cases reported where the largest number of children were abused for between one and two years.[11] Clearly many children are abused over a long period of time. It may very well be that with the publicity surrounding sexual abuse, the growing aware-

Table 2.5. Duration of sexual abuse (274 families)

Duration of abuse	No.	%	%*
Once only	22	5	9
<6 months	43	11	18
6 months to 1 yr	41	10	17
1— 2 yrs	50	12	21
2— 4 yrs	37	9	15
5— 7 yrs	31	8	13
8—10 yrs	12	3	5
>10 yrs	5	1	2
Not known	170	41	—
Total	411	100	100

* Percentage of those cases where the information was available.

ness among families and professionals of the signs and symptoms of abuse, and the readiness to listen, children are now being heard, rather than tolerating and adapting to long periods of abuse.

The Perpetrators—Relationship to the Victim

Table 2.6 shows the relationship of the perpetrator to the victim. Because the emphasis of referrals is on the treatment of sexual abuse within the family, not surprisingly the majority of cases are abused by family members. Thus in our sample parents are the predominant abusers in 46 per cent of the cases, followed by step-parents, other relatives, a group of trusted members within the family context, and

Table 2.6. Relationship of perpetrator* to victim
(274 families)

Relationship	No.	%
Parent	127	46
Step-parent	75	27
Other relative	25	9
Friend of household e.g. boyfriend	20	7
Neighbour	8	3
Community leader	5	3
Stranger	3	1
Not known	11	4
Total	274	100

* Seventy-five per cent of the perpetrators were houshold members.

a very small number of strangers. Seventy-five per cent of the perpetrators were household members, while others were occasional visitors or were visited by the child. Of the known perpetrators 96 per cent were men and 2 per cent were women. In the remaining cases the families included multiple abusers where there had been some form of group sexual activities which may have involved mothers as well as fathers or stepfathers. There was a very small percentage of perpetrators who were over 60 or young adolescents, but the majority were in the age-group expected of parents.

DESCRIPTION OF FAMILIES WHERE SEXUAL ABUSE HAS OCCURRED

In the study of 274 families referred to the sexual abuse project we made some observations of the sort of families where sexual abuse had occurred. Because this information was partly gained retrospectively from case notes, and partly from information from referrers, the amount of information is limited but there are some indications about the families from the findings presented here.

Description of the Family (Family Situations)

The family situation at the time of the incident is shown in *Table 2.7* and it will be noted that only 39 per cent of the families were nuclear families. There were a variety of other family constellations including stepfamilies, single parents, common-law relationships and a smaller proportion of foster families and extended multigenerational families. Comparison with general population studies indicates that there is a greater variety of family constellations in a population where sexual

Table 2.7.   Family description

Family description	No.	%
Nuclear family	106	39
Stepfamily	64	23
Single parent (divorced)	34	12
Cohabitation and common law	30	11
Single parent (unmarried)	19	7
Foster family	11	4
Extended family in same household	7	3
Not known	3	1
Total	274	1

Table 2.8.   Length of time household had been together
(the household membership at the time of the incident)
(274 families)

Duration of household	No.	%
1. >10 yrs	81	29
2. 8–10 yrs	37	14
3. 5–7 yrs	38	14
4. 3–4 yrs	22	8
5. 1–2 yrs	29	11
6. Not known*	67	24
Total	274	100

* In *some* cases, the referring agent did not know how long
the household had been together.

abuse occurs compared to the general population. This may confirm notions that sexual abuse occurs where there is disruption, separation, divorce and step-parents. Despite this, an examination of the length of time the household has been together (*Table 2.8*) shows that 57 per cent of the families had been together for five years or more years and over a quarter of the families had been together for more than 10 years. Therefore although there may be considerable dysfunction within the families themselves, the structure itself may be stable. Theories which describe the abuse of a child as a means of structuring and stabilizing families may account for this observation about the length of time the families have lived together. Follow-up information (to be described in Chapter 12) will indicate how considerable the changes in family structure can be following disclosure. These changes may, of course, be due in part to the interventions of professionals, but they also may relate to the way in which family dysfunction and dysharmony are maintained at a tolerable level by secret abusive relationships with one or more children.

Occupations within the Families

Table 2.9 shows the occupational levels of the family. There is a considerable predominance of skilled manual, partly skilled and unskilled economically inactive families. This may well confirm a stereotype that sexual abuse occurs in lower social class groups with high unemployment and chaotic lifestyles. Of the known adults 62 per cent had educational qualifications. However, Parton[9] and others have shown that the recognition of abuse within the family occurs within those families in contact with social services agencies in the first instance.[12,13] Baker and Duncan's study has shown that when adults

Table 2.9. Adult occupation (274 families)

Occupation	No.	%
Professional	24	4
Intermediate/managerial	16	3
Clerical	7	1
Skilled manual	54	11
Partially skilled	58	11
Unskilled	62	11
Economically inactive (students, housewife, never on work force)	101	18
Not known	227	41
Total	549	100

are asked about abusive experiences which occured in childhood, all social classes are represented equally.[14,15] Yet in cases referred, the upper social class groups are greatly underrepresented. It may well be that families from these backgrounds have more skills in hiding the facts of abuse, or use practitioners who do not report or abide by the guidelines adopted by hospitals or other agencies.

There are very real issues within professional groups regarding whether or not to report cases. We follow a policy of not maintaining confidentiality where the protection of a child is at issue. In the inter-disciplinary working party which met under the auspices of the CIBA Foundation report it was recommended that sexual abuse of a child was a situation where medical confidentiality should be breached for the sake of the protection of the child. The involvement of social service care agencies is the only way to assure the protection of a child. Treatment with a probation order is essential to achieve change of the perpetrator. It is essential that 'treatment' should be the aim of all professionals in a context of 'safety' for the child, so that a phenomenon which crosses class boundaries is dealt with equally.

THE EFFECTS OF SEXUAL ABUSE ON CHILDREN

Physical Effects

To describe the effects of sexual abuse it seems sensible to start with the way the child responds. The physical effects depend on the actual pattern of abuse and the age and stage of development of the child; for instance, attempted intercourse with a very young child will have a different effect than with an adolescent.

There may be direct evidence of genital damage, tearing of the vaginal wall or rectal damage and ulceration. There may be bleeding, inflammation, infection and discharge with vulvovaginitis, or evidence of sexually transmitted diseases of the mouth, vagina or anus. Pregnancy is a possibility in teenagers.

Very often, however, there are few physical changes to observe. Force may not be used, there may be no penetration. Goodwin[15] has stated that less than 30 per cent of sexually abused children show physical changes. There is some evidence now[17,18] that attempts to penetrate, whether by finger or penis, do produce a difference in the transverse diameter of the vagina which can be measured (e.g., above 4 mm). Also signs of laxity of anal tone or trauma to the anus can be recognized in young children. Such physical signs and the possibility of child sexual abuse should be in the minds of practitioners who see children with vulvovaginitis and other genital and anal symptoms.

Traumatic and Psychological Effects

Are there direct psychological effects which draw attention to the possibility of a child being involved in a long-term abusive relationship? The best way of describing such direct psychological effects is based on the pattern that Figley and McCubbin[18] has described as 'traumatic stress disorder'. This may appear while sexual abuse is occurring or it may well appear as a post-traumatic syndrome after the abuse has stopped. The delay in symptom formation may well come about through the creation of a defensive protective wall which insulates a child from stressful experiences until a less abusive context comes about after disclosure, then the child lets herself feel.[19] The characteristics of acute, chronic or delayed traumatic stress disorders are:

1. Flashback of the traumatic experience itself which gives the individual an impression of re-experiencing the abuse. This can occur spontaneously or in the context of someone who may be showing ordinary physical closeness and affection. Such a response can produce considerable confusion, because the individual becomes unsure about the nature of people's response to him or her.
2. Withdrawal in the form of psychic numbing, reduced responsiveness, detachment and estrangement and frozen watchfulness.
3. A sense of heightened anxiety. This may show itself in the form of hyperalertness, sleeplessness, nightmares which often have similar forms to the abuse itself or have a punishing quality. This may arise out of a sense of guilt for what may have happened to a close member of the family or someone to whom there may be a good deal of ambivalence or mixed feelings.

4. There may be memory impairment, and blankness or a sense of loss, depression and irritability.

Specific Signs of Traumatic Stress Disorder in Sexual Abuse

The particular form of such responses in sexual abuse depends on a number of issues, including:

1. The age of the child.
2. Whether the abuse is accompanied with physical trauma.
3. Whether the abuse is long-standing.
4. Whether the abuse started in a limited way and then gradually increased in intensity.
5. Whether the family context negates and ignores emotional responses in children.
6. The character of the family, that is the way in which communications, feelings, closeness or distance, and alliances between people are negotiated.

Thus the pattern seen clinically depends in part on the internal 'digestion' of the experience by the individual and the way that the family and the social context processes it.

Some characteristic responses seen in sexual abuse are detailed below.

Responses connected with poor self-esteem

A pervasive loss of self-esteem is a characteristic response of sexually abused children. This may be shown through school failure mediated by poor concentration, depressed mood, withdrawal, and a general sense of unhappiness. Loss of self-esteem may also be manifested by a failure of self care and what Goodwin[15] has called the Cinderella syndrome. This syndrome described children who chose to wear ill-fitting clothes and who cared poorly for themselves—hair, skin, hygiene—despite living in a context which would not necessarily be associated with poor care and neglect. In older children failure of self-esteem may be connected with depressive feelings of such magnitude that over-dosing, self-mutilation and running away from home can occur. Various roles can be taken or assigned, including taking on a victim role, becoming the family scapegoat, expecting to become an abuser or to be abused.

The feeling that abuse is deserved is described by Summit[20] in 'the sexual abuse accommodation syndrome'. This syndrome described the experience of being caught in a traumatic situation, being entrapped in a family context of silence and disbelief. Children may well try to draw attention to the fact of their sexual abuse, but in such a way as not to be believable—to continue to obey the rule of silence. Allegations are made which are wild and untenable, for example, an immature 12-year-old thought she was pregnant, so her statements were dismissed. Two years later an examination showed sexually transmitted disease and vaginal scarring. If there is a direct allegation, a withdrawal is made in a self-sacrificial way so as to make professionals believe that the whole matter was a fantasy or a lie.

Jane, aged 16, and Catherine, aged 14, having gone to the police to talk about abuse, withdrew their statement under threat from their father, who said he would commit suicide. They instructed a solicitor to challenge a Care Order made on them in court. Eventually a judge in a Higher Court, encouraged by a psychiatrist who stated that this pattern of allegation and withdrawal was common, judged there had been abuse and excluded the father from the home. He returned secretly and used his controlling position to induce silence, until the mother was able to inform professionals of her concerns. The father could then face the realities of his abusive behaviour and accept treatment.

Psychosomatic responses

Another common response to trauma is expression through somatic pathways, or triggering of psychosomatic responses. There may be general regression to earlier stages of functioning, including wetting, soiling, self-comforting behaviour, clinging; or there may be specific responses, including abdominal pain, headache, limb pain, hysterical fit, faint and weakness, and illness behaviour. There may be triggering of syndromes, for example, asthma, eczema or anorexia nervosa.[22]

Sexual confusion and repetitions of sexual activities

One of the commonest ways in which children deal with the traumatic experience of being sexually abused or being involved in a sexually abusive relationship which cannot be comprehended is to identify in some way with the experience, by adopting an active sexual role or by expecting and seeking sexual contacts. Such heightened sexuality is described as the 'sexualization' of behaviour. Where compliance is obtained through the use of force and threat, a solution is to adapt and accommodate to the role, which is then internalized so that the child or young person repeatedly enacts the same behaviour with other adults—grabbing an adult's genitals publicly, re-enacting with other children sexual activities similar to those to which they have been subjected, for example, a five-year-old girl taking another into a lavatory, undressing and digitally exploring her vagina. Such behaviour may have a 'signalling' function which draws attention to a the child's high level of anxiety and tension.

There may be a pressure towards masturbation of high intensity, again depending on the age and developmental stage of the child. A young child will be less aware of the socially inappropriate nature of the behaviour and will be much more open in his sexual patterns of behaviour and interaction. The older child may be promiscuous or far more embarrassed by his experiences, and will try to block off sexual responses, refuse to speak about experiences, reverse them by turning their passive role into activity. Philip, aged 14, was abused by his father; once his father was imprisoned, he then felt it was necessary to prove he was not homosexual by fighting boys in his school.

There may be a process of identification either with the perpetrator or with the victim. This identification with the aggressor, for instance, can lead to enactment of abusive sexual behaviour towards younger children, either in a homosexual or heterosexual way. Hence the cycle is completed and the victim becomes offender, creating another victim. Sexual feelings may be inhibited totally, extending to the imaginative life of the individual. Intense fear is connected with sexual feelings, even ordinary affectionate approaches are experienced as repetitions and recreations of abuse such is the intensity of the traumatic responses. The wish to avoid any activity associated with traumatic experiences is common for many years. Once the desire to talk is facilitated there is often a wish to get rid of what is felt to be dirty or messy.

Macarthy[22] has pointed out that sexual experiences at various stages of sexual development ('oral', 'anal', 'genital') amplify these experiences. As a result the sexual experiences become highly associated with oral, anal or urethral reactions with associated intense fantasies which may be erotic and highly unpleasant. Not surprisingly, perverse impulses[23] and feelings associated with sexuality result in later associated frigidity, avoidance of sexual relationships and intense anxieties and fears in relation to the contact and handling of children, even resulting in physical abuse.[15]

Emotional problems and sexualized behaviour

To assess the degree of problem behaviour within children who have been sexually abused, we collected information both in the retrospective cases and prospectively about the sexualized behaviour of victims and siblings and other complaints. Unfortunately, because information was not collected systematically from the families directly, we have a limited amount of information available on siblings. However, *Tables 2.10* and *2.11* indicate that the frequency of sexualized behaviour was far higher in victims than in siblings, and other forms of problems were again far higher in victims than in siblings. This included a variety of emotional, behavioural and affective responses. This information is to be treated with great caution since there may

Table 2.10.   Reported signs of overly sexualized behaviour at intake (274 families)

Overly sexualized behaviour at intake	No.	%	%*
Victimized children (suspected or proven)			
No signs	162	39	51
Moderate or slight signs	53	13	17
Definite or serious signs	102	25	32
Not known	94	23	—
Total	411	100	100
Non-victimized siblings			
No signs	151	42	90
Moderate or slight signs	10	3	6
Definite or serious signs	7	2	4
Not known	194	53	—
Total	362	100	100

* Percentage of cases excluding the 'not known' category.

Table 2.11.   Signs of emotional disturbance or behavioural problems at intake (274 families)

Signs of emotional disturbance or behavioural problems	No.	%	%*
Victimized children			
No signs	36	9	11
Moderate or slight signs	122	30	36
Definite or serious signs	180	45	54
Not known	73	17	—
Total	411	100	100
Non-victimized siblings			
No signs	135	29	54
Moderate or slight signs	21	14	26
Definite or serious signs	39	11	20
Not known	167	46	—
Total	362	100	100

* Percentage figures excluding the 'not known' category.

well be an expectation by referrers that a child involved in sexual activities with an adult is bound to show inappropriate sexualized behaviour and it may well be that when we come to look at children systematically we may find less differences between children and their siblings. Collecting systematic information on these issues is very important since it has become clear that the impact of sexual activities on children is so pervasive.

EFFECTS IN RELATION TO AGE AND STAGE OF EMOTIONAL DEVELOPMENT OF CHILDREN

The way in which abuse develops in adult life depends on the sort of roles and relationships which emerge from the patterns described. A wide variety of later effects have been pointed out, including prostitution,[24] delinquency,[25] marital failure due to sexual difficulties,[26] parenting problems,[27] long-standing problems of self-esteem.[28] The extent of problems is in part related to the type and duration of abuse.[29,30] Boys tend to identify more with the perpetrator roles, girls with victim roles, but the reverse is possible.

Patterns in Relation to Age and Stage of Development

1. *Preschool children* show direct physical responses, sexualisation of behaviour and regression in terms of wetting and soiling behaviour.
2. *School-age children* commonly show patterns of pervasive low self-esteem, problems in school, sleeping difficulties, psychosomatic reactions, abdominal pains and some aspects of the sexualization patterns, although perhaps not so frequently as the preschool children.
3. *Adolescents* commonly show patterns of loss of self-esteem, running away when they become aware that what is happening to them is inappropriate, signs of the sexual abuse accommodation syndrome, wild allegations and withdrawals, self-mutilation, depressed mood and, of course, pregnancy.
4. *Adults* are more likely to show the delayed form of sexual abuse response with denial for many years and a major avoidance of knowing what they know except at a very vague level. The onset of pregnancy and childbirth can stimulate an intense flooding of memories, with severe mood swings, suicidal behaviour and perhaps the onset of avoided traumatic responses including rage and retaliatory wishes towards the abuser. Alternatively, response

may be delayed until the baby is born, and the closeness and intensity to the infant appears to trigger off intense memories.

The response may be delayed until children grow to an age when the individual parent was abused, when a reabusive pattern occurs either through self or through partner. The prevalance of previous abuse among abuser and their partners is high (*see* later).

PRECONDITIONS OF ABUSE

There is no one explanation of why children are sexually abused. Over 90 per cent of abusers are men, and a number of attempts have been made to try to explain the phenomenon. Groth,[30] for instance, has described fixated and regressed offenders. Fixated offenders are those individuals who have emerged from their own childhood with a sexual orientation towards children. Regressed offenders are those individuals who may have reached an adequate sexual relationship with an adult, but in the presence of particular crises, for example, the illness or death of a partner, find themselves turning towards a child sexually.

Although this seems to be a helpful division, in practice it does not help distinguish between those individuals who may well have had very similar experiences in childhood in terms of their own sexual abuse, or involvement in a family where sexual abuse was a pattern. Both fixated and regressed offenders can come from these types of childhood.

The Stages Leading Towards Sexual Abuse

Finkelhor[10] has attempted to capture the complexity by looking at both individual and social factors. Focusing on the perpetrator's role in sexual abuse, he looks at four 'preconditions' which have to be met to allow for sexual abuse to occur:

1. Factors which motivate an individual towards a sexual interest in children and to sexually abuse children.
2. A second stage when inhibitions against putting such motivations into action are overcome so that action is seen to be acceptable.
3. A third stage overcoming external inhibitions to abuse, connected with the absence of protection of the child.
4. A fourth stage to do with factors which help overcome the child's resistance to being abused.

Precondition 1: Factors relating to the motivation towards sexual abuse

(i) Emotional congruence. Sexual interest in a child has to be congruent to both the individual and the family's beliefs, views and experiences. These are families who seem to have quite an open belief shared by all members that children have sexual roles, and are expected to take them on.

The Jones family lived in an isolated farming area, the stepfather had been charged previously with animal abuse, and the children of the family openly took turns to be stepfather's sexual partner. Initially the social worker thought this to be a 'subcultural' norm of isolated areas, but once she talked in depth to the children she realized that they had no choice and a great deal of compulsion and threat was used; the children were relieved when the abuse stopped.

Adult and children's roles may be confused within the family, so that if children are expected to take on parental roles, and vice versa, then in this confusion and blurring, a sexual relationship is seen as being a natural aspect of the patterns of relationships. In the C. family Sheila, aged 15, found herself in a parental role while her father, her sister, and two brothers were involved sexually with each other, as if they were a sibling group out of control. The mother seemed to be on another level, isolated and peripheral, involved with her own sick mother rather than the family.

(ii) Traumatic conditioning and its effect. Perhaps the individual adult who has been a traumatized child through sexual abuse may deal with his experiences by projecting his traumatized child self onto his own child, without in any way seeing clearly the consequences of these actions. Adults speak about being able to tell themselves that sexual relationships with children are permissible because this was how they grew up in their own families, and this was what was expected.

David was horrified to 'discover' he had repeated abuse to his children's friends and had 'blocked out' his experience of abuse in the institution in which he had been placed when his parents separated. Allied to traumatic conditioning may be an experience of getting emotional needs met through sexual activity as a language of closeness and distance. John described an empty unloved childhood and found 'closeness' as an adolescent when he discovered sexual relationships. Ordinary closeness thus meant a sexual relationship and he avoided relationships with men. The problem was that when he wanted to get close to a stepdaughter, the only route he knew was through sexual channels. An attempt to comfort became sexual abuse.

(iii) Blockage of sexual outlets. Perhaps associated with traumatic conditioning is blockage of sexual outlets, with intense anxiety over

adult sexuality, fear of adult females connected with failures and disappointments in sexual activities. A sexual interest in children is a solution to a multitude of experiences and relationships. Brian, an unconfident teenager, married the first girl he met, as inexperienced as himself. He described their sexual relationship as never being right. When playing hide and seek with his daughter's friend of four years of age, he found himself sexually abusing her, and during the act was convinced the little girl was encouraging him and responding, unlike his wife!

Precondition 2: Factors predisposing to overcoming internal inhibitions

Finkelhor[10] describes a variety of associated factors, for example, alcohol, drug abuse, psychotic illness, impulse disorders, senility, problems of intellectual achievement. He also identified a societal toleration of inappropriate behaviour while intoxicated, and general societal problems in recognizing the needs of children. In the J. family both parents were addicted to hard drugs, there was persistent disorganization and their seven-year-old showed sexualized behaviour for many months in school before these factors were recognized by the professionals in the community so that the diagnosis of sexual abuse could be made. The presence of drug addiction and toxic states means that parents who should be exercising a protective relationship cannot do so. This may allow perverse individuals to be present in the family. Mrs. J., a long-time addict, had a series of casual short-term relationships, some addicted, who drifted in and out, and two separately abused her 12-year-old daughter.

Precondition 3: Factors which predispose to overcoming external inhibition of the child

These include illness of mothers and mothers with distant, unprotective, punitive relationships with their children. There may be rigid patterns of complimentary male and female roles, for example, dominance and submission, so that there is no room for protective behaviour on the part of a parent who has a compliant rôle. The H. family managed to 'marry' their daughter Anne, who had brain damage following an alcoholic bout, to an older man. He became increasingly close to Anne's daughter, who became the 'wife', while the mother took a child role.

Further predisposing factors which can overcome external inhibitions are unusual opportunities to be alone with children, for example, mothers working when fathers are at home, unemployed, ill or handicapped. Step-parenting represents a further risk. There is a widespread notion among abusers that having sex with a child who is not your own is acceptable but to have sex with a child who is 'flesh and blood' is not. It is noticeable that the legal system also regards non-related sexual contact as a lesser offence.

John H., who had been very attached to his mother, married for the third time following her death. He became 'one of the children', and found himself experimenting like a teenager with his stepdaughter: experimenting for him, abuse for her.

Precondition 4: factors predisposing to overcome a child's resistance

The child who is emotionally immature, mentally or physically handicapped, scapegoated or deprived, or who has particular lack of knowledge about sexual matters in a context of poor information on sex generally within the family, seems particularly vulnerable. A situation of particular trust (e.g., a father and child living together), a child in a 'parental' role who sees him or herself as responsible for the parents remaining together, are all factors which predispose to overcoming a child's resistance.

Vanessa M., a 15-year-old, mildly handicapped girl, had a long-standing scapegoat role, which increased when a new stepfather joined the family. She increasingly became the focus of aggressive and sexualized teasing, her underwear being pulled down, and she became increasingly confused and provocative in school until the pattern was recognized.

FACTORS CONTRIBUTING TO ABUSE

Factors in the Family

We examined some of these recent and long-term issues in our research at intake, *Tables 2.12* and *2.13* show the contributing factors to the abuse as seen by the referral agents concerning the perpetrator and the other adult in the family. Again these figures are not derived from direct interviewing but from the information gathered by agencies in contact with families before referral. However, there are indications of high levels of alcohol abuse, the habitual use of violence, unemployment, the absence of the other adult, and considerable incidence of marital problems and sexual difficulties. There are a small number of parents who show evidence of subnormality, drug abuse

Table 2.12.   Factors contributing to abuse concerning the perpetrator (274 families)

Factors	Recent	Long-term	Not present	Not known
		Duration of contributing factors		
Alcohol abuse	11 (4%)	41 (15%)	15 (5%)	207 (76%)
Drug abuse	1 (—)	12 (4%)	22 (8%)	239 (87%)
Physical illness	3 (1%)	15 (6%)	21 (8%)	235 (86%)
Psychiatric illness	10 (4%)	17 (6%)	20 (7%)	227 (83%)
Violence	13 (5%)	60 (22%)	16 (6%)	185 (67%)
Unemployment	17 (6%)	43 (16%)	23 (8%)	191 (70%)
Absence of other adult at home	26 (9%)	44 (16%)	16 (6%)	188 (70%)
Marital problems	13 (5%)	118 (43%)	16 (6%)	127 (46%)
Sexual problems	19 (7%)	83 (30%)	10 (4%)	162 (59%)
Subnormal IQ	1 (—)	13 (5%)	28 (10%)	232 (85%)

Table 2.13.   Factors contributing to abuse concerning the other adult in the household* (274 families)

Factors	Recent	Long-term	Not present	Not known
		Duration of contributing factors		
Alcohol abuse	3 (1%)	12 (5%)	19 (9%)	198 (85%)
Drug abuse	—	2 (1%)	19 (9%)	203 (90%)
Physical illness	9 (4%)	23 (10%)	18 (9%)	182 (77%)
Psychiatric disorder	7 (3%)	26 (11%)	17 (9%)	182 (77%)
Violence of perpetrator	9 (4%)	45 (20%)	15 (8%)	163 (68%)
Unemployment	4 (1%)	18 (9%)	21 (10%)	189 (80%)
General marital problems	8 (3%)	122 (60%)	7 (2%)	95 (35%)
Sexual problems	5 (2%)	67 (30%)	13 (5%)	147 (63%)
Subnormal IQ	—	8 (4%)	22 (10%)	202 (86%)

* The other adult in the household is primarily the mother. Two hundred and thirty-two adults were present.

and physical illness. These figures are in excess of what would be expected in the population generally, and reflect the preconditions described above.

Factors in the Family of Origin

We also asked some questions about factors from the family of origin of the parents, particularly those factors concerned with previous experiences of sexual abuse as a child, alcoholism or criminality (*Table 2.14*). There is an indication that even at the early stages of the investigation of cases, there is description of abuse in the childhood of

Table 2.14.   Previous history from family of origin of adults in household (274 families)

Previous history	Perpetrator	Other adult	Both	Not applicable	Not known
Sexual abuse	14 (5%)	32 (12%)	8 (3%)	9 (3%)	211 (77%)
Alcohol abuse	9 (3%)	9 (3%)	1 (1%)	13 (5%)	242 (88%)
Drug abuse	2 (2%)	2 (2%)	—	14 (5%)	256 (92%)
Psychiatric disorder	11 (4%)	19 (7%)	2 (1%)	12 (4%)	230 (84%)
Physical illness	7 (3%)	9 (3%)	—	11 (4%)	247 (90%)
Chaotic family	23 (8%)	48 (18%)	23 (8%)	7 (3%)	173 (63%)
Violence	17 (6%)	29 (11%)	6 (2%)	9 (3%)	213 (78%)
Criminal record	15 (6%)	7 (3%)	4 (1%)	14 (5%)	234 (85%)

perpetrators and significantly their partners. This phenomenon has been noted in terms of the choice of partners and the recreation of earlier patterns in the present family. During treatment there is often a far greater description of earlier abuse than is given at the onset of the work.

References

1. Johnson A. (1886) *Lectures on the Surgery of Childhood*. London.
2. Masson J.M. (1984) *Freud: the Assault on Truth*. London: Faber and Faber.
3. Brouardel P. (1909) *Les attentats aux Moeurs* [Offence against morals]. Paris: J.B. Baillière.
4. Tardieu (1860) A medico-legal study of cruelty and brutal treatment inflicted against children. *Aurales of hygiene publique et de medicine legale*. 2nd series, 361–398.
5. Schecter M.D. and Roberge L. (1976) Sexual exploitation. In: Helfer R. and Kempe C.H. (eds), *Child Abuse and Neglect: the Family and The Community*. Cambridge, Mass: Ballinger.
6. Dingwall R., Eekelaar J. and Murray T. (1983) *The Protection of Children*. Oxford: Blackwell.
7. Eekelaar J. (1973) What are parental rights? *Law Quarterly Review* 89, 210–34.
8. Eekelaar J., Dingwall R. and Murray T. (1982) Victims or threats? Children in care proceedings. *Social Welfare Law* 68–82.
9. Parton N. (1985) *The Politics of Child Abuse*. London: Macmillan.
10. Finkelhor D. (1984) *Child Sexual Abuse: New Theory and Research*. New York: Free Press.
11. Furniss T., Miller L. and Bentovim A. (1984) A therapeutic approach to sexual abuse of children. *Archives of Disease in Children* 59, 865–870.

12. Creighton S.J. (1985) An epidemiological study of abused children and their families in the United Kingdom 1977–1982. *Child Abuse and Neglect* **9**, 441–448.
13. La Fontaine J. (1987) The social class of families referred to a sexual abuse project (in preparation)
14. Taylor B. (1981) *Perspectives on Paedophilia*. London: Batsford Academic.
15. Goodwin J. (1982) *Sexual Abuse, Incest Victims and their Families*. Bristol: John Wright.
16. Cantwell H.B. (1983) Vaginal inspection as it relates to girls under 13. *Child Abuse and Neglect* **7**, 171–176.
17. Wilde N.H. (1986) Sexual abuse of children in Leeds. *British Medical Journal* **292**, 1113–1116.
18. Figley C.R. and McCubbin H.I. (1983) *Stress and the Family*, Vols 1 and 2. New York: Bruner/Mazel.
19. Kinston W. and Rosser R. (1974) Disaster effects on mental and physical states. *Journal of Psychosomatic Research* **18**, 437–456.
20. Summit R. (1984) The child sexual abuse accommodation syndrome. *Child Abuse and Neglect* **7**, 177–193.
21. Oppenheimer R., Howells K., Palmer M.L. and Challoner D.A. (1985) *Adverse Sexual Experience and Clinical Eating Disorders*. Leicester: University of Leicester.
22. Macarthy B. (1983) Therapeutic Problems in Working with Victims of Incest. Paper given to Royal College of Psychiatrists' Annual Conference.
23. James J. and Meyerdring J. (1979) Early sexual experience as a factor in prostitution. *Archives of Sexual Behaviour* **7**, 31–42.
24. Maisch H. (1972) *Incest*. New York: Stern and Day.
25. Meiselman K.C. (1978) *Incest: a Psychological Study of Causes and Effects with Treatment Recommendations*. San Francisco: Josey-Bass.
26. Goodwin J., McCarty T. and Di Vasto P. (1981) Prior incest in abusive mothers. *Child Abuse and Neglect* **5**, 1–9.
27. Steele B. and Alexander F.W. (1981) Long-term effects of sexual abuse in childhood. In: Mrazek P.B. and Kempe C.H. (eds), *The Effects of Child Sexual Abuse: Methodological Considerations in Sexually Abused Children and their Families*. Oxford: Pergamon.
28. Mrazek P.B. and Mrazek D. (1981) In: Mrazek P.B. and Kempe C.H. (eds), *The Effects of Child Sexual Abuse: Methodological Considerations in Sexually Abused Children and their Families*. Oxford: Pergamon.
29. Bentovim A. and Okell Jones C. (1986) Sexual abuse of children: fleeting trauma or lasting disaster. In: Anthony E.J. (ed.) *Year Book of the Institute of Child Psychiatry*. London: Wiley.

30. Groth A.J. (1982) The incest offender. In Sgroi S.M. (ed.), *Handbook of Clinical Intervention in Child Sexual Abuse*. Lexington, Mass.: Lexington Books.

CHAPTER 3

Understanding the Phenomenon of Sexual Abuse—A Family Systems View of Causation

Arnon Bentovim

A SYSTEMS INTRODUCTION

How can sense be made of the phenomenen of sexual abuse? The very title of this book, 'Sexual Abuse', defines the problem as sexual activities which are abusive. A view is advanced that an adult involved in sexual activities with a dependant child or young person, by reason of authority, is subjecting that child to a form of sexual abuse, even if the activities themselves are not carried out with force and threat. We are concerned here with such activities occurring within the family, or family context. The adult who abuses is the perpetrator, the child who is abused is the victim. It may be necessary to remove the child from the family for his or her protection, or the perpetrator for appropriate punishment. Treatment may follow to deal with the trauma or to help the perpetrator to change his abusive attitude. A survey of professional responses to child sexual abuse in the family by Mrazek et al.[1] indicated the predominance of protection and punishment over any form of treatment in a large number of reported cases.

We know from our orientation as child and family psychiatric practitioners that a definition of a problem into pure cause and effect does not always help us work in a therapeutic manner. It helps to see that individuals are locked into 'required roles' through mutual reinforcement processes, and 'feedback patterns' which are both problem-inducing and problem-maintaining, recur between individuals. Activities once they are initiated may come to be mutually reinforced, so that a father may well describe his daughter coming to him once he has made a first move. This in no way absolves him from his adult responsibility, but we need to understand the complexity of behaviour to understand the phenomenon fully. Why does the child continue with an activity which he or she may feel to be both pleasurable and abusive? Why does the father continue to behave in ways which he knows to be wrong and abusive, no matter how much he tries to deceive himself?

Extending the System beyond Victim and Perpetrator

The notion of 'victim' and 'perpetrator' does not include the involvement of other individuals, for example, the siblings or the other parent, who appear to be neutral. It is as if they have no role in the problem, and are passive bystanders. Yet we know in other fields that the child who is refusing to eat food or attend school, or becomes a focus through a severe psychosomatic state, may be drawing attention away from other problems, for example, concern about a potential marital failure, or another sibling who may be handicapped physically or mentally. Such issues may be perceived as having a catastrophic potential and must be avoided at all costs, even though the consequences are a life-threatening state in another individual.[2,3]

This view of individual states and their connection to the family system sees causality as 'circular' rather than 'linear'. It sees individuals 'caught in a dance' with one another. To be effective, therapy has to pay equal attention to all members. The therapist owes an allegiance to all members of the family and has to see and deal with the contribution of each. He may have to decide that the cost to an individual of having a particular role may be worth accepting for a time to help the family as a whole. The therapist may appear to side with the family's view at one phase of the work. To create change he may connote and reframe the child's impossible behaviour as being unconsciously helpful to the family, even though the child is being self-destructive and self-sacrificial in the process. He may even confront the family with a view that the child's illness is his or her way of trying to help to avoid other problems. Such an approach is more helpful than trying to remove and rescue a child, since in the long run other children will be inducted into the same role, and it is better to try to create change within the family and use their strengths to create change rather than to disrupt and create further turmoil.

DILEMMAS OF A FAMILY SYSTEMS APPROACH

If the sexual abuse of children is a family systems problem which involves a wider circle than the victim and perpetrator, then a family systems approach to treatment seems to follow logically. Yet as Jacobs[4] has pointed out, there are some major dilemmas for a therapist in working in the field of sexual abuse.

Therapist's Responsibility

The therapist's primary responsibilities are seen as protecting the rights and promoting the welfare of his or her clients. The dilemma with multiple clients is that in some situations an intervention that serves one person's best interests may be counter-therapeutic to another. If the family is the client a family therapist with his particular notion of responsibility might find himself having to promote the welfare of one or the other of his clients—a child in the family as against a parent. This action may prove to be to the detriment of the family, particularly if, for instance, a child has to be removed from the family where that child may have an important role to maintain such as in the 'togetherness' and therefore the integrity of the parents' marriage.

Margolin's[5] view is that if there is evidence of abuse, "It is the therapist's ethical responsibility to abdicate the role of relationship adviser and help the threatened person to find protection".

Confidentiality

Margolin holds the view that it is the therapist's responsibility to safeguard information obtained in the therapy session. Exceptions are: "To avoid clear or imminent danger to the client or others, or when a specific requisite of the law takes precedence".

Boszormenyi-Nagy[6] has put forward a useful conceptual framework in which to think about these issues. He describes a 'Relationship Ethical' model which includes the principal of interpersonal consequence, an important aspect of close relating:

1. Individuals are ethically and legally responsible for their actions.
2. Responsibility for consequences rests most heavily with respect to the interests of future generations. He states: "The future life prospects for the young, and even for as yet unborn children, represent the highest ethical priority for their parents".
3. The chain of consequences points towards the interests of posterity. Consider the case of the incestuous father's family. Besides being a part of the system of recursive current transactions, the incestuous parent's acts reflect consequences resulting from his formative past. In contrast, the abused child lives in a formative present which may

have lasting consequences for her future survival. Moreover, if she is lastingly affected, she may have a corresponding impact on her children.

The therapist thus has to accept that there is a larger societal system that he is part of. A parent has a responsibility to socialize a child appropriately and to ensure his welfare and safety from abuse. A therapist through his caring role and professional status shares this responsibility when he is connected to the family. There may be no way forward for the therapist and the family as a system, unless this issue is grasped and the abuse is stopped by bringing in those agencies who have a responsibility for providing services for children who have been abused.

The therapeutic aim then has to be to help the family to take on these societal responsibilities and face the care and criminological issues connected with failure to care, protect and socialize. The theme to be developed in this book is that therapeutic work has as its aim to help families to convince care and control professionals that the family is changed sufficiently to satisfy community standards of care and protection.

A SYSTEMS MODEL OF THE INITIATING AND MAINTENANCE OF SEXUALLY ABUSIVE BEHAVIOUR

Kinston and Bentovim[7] and Bentovim[8] have attempted to provide a coherent way of thinking about families seen generally in clinical practice, and where violence has occurred. It is necessary to think in terms of seven levels to be able to give a meaningful description of families. These levels are:

1. Elements of interaction.
2. Cycles of interaction.
3. Active meaning systems.
4. Dimensions of the family and family life.
5. Formulation of the family.
6. The practical goals for the family in a therapeutic context.
7. The generality of families and family life.

First Level—Elements of Interaction

Elements of interaction describe meaningful interactions observed in families where sexual abuse occurs. These would encompass touching of a child's genitals digitally, oral–genital contact, attempted anal or vaginal intercourse, a variety of violent sexual actions and sexual uses of children. These are fundamental to an understanding of sexual abuse, but they make little sense clinically unless they are gathered together into 'patterns' or cycles describing actions and reactions around the specific sexual acts.

Second Level—Cycles of Interaction

Such elements become coherent when combined into episodes or cycles of interaction. They would describe for instance the teenage daughter who cannot sleep, coming to her parent's bed and her father having intercourse with her while her mother sleeps. This pattern may have commenced previously with a cuddle to calm the child down before returning her to her own bed, such a pattern increasing in intensity until intercourse occurs, mother continuing to sleep throughout. Another pattern would be a mother going out to work early in the morning, and a stepfather regularly digitally penetrating his stepdaughter. A son of 14 goes out to work with his father, and during a lunch break the father abuses him anally. A daughter of six habitually has a sleep with her father on a Sunday afternoon, he wakes up to find that his daughter is playing with his penis and he then uses her hand to masturbate him until he ejaculates. Such cycles or episodes build up over time to create the sexually abusive syndromes described here. However, in clinical practice it is essential to put such episodes into the context of what they mean for the family in question.

Third Level—Active Meaning Systems

Active meanings describe the 'context' of events, they may be recent or long-standing in origin. The father who has intercourse with his daughter may have had a sister who was sexually abused by his father. The stepfather who digitally penetrates his stepdaughter may be finding it impossible to deal with a major conflict with this wife, their sexual life may have failed, and he is using the only emotional language he knows—sexuality—to get some degree of closeness to his wife through her daughter. The father who abuses his son may be married to a woman who had been abused sexually herself and could not respond to him sexually, and he may have abused a daughter earlier.

It is possible to see such patterns as a circular phenomenon in terms of time. *Figure* 3.1 attempts to put the phenomena into a time frame by showing that the individual caught up in an abusive interaction himself carries forward abusive responses into the longer term, into choice of partner in adulthood, into patterns of sexual relating and parenting,

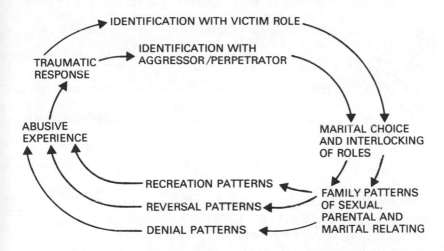

Figure 3.1. The intergenerational cycle of sexual abuse.

and then to the way in which subsequent children are dealt with which
re-enacts the whole cycle, thus giving a particular significance and
meaning to sexual activities between adults and children. This figure
indicates that events which occurred either in the childhood of the
parents, that is in the family of origin, or which occurred in the current
family to the parents as adults, were dealt with in characteristic ways.
Particular events and experiences come to be seen as especially
relevant and come to have such significant meanings that they orien-
tate family members towards the world and expectations of it.
Individuals will choose each other as partners on the basis of such
experiences, and in turn these same views and expectations will
influence the way in which children are treated and inducted into the
same family system. They will come to share the same beliefs and
meanings, for example, the roles of parents and children, how they
should relate to each other, by whom and how this control should be
exercised, the role of violence and sexual attitudes and activities.

Recurrence of abusive patterns

Some families seem to *recreate* the pattern of relationships that
occurred in their family of origin, focusing around stressful events and
relationships. So as its simplest fathers abuse as their fathers abused,
daughters are abused as their mothers were. In Tony's family, he
abused his daughters as his father had his sisters, in Joan's family, her

daughter Mary was abused by her stepfather as she had been by her father. There are of course many other intervening variables, but such patterns do re-occur.

Reversal of abuse patterns

Some families seem to attempt to reverse or try and overcome the effects of such events. A women such as Sheila chose a younger 'dependent' man who appeared very different from the bullying father who had abused her. Yet choosing an opposite may mean that the father is on the same level as the daughter and may abuse her in a distortion of brother–sister exploring.

Denial patterns in relation to abuse

Other families appear to totally deny and falsify their experiences and constantly displace them by enacting minor disasters to prevent the major disaster which was to be feared and which was always to be avoided. For instance, a child may be sexually abused to prevent a major disaster—'at least I did not go outside the family and realize your worst fear—a marital break up which occurred when your previous husband had an affair and left you'—was the explanation for the abuse of a 15-year-old stepdaughter.

Level Four—The Dimensions of Family Life in Sexual Abuse

Although these three patterns are helpful in understanding some of the threads that appear in families who abuse sexually, further organization is necessary to gather such observations together to be able to fully understand the phenomenon of sexual abuse in the particular family that is being worked with. Bentovim and Miller[9] have described the particular dimensions noted in severe family breakdown, whether caused by physical, sexual or other forms of abuse or abandonment. There are two particular family types which bring together the sexual abusive interaction, cycles and active meanings, described as:

    A. Endogamic—conflict-avoiding families.
    B. Disorganized—conflict-regulating families.

A. Endogamic—conflict-avoiding families

Basic pattern

This family type, which has been described by Rosenfeld[10] and Furniss,[11] is illustrated by a family who develop a highly enmeshed pattern of interaction influenced by stressful events and relationships in the families of origin and the current family. The characteristics are shown in *Figure* 3.2, which describes an intense over-involvement between a father and a daughter, and a more distant and hostile relationship between mother and daughter. The relationship between the parents on the surface seems good, but conflict is avoided actively between them. The feared disaster here is that conflict between parents is expected to result in destruction and marital breakdown. The care of the children is usually good enough, but the sexually abusive relationship often emerges out of a long-standing sexual failure in the marriage, perhaps connected with previous abuse of the mother.

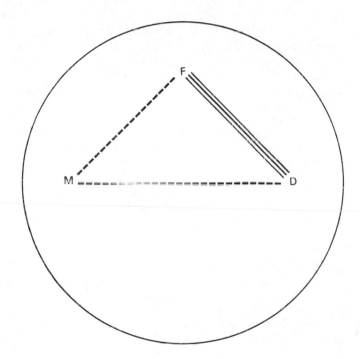

Figure 3.2. Endogamic and conflict-avoiding patterns of family relating: variation 1 (*see* Furniss[14]). ────, Boundary; ══, enmeshed relating; ─────, distant ambivalent relating. F, Father; M, mother; D, daughter.

It appears on the surface as if the father is then using both mother and daughter and that he is occupying the dominant role in the relationship, above mother and daughter who are at a dependent level to him. There is usually intense secrecy and very poor communication about anything to do with sexual matters in the family, and the longer the distant relationship between mother and daughter is perpetuated, the less able the daughter is to speak about sexual issues and can only maintain silence or make allegations which are unbelievable. At the same time the daughter's disappointment at not being heard is intense. As mother and daughter become more distanced father and daughter become nearer and the more the strain grows between the parents, eventually activating conflict. However, some conflict between parents would be a disaster, mother's anger is directed towards the daughter, who then has to get closer to father, which reduces the conflict again.

In this pattern of interaction[5] the function of the sexually abusive, incestuous relationship is to reduce major conflict between the parents and keep it at a tolerable or even absent level. Conflict can be avoided, despite what could be seen as cause for major marital disaster.

In these situations a daughter will often disclose her abuse as she approaches adolescence, perhaps to 'save' a younger sibling. The explosion that follows is often profound and the conflict explodes between the parents with a sense of betrayal and outrage. Professional interaction and work at this point have to be carried out carefully to avoid the sort of pattern Furniss[14] described, where subsequent conflict is buried again between the parents when, for instance, the daughter is removed, and the parents then come together and see her as the *moral* evil, the 'cause', or alternatively professionals who removed the daughter are seen as enemies. Alternatively, if a father is removed, mother and daughter bury their differences to see him as the source of all badness. Inevitably conflict surfaces between them with a variety of unhappy results.

Case example

Susan aged 14 was the oldest of three children—the younger two, boys. Her father described himself as the one who got all the punishments at home, his sister was the favourite and had been abused by their father. Susan's mother was quite a neglected child and each parent had a very poor self-image. The father became absolutely convinced he was not satisfying his wife sexually, but could never tell her his fears. Their relationship seemed excellent—they never argued. He had always felt close to Susan, and gradually he felt that her response to him, the ordinary daughter–father love, was making him feel he could satisfy someone. He initiated increasingly sexualized contact including digital penetration, and was convinced Susan's continued coming to him implied she was consenting and wanted the contact. She could not tell her mother and was becoming increasingly distant from her. She finally confided in a friend and her family, and lived with them for a time. When Susan and the family were seen, the couple were 'clinging together', mother said sex had always been fine and could not understand her husband's concerns, she needed her husband and vice versa. Susan was in care. She was desperate to get closer to her mother and furious with her father, but her behaviour pushed her further and further away from her mother—while the further she was away the closer the parents' own relationship. The boys remained in total ignorance.

Other patterns in conflict-avoiding families

Mothers as caretakers. Furniss[14] has pointed out that behind the father who seems to be taking control of the family and using mother and daughter for his own needs, is a mother who sees her husband and daughter as a pair of teenage children (*Figure* 3.3). Work with such families often reveals that the parents have chosen each other on a parent–child basis, so that mothers may emerge from the sort of families we have described and take on a compulsive care-taking role, while fathers again find themselves taking the little-boy role in the marriage. Not surprisingly with the difficulty in making adult relationships, fathers and daughters can sometimes appear like a pair of children with none of the ordinary boundaries that parents and children should have.

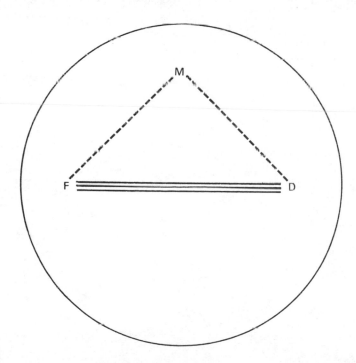

Figure 3.3. Endogamic, conflict-avoiding pattern of family relating: variation 2.

Case example

Bill had been married twice previously and Jean once. She had two daughters (15 and 13) who lived with her, Bill had two sons who lived with his ex-wife. Jean was older than Bill, very independent, but very hurt at the rejection by her ex-husband. She was much attracted to Bill but perceived he had absolutely no responsibility with money, drank too much and turned to his mother for support. She made it clear she would not go out with him, or be with him unless he 'became responsible', which he did; indirectly she became the 'parent'. He found himself behaving like an adolescent with her daughters, and in rough and tumbles 'found himself' acting in a sexual way with them. They told their mother, but she 'tried to keep it in the family'. The mother tried to control and monitor the situation, but the parents' sexual relationship deteriorated. He was convinced his actions were not harmful and in a defiant way reabused the children. The girls told their mother who reported the stepfather who left the home. The girls stayed with their mother, but the couple 'united' later through opposition to the social work agency who wanted to ensure the girls were protected.

Children in parental roles. Another twist in the triangle (*Figure* 3.4) is where the child can take on a parental role and thus be seen at the top of the triangle. The child who talks about her anxiety about her

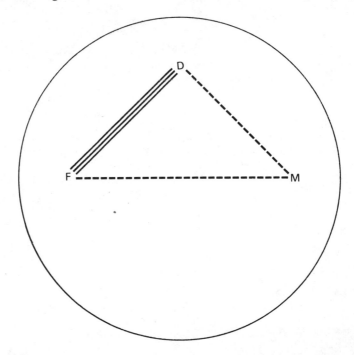

Figure 3.4. Endogamic, conflict-avoiding pattern of family relating: variation 3.

parents' splitting up, about the marriage breaking down, about the terrible things that would happen to the family if the police came in, about the possibility of her father going to prison, may take on a self-sacrificial role, almost as if she is a grandparent looking after the parents.

Case example
Lyn aged 16 described the way her stepfather turned to her when he was rejected by his own daughter. Lyn 'allowed' her stepfather to continue his sexual advances, as she was convinced he might leave her mother and return to his original family. She became pregnant but hid the fact until the eighth month when the facts came out.

Father and daughter as a couple. A further twist (*Figure* 3.5) is where a father and daughter are seen as the couple and the mother almost as the dependent child. This may occur particularly where there is an illness or some form of handicapping condition in the mother, so that genuinely father and daughter take a care-taking role, or where the mother feels herself to be pushed out and excluded and 'has to go to bingo'. Lorraine's mother described her helplessness when her

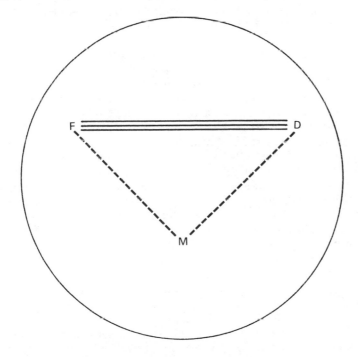

Figure 3.5. Endogamic, conflict-avoiding pattern of family relating: variation 4.

husband and Lorraine were "kissing and cuddling on the couch", "I knew it was wrong to leave them, but no-one would listen to me."

These families, as well as having profound secrecy between themselves about emotional differences and sexual matters, also create a very strong boundary between themselves and the community. They may well be isolated from the extended family or professionals. John described himself as "the black sheep" in the family when his mother left them, his father favouring his brothers. John never saw his family. His wife Joan had not seen her family for years. They themselves worked different shifts and passed 'like ships in the night'. John started to abuse their 15-year-old daughter when Joan was working at night, and they appeared as the parental couple, while the mother seemed abandoned by both.

The possibilities of helping conflict-avoiding families and the dangers of openness

It is difficult to know exactly what proportion of cases seen in practice fall into this 'conflict-avoiding' category. They do represent a significant proportion of those cases where there is acceptance of allegations, a high level of guilt, and a desperate wish that the abuse could stop.[12]

Relief is often expressed when matters come into the open, and there is often a positive attitude towards the possibility of help and change with professional involvement. Perhaps these families represent a group where previous losses create a need for the marriage which is very powerful and a fear of conflict therefore very high. Parents may well wish to remain together even though it may mean that a child is rejected. At the same time there is a persistent hidden competition and rivalry between mother and daughter. Despite the feeling of abuse the daughter may have a sense of triumph over her mother which often needs considerable attention if there is to be any real therapeutic change.

The absence or disappearance of conflict between parents is often persistent, and the stubborn enmeshment and denial of difference is frequently a major sticking point in therapeutic work. Long-term abusive patterns as a way of avoiding major conflicts, possibility of loss, abandonment and other disasters do take on an addictive quality. It is only too easy to 'batter' or 'seduce' the professionals to fight amongst themselves by proxy.[13]

It is not surprising, therefore, that what may have to be faced is a sense of guilt, shame and anger of such a high order that suicidal attempts by perpetrators, by their wives, as well as by the young people themselves, may occur, or be threatened as a consequence of disclosure, separation or confrontation. Abuse can become an addictive pattern which helps keep such fears at a distance.

Case example

John and Janet sat locked hand in hand throughout groups, touching each other, never arguing, never showing any anger at his abuse of three of their children. If it happened again, she would immediately forgive him, the children were always close, affectionate, often in physical contact. John spoke about the tradition in his family that when people grew up, they never met again. He could not bear to lose his children, his sexual behaviour was his way of expressing closeness. His wife who had been abused by a brother she had never confronted, gazed into his eyes. Only one of the three daughters could express any difference—and she chose to stop going to her therapy group for a time. Perhaps this was the only way of convincing the professionals that this 'compliant' family, who did everything they were asked to by professionals, had another face.

B. Disorganized—conflict-regulating families

Basic pattern

Traditionally the second major family type observed within the family constellation where sexual abuse occurs was called the 'promiscuous pattern'.[8] This is such a negative connotation that it is preferable to refer to this type according to the characteristics of disorganization, chaos and the regulation of conflict within the family.[7] *Figure* 3.6 represents a far less structured family than the previous pattern. Instead of a confusion about who is the emotional parent, father, mother or child, there is a confusion about who is the actual parent. In the previous type, the care, control and stimulation of the children by the parents are adequate.

By contrast, in these disorganized families there may be far more in the way of chaos and poor care. The family may be known as a 'problem family' and are characterized by poor boundaries both between the generations and between individuals. There is often a far higher degree of violence and punitiveness in communication patterns. Alliances may shift and involve various children rather than one. There may be a sexual relationship between the father and several of the children of what may be quite a large sibship. It may become clear on seeing the family that one of the children takes a parental role, and it is as if that child is in the parental position, while the father, mother and siblings are like a set of arguing, squabbling children on the same level. Mothers may be involved in group sexual activities with father and children. Sexual activities may be restricted to the family circle or include outside contacts.

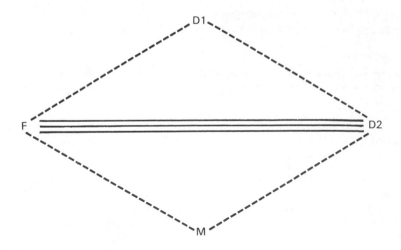

Figure 3.6. Conflict-regulating, chaotic family patterns of functioning in sexual abuse (*see* Furniss[14]). D1, Daughter 1; D2, daughter 2.

Case example

The Jones family had been a concern to Social Services Departments for some years, there were a number of long-standing problems. John the 15-year-old was encopretic, Margaret the 16-year-old had a mild degree of handicap. The mother had had a number of cohabitees, and the most recent had immediately demanded that he be called 'Dad' when he moved in. He shouted at and bullied the children, and their mother stood by 'helpless'. Sheila the 12-year-old seemed 'sensible', and always kept out of squabbles. Mother, stepfather and the two oldest children seemed like squabbling children. John was hit when he soiled, Margaret was experimented with sexually 'to introduce her' to 'grown-up' behaviour. Sheila seemed to take over the 'maternal role' and was the only person who could blow the whistle on the noise and confusion. There was far less in the way of secrecy within the family, and sexual contact was disqualified as nothing serious. Others outside the family were accused, and there was an atmosphere of confusion and doubt. The child who had 'talked' was seen as a traitor.

The function of the sexual abuse seems to be a way of temporarily reducing conflict within the family.[7] Sexual relationships serve a regulatory function so that instead of a level of violence continuing which would become explosive, there are peaks and troughs and the use of sexuality is like a tension-reducing drug. The major secrecy is between the family and the outside world.

Characteristically each of the adults and children may speak at great length about sexual activities on a one-to-one basis, but seeing the family together, the rule of silence takes over, or a shifting pattern of scapegoating and blaming is seen. There may well be a multiplicity of factors already covered which may predispose to this particular family pattern, including alcohol misuse, drug addiction, limitation of intellectual functioning, major levels of privation and poor care, punitiveness and previous sexual abuse of the individual who is caught in a repeating pattern.

The effect of disclosure

Disclosure causes far less in the way of explosiveness but will certainly produce a rallying around of the whole family against the agencies attempting to work with the family or the child who has disclosed. Perhaps the major fear and disaster in these families is dissolution, separation and abandonment. The sacrifice of children one by one to maintain total family togetherness and the exclusion of the external world is a basic function. Many professionals are mortified when they learn that there have been major sexually abusive activities in a family they have been working with for many years. They may have provided family aides, and taken a major parental role themselves. The changes which can be achieved in these families are limited.

Alternative care for a family of six to eight members becomes a daunting prospect, even though they may demand it. Chapter 12 shows that it is possible, using a structured approach to the work, to achieve limited changes, even in families whose chaotic functioning pulls in professionals of all disciplines.

These are the families which are likely to show high levels of physical abuse and sexual abuse. It would be helpful for there to be a routine enquiry in all families where there are high levels of physical abuse and neglect in the chaotic context described here, to assess the possibility that sexual abuse may also be occurring as part of poor boundaries of feelings and action.

Level Five—The Formulation of the Family

Having looked at the elements, cycles, active meanings and dimensions of sexually abusive families, the clinician needs to be able to make sense of the specific case he has seen. The clinician needs to attempt to understand what have been the factors in this family that specifically maintain and have initiated the sexually abusive behaviour, what sort of interactions appear thereby to be avoided. What are the specific factors in the family of origin or current family which seem to have given rise to such a degree of fear and anxiety that sexually abusive patterns of behaviour have become initiated?

We have found that a number of specific issues also need to be examined, and these are described in more detail in Chapter 8.

1. Is there proper responsibility for the abuse taken in the family?
2. Is there a particular sense of scapegoating of the abused child or children?
3. Is there evidence of hostility within the family?
4. Is there evidence of warmth in the family?
5. The position of the victim in the family.
6. The relationship between the parent and the abused child.
7. The quality of the marital relationship.
8. General family patterns, particularly those linked with rigidity, enmeshment or lack of boundaries.

Level Six—The Potential for Treatment, Actual and Ideal

It will be seen that assessment of the family takes place in the statutory context of the referral agencies, and those in the community whose responsibility it is to give a service to abused children and their families. It is essential to specify the possible outcome, given the availability of treatment, in relation to the particular characteristics of the family. In Chapter 8 categories of outcome will be given in terms of 'Hopeful outcome cases', when there appears to be a reasonable taking of responsibility for the abuse, a degree of flexibility of family operations and a basic attitude of cooperativeness with the professionals and a potential for change within the assessment process. 'Doubtful outcome cases' are those where there is greater uncertainty about parents taking responsibility, children's needs are not seen as primary, there is limited flexibility and potential for change within the family system, and reflections with the helping professionals may be ambivalent and mixed. However, there may be some potential for hopefulness here, but perhaps not enough to convince the professionals that the family is hopeful, for example, because of a failure to take responsibility for the abuse, a failure to recognize children's needs, a failure to acknowledge long-standing family problems and the rejection of professionals.

Even families with hopeful characteristics may well have a poor prognosis when statutory agencies cannot develop a therapeutic aim between themselves, or where there is an absence or overload of therapeutic services and a variety of group, individual and family work which is needed to create change is not available. Different family types and constellations require different therapeutic strategies. Furniss[14] has described the therapeutic tasks necessary to create a safe outcome for children who have been abused. The tasks move through phases of assisting the parents to be able to take responsibility for the care of their child even if they are living separately, to restore the relationship between the non-abusive parent and the abused child to deal with the competition, rivalry and disappointment inherent, and to focus on the marital relationship where the fear of conflict so often acts as the motivating factor for sexual abuse. Finally, the relationship between the perpetrator and the victim can be addressed, but often later in the work once other issues are dealt with. In disorganized families often a great deal of work has to be done to meet the aim of ensuring the basic necessities of care, control and stimulation are achieved before the relationships between individual members can be addressed.

Level Seven—The Generalities of Family Life

It is impossible to be able to fully describe and think about sexually abusive families without putting them into contexts of the generalities of family life. It is very easy to be idealistic about particular families and feel that the degree of disorganization and abuse means that break-up and placement of children away is the only solution. And yet, if there is an appropriate awareness of the range of family life ranging from the most organized and competent, to the least, then it will be possible to know what the limits of achievement are for the particular family that is being worked with. This may mean that paradoxically a family who functions well in many spheres may not be able to provide for the care of a child because of the potential for sexual abuse recurring. Yet another family who may be much more borderline in their general function may be able to have a child rehabilitated when the particular issue of sexual abuse is better resolved.

References

1. Mrazek P.B., Lynch M. and Bentovim A. (1983) Sexual abuse of children in the United Kingdom. *Child Abuse and Neglect* **7**, 147–154.
2. Byng-Hall J. (1980) Symptom bearer as marital distance regulator: clinical implications. *Family Process* **19**, 355–365.
3. Kinston W. and Bentovim A. (1980) Creating a focus for brief marital and family therapy. In: Budman S.H. (ed.), *Forms of Brief Therapy*. New York: Guilford Press.
4. Jacobs B. (1986) Incest: The Relationship between Ethics and Therapy in a Non-statutory Family Therapy Agency. Dissertation, Institute of Family Therapy, London.
5. Margolin B. (1982) Ethical and legal considerations in marital and family therapy. *American Psychologist* **37**, 788–801.

6. Boszormenyi-Nagy I. (1985) Commentary: transgenerational solidarity—therapist's mandate and ethics. *Family Process* **24**, 454–456.
7. Kinston W. and Bentovim A. (1987) A Seven Level Description of Family Systems—in preparation.
8. Bentovim A. (1987) Violence in the family—definitions, assessment and management. In: Bluglass R. and Bowden P. (eds), *Text Book of Forensic Psychiatry*. Edinburgh: Churchill Livingstone.
9. Bentovim A. and Miller L. (1984) Family assessment in family breakdown. In: Adcock M. and White R. (eds), *Good Enough Parenting*. London: British Agencies of Adoption and Fostering.
10. Rosenfeld A.A. (1979) Endogamic incest and the victim-perpetrator model. *American Journal of Psychiatry* **133**, 406–10.
11. Furniss T. (1984) Conflicting—avoiding and conflict regulating patterns in incest and child sexual abuse. *Acta Paediatrica Scandinavica* **50**, 299–313.
12. Mrazek B.P. and Bentovim A. (1981) Incest and the dysfunctional family system. In: Mrazek P.B. and Kempe C.H. (eds), *Sexually Abused Children and their Families*. Oxford: Pergamon.
13. Furniss T. (1983) Mutual influence and interlocking professional-family processes in the intervention of professionals in families of sexual abuse. *Child Abuse and Neglect* **8**, 210–223.
14. Furniss T. (1983) Family process in the treatment of intra-family child sexual abuse. *Journal of Family Therapy* **4**, 263–279.

CHAPTER 4

Recognition and Assessment of Child Sexual Abuse

Eileen Vizard and Marianne Tranter

INTRODUCTION

It is over 100 years since Dr Athol Johnston,[1] while working at The Hospital for Sick Children, Great Ormond Street, London, described a series of cases of children who had presented with recurrent fractures of the bones, and believed them to be due to rickets, a common disease at the time. In the same year in Paris, child sexual abuse was being demonstrated in the post-mortem findings of children who had been physically abused in other ways and these observations were being described and written about in the medical literature.[2] Nevertheless, it was not until 1980 that sexual abuse was included in the Department of Health and Social Security's statistics as a definition of child abuse, and thus it is only very recently[3] that we have to come to accept child sexual abuse as a very serious form of child abuse.

An American paediatrician, Suzanne Sgroi, comments that "recognition of sexual abuse is entirely dependent on the individual's inherent willingness to accept that the phenomenon actually exists".[4] Hence there appears to be a difference between hearing about accounts of sexual abuse and actually believing that it does happen. In other words, seeing and hearing is not necessarily believing in relation to child sexual abuse.

It is important to note that we live in a culture which is very strongly resistant to accepting this problem, and this resistance can be seen in professionals as well as in the general public. Sexual abuse has not been newly discovered; like other forms of abuse, it has always existed. Despite public interest in sexuality as a topic there is a high degree of secrecy and privacy surrounding personal sexual activities and especially sexual activities which break social roles and taboos. As

David Finkelhor has commented, "we cannot think about sexual abuse as a phenomenon without looking carefully at the ways in which the attractiveness of children is used in areas such as media advertising, so that we acknowledge the societal contribution to the problem, rather than seeing it as a problem of individual pathology".[5]

The issue being raised here is the fact that society appears to have double standards in relation to childhood sexuality. On the one hand there is adherence to a notion of 'childhood innocence' and purity with respect to sexuality, while on the other hand there is notion of 'Lolita-like' children, who almost invite assault, so the notion goes. It is the latter of these two alternatives which appears to fuel the sexual usage of children, in, for instance, the thriving 'kiddie porn' industry. In this way, it could be said, society is seen to be protecting children, overtly, while condoning their abuse covertly.

David Gil[6] has taken this point further, in his Marxist analysis of child/woman abuse, seen as the inevitable consequence of an exploitative capitalist society. In other words, in a society where there must be 'winners', Gil would argue, it is no surprise that vulnerable individuals, such as children, will be 'losers' and that if we accept the core abuse in child sexual abuse as being a misuse of *power*, then, the argument goes, a capitalist system will inevitably abuse women and children. However extreme such an analysis may seem, it is important to remember the lasting impact made by feminists, on social awareness of rape, wife battering, and to note that recent police initiatives in improving their interview techniques for rape victims have stemmed from such sociopolitical pressures.

THE RECOGNITION OF CHILD SEXUAL ABUSE

Historical and General Issues

As mentioned previously, while the recognition of child sexual abuse is dependent partly on the willingness of society to acknowledge its existence as a major form of child abuse, it is also dependent on the development of diagnostic and assessment skills in the relevant professionals such that the problem can be correctly identified. Parallels may be drawn between the recognition of child sexual abuse and the recognition of physical abuse some 15–20 years ago. At that time, important developments in diagnostic skills were being pioneered by paediatricians such as Henry Kempe. Recent work by paediatricians in Leeds[7,8] has highlighted how sexual abuse may present directly, and blatantly, with sex rings, but has confirmed the results of earlier studies, showing the chronicity of sexual abuse, and its early onset, with an average age for onset of 8.6 years in cases referred in 1984. The Great Ormond Street case-load shows a clear trend for even younger children to be referred, and indicates that even in children of seven years and under, sexual abuse may be a chronic problem (*see* Chapter 2).

Reviews of the literature[9] describe a range of presenting symptoms, which should alert the clinician to the possibility of child sexual abuse, and these signs, symptoms and sequelae,[10] are described elsewhere, and later in this book, in the hope that professionals working in the community, in education, health and social services, may become aware of such presenting features. A recent study[11] has indicated the need for vigilance on the part of hospital physicians (both medical and surgical), when dealing with indirect or 'masked' medical presentations of child sexual abuse. In these cases psychosomatic abdominal pain and behavioural problems, such as drug overdose, were second only in frequency, to more obvious genital symptoms, such as discharge and pruritus, in a group of children presenting with a range of symptoms, who were only later shown to have been sexually abused. This links also with recent work on a smaller scale,[12] indicating that two-thirds of adult female anorectic patients gave a history of a range of unwanted adverse sexual experiences in childhood, while one-third of the population claimed more serious genital sexual contact with an adult, in childhood. Aetiological claims cannot be made on the basis of such small numbers ($n = 78$), but nevertheless links are emerging between eating disorders in childhood and child sexual abuse. This all lends weight to the notion of 'masked medical' presenting features for child sexual abuse.

Definitions of Child Sexual Abuse

A full definition of child sexual abuse is as follows: the involvement of dependent, developmentally immature children and adolescents, in sexual activities which they do not fully comprehend, to which they are unable to give informed consent or which violate the social taboos of family roles. This includes rape, paedophilia and incest.[13]

How the Abuse Starts

The following spectrum of behaviours will often start non-intrusively with showing or touching of genitals, and will then become progressively more serious and penetrative over time. The initial stages of abuse may be non-coercive with the adult spending plenty of time in engaging the child's trust in something which is often represented as a 'game', 'our little secret', etc. Children will usually go along with this readily.

A typical progression in seriousness of child sexual abuse might be as follows:

1. Pseudoeducative contact, e.g., mutual exhibition of genitals, sometimes while giving a child information about the facts of life.
2. Masturbation of the adult by the child.
3. Mutual masturbation.
4. Oral–genital contact.
5. Vaginal intercourse.
6. Anal intercourse/buggery—as it is sometimes called.
7. Other forms of sexual play and fondling between children and adults.

It is important to stress here, that although rapacious and violent intrafamilial child sexual abuse does occur (as does stranger abuse), the majority of children (*see* Chapter 2) are *not* engaged in brief, 'once-only' incidents of molestation, and *are* coopted into long-term abuse, which escalates in seriousness over time.

Clinically, this point cannot be over-emphasized, since it would be naive to accept the initial, tentative disclosures of abuse, by older children for instance, when they may admit to intercourse having happened 'just once or twice' on a first interview. It is helpful to view such tentative disclosures as a sort of 'testing the water', to see if the listening adult will be receptive and believing of a more extensive disclosure. In simple terms, we as clinicians should ask ourselves: 'How many months/years, did the abuse take to build up to sexual intercourse, which "just happened once or twice"'. This may help to put the disclosure of abuse in a longer-term context, and also, of course, has implications for child protection and later issues of permanency planning.

Who is Responsible for Child Sexual Abuse

It is important to note that sexual acts between adults and children occur at the adults' behest and for their sexual gratification, as described above.

Children do not often seduce adults, as it is sometimes believed. Research has indicated that in 97 per cent of cases, according to respondents in one survey,[14] the sexual relationship was initiated by the adult. Similarly, it has been reported that many girls, and boys, claim that their partners used some kind of force to ensure participation.[14] The forceful measures ranged from actual physical constraint to the threat that they would be punished if they did not cooperate.

Finkelhor goes on to make the point that, even if respondents did not report overt coercion, it was difficult not to see elements of coercion in the differences in age or authority of the parties involved. This means that small children are, in the natural order of things, subject to various social pressures from older children and adults, which condition them into acquiescence and make resistance to assault difficult.

While Freud's work on infantile sexuality has been helpful in alerting us to the existence of sexual impulses and wishes in childhood, it should be pointed out that these theories were derived largely from retrospective work with adult patients. With the exception of one particular child (Little Hans), analysed jointly by Freud and the child's father, Freud did not work directly with children. However, this lack of an observational data-base for Freud's views on infantile sexuality has recently been compensated for by a British study, where the behaviour of non-abused children was observed.[15] This is discussed briefly in Chapters 5 and 6 on interview techniques, and it is now clear that persistent sexualization in children is a type of learned behaviour and should be taken seriously until further investigation excludes child sexual abuse.

However, it is also correct that when non-abused children behave in a sexual or provocative way in the short term, this may be seen as part of their normal development, whereby sexual and social roles are 'tested out' on trusted adults, usually parents or care-takers. These adults are expected to provide limits for the child's behaviour, and to respect the child's rights to mature physically and emotionally, without inappropriate sexual or social responses from adults. There is a distinction between such short-term 'testing out' behaviour, found in many families, and the compulsive sexualization found in sexually abused children.

Since the vast majority of sexually abused children (around 75–90 per cent) are molested by someone they know,[16] they may therefore become deeply confused about the blurring of these roles as mentioned. On the one hand they may wish to please a care-taking parent or family friend and to trust them, but on the other hand, the process of being involved in puzzling sexual activities which are sometimes physically and emotionally traumatic may undermine the child's capacity to trust his or her own judgement. In such circumstances, any notion of informed consent needs to be viewed cynically.[17] Certain aspects of a sexualized relationship may be enjoyed by the child, but this too leads to confusion, since the child often starts to realize that the activity is inappropriate as intellectual and moral development proceeds. A sense of guilt and shame and an erroneous belief that the child is in some way responsible for the relationship may also be serious sequelae of the abuse, and may inhibit disclosure. Such feelings are, of course, compounded by the threats or comments made by the perpetrator to the child, such as: 'If you tell, your mother will have a breakdown, and it will be your fault'.

SIGNS AND SYMPTOMS OF SEXUAL ABUSE

Physical Signs and Symptoms

The recognition of child sexual abuse depends on the professionals concerned putting all signs and symptoms into a wider psychosocial context and avoiding rushed, ill-informed or premature diagnoses.

Hence, in order to recognize the problem, it should be noted that child sexual abuse may present in different ways, to different professional persons, working in different locations. Therefore, academic underachievement, for instance, and behavioural disturbance may be part of the presenting pattern, within a school context, whereas more overtly medical signs and symptoms, such as bedwetting and genital discharge, may present in a medical setting.

In the case of children, where the medical examination is negative for instance, the diagnosis will rest on an assessment of family-background risk factors, and the psychiatric interviews with the child and family. To underline this point, Suzanne Sgroi[4] has said: "Absence of (medical) proof, is not proof of absence".

Sexually Transmitted Diseases

Sgroi[4] has commented on the medical professions 'double standard' in diagnosing venereal disease as sexually transmitted in adults, but as somehow, non-sexually/innocently transmitted in children. The reality is that between 4 per cent[18] and 13 per cent[19] of sexually abused children, have a sexually transmitted disease (STD). This may be gonorrhoea, or one of the less obviously venereal organisms such as *Gardnarella vaginalis* or *Chlamydia trachomatis*, which have recently been linked with sexual abuse in children. While estimates of the prevalence of gonorrhoea infection in sexually abused children vary, it has been claimed that 37 per cent of the referrals to a paediatric gynaecology clinic[20] were infected with *Neisseria gonorrhoeae*.

Gonorrhoea vulvovaginitis in the prepubertal child usually appears as a purulent vaginal discharge with secondary vulvitis. However, a thin mucoid discharge in an asymptomatic child may also indicate infection with *Neisseria gonorrhoeae*. Testing for gonorrhoea is with swabs from the oropharynx, vagina and rectum, for which Gram's stain and VDRL culture are required.

Multiple venereal infections are common, and 45 per cent of adults infected with gonorrhoea also have infection with *Chlamydia trachomatis*.[20] Serological tests for syphilis should also be made on first examining the child, and again on follow-up four to six weeks later. Testing for other STDs should also be carried out at this time.

Chlamydia trachomatis is now recognized as the most prevalent, sexually transmitted pathogen in the adult population,[20] and can, therefore, be transmitted to children during sexual abuse. *Chlamydia* also occurs in symptosomatic control children, but is found more frequently in children with a history of recent or past child sexual abuse. Since *Chlamydia* is an obligate intracellular organism, it must be identified in tissue culture over 10 days or so, although recent immunofluorescent slide testing using monoclonal antibodies from a blood sample has meant that results may be available in 24 hours or so. Swabs of the endocervical canal, to gather these particular cells, are needed to culture *Chlamydia*. Swabs taken from a pool of vaginal discharge may not actually contain these infected cells. Use of a paediatric speculum may be necessary to view the endocervical canal itself, and this of course may present problems in very young children, where the hymen is relatively intact. Swabs for *Chlamydia* should also be taken from the rectum and the conjunctiva of the eyes.

Trichomonas vaginalis is a parasitic organism which prefers an oestrogenic environment, and is therefore seldom found in pre-pubertal children. Like other organisms mentioned *Trichomonas* is a STD, and although non-sexual transmission of this, and other organisms, is known, review of the literature on non-sexual transmission of STDs indicates that sexual abuse of an infected child must first be excluded. *Trichomonas* presents with a copious, frothy, yellow-grey discharge with a foul smell. Itching, hyperaemia of the vulva, vulvovaginitis and dysuria may also be present. A fresh-saline, wet-mount vaginal swab from an infected child may show football-shaped trichomonads.

Gardnarella vaginalis is another organism which prefers an oestrogenic vaginal environment, and therefore infection is unusual in the preadolescent girl, and should raise suspicions about child sexual abuse which needs to be excluded. Presenting symptoms include a profuse pruritic and foul-smelling vaginal discharge. Hammerschlag et al. looked at vaginal cultures from 100 healthy girls between two months and 15 years, and found a range of bacteria present in these children.[22] *Gardnarella vaginalis* was present in 13·5 per cent of these children, but it is not clear if and how, and a history of child sexual abuse was excluded in this population, making it difficult to interpret such data.

Other genital conditions are caused by organisms for which an aetiology of child sexual abuse should be excluded; these are condyloma acuminatum, molluscum contagiosum, herpes simplex, lichen sclerosus and anogenital warts, and persistent thrush (*Candida albicans*), recalcitrant to treatment in a young child.

Non-specific vulvovaginitis

Redness and irritation of the vulval and vaginal areas is held, by lay and professional people alike, to be a common childhood complaint due to poor hygiene. How true is this, and are there features which distinguish non-specific vulvovaginitis from vulvovaginitis associated with child sexual abuse?

It has been said[20] that since the prepubescent vulva is a hairless area, with small labia minora which open readily on squatting, this anatomy may allow easy introduction of pathogens, either from poor hygiene practices, such as wiping faeces from anus to vagina in toiletting, or from squatting in dirt during play. Since the prepubescent vaginal and vulval mucosa is not oestrogenized, the pH of these tissues is neutral, allowing for easier permeability by pathogens. In fact, one study[23] has shown that 70 per cent of cases of non-specific vulvovaginitis derive from poor perineal hygiene and faecal contamination. Therefore, in such cases, culture of vulval or vaginal swabs may yield coliforms, hence giving a clue to the aetiology.

Paediatricians have previously noted the role of tight, synthetic clothing or underwear in promoting vulvovaginitis, and enquiry should be made for a history of wearing such clothes. Similarly, local irritants such as new soaps, so-called 'feminine deodorants', etc. may cause transient vulvovaginits. In relation to this aetiology, the possibility of sexual abuse involving deliberate application of irritants to the child's genital region, or application of allergenic lubricants to the vulval area, should be considered.

Another common cause of vulvovaginitis may be the insertion of foreign bodies into the vagina, resulting in a foul-smelling vaginal discharge. Culture of such a discharge will show non-specific, mixed, bacterial growth, as indeed is found in the other examples of non-specific vulvovaginitis listed above. However, the clinician should enquire about the *circumstances* of foreign-body insertion—could this have been done by an abusing adult, or was it part of a pattern of compulsive masturbation by a sexually abused child? In relation to masturbation by the child leading to vulvovaginitis, this behaviour as an aetiological explanation is often put forward. However, in a non-abused child masturbation is usually a pleasurable, short-lived phenomenon, leaving presumably very minor (if any) physical signs. Masturbation continued long enough to produce vulvovaginitis, despite discomfort to the child, may have a compulsive quality and be non-gratifying to the child. Such a history is suggestive of child sexual abuse and warrants further investigation.

However, while the medical examination can and should be undertaken sensitively, by a trained doctor, negative findings are often the norm where sexual abuse has occurred. Of 55 per cent of girls with positive findings of child sexual abuse, 35 (63·6 per cent) had intact hymens, although 15 out of the 20 not intact hymens (i.e., 75 per cent of this group) showed signs of healing, assumed to be evidence of earlier abuse.[24] It is particularly true with very young children that fondling, masturbation or oral–genital abuse will leave no signs. The recent confirmation[25] that anal interference in very young children is both common and overlooked should, nevertheless, encourage the examining doctor to check the anal orifice, and to take swabs from the anus, as well as from the vagina and mouth. For instance, in a little girl complaining of 'a sore botty', it should not be assumed that this refers only to the vaginal area, since vaginal penetration is relatively unusual in very young children, whereas penile penetration of the anus is perhaps the commonest form of perineal intercourse in both sexes of this age.

Physical and Behavioural Signs and Symptoms— A Developmental Perspective

Many of the signs and symptoms related to child sexual abuse may be found in children of all ages. However, it is helpful to remember that certain patterns of presenting symptoms are associated with particular age-groups, as detailed below.

Five years and under

Injury or behaviour disturbance, rather than verbal disclosure of sexual abuse, is the presenting norm in this age-group. The verbal capacities of, say, three-year-old children will vary, so that one child may be virtually inarticulate, while another *can* communicate in simple words. However, as is described in Chapter 5, play, not words, is the natural medium for communication at this age, and this should be remembered in the assessment interview. Therefore, lacking words, a small child may well present with bodily symptoms or behavioural disturbance. Recurrent urinary tract infections have been repeatedly linked clinically with child sexual abuse and are commonly seen in children referred for assessment of sexual abuse. However, to date no study has been done to find the prevalence of child sexual abuse among, for instance, children with recurrent urinary tract infections. Since 2 per cent of young school-entrant female children have asymptomatic bacteria,[26] it would be interesting to know what percentage of this group have been sexually abused.

Venereal infections of the mouth, anus or vagina, associated non-accidental injury and compulsive masturbation, are common symptoms found in this age group. Frozen watchfulness (typical of a child who has been abused, and who is fearful about speaking without parental permission), anxious attachment, as demonstrated by over-clinging behaviour towards parents or care-takers, can be found in sexually abused children and may link to the finding that, at least 15 per cent of sexually abused children have also been physically abused.[16] Physical abuse and non-accidental injuries may, therefore, be presenting signs of *sexual* abuse in this age group.

Five to 12 years

Psychosomatic illness and behaviour disturbance. In this age-group, children are pretty well able to communicate in words, but emotionally a child of this age is still very dependent on the family and on parents, and is therefore particularly susceptible to the blackmail and coercion described earlier, which makes a verbal disclosure so difficult. One way out of this dilemma may be for the child's body to develop psychosomatic symptoms of his or her distress, or to present with very disturbed behaviour, in the hope that an adult will notice and ask the right question. Recurrent abdominal pain, bedwetting, soiling, sudden changes in bahaviour patterns at school, over-sexualized behaviour towards other children and adults, sexualized drawings and play, are therefore some of the ways in which these children may present.

Other common behavioural characteristics of sexually abused children can include a sudden change in behaviour or personality; an increase in aggressive behaviour; withdrawal from group activities; depression; anxiety, irritability or fear, particularly fear of being left alone with men; excessive crying; unusual avoidance of touch; regression to use of babyish speech or behaviour; overcompliance; an expressed wish not to go home from school or from visits to relatives; also sleep disturbances (bedwetting or nightmares). Academic under-achievement is a common reason for referral to children's agencies, and, of course, there are a number of reasons for such a problem, including special educational needs in a developmentally delayed child. However, a sudden *change* in academic achievement usually shown by poor concentration, lack of motivation to work, etc., may indicate a home-based anxiety, such as sexual abuse.

It is worth noting that the compulsive masturbation seen in younger children, and the over-sexualization seen in both preschool and school-age children, is qualitatively different from ordinary sexual exploratory play, such as 'mummies and daddies' or showing of genitals. Over-sexualization which persists, in public, despite sanctions and prohibitions, is again a type of learned behaviour, and it is strongly associated with child sexual abuse. An example would be the boy who repeatedly grabs the genitals of male teachers, and makes sexual comments such as 'Can I suck your willie till the milk comes out?' This really cannot be seen as normal sexual exploratory behaviour, and once more 'innocent' explanations, such as access to unsupervised viewing of pornographic videos, has been ruled out, the possibility of sexual abuse should be instigated.

Twelve to 18 years

Self damage or disclosure. These children are old enough to disclose in words, and sometimes do. They are frequently *disbelieved.* All possible allegations or direct disclosures of sexual abuse in this age-group should be taken very seriously by professionals, as false allegations are rare,[27] whereas false retraction of allegations is extremely common.[28] Most incest victims attempt to tell once or twice and then give up for the rest of their lives. The onus is on us as professionals to hear the child. Self-mutilating behaviour, overdosing, alcohol and drug abuse, are some of the other ways in which child sexual abuse victims will damage themselves.

Prostitution (common in girls), and sexual assaults (common in boy victims of child sexual abuse), can indicate a past history of child sexual abuse, and show that the child is repeating patterns of learned behaviour, originally associated with the sexual abuse. Sexual assaults on younger children may be a worrying indication that the abusing child has tried to deal with his/her own victimization by a process of identification with the aggressor. Prevalence figures are lacking for the percentage of teenage boys who assault younger children, and who were victims themselves. However, many studies, exemplified by work of Groth and Burgess,[30] indicate a very much higher than expected rate of childhood sexual abuse and incest in the histories of convicted child molesters (32 per cent of a group of 106 molestors). David Finkelhor,[31] however, warns against making simplistic victim-to-perpetrator, cause-to-effect links, since many victims do *not* grow up to offend.

Running away from home and teenage pregnancies should be seen as possible signs that a child is trying to escape from incestuous abuse. A high percentage of teenage runaways have a history of child sexual abuse and incest on subsequent enquiry, and survival options for such runaway teenagers are limited to risk-filled activities such as prostitution (with nearly 90 per cent of prostitutes having a family history of child sexual abuse) and petty crime, while suicide attempts and depressive symptoms may be other ways in which a desperate adolescent will seek to draw professional attention to undisclosed child sexual abuse or incest.[29]

Similarly, teenage pregnancy itself *may* be related to a history of child sexual abuse, incest or rape. The frequency of incest pregnancy varies in different studies. De Francis[32] found that 29 out of 269 incest victims in a New York Population (i.e., 11 per cent of the sample) were pregnant. This figure is representative of other studies reviewed by Goodwin and Roybal.[33] From a clinical point of view, awareness of incest pregnancy, and making specific enquiry in young pregnant girls may help to open up a closely guarded secret.

By contrast, teenage pregnancy where the identity of the father is known to be someone outside the family circle, but where the *reasons* for becoming pregnant are difficult to ascertain, may be another sort of 'escape route' for a girl trapped in chronic, intrafamilial sexual abuse, and may also represent a cry for help. Dissociative phenomena, frank psychotic illness, and, very rarely, homicidal attacks towards the perpetrator, are more unusual presenting signs of child sexual abuse.

Recent work[34] has linked the so-called 'multiple personality' with early experiences of child sexual abuse, and clinically the processes of splitting, projection and denial (of early abusive experiences) are seen commonly in incest victims who often seem to suffer patchy amnesia for past events.

Anorexia nervosa and eating disorders may be linked to child sexual abuse, as mentioned earlier, as ways of denying sexuality by the child victim, and can certainly been seen to reflect a low self-esteem and poor body image.

Any of the above-mentioned indicators *alone* does not necessarily mean that the child has been sexually abused, but may be indicative of a child under stress, and should be assessed in an overall context. However, if more than two to three extreme or persistent behaviours or symptoms are noted, sexual abuse may be indicated and further investigation and explanation of the source of a child's symptom is needed.

It is important to remember, therefore, that signs and symptoms are not diagnostic in isolation, but that they must be seen in a context which includes relevant issues from the past family history, as well as *risk factors*.

RISK FACTORS FOR CHILD SEXUAL ABUSE

Many of the risk factors associated with physical child abuse now seem to link with child sexual abuse. Importantly, we should note—a family history of child sexual abuse or incest, a criminal record of violence, a criminal record of indecent assult or incest with children, alcoholism usually in the male perpetrator, psychiatric illness, often in the mother. Recent or concurrent sexual abuse of siblings is a risk factor for the referred child, with one-third of the sibling group of referred sexually abused children, in one study,[35] subsequently being discovered to have been sexually abused.

Physical abuse of the child is also associated with sexual abuse, and as mentioned earlier children may be battered or coerced into silence about incest. However, some of the sociodemographic characteristics of physically abusing and sexually abusing families may be shared, so that some sexual abuse, for instance, may be occurring in families who are demonstrably violent or deprived in the first place, and where physical coercion of a child into silence may be part of that family's own behaviour pattern.

Physical and mental handicap in the child are factors which seem to make some handicapped children vulnerable to abuse and exploitation. Certainly, the vulnerability of handicapped, institutionalized children to sexual abuse by their care-takers, has been the subject of national scandals recently, in this country and elsewhere. However, more child-linked risk factors, such as physical appearance, victim style body language, etc. may seem clinically relevant, but have not yet been substantiated with research. Similarly, looking at the empirical findings for risk factors in a number of studies, Finkelhor[36] was able to state that ethnicity and social class do *not* act as risk factors since child sexual abuse seems to be normally distributed in the population.

David Finkelhor's earlier study[37] looked at psychosocial characteristics of the student respondents to his anonymous questionnaire on family attitudes towards sexuality and childhood experiences of sex. Factor analysis of the data collected allowed him to construct a 'risk factor check-list', which is reproduced in *Figure* 4.1.

Finkelhor is quite rightly sceptical about the possibility or advisability of ever devising a reliable screening test for the problems of physical or sexual abuse. However, he goes on to say that such a check-list can be a device for sensitizing professionals about the kinds of backgrounds which put a child at risk for sexual victimization, as well as providing research data.

As mentioned, recent data from the NSPCC[38] seem to indicate that there may be an overlap between those risk factors which we know of for physical abuse, and risk factors for sexual abuse. For instance, it

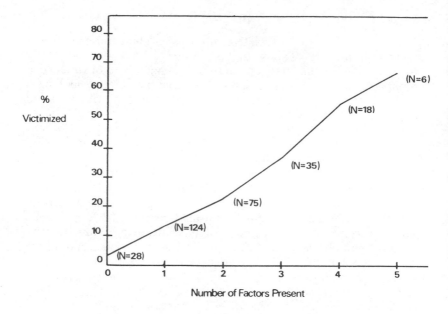

Risk factors for Girls

i.	Stepfather	v.	Sex-punitive mother
ii.	Ever live without mother	vi.	No physical affection from father
iii.	Not close to mother	vii.	Income under $10,000
iv.	Mother never finished high school	viii.	Two friends or less

Fig. 4.1. 'Risk factor check-list' (Finkelhor David, *Child Sexual Abuse—New Theory and Research.* The Free Press, MacMillan, 1984.

may be that unemployment, large family size and single-parent status are risk factors for sexual abuse. Single-parent status coupled with unemployment, for instance, may mean that more unrelated, male cohabitees of the mother, in a possibly abusing family, have un-supervised access to young children. Since Finkelhor has shown that having a stepfather puts girls at five times more risk of child sexual abuse, we can begin to see how such factors may knit together to make a worrying background of possible risk.

Jean Goodwin[39] has shown that there is a higher than average prevalence of childhood sexual and physical abuse, in the histories of mothers, where the child is referred for assessment of child sexual abuse. Since, as discussed earlier, studies agree on a high prevalence of childhood incest and childhood sexual abuse among male sex offenders, this can be put together with the other data about the sequelae of incest, mostly of a self-destructive nature, so that certain repeating and cyclical patterns become apparent (*see* Chapter 3).

In other words, as for physical abuse, sexual abuse appears to be repeated across generations, and to be recreated in new families of procreation and, indeed, in second family situations upon remarriage. Having been sexually abused once seems to 'set up' a child to become abused again. Groth[40] describes the innate skill of a sex offender in picking out potential victims from the schoolyard, on the basis of 'victim-like' body language, non-assertiveness, etc. This is readily borne out in clinical practice with young sexual abuse victims, where guilt and low self-esteem make assertiveness difficult.

Hence, the past history is an important assessment issue in formulating the present problem. It has been said[41] that the best (forensic) predictor of future behaviour is past behaviour, again a reference to the importance of patterns in assessment.

ASSESSMENT OF CHILD SEXUAL ABUSE

The assessment process can be considered in the following sequence of steps:

1. Consultation — with the network
2. Consideration — of the information
3. Construction — of an hypothesis
4. Confirmation/ refutation — of the hypothesis in the medical examination and in the psychiatric interview
5. Consensus — about findings and conclusions
6. Conjoint action — with the network to protect child and provide therapy

The Status of Concern

One of the difficulties in the assessment of child sexual abuse, and in the Management of Disclosure (*see* Chapter 7), relates to the *status of concern*.

In other words, is this a case at a very early stage, i.e.:

(i) a. *Early stage* — *Suspicion* of child sexual abuse;
     b. *Early stage* — *Allegation* by adult;
     or is it at a
(ii) *Later stage* — *Allegation* of child sexual abuse;
     or is it at a
(iii) *Much later stage* — *Disclosure* of child sexual abuse;

The ways in which the four stages of cases present to the professional, and the management issues in these different circumstances, are described in Chapter 7 on the 'Management of Disclosure'.

Nevertheless, whatever the *status of concern* about the case, the professionals involved will need to consider all six steps above in the process of assessment. The order in which these steps are considered may very well differ from case to case. For example, in (i)(*a*), *Early stage*: a *suspicion* of sexual abuse, the assessment process will probably emphasize Step 1, consultation with the network, and Step 2, consideration of the information, in order to see *whether* Step 3, Construction of an hypothesis, innocent or otherwise, can be found to account for suspicion itself (*see Figure* 4.2).

The Need for Information

At this point in assessment, Steps 1 and 2, it is vital that as *much information as possible* is made available to the network. If the professional holders of such information are themselves of a *low* level of awareness of child sexual abuse, then great resistance may be encountered in actually persuading these colleagues that the information which they hold in their own (medical/social work/police) file may be of relevance to the rest of the group. For example, a GP attended a case conference on a four-year-old female child, whose teacher was suspicious of sexual abuse on the basis of the child's behaviour only. Having explained the nccd for information sharing to the group, the chairperson gathered various items of information about the family background, and asked the GP if these was anything relevant in the notes. The GP replied, angrily, "Well not unless you count some recurrent vulvovaginitis, a few weeks ago; but on that basis, half the four-year-olds in my practice would be abused!".

The point here is that information may need to be specifically enquired for, possibly even *listing* some of the common signs and symptoms to doctors, relevant family risk factors to social workers, and criminal record, in *all* possible perpetrators, to police colleagues. This quiet persistence is often rewarded, as in the example mentioned, and can *change* the status of professional concern, moving a (i)*a. Early stage*; *suspicious* case, further along the spectrum towards, or away from, a confirmed case of sexual abuse.

(ii) *Later stage*: in the case of an *allegation* of sexual abuse by a child, the *status of concern* will be considerably higher. Current practice[42] recommends that an allegation of child sexual abuse *by a child* should be taken seriously, and believed, until proved otherwise.

In such a case, the assessment process would start with Step 3 (Construction of an hypothesis), and would say, for instance, that this child is alleging sexual abuse, because it *has* occurred, and that we must test this assumption by Steps 2 (Consideration of the information) and 4 (Confirmation/refutation by medical and psychiatric examination).

Having clarified the status of concern—is this a confirmed case or not—the network then needs to consider Steps 5 (Consensus about findings and conclusions) and 6 (Conjoint action—to protect and treat the child). Throughout the assessment process in a case of alleged sexual abuse (as with all other types of cases), the concerned professional will need to engage in Step 1 (Consultation with the network) from the beginning, and through until treatment (if any) begins.

In the case of a perpetrator confessing, him or herself, to child sexual abuse, this is taken as a disclosure (iii) *Much later stage* (p. 77).

Family Context of Allegations

What if the allegation is made by a family member? (i.e. Early stage allegation by Adult (i)b.) In this case, no testable hypothesis can be made, until consultation, information gathering and, possibly also, the medical and psychiatric examinations, have occurred. In other words, rather *more* weight is given to an allegation from a child, than from a family member, in the first instance.

It should be remembered that the family *context* in which an allegation of child sexual abuse is made is vitally important. In relation to the rare instances of false allegation by a *child*, a family background of parental conflict, or maternal psychiatric disorder may be associated with 'opportunistic lies', or with *folie à deux* allegations.

Similarly, and of current concern, is the *possible* association between false, parental, allegations of child sexual abuse, by the other spouse, in contested custody and access cases, where the diagnosis of child sexual abuse would be a vital factor in deciding on the best interests of the child.

In such cases, where adequate measures have been taken to protect the child (*see* Chapter 7), the assessment process may well benefit from being extended to include two or more meetings with the child to counteract the often over-excited and litigious attitudes of the parents. This extended assessment may also allow time for the child to open up and talk to the interviewer, particularly if the child has been made very aware, by the parents, that anything said, or anything not said, will be damaging to one or other of the parents. Finally, although it is vital to exercise caution in making a diagnosis of child sexual abuse in access cases, and to *avoid*, therefore, the possibility of *false-positive* diagnosis, nevertheless, there is no doubt that child sexual abuse *does* occur on access visits, and may have a special connotation, for the perpetrator, of 'spoiling' something (the child) which belongs to the custodial parent.

Therefore, in cases of adult allegations of child sexual abuse (*see Figure* 4.2), assessment will generally follow the lines (ib) where a medical examination may be needed, a psychiatric examination is likely to be needed, and the hypothesis formation may *have* to wait until later.

(iii) *Much later stage: disclosure* of sexual abuse (*see Figure* 4.2), whether by the victim, by the perpetrator, or by the process of assessment itself, will usually require some sort of Conjoint action (Step 6) with the network, to protect the child and to provide therapy (*see* Chapter 7). However, it is important at the point of disclosure to be thinking of *risk to other children*, either in the home of the child concerned, or elsewhere within range of the perpetrator. Information should also be gathered about these children, in Steps 1 and 3, and action (Step 6) taken to protect them, if necessary. *Figure* 4.2 demonstrates, notionally, how the various Steps (1–6) in the assessment process might be used in each of the four case types, (i)–(iii), described above.

It will be seen from the above that the processes of recognition, assessment and management of disclosure are all interlinked and that the whole professional network, not just the key worker or therapist, is

Steps in assessment of child sexual abuse

	1	2	3	4	5	6

(ia) Early stage: suspicion

o ------->-------->

(ib) Early stage: allegation by adult

o ------->--------> ?<---- ? Need for medical examination

(ii) Later stage: allegation by children

Test   Test

<------- o ------->--------->-------->

(iii) Much later stage: disclosure by child/perpetrator

<-------<-------<------- o ------->-------->

Fig. 4.2.   Possible use of Steps 1–6 in the assessment process of case types (i)–(iii)

closely involved in supporting this process. This needs to be said, although it may seem obvious, since anxiety about the assessment of a sexual abuse suspicion, allegation or disclosure, can lead professionals into *over*-estimating certain tasks (e.g., the medical examination), and *under*-estimating others (e.g., the role of the police). As with all forms of child abuse, the major task in assessing child sexual abuse is to be sure that the child is safe.

Steps 1–3, 5 and 6, are discussed within a management context more fully in Chapter 7. Therefore we will now look at Step 4 in the assessment process.

Confirmation or refutation of sexual abuse—
the medical examination and psychiatric interview

More haste, less speed. Although the medical examination should occur quickly after an allegation or disclosure of *recent* sexual abuse, so that appropriate samples can be taken before this potential evidence vanishes, this is not necessary in all cases of sexual abuse—where the abuse stopped some time previously. Therefore, some initial idea of the timing and *duration* of the abuse will be needed to decide whether or not the medical examination is necessary.

Looking again at the three different types of cases (i) Early stage suspicion, (ii) Later stage allegation, (iii) Much later stage disclosure, how should a decision be made about the medical examination in each of these situations? The first thing to point out is that the medical examination is only part of the examination of the child, and that a negative result from the medical examination does *not* exclude child sexual abuse (*see* p. 79).

Therefore, returning to *Figure* 4.1, if the assessment process has reached a point at which the network has constructed a hypothesis that child sexual abuse may possibly have occurred, Step 3, then it is reasonable to move onto the first part of Step 4—the medical examination/psychiatric interview. It will be apparent in early stage cases of suspicion (ia), and of allegation by adult (ib), that such a hypothesis cannot be made, and that a medical examination is probably not justified. Another way of looking at this is to suggest that a medical examination *should* be carried out on all children where there is a recent allegation by the child, or confession by the perpetrator. An important exception to this would be those cases where, for whatever reason, the abuse is known to have stopped a long time previously and where there is no suspicion of injury to the child. Of course, ascertaining these facts may be difficult, and if there is *doubt* a sympathetically conducted medical examination should be undertaken to reassure both child and family that all is well.

The physical examination[44]

1. General physical examination.
2. Specific examination of the genital and anal areas.
3. Screening for problems related to sexual activity, such as sexually transmitted diseases and pregnancy.
4. Collection of items necessary for forensic evaluation.
5. Reassurance.

It is worth remembering, in relation to point 1, that non-accidental injury (NAI) of one sort or another occurs in *at least* 15 per cent of sexually abused children, and that the physical examination of a stripped child is essential in order to detect bruising hidden by clothing, for instance.

Some clinicians advocate doing the medical examination in two sessions, in order to build up a rapport with the child, and to complete parts of the examination which were initially difficult to do, possibly due to fear on the part of the child, on the second occasion. Again, the delay involved and the effect on the forensic evidence, as well as a possible exacerbation of anxiety in the child, need to be taken into account by the examining doctor.

Who should do the medical examination? The answer is, a trained doctor, probably an experienced police surgeon, or a specifically trained paediatrician, who has access to and is familiar with police forensic materials and procedures. It is far better to *wait* a few hours, or even a day if necessary, in order to obtain the services of the best-trained doctor, although there are important exceptions to this, including cases where ejaculation is suspected to have occurred within the last 72 hours. However, the disadvantages of waiting for an experienced doctor mean that not only will the samples gathered be acceptable to the police, but also the trained doctor's evidence will carry far more weight in court than would that of an inexperienced GP colleague. It may, in certain areas, be possible for a paediatrician and police surgeon to do a joint medical examination of the child, and again, this may be helpful.[45]

Similarly, the trained doctor will be much more likely to *succeed* in doing these very intimate, and possibly frightening, examinations with children, than say a nervous, hasty casualty doctor, who may inadvertently cause vaginismus in a female child, or refusal to examine the anus in either sex.

While it is obviously right, necessary and helpful, for day-nursery staff to look superficially at the genitals of small children in their care, in the process of cleaning/nappy changing, it is *not* appropriate for such staff or for teachers to attempt to look 'inside' the child's vaginal or anal orifice, or for that matter to 'persuade' a weeping child to let them have a 'look-see'. The inexpertly performed 'look-see' may spoil valuable forensic evidence, sensitize the child against later examination and, most importantly, may reinforce in the child a sense of having no control over his or her own body.

Pursuing this argument for examination by suitably qualified medical personnel, it follows that, for a small number of very frightened and resistant children who have been badly physically damaged or emotionally traumatized by the abuse, an examination *may* need to be done under a general anaesthetic, in order to allow a clear view of the genital organs and to decide on possible treatment. One difficulty here may be the physiological relaxation of the anal sphincter under general anaesthetic, a phenomenon which could lead to difficulties in the interpretation of an apparantly dilated or stretched sphincter. However, in more relaxed and compliant children a clear macroscopic view may be greatly aided by the use of an instrument called a colposcope, which can give a magnified view of very fine details on the genital region. Recent research[24] has indicated that tiny petechial haemorrhages (very fine tears) around the perineal body, and very subtle bruising, can be picked up using this instrument. In children, where only *attempted* penetration has occurred, it is estimated that 50 per cent of abnormalities can be visualized using the colposcope. A macroscopic 'eye' view of the genital area (looking at female genitals or at the anus) might register normal appearances, and conclude that nothing had happened. However, it should be emphasized that novel instruments are no replacement for first-hand clinical experience. Since police surgeons and paediatricians may have complementary skills in relation to forensic and paediatric matters, the notion of learning from each other, by conducting *joint* medical examinations of child sexual abuse victims has recently been noted by both the Association of Police Surgeons and the British Paediatric Association.

Recent work by Hobbs and Wynne[25] has pointed out the surprising frequency of anal interference in children of both sexes, and has suggested that until now many practitioners may have omitted to part the child's buttocks, particularly if the suspected victim was a little girl, and to check for bruising, anal tears or poor anal tone. Clinical experience, in psychiatric interviews with children, strongly confirms that anal interference with digital, penile, or object penetration may be a very common type of abuse with very young children and yet may leave no marks. The same team have looked at the range of measurements of the transverse vaginal diameter in sexually abused girls, and have suggested that a transverse vaginal diameter of more than 5 mm is compatible with child sexual abuse. However, it is very important not to overemphasize the value of such a measurement—rarely children are born with imperforate hymens, or with no hymen at all. Police surgeon colleagues report that the appearance of the vaginal orifice in female babies can vary tremendously, and of course the actual process of measuring such an area in an anxious child requires maximum skill and experience. Nevertheless, the refining of medical examination techniques is greatly to be welcomed, although, as Finkel says, "Sexual abuse can rarely be diagnosed with forensic tests".

However, at times such forensic investigation may be needed and, in order to utilize colposcopy and other technology, hospital-based investigation may be necessary. This links to the possibility of routinely admitting all suspected sexually abused children who need an examination to hospital for assessment, both medical and psychiatric, as well as allowing the development of a multidisciplinary management plan, while the child remains safe from reabuse within the hospital. In the UK different areas have evolved different guidelines on the management of disclosure. However, the 1986 DHSS guidelines on the management of child abuse cases state that the child should not be subjected to repeated medical examinations, and that the examination should be conducted in an 'adequate clinical setting', for example, a local hospital, or specially equipped room at a police station.[42]

Certain boroughs in London[43] have developed a procedure for medical and psychosocial assessment of the suspected sexually abused child, to be undertaken in a hospital setting, with discharge when results of the tests are available and the security of the child is established. Early reports indicate that this is a helpful way in which to overcome some of the difficulties described above.

The final stage of reassurance cannot be over-emphasized in relation to the medical examination, and this ties in with the issues raised in the Practice Guide in Chapter 6. The examining physician must be sensitive to the child's vulnerability and must be aware that rough 'business-like' or even 'over-jolly' approaches to such children, may be a clear indicator, to the child, that the *doctor* is nervous and ambivalent about the examination.

Helpful medical and forensic texts are now available for medical practitioners. These should also be read by other mental health practitioners, to inform them about the approach to the whole examination, to de-mystify the medical aspects of it and, finally, to help in the post-examination management of the child.[9]

References

1. Johnston A. (1886) *Lectures on the Surgery of Childhood*. London.
2. Tardieu A. (1878) *Etude Medico-Legale sur les Attentats Aux Moeurs*, 7th edition. London, Paris: Ballière et fils.

3. Kempe R.S. and Kempe C.H. (1978) Chapter 4. Incest and other forms of sexual abuse. In: Burner J., Cole M. and Lloyd B. (eds) *Child Abuse, the Developing Child*. Milton Keynes, Open University Press.
4. Sgroi S.M. (1977) "Kids with clap"—gonorrhea as an indicator of child sexual assault. In: *Victimology* **II**, 251–267.
5. Finkelhor D. (1984) Chapter 1. Sexual abuse as a social problem: In: *Child Sexual Abuse: New Theory and Research*. New York: Free Press.
6. Gil D. (1985) Chapter 2. The political and economic context of child abuse. In: Newberger, Eli and Bourne (eds), *Unhappy Families—Clinical and Research Perspectives on Family Violence*. Boston: PSA.
7. Wild N.J. and Wynne J.M. (1986) Child sex rings. *British Medical Journal* **293**, 183–185.
8. Wild N.J. (1986) Sexually abused children in Leeds. *British Medical Journal* **292**, 1113–1116.
9. Sgroi S. (1982) *Handbook of Clinical Intervention in Child Sexual Abuse*. Lexington, Mass.: Lexington Books.
10. Vizard E. (1984) The sexual abuse of children, parts I & II. *Health Visitor* July, August.
11. Hunter R.S., Kilstrom N. and Leda F. (1985) Sexually abused children identifying masked presentation in a medical setting: *Child Abuse and Neglect* **9**, 17–25.
12. Oppenheimer R., Howells K., Palmer R.L. et al. (1985) Adverse Sexual Experience and Clinical Eating Disorders. A Preliminary Description. Unpublished paper. University of Leicester.
13. Schechter M.D. and Roberge L. (1976) Sexual exploitation. In: Helfer R.E. and Kempe C.H. (eds), *Child Abuse and Neglect: the Family and the Community*. Cambridge, Mass.: Ballinger.
14. Finkelhor D. (1984) Chapter 3. Victims. In: *Child Sexual Abuse: New Theory and Research*. New York: Free Press.
15. Glaser D. (1986) The Response of Young, Non-sexually Abused Children to Anatomically Correct Rag Dolls. Talk given to ACPP, November 1985.
16. Mrazek P.B., Lynch M. and Bentovim A. (1981) Chapter 3. Recognition of CSA in the United Kingdom. In: Mrazek P. B. and Kempe C.H. (eds), *Sexually Abused Children and their Families*. Oxford: Pergamon.
17. O'Carrol T. (1980) *Paedophilia—the Radical Case*. London: Peter Owen.
18. Goodwin J. and Fried J. (1978) Rape. *New England Journal of Medicine* **298**, 167.
19. White S.T., Leda F.A., Ingram D.L. et al. (1983) Sexually transmitted diseases in sexually abused children. *Paediatrics* **72**, 16–21.

20. Arsenaut P. and Gerbie A. (1986) Vulvovaginitis in the pre-adolescent girl. *Paediatric Annals* **15**, 577–585.
21. Neinstein L.J., Goldenring S. and Carpenter E.V. (1984) Non-sexual transmission of sexually transmitted diseases: an infrequent occurrence. *Paediatrics* **74**, 67–75.
22. Hammerschlag M.R., Albert S., Rosner I. et al. (1978) Micro-biology of the vagina in children: normal and potential pathogenic organisms. *Paediatrics* **62**, 57–62.
23. Huffman J.W., Dewhurst C.J. and Caprato V. (1981) *The Gynaecology of Childhood and Adolescence*, 2nd edition, p. 124. Philadelphia: Saunders.
24. Eros W.F., Conrath T.B. and Byer J. (1986) Forensic evaluation of the sexually abused child. *Paediatrics* **78**, No. 3., September 1986.
25. Hobbs C. and Wynne J. (1986) Buggery in childhood—a common syndrome of child abuse. *Lancet* **3**, 792–796.
26. Kunin C. (1979) *Detection, Prevention and Management of Urinary Tract Infections*, 3rd edition. Philadelphia: Lea and Febiger.
27. Goodwin J. (ed.) (1982) Chapter 2. False accusations and false denials of incest: clinical myths and clinical realities. In: *Sexual Abuse: Incest Victims and their Families*. Bristol: John Wright.
28. Summit R. (1983) The child sexual abuse accommodation syndrome. *Child Abuse and Neglect* **7**, 179–193.
29. Lindberg F.H. and Distaddeis J. (1985) Survival responses to incest: adolescents in crisis. *Child Abuse and Neglect* **9**, 521–526.
30. Groth N.A. and Burgess A.W. (1979) Sexual traumas in the life histories of rapists and child molestors. *Victimology* **4**, 10–16.
31. Finkelhor D. (ed.) (1986) Chapter 4. Abusers: special topics. In: *A Sourcebook on Child Sexual Abuse*. Beverley Hills: Sage Publications.
32. De Francis V. (1965) *Protecting the Child Sex Victim*. Denver: American Humane Association.
33. Goodwin J. and Roybal L. (1982) Chapter 12. The incest pregnancy. In: Goodwin J. (ed.), *Sexual Abuse: Incest Victims and their Families*. Bristol: John Wright.
34. Coons P. M. (1986) Child abuse and multiple personality disorder: review of the literature, and suggestions for treatment. *Child Abuse and Neglect* **10**, 455–462.
35. Berliner L. and Stevens D. (1982) Clinical issues in child sexual abuse. In: Conte J.R. and Shope D. (eds), *Social Work and Child Sexual Abuse*. New York: Haworth.
36. Finkelhor D. (ed.) (1986) Chapter 2. High risk children. In: *A Sourcebook on Child Sexual Abuse*. Beverley Hills: Sage Publications.
37. Finkelhor D. (1979) *Sexually Victimised Children*. Glencoe: The Free Press.

38. Creighton S. (1985) An epidemiological study of abused children and their families in the UK between 1977–1982. *Child Abuse and Neglect* **9**, 441–448.
39. Goodwin J. (ed.) (1982) Chapter 13. Physical and sexual abuse of the children of adult incest victims. In: *Sexual Abuse: Incest Victims and their Families*. Bristol: John Wright.
40. Groth N. (1979) *Men Who Rape*. New York: Plenum.
41. Scott P.D. (1977) Assessing dangerousness in criminals. *British Journal of Psychiatry* **131**, 127–142.
42. DHSS (1986) Child Abuse, Working Together. A Discussion Document. London: HMSO.
43. Hall A. and Harris R. (1986) Personal communication guidelines for response to CSA, used in London Borough of Tower Hamlets.
44. Finkel K.C. (1983) Recognition and Assessment of the Sexually Abused Child—Guidelines for Physicians. Prepared for Committee on Child Welfare, Ontario Medical Association, Toronto.
45. Association of Police Surgeons of Great Britain and The British Paediatric Association, 10th July 1987. Agreed Joint Statement on Child Sexual Abuse.

CHAPTER 5

Helping Young Children to Describe Experiences of Child Sexual Abuse— General Issues

Eileen Vizard and Marianne Tranter

INTRODUCTION

The aims of this chapter on interviewing young sexually abused children are: to provide information for professionals engaged in this work, to share a body of clinical experience arising out of this work and, hopefully, to provide a basis for the training of clinicians who need to interview young sexually abused children. The clinical material described in this chapter is based on nearly five years' work, in the Child Sexual Abuse Team at The Hospital for Sick Children, Great Ormond Street, London. The demographic characteristics of these children, and their families, as well as follow-up information on treatment outcome, are described in Chapter 2 of this book. Clinical examples, and conclusions about the observed behaviours of children in the room, are taken directly from the Great Ormond Street Team's experience in working with some 600 children.

Deleterious Attitudes to Abused Children

Historical and cultural perspectives in relation to the recognition of child sexual abuse have been described elsewhere.[1] Nineteenth-century medical and psychiatric attitudes towards the untruthfulness of children and their tendency to fantasize about sexuality,[2] coupled with the legal reflection of this perception in our present law which does not accept the uncorroborated evidence of a child under 10 as valid, have unfortunately combined to put the young child victim of sexual assault in an impossible position. If the child tells someone in authority about the abuse, he or she may not be believed. Even if they are believed, the lack of medical evidence which is usual in such cases may result in the adult abuser exercising his right under law, to test the evidence of his victim in the court system through cross-examination.

However, while an adversarial stance may be perfectly suitable for adult parties in the court system, it is clearly developmentally inappropriate for small children to be exposed to hostile cross-examination by an adult. Indeed, clinical experience has demonstrated that, following disclosure, child victims of sexual abuse are subject to tremendous pressure from adults, both inside and outside their family, to recant.[3] When police prosecution of an offender does not ensue, perhaps due to lack of corroborative evidence, retraction by the child of the original allegation is very common, and may be the only way in which that child will be accepted by the rest of his or her family. One might say, therefore, that all the dice are loaded against the young child sticking to his or her story, and in favour of a retraction of the allegation, which then feeds further into stereotyped notions about children being untruthful. Hopefully, this situation will not continue, since both adult victims of child sexual abuse, and adult perpetrators of these crimes, are now speaking out in the media and on television, confirming in explicit detail the clinical stories which have been heard from young child victims for a number of years.[4] Adult victims confirm that sexual abuse in the family is seldom a once-only incident, but is usually a long-standing pattern of abuse going back many years into early childhood.

Failures in Management of Sexual Abuse

The lack of treatment available for recidivist sex offenders may have serious implications, as in the case of one very elderly offender in his seventies who admitted to a total of 77 previous undetected sexual assaults on young children, escalating in seriousness and culminating in a child murder. While abuse by this type of deeply disturbed offender, which, given the current dearth of treatment facilities for children, resulting in detection, may indicate a 'cry for help' from the offender, which given the current dearth of treatment facilities for offenders, may well go unheeded. Recent studies show that a large number of child molesters report sexually abusive experiences from their own childhoods,[5,6] hence confirming the clinical impression of cyclical patterns of abuse across generations, whereby victims become perpetrators and so on.

In approaching an interview with a young sexually abused child, considerations of outcome may be relevant, since worries about the fate of the alleged abuser (i.e., prison or help) may inhibit a child from disclosing sexual abuse. While false reassurance should never be given to children about such long-term issues as outcome for the alleged abuser, the therapist should nevertheless bear these issues in mind, since the child will certainly be doing so.

Finally, it is extremely important that the individual interview with a young child is put well and truly into an overall assessment context. A final diagnostic statement about child sexual abuse will be based on consideration of a whole range of family background issues, risk factors, reported circumstances around the abuse, medical evidence, as well as what occurs in the interview.

A Clinical Approach

The main role of the clinician should still be a therapeutic one of facilitating disclosure,[7] in order to afford the therapeutic relief described at the end of the structured interview format in Chapter 6. Even if an investigative component is included in the clinician's aims for the interview, it should be remembered that in uncorroborated cases of child sexual abuse the criminal law burden of proof, aiming to establish proof 'beyond all reasonable doubt', can seldom be applied. In civil law,[8] judicial decisions about child abuse are made on 'the balance of probabilities'. Therefore, clinicians should remember that they are not expected to operate as policeman, for instance, persistently or relentlessly questionning the child about sexual abuse.

An overall clinical view should be taken of the child's emotional state and preoccupations, the child's relationship with parents or caretakers, and with peers, the child's progress at school, and the family background, which might or might not put the child at risk of sexual abuse. In other words, the importance of the individual interview with the child should *not* be over-emphasized, since this may lead to the missing of vital background information, which could inform the interview itself. However, the importance of the individual interview should not be under-emphasized, since this may lead to a failure to see the child separately or to a tendency to 'pre-judge' the diagnosis in advance of the interview and hence introduce bias.

DEVELOPING A NEW APPROACH

In common with American treatment projects for sexually abused children and their families[9,10] the Great Ormond Street Child Sexual

Abuse Team noted a steady fall in the age at referral among children presenting within the first three years of establishing the treatment project. Initially, large numbers of teenage girls were referred, changing over the subsequent months and years to include referral of boys, then referral of young children under ten and, finally, to the present situation, where many young children under seven, including an increasing number of children below three years of age, are now referred for assessment (Chapter 2). With increasing awareness of child sexual abuse, other treatment projects in England are confirming this experience, so that clinicians are now faced daily with the referral of young children from early infancy to puberty, for assessment of possible child sexual abuse. An approach to interviewing adolescent children is described in Chapter 6, and this chapter will concentrate on working with young children, under the age of ten, to help them discuss possible abusive experiences.

Initially, assessment of adolescent children in the Great Ormond Street team was undertaken in the context of the family interview, which might or might not include the alleged perpetrator of the sexual abuse. The team approach to family work, described in Chapter 8, is systems-based, and seeks to understand the meaning of the abusive behaviour within the overall context of a family. Therefore, it may seem reasonable to begin to explore the incestuous behaviour, including an assessment of its extent, within a family context. There are pros and cons to this approach, in relation to early assessment of adolescents. One major disadvantage may be that the right of the young person to be seen as an individual, and not a wholly dependent member of the family, is overlooked.

The Need for Individual Interviews with Children

However, in practice, it soon became apparent to the Great Ormond Street team that there was also a need for a separate individual interview with younger children, albeit for different reasons from those relating to the adolescent boy or girl. Briefly, it was noted that young children may be inhibited from talking about abuse in a large family group, and will almost certainly be inhibited if this group includes the alleged perpetrator. Even more importantly, young children may be subtly invalidated by other family members during a disclosure (see Chapter 6), and may retract the disclosure. Apart from these considerations, it became clear that different approaches to the process of assessing and talking with young children needed to be developed, since many children were either pre- or poorly verbal, or simply too frightened to put their experiences into words.

The Use of Play

The question may be asked, 'Why use play with young children, why not simply ask them what, if anything, has happened?' There is nothing whatever to stop the interviewer simply asking, even a very young child, what has happened (*see* Chapter 6 for details), but it should be remembered that children are *not* 'mini adults', and cannot be treated as such. In other words, a small child cannot reasonably be expected to sit on a chair and engage in a continuous verbal dialogue with an adult over a long period of time. This is not natural behaviour for children, and may be tedious, even for slightly older children approaching puberty, who may need drawing materials or other play material provided in order to facilitate communication. In fact, investigating police officers are now only too well aware that the tendency to treat little children as if they were 'mini adults', as in the traditional police interview, is now outdated and inappropriate. More importantly, police colleagues realize that they may be losing potentially valuable evidence from the child, and recent training initiatives by the Metropolitan Police have encouraged investigating officers to take a more imaginative approach towards interviewing small children, and to undertake this work in conjunction with a specialist social worker.

If children cannot or will not communicate through speech, are there any other forms of communication which may tell us what has been going on? Children have always communicated their feelings and experiences through play, drawing and body language, as well as through symptoms and behaviour. Being already aware of these issues, and becoming aware of the difficulties facing the young sexually abused child, an approach developed which allowed the clinician and the child to communicate through play, and in words. This approach was more developmentally appropriate for young children, and took into account some of their special needs.

It is assumed, throughout this chapter, that children's play in such a therapeutic context is not a trivial matter, and that it does have meaning which can be understood by the trained observer. Although the approach described in the Practice Guide (*see* Chapter 6) is a form of structured play using dolls, the importance of fantasy play, using a range of play materials, should not be underestimated. A child's fantasy communications in an interview which aims to explore the possibility of sexual abuse, among other things, may relate indirectly to abusive experiences, or to relevant aspects of home life. For instance, a wild little five-year-old girl, seen for assessment of possible sexual abuse, spent the first 10 minutes cutting out sets of sharp paper teeth while she described her 'dream' of the big shark in the sea eating up all the little baby fish, and even the friendly shark being unable to resist nibbling the fingers and toes of the baby fish. This child went straight on to demonstrate a range of sexual behaviours with the dolls, which included her own involvement with bestiality. However, on direct verbal enquiry of the child, she denied that anything had happened, curled up in the chair, and said, 'Don't tell them what I told you'. Therefore, the meaning of fantasy communication is relevant to an assessment of child sexual abuse, but may also be subtle, and at times difficult to interpret.

The issue of fantasy

Something more needs to be said about the issue of fantasy in relation to play techniques with young suspected sexually abused children. Persisting Freudian notions about Oedipal wishes towards the parent of the opposite sex, coupled with a negative societal perception of children and women,[11] have also fed into the assumption that when children talk about sex, they may well be lying. However, is this true? Why should children lie about sexual matters, why should their fantasy play, their verbal communications, or their behaviour patterns, be sexualized to a noticeable extent, as often is the case with sexual abuse victims? As has been indicated above, the content and meaning of fantasy play may be directly relevant to an abusive experience. Clinical experience strongly confirms that young children are *not* natural liars, and that the whole of their development is characterized by a search for truth and understanding, which may be expressed in different ways.

This is not to say, naively, that children never tell lies. Of course they do, and this discussed on p. 97, but like all of us, children will lie for a reason. Fear of disclosure, often based on the reality of threats to the child, may completely prevent that child from putting a sexually abusive experience into words. However, something about the naturalness of play and the use of play materials, including 'anatomically correct dolls', helps children to bypass the need to articulate the feared words about abuse, while providing them with an age-appropriate method of demonstrating what has happened.

Developmental issues

Finally, from a developmental point of view, young children may have great difficulty in expressing real events in abstract words, either due to poor verbal skills, or to inhibition as mentioned above. The natural egocentricity, and concreteness in thinking of young children[12] means that they will identify readily with, for instance, line drawings of children and adults, puppets with friendly faces, or with anatomically correct dolls. Any difficulties in symbolizing an abusive experience, and reproducing this in words, may therefore be bypassed by simple re-enactment of the abuse using play material. In most children there is a clear distinction between the sort of fantasy play described earlier, random oversexualized play using the dolls, and a hesitant, but convincing demonstration of sexual abuse, which can be repeated consistently, using the dolls, and which may also be described in words.

Therefore, a new approach developed, which was based on the assumption that young children, who may have been sexually abused, need to be seen separately at some point by a trained clinician in order to evaluate the nature of their experience. It has been found helpful to use a range of play materials, including the anatomically correct dolls, and to bear in mind other and concurrent forms of communication from the child, such as observed behaviour in the room, which may also carry a message about sexual abuse. It has become very clear that considerable training is necessary for this work, particularly in cases where the abuse may have been chronic, where children may have been coerced into silence, or where there are communication difficulties. Even the most experienced clinician needs supervision and support from a team who can point out errors, sharpen skills and, above all, provide another view of the child's communication.

THE INDIVIDUAL INTERVIEW

Aims of the Interview

In all cases, one aim for the interview must be to help the child, whether this is by assessing the degree of risk to that child, or by allowing the child the opportunity to ventilate his or her feelings about the abuse. It should be remembered that while the first disclosure interview is usually cathartic and often therapeutic for the child, subsequent interviews may be needed to be handled rather differently. In other words, the child should not be subjected to repetitive questioning about the details of the abuse, which in itself may feel intrusive and abusive to the child. Unwitting identification by the clinician with individual members of the abusing family (mirroring)[13] (Chapter 7) *may* result in either inadequate questioning which does not grasp the nettle in relation to sexual abuse, or conversely may result in relentless and perhaps repetitive questioning, which may produce nothing new. In this context, the attitude of the interviewer is important (*see* Chapter 6).

There are five possible aims for a clinician interviewing a suspected sexually abused child, or a child who has been sexually abused:

1. Disclosure by the child, perhaps for the first time, of a sexually abusive experience.
2. 'Recap' of an earlier disclosure of sexual abuse, when it is suspected that further abuse may have occurred, which has not been fully disclosed.
3. Clarification about the degree of possible risk to the child, with a view to child protection measures.
4. Gathering evidence for criminal proceedings.
5. Assessment of the therapeutic needs of the sexually abused child, where specific discussion of the sexual abuse may have to occur in order to understand the child's emotional and treatment needs.

Doubtless there are other interview aims which will be specific for different cases in differing situations. For instance, the only too prevalent abuse of younger children in children's homes, by older children in the same institution (which is a great deal more prevalent than was previously suspected), or by professional care-takers, requires a particularly sensitive approach to interviewing these children. Here the aims may be not only to facilitate private disclosures, but also to find out which other children are at risk.

Inevitably, the aims of the interview will relate closely to who does the interview (*see below*), and in any case since the professional conducting the interview should never be operating in isolation, all these issues need to be agreed by the professional network *before* the interview commences. A simple example of the consequences of not thinking ahead would be the case where an 'emergency' assessment of an allegation of sexual abuse, made by a child in school on a Wednesday, is dealt with in an individual interview, late on a Friday afternoon. What are the aims of this interview? If a first-time disclosure of abuse occurs, what can be done with it at 5.30 p.m. on a Friday evening? Has anyone thought ahead to the implications of a disclosure, both for the child and for the parents? Are medical, police and social work colleagues alerted and standing by in case of disclosure? Has adequate background research been done on the case, to inform the prospective interviewer? These and many other questions need to be answered before the aims for such an eleventh-hour interview can be clarified.

It is clear that protecting the child from the risk of continuing abuse (as in aim 3 above) needs to be a priority in the investigation of child sexual abuse. However, children are best protected by a multiagency approach to child abuse,[14] which underlines the need for prior preparation, as described above.

Finally, the clinician should remember that, whatever the aims of the interview, if child protection issues or criminal proceedings are involved in the case, then the clinician may be required to give evidence in civil or criminal proceedings about the content of the interview with the child. There may be specific implications here, in relation to confidentiality and interview techniques, if the clinician chooses to videotape the interview. In any event, very careful record keeping, in the form of written notes, should be a part of the assessment process, and it should be remembered that these notes may also be used as evidence in subsequent court proceedings.

Approaches Used—Who Does the Interview?

The question of who does the initial interview, or subsequent interviews of the child, depends partly on whether the case is at an early or at a later stage, and partly on the aims for the interview. Ideally, in the early stages of the management of disclosure, a joint approach is now advocated.[14] This might entail a trained police officer and a trained social worker working together jointly to take a definitive statement from the child, and would have evidential value, which would avoid the child having to be interviewed again.

In some areas this joint approach is now occurring, but in practice, an initial interview by the duty social worker, for instance, may have to be followed by another police interview, and possibly by yet another psychiatric interview, to look at treatment needs. National guide-lines are urgently being constructed, to ensure a more coordinated response to the early management of disclosure. However, since both criminal and child-care issues are involved, it is clearly better that professionals such as paediatricians, casualty officers and police surgeons, psychiatrists, psychologists, and psychotherapists, etc. do *not* engage single-handedly in the diagnostic interviews in the early stages.

Unless police and social work colleagues are linked in to the assessment process at the very beginning, well-intentioned diagnostic interviews conducted by other professionals may need to be replicated later. This is not to say that other professionals cannot talk, in a preliminary way, to a child who is starting to disclose sexual abuse in, say a casualty department. However, the approach here should be to assess whether or not the police and social services department need to interview the child. If such an interview is to take place, the clinician concerned should explain to the child that he/she can tell the *details* to some people with a special interest in the subject later on. In this way, the child is saved from repeating the information twice.

Once an initial disclosure of sexual abuse has occurred, the child may be placed in care, or with relatives, or the perpetrator may be required to leave the home so that the child is safe. If a child is placed in care, it may become apparent that there are further details about the abuse yet to be disclosed, or the child may become symptomatic and disturbed, for instance, starting to sexually abuse other children in care. Similarly, children who have been received into care some time previously, and where there has been no initial admission of sexual abuse, may subsequently indicate by their behaviour or in words, that a disclosure is imminent. In these situations, it may be helpful for someone within the care system who is well known to the child, such as a key worker or a foster mother, to spend some time reassuring the child, and encouraging the child to talk, if possible, about his experiences.

This is not to suggest that foster parents and children's home workers should be expected to conduct detailed initial interviews in relation to sexual abuse. That would clearly be inappropriate, in view of the training required. However, children may take great comfort and encouragement from preliminary discussion and reassurance from someone whom they trust, and this in itself may facilitate fuller disclosure in a later interview. It is likely that at a later stage in the management of disclosure a specialist team may need to be consulted about interviewing the child to assess treatment needs. Once referred to a specialist agency, however, contact should still be maintained with the referring agency, as it is usually very helpful for the referring social worker to accompany the child to this interview, and to be made aware of the outcome of the interview itself.

The approach used in interviewing a suspected sexually abused child will depend partly on the aim of the interview as mentioned above. Therefore, where the main aim is to provide evidence for criminal proceedings (*see* Appendix 1), for instance, the interviewer will usually be a police officer, specially trained in interviewing young children, and with an understanding of the laws of evidence. Working either jointly with a social work colleague or alone, this police officer will take care to avoid leading questions, will try to gather as much corroborative evidence about the circumstances of the abuse as possible, and will try to help the child to make a verbal disclosure in the first instance, probably only using the anatomically correct dolls as an illustrative recap of what has already been said in words.

The range of questions asked in this sort of investigative interview will be strictly limited, but other forms of communication, such as body language, the observed behaviour of the child in the room, the emotional state of the child and so on, will be carefully noted. At the end of such an interview, the investigating officer will make a decision about the likelihood of sexual abuse, which will be based on narrow criteria relating to the child's response in the interview, and external corroboration. As a result of this conclusion, criminal proceedings

may or may not be brought. Nowadays all such investigative interviews, if not conducted jointly, will need to be reported back to the
professional network, so that subsequent help and therapy may be
offered to the child and the family.

However, a different approach may be taken when the aim of the
interview is either (2) or (4) (as on p. 91). When abuse has been
established, the task of the clinician is either to gather fuller
information, or to make an assessment of treatment needs, then the
approach to interviewing the child can be more flexible than that
described above, and would be essentially clinical and child-centred.
With this clinical approach the intention is to help the child to work
through conflicts and anxieties about possible abuse, in order to obtain
a degree of therapeutic relief by the end of the interview. Since it is
likely that the clinician will be dealing with a child who has some
resistance to discussing the abuse, a sensitive and flexible approach is
required. Simply asking the child to say what has happened may be
greeted with silence and a range of questioning techniques (*see*
Chapter 6) may need to be used.

The Play of Non-abused Children with Anatomically Correct Dolls

To date, only one study has been reported looking at the responses of
non-sexually abused children to anatomically correct dolls.[16] In this
study, 80 children between the ages of three and six, including both
boys and girls, were allowed a free play period with anatomically
correct dolls, and this play session was videotaped. General as well as
specific responses to the dolls were looked for, as well as the degree of
familiarity with the doll's sexual anatomy, and an attempt was made to
link these observations to the demographic characteristics of the
children studied. Preliminary analysis indicates that only three
children out of 80 showed any persisting interest in the sexual anatomy
of these dolls, or demonstrated sexual acts using the dolls. The
remaining children, after a cursory look at the dolls' bodies, chose to
engage in pretty repetitive day-to-day play with the dolls, such as
washing their faces, putting them to bed, getting them up for their
breakfast, telling them off if naughty, taking them to school and so on.
Grossly excited, or very inhibited or phobic reactions towards the dolls
were not noted, although three children did show some specific
interest in the genitals of the dolls, and one child attempted to
demonstrate a sexual act with the dolls. The impression given by these
young non-abused children was that the dolls themselves play no
particular role in sexualizing the behaviour of the children, simply
because these dolls have genitals, in contrast to criticisms previously
made, about the use of the dolls.

Another study undertaken in Louisiana State University,[17] compared the behaviour of sexually abused and non-sexually abused children in play with anatomically correct dolls, and found a significant excess of sexual play with the dolls in the abused group. However, this is a very small sample, with 10 matched pairs of children between the ages of three and eight being allowed free play periods with the dolls both dressed and then undressed by the child. Since two of the control children were in the care of the state, it is not clear whether they had been exposed to sexual behaviours or even abuse before the start of the study, or whether this can be excluded. However, it was found that 9 out of 10 of the abused children, compared with 2 out of 10 of the non-abused children demonstrated sexual behaviour between the dolls. These sexual behaviours included vaginal, oral and anal forms of intercourse, as well as the child showing touching of the dolls' genitals in play (for other than hygenic purposes, such as changing a nappy).

Specifically, six of the abused children compared with one of the control children showed vaginal sexual intercourse, and three of the abused children compared with none of the control children showed additional sexualized play with the dolls, such as re-enactment of the abuse situation. Interestingly, and picking up on the issue of day-to-day play and non-sexual behaviour demonstrated by the children in the previous study, eight out of the control children compared with only one of the abused children showed non-sexual behaviour and play using the dolls. This study also described the effect of the interview itself on the behaviour of the children, as one abused child masturbated openly after showing the play, while another abused child refused to touch the dolls and showed signs of emotional disturbance. Similarly, a three-year-old abused boy in the study, punched and stabbed the perpetrator doll with a crayon, reflecting the Great Ormond Street team's clinical experience of the value of the dolls when used to provide therapeutic relief for pent-up angry feelings.

The Meaning of Sexualized Play

Although the results from these studies are interesting, they need to be replicated and expanded to include observational data on a range of children from different social and ethnic backgrounds. Another important issue, currently contaminating our assessment of the meaning of childrens' sexualized play, is the proliferation of home-shown pornographic movies. The majority of children nowadays have access to a video recorder, and a substantial number of children have video equipment in their own homes. Increasing numbers of children are now being referred with sexualized behaviour and demonstrations of explicit sexual acts with other children at school, for example, which seem to be based on their memory of having viewed pornographic videos, rather than relating to a personal experience of sexual abuse.

However, sexually abused children are often used in subtle ways by abusing adults, such as forcing them to watch pornographic videos with the adult, or reinforcing a child's casual interest in pornographic material which may be freely available in the home. In this way, children's behaviour may become sexualized, and it will be very important for the interviewing clinician to establish the background facts and risk factors around this particular child before jumping to the conclusion that the child has been directly sexually abused. This is not in any way to minimize the harmful effects of such subtle corruption of children, but rather to create a space in the interviewer's mind for the reality that a whole spectrum of sexually abusing activities are possible with children, including the passive viewing of pornographic material. Studies have indicated that children are likely to be affected by viewing gratuitous violence on television,[18] and clinical experience is now indicating that children may act out some of the sexual behaviours which they witness in pornographic films. Research is needed to clarify the vulnerability factors which allow certain children to become very sexualized by such experiences and, by contrast, the protective factors which allow other children to survive in risk-filled households.

The Behaviour of Sexually Abused Children with Anatomically Correct Dolls

Clinical experience in working with sexually abused children has indicated that, although they all respond individually to the interview situation, certain patterns do seem to emerge. For instance, children who have been sadistically abused, or kept quiet through the use of threats, may show an avoidance of the dolls in the free-play session, or a positively frightened reaction to the male doll, or more specifically, fear of the genitals of the male doll. Such children may engage chattily with the interviewer, but may suddenly back off and refuse to undress the male doll or to hold the doll at all.

Sexually abused children from multiproblem families, where the tendency may be to act out rather than to talk out feelings, may well be children who demonstrate over-sexualization in their play with the dolls, and in their presentation in the room. Such children may repeatedly demonstrate sexual acts between the dolls, may occasionally engage in sexual contact with the doll itself, for example, a non-verbal three-year-old, who insisted on biting and sucking the clothed penis of the male doll, while roaring with laughter and indicating that this was a game. Very disturbed chaotic sexually abused children may become sexually aroused by the interview process, may masturbate or make sexual overtures to the interviewer.

In between these two extremes are a range of reactions shown by sexually abused children who have had differing experiences of abuse. Many sexually abused children have positive loving feelings towards the abuser, and this may come out in the play with the dolls. For instance, deprived sexually abused children may show the abused child doll hugging and holding the abuser doll, and may indicate that this was a major source of comfort and caring for them. Other sexually abused children (possibly those with a slightly better therapeutic prognosis) may show very great anger towards the perpetrator doll, kicking at its genitals, attacking and abusing it in many different ways. It is interesting to note that even in older prepubescent and occasionally intellectually subnormal or very inhibited adolescents, the anatomically correct dolls may provide a means of emotional communication for these children.

Diagnostically, it is not difficult to pick out the play of a chaotic, emotionally disturbed sexually abused child as being obviously significant. However, the difficulty may arise in interpreting the play of much more inhibited children, since general inhibition in play is certainly not indicative of sexual abuse, and may be present for a number of other reasons. These and other considerations have led to the development of a structured interview format which included a preliminary free-play period, so that the clinician can get a sense of the child in spontaneous play without therapist intervention.

SOURCES OF ERROR IN INTERVIEWS

False Allegations

There is a great deal of professional concern at the moment about the possibility of false allegations of child sexual abuse,[19] which may mislead a clinician into making a false-positive diagnosis. The available evidence suggests that false allegations do indeed occur, more often involving older children, frequently in the context of an access dispute, and most frequently when the child is used by one or other parent in a dispute to make a false allegation of sexual abuse in order to strengthen their legal case. In an American study,[20] it was found that only 21 out of 267 'unfounded' cases involved false allegations by a child (this was 1·5 per cent of *all* 576 cases), whereas 17 out of 21 'unfounded' cases were false allegations by an adult (6·6 per cent of all cases). This study demonstrates, therefore, that adults were more likely to lie on behalf of children than children were to lie them-selves. Nevertheless, with 1·5 per cent of all cases being false allegations by a child, and 6·5 per cent false allegations by an adult, it is clearly important that the interviewing clinician is aware of this as a possibility, and does not adopt a credulous 'children never lie' attitude, particularly in hotly contested custody cases. Interestingly, all the children who made false allegations had been previously sexually abused, and it is now thought that these children were probably suffering from a post-traumatic stress disorder at the time that the false allegation occurred. Furthermore, another study by Jones and Seig[21] indicated that out of 20 vicious custody disputes, where allegations of sexual abuse were involved, only four proved to be false allegations. In 14 of the cases the allegations were clearly true, and were thought to be the actual basis for the viciousness of the battle.

Goodwin[19] described false accusations of incest by children as often being 'opportunistic lies', where a desperate child fabricates an incest story because of acute unhappiness at home. In these instances, the presence of an adult confederate has been noted, with the child easily admitting to the lie on direct questioning. Earlier reports[22] have linked repeated false allegations by children with more specific psychiatric pathology in the child. However, it must be remembered that earlier writings about false allegations in relation to incest were influenced by Freudian theory about such reports being based on fantasies, with the possibility that earlier workers took the false allegations at face value, without specifically excluding the possibility of abuse. Having said all this, it is still clear that false allegations *do* occur, often in a context of custody disputes, more frequently with older children, and most often under pressure from one of the child's parents.

False Retractions

Sometimes called false denials of incest or sexual abuse, these are situations which classically tend to occur when the original allegation of sexual abuse or incest cannot be substantiated by corroborative evidence, and where charges against the offender are therefore not taken out or dropped. This often means that the alleging child stays at home with the alleged perpetrator, or is actually returned home from care. It has been found[21] that 25 out of 309 cases of 'founded' (i.e., substantiated) sexual abuse involved false denials. However, we do not know what proportion of these children were denying the original allegation, under the circumstances described above, which would be likely to promote false denial, and how many were denying despite the fact that prosecution and child-care measures proceeded.

Clinical and police investigative experience strongly indicate that when prosecution cannot be pursued, it is only a matter of time before a child returned home under these circumstances, will falsely deny the original allegation. Even children who are kept in care, but whose allegations of sexual abuse are not supported by the family, show a tendency to drift towards partial false denial of their allegations over time. This indicates, perhaps, the beginning of a tendency in these child sexual abuse victims to devalue their own perception and judgement of events, when faced with lack of adult support. It is clear that false denial of a real sexual abuse must be damaging to victims and must feed into the development of low self-esteem in the long-term.

It has been noted that refusal to talk or testify about incest and sexual abuse is more common than false denial, perhaps affecting as many as 30 per cent of victims.[19] This is certainly confirmed from work with adult victims of incest, and given the recent trend for more adult male victims of sexual abuse and incest to speak up about their experiences, it may be that silence about sexual abuse experiences is more common in male victims than in female victims.

Lack of Background Information

Circumstances may dictate who undertakes the interview, the approach to interviewing the child, and the venue used. A crisis disclosure interview, therefore, may of necessity mean that the interviewer knows little or nothing about the child. It could be argued that this is an advantage for the interviewer, since a more objective approach will therefore be used. This may indeed be true, but there are specific dangers, particularly in relation to interviewing very young children with impaired verbal skills. Lack of adequate background information may mean that the interviewer simply does not ask relevant questions, and if the child is unable to communicate spontaneously, important information may be missed.

Even with older, articulate children, the reality is that many of them have been somehow pressured or coerced into silence, and may be very fearful of disclosure.[23] If the interviewer is aware of the salient background features of the case, then questions about specific issues may release the child from a fearful silence and help communication. Hence, an obvious difficulty under these circumstances is the possibility of a false-negative diagnosis. Returning to the issue of false allegations, it is clearly important that when this is suspected, or thought possible, the disclosure interview is either postponed until adequate information about the family is available, or possibly that the interview is repeated by a more skilled person at a later date.

Again, it could be argued that a substantial lack of background information will not exclude false-positive diagnosis, since certain interviewers, perhaps with an overly child-centered approach, may misinterpret aspects of the child's behaviour or play in interview as indicating sexual abuse. Although there can be no question of a disclosure interview establishing the truth 'beyond all reasonable doubt', as might be expected in criminal proceedings, nevertheless, common-sense precautions to make sure that the relevant facts are known before the interview will clearly avoid many of the dangers described above.

False-negative and False-positive Diagnoses

In cases where there is no corroborative medical evidence or direct witnesses of the abuse itself, the diagnosis of child sexual abuse will ultimately rest on the clinician's overall interpretation of the family context, the child's behaviour in the room, the child's statement and play, and possibly statements from other adults. Assessment is therefore of necessity complex, and no single 'test' will clinch the diagnosis. Therefore, there is unfortunately plenty of scope for falsely negative and falsely positive diagnoses.

What can be done to minimize these problems? First of all, it has been noted, that inexperience in the interviewer is associated with a higher level of false-negative diagnoses.[24] This of course applies equally to doctors conducting the medical examination of suspected sexually abused children, since seeing (physical findings) is not necessarily believing (in the possibility of child sexual abuse). Cases are still frequently reported in which GPs or casualty officers will examine a child, note a range of physical findings, such as vaginal discharge, anal tears, genital bruising, and so on, but nevertheless record in their notes that sexual abuse has been excluded. Similarly, in a psychiatric interview, inexperienced clinicians may miss the vital clues from a child, through body language or doll play, which indicate that they have something more to say. In a sense, sheer ignorance, or lack of training, should be easily remediable, leading to increased sensitivity to work with sexually abused children, a capacity to recognize the signs and symptoms of the problem, and the skills with which to properly pursue the issue in a disclosure interview. Given the increasing numbers of children now referred by professional colleagues for psychiatric help in relation to sexual abuse, it is clear that this process of education is indeed occurring. However, an ideological bias, whether overly child-centred or feminist on the one hand, or overly sceptical or Freudian on the other hand, may lead the interviewer into false-positive or false-negative diagnoses respectively. Again, training should help to eliminate such biases, often based on a human fear of having to work at close quarters with such distressing and distasteful subject matter.

The issue of false-positive diagnoses has been criticized recently[25] in connection with techniques which were designed to help frightened and conflicted children talk about their sexual abuse experiences. Using the criminal law concept of establishing proof 'beyond all reasonable doubt', a judgement on a wardship case, where sexual abuse was alleged, stated that: 'one more question . . . . would have established the truth'. However, this suggests that child abuse can, and should, be established 'beyond all reasonable doubt', an approach which seems to 'fly in the face' of all child protection practice, in the civil courts, over the past 15 years or so. This tradition has expected the judge to decide about the risk to the child of possible abuse 'on the balance of probabilities' only, therefore an expectation that clinicians can and should establish 'the truth' of the matter (rather than commenting on links between the child's past experiences and present needs) is puzzling. It is agreed that psychiatric interview techniques involve the use of leading questions, one purpose of which may be to facilitate a spontaneous response on behalf of the child. However, it is easy to see that an inexperienced, overly child-centered interviewing technique, which leans heavily on the use of leading questions, may run the risk of false-positive diagnosis. This would seem more likely with very young children, when much depends on the interviewer's interpretation of the child's responses, hence allowing scope for inter-viewer bias. Again, vigorous training and continuing supervision of all disclosure interviews with children may be one way of attempting to overcome such inadvertent bias.

Finally, it should be remembered that while false-positive diagnosis of sexual abuse carries enormous and worrying implications for the civil liberties of the alleged abuser,[26] his reputation and his right to access over his children, on the other hand, false-negative diagnosis may mean that an abused child is returned home to a process of false denial and possible continuing victimization. It should be remembered that other children may continue to be abused by the alleged perpetrator, and that under these circumstances help will not be given to the adult concerned.

The Use of Leading Questions

It is clear that the use of leading questions in interviews which are intended to provide evidence for criminal proceedings may seriously undermine or invalidate the evidence obtained. Although leading questions are very often both necessary and helpful for frightened anxious children, they will almost certainly be viewed in a negative light in court. In civil proceedings, for instance, child-care proceedings, or disputed access proceedings, where a disclosure has been made as a result of leading questions, the value of the evidence may be seriously questioned.

How then is a clinician to reconcile these difficulties with the therapeutic need to help a child overcome a resistance to talking about abuse? A recent judgement in the high court on wardship,[27] has indicated that when leading questions are used in order to facilitate a subsequent spontaneous response on behalf of the child, they may have some value. However, this requires alertness on behalf of the clinician, to ensure that after a spontaneous response is given, the questions immediately following revert to being open and non-directive, to allow any further spontaneous contributions from the child. Only when faced with anxiety, or a total blocking, should the interviewer resort to leading questions. In this way it is unlikely that an entire interview could be constructed on the basis of leading questions only.[30,31]

Of course, if the aim of the interview is to explore the meaning of the abuse with the child, in order to understand the child's feelings and to make an assessment for later therapy (see Aim 5, p. 91), or if the interview itself is to be part of a continuing therapeutic process, then leading questions may be both necessary and appropriate, in order to help the child communicate. Indeed, it could be said that the majority of questions used in ordinary adult and child psychiatric practice are leading, aimed as they are at overcoming the frequent resistance of the presenting patient to discussing their problems. Many adult and child psychiatric patients clamour for help and may then 'clam up' in the interview. Skill and experience in helping patients to face their problems involves the use of techniques which are far from straight-forward.

Interestingly, in view of the considerable controversy among lawyers in relation to the use of leading questions in such interviews, the law itself recognizes the need for an alternative questioning style, by building in straightforward questions in examination in chief of a witness, but allowing defence counsel the opportunity to put leading questions to the witness in cross-examination.[28] It remains to be seen whether recent proposals to include videolink cross-examinations of child witnesses in sexual abuse cases, within new legislation,[29] will actually result in defence counsel for the alleged abuser putting leading questions to the child in cross-examination. If this should be the case, it will be interesting to reflect upon the meaning of the current controversy, whereby clinicians have been strongly criticized for using these questioning techniques in order to understand and protect children, whereas lawyers may be free to use the same approach in order to protect the perpetrator.

References

1. Vizard E. (1987) The historical and cultural context of child abuse. In: Maher P. (ed.), *Child Abuse, the Educational Perspective*. Oxford: Basil Blackwell.
2. Freud S. (1933) Femininity. In: *New Introduction Lectures on Psychoanalysis*, Standard Edition, 1964, Vol. 17.
3. Summit R. (1983) The child sexual abuse accommodation syndrome. *Child Abuse and Neglect*, **7**, 177–193.
4. BBC (1986) *Childwatch*, Esther Rantzen. 30 October.
5. Groth N. A. and Burgess A. (1979) Sexual trauma in the life histories of rapists and child molesters. *Victimology* **4**, 10–16.
6. Finkelhor D. (1984) Perpetrators. In: *Child Sexual Abuse: New Theory and Research*. Glencoe: Free Press, Chap. 4.
7. Jones D. P. H. and McQuistan M. (1986) The process of validation. In: *Interviewing the Sexually Abused Child*. Vol. 6 of a series, 2nd edition. The C. Henry Kempe National Center for the Prevention and Treatment of Child Abuse and Neglect, Chap. 5. Denver, Colorado.
8. Vizard E. (1986) How certain can we be? *Family Law* **16**, 313–314.
9. Kempe C. H. and Kempe R. (1984) Definitions and incidence. In: *The Common Secret—Sexual Abuse of Children and Adolescents*. New York. W. H. Freeman, Chap. 1.
10. Giarretto H. (1981) A comprehensive child sexual abuse treatment project. In: Mrazek P. B. and Kempe C. H. (eds), *Sexually Abused Children and their Families*. Oxford: Pergamon, Chap. 4.
11. Rush F. (1980) A Freudian cover up. In: *The Best Kept Secret—Sexual Abuse of Children*. New York: McGraw-Hill, Chap. 7.
12. Piaget J. and Inhelder B. (1973) *Memory and Intelligence*. New York: Basic Books.
13. Dale P., Waters J., Davies M. et al. (1986) The towers of silence—creative and destructive issues on therapeutic teams dealing with sexual abuse. *Journal of Family Therapy* **8**, No. 1, February.
14. DHSS (1986) *Child Abuse, Working Together. A Discussion Document*. London: HMSO.
15. BBC (1986) *Panorama: Family Secrets*. 8 September.
16. Glaser D. and Collins C. (1986) The Response of Young, Non Sexually Abused Children to Anatomically Correct Rag Dolls. Paper presented to Association of Child Psychiatrists and Psychologists, 19 November.
17. Templeton S. and Weber C. (1985) An Assessment of the Behaviour of Sexually Abused and Non Sexually Abused Children with Anatomically Correct Dolls—Research Report. Louisiana State University (unpublished).

18. Sims A. and Melville T. (1985) Survey of the opinion of child and adolescent psychiatrists on the viewing of videos by children. *Bulletin of the Royal College of Psychiatrists* **9**, 238–240.
19. Goodwin J. (ed.) (1982) False accusations and false denials of incest victims and their families. In: *Sexual Abuse: Incest Victims and their Families*. Bristol: John Wright.
20. Jones D. P. H. and McGraw J. M. (1986) Reliable and fictitious accounts of sexual abuse to children. *Journal of Interpersonal Violence* **2**, 27–45.
21. Jones D. P. H. and Seig J. M. (1986) unpublished observations. Mentioned in Krugman R. D. (1986) Recognition of sexual abuse in children. In: *Paediatrics in Review,* Vol. 8.
22. Selling L. (1942) The psychiatric aspects of the pathological liar. *Nervous Child* **1**, 358–388.
23. Finkelhor D. (1984) Victims In: *Child Sexual Abuse—New Theory and Research*. London. MacMillan Free Press, Chap. 3, p. 23–32.
24. De Francis V. (1967) *Protecting the Child Victim of Sex Crimes Committed by Adults*. Englewood: American Humane Society.
25. *The Times* (1986) Re. E. C. a minor and G. C. a minor. Mr. Justice Ewebank. 16 July.
26. *The Times* (1986) Times Leader—The Protection of Children. 10 October.
27. (1986) Re. W. minor. W. Justice Waite. 23 May.
28. Cross R. and Wilkins N. (1986) Testimony—Article 28. Cross Examination 94–100 In: Tapper C. (ed.), *Outline of the Law of Evidence*. London: Butterworths, Chap. 4.
29. Williams G. (1987) Videotaping children's evidence—criminal law. *New Law Journal* 30 January, 108–112.
30. Vizard E. (1986) How certain can we be? *Family Law* **16**, 313–314.
31. Vizard E. (1987) Interviewing young sexually abused children. *Family Law* **17**, 28–33.
32. Sgroi S. (1982) *Handbook of Clinical Intervention in Child Sexual Abuse*. Lexington, Mass.: Lexington Books.
33. Groth A. A. (1984) *Anatomical Drawings for Use in Investigation and Intervention of Child Sexual Abuse*. Newton Center, Mass.: Forensic Mental Health Association.

CHAPTER 6

Helping Children to Describe Experiences of Child Sexual Abuse—A Guide to Practice

Eileen Vizard and Marianne Tranter

MANAGEMENT ISSUES

Seeing the Child Alone Again

As mentioned in Chapter 5, clinical experience has indicated that most young children need to have an interview which is separate from the family in which sexual abuse is alleged to have occurred. The reasons for this are that young children are still developmentally and emotionally very dependent upon their parents and care-takers. If abuse has occurred in the family home, and if a subsequent interview with a child includes either the non-abusive parent, or possibly both the non-abusive and the abusive parent, the child will continue to function as a dependent part of that family group, and will be unlikely to make a spontaneous disclosure of abuse.

This is putting the situation at its mildest, in that the passive presence of parents and relatives, who have been part of such an abusive household, will certainly inhibit the child from disclosure, but more active and subtle attempts at inhibiting the child from talking may also occur. For instance, a non-abusing but unconsciously colluding mother may insist on being present in the interview in order to reassure the child. Close holding of the child, cuddling and 'encouraging' squeezes of the child at difficult moments in the interview, serve as a subtle reminder or warning to the child that his or her loyalty is first of all to the family. Other manoeuvres which can be positively distracting include helpfully stroking the child's hair or wiping the child's nose just as a crucial question is being asked, loudly instructing the child to 'tell the doctor', or making comments such as 'don't worry about mummy, I'd rather know the worst'.

The Effect of a Parent's Presence

Obviously, in those unusual cases of false allegation of sexual abuse, the presence of the mother or another family member in the room can only serve to cloud the issue, and to prevent the interviewer from getting a sense of what has really happened. From time to time, it may appear that siblings who have participated jointly in sexual abuse activities with an adult, or with each other, should be seen together by the interviewer. This is usually helpful, but not only can older siblings exert a considerable influence over their younger siblings to tell the same story (and hence mask a possible false allegation), but where there is genuine abuse a younger sibling may have valuable extra information which he or she is unwilling or unable to share in the presence of a brother or sister. For this reason, a brief period with both siblings together, followed by separate individual interviews, is one way around the difficulty.

It is often said that separation anxiety from the mother makes separate interviewing of very tiny suspected child sexual abuse victims difficult or impossible. It is quite true that a natural response from a small child is to protest loudly on being separated from his or her parent. However, ordinary clinical experience in working with other types of childhood disorder indicate that a preliminary meeting with the parents, social worker, or other professionals concerned and the child, allowing the child an opportunity to meet the therapist and explore the room, can also function as a sort of 'handover' to the interviewing clinician. After a preliminary meeting of this sort, which may be quite brief, the child can be shown where mother, or foster mother, will be waiting for them, and can be pleasantly and firmly taken into the room with the interviewer. Preliminary work should have been done with the mother or foster mother prior to the interview, to ensure that there are no ambiguous messages from the adult to the child about separation, such as intensely close hugs, tears or implications that the interview may be of stress to the child. It should be made clear to the mother or foster mother, that there may be certain things which are difficult for any child to talk about in a group, and that this would include sexual abuse experiences, and that there- fore the child has a right to a private individual interview. Resistance to this notion of the child being seen separately may have innocent explanations, such as a natural fear of the child getting upset. However, a persistently obstructive attitude about a separate inter- view for the child needs to be seen in the context of possible adult fear of the child 'spilling the beans'. If statutory powers are not involved in the case at this stage, and parental permission is refused for a separate interview with the child, it may be necessary to regroup professionally, perhaps with a case conference, to decide if and how the assessment should proceed.

Children in Care

In certain cases of children recently received into care following a disclosure of sexual abuse, the degree of trauma to the child may be such that acute fear and terror are experienced at the prospect of meeting someone new to discuss the abuse. If all the above measures have been tried in order to see the child separately, but, in this instance, the child is refusing, it may be necessary for a trusted adult to stay in the room with the child during the interview. Should this happen, the interviewer needs to take charge of the situation, so that the right sort of questions are asked by the interviewer, and that there are no unfair expectations made of the foster mother, or child-care worker, that they somehow conduct the diagnostic interview, while the interviewer watches. This could be quite rightly criticized later, on evidential grounds, if the interview is to feature in legal proceedings. Even if the care-taker's intention is to make a preliminary therapeutic contact, it will clearly be necessary for the trusted person not to intrude inappropriately into the relationship between the child and the interviewer.

Older Children

With older children, an immediate problem facing the interviewer may be posed by the child who promises to tell everything, as long as it goes no further. Child sexual abuse victims cannot be helped by one person alone, and therefore guarantees of spurious confidentiality, at the outset of the interview, will deprive both the child and the interviewer of later support and advice. Rather, the interviewer needs to develop skills in reassuring the child that unnecessary repetition of the more intimate details of the case will not occur, since the interviewer has respect for the child's feelings in this matter. At the same time the safety of the child, and of other children, will come first, and in order to help the child properly the interviewer should tell him or her that it will be necessary to talk to some other people. The manner in which this reassurance is given is almost as important as its content, since the child is genuinely seeking a sign that the interviewer is a trustworthy and responsible person, and in that sense is different from the abuser. On a deeper level, the child may also be seeking reassurance that the interviewer cannot be tempted into keeping inappropriate secrets between the two of them, again like the abuser.

PRACTICAL PROCEDURES

'Loo Stops', Food and Drink Etc.

All children (and perhaps for that matter some anxious adolescents) who are about to experience such a diagnostic interview, should be taken to the toilet immediately beforehand. Older children may be asked if they need to go, and the toilet pointed out, but much younger children may be needed to be taken in order to empty their bladders before the interview begins. This is not a trivial matter, since the anxiety of talking about sexual assault is such that it is not at all uncommon for children to involuntarily wet themselves when distressed. This is embarrassing and adds further to the child's distress, and can easily be avoided by a preliminary visit to the toilet.

With young children, feeds from bottles, drinks and snacks should all be given a good half an hour before the interview, to allow their stomachs to settle, and the 'loo stop' subsequently, to be timely. It is generally better to gently remove bars of chocolate, bottles of squash and other food items from the child before they enter the room. Similarly, children should be firmly and pleasantly prevented from bringing in a range of their own toys, since the interviewer will have specific materials available in the room.

Equipment Needed

The decor and style of the interviewing room will obviously depend on its location—in a hospital, social services department, clinic setting, etc. However, a natural and homely atmosphere should be created with a range of easy chairs, as well as small child chairs, informally arranged, but including a low-level table accessible to small children. Obviously, personal possessions belonging to the interviewer or owner of the room may inevitably intrude, but it should be remembered that while these will add to a sense of informality, they can also provide annoying distractions for restless children who do not wish to engage in the task in hand. Similarly, it has been found that free access to a large number of tantalizing and interesting toys which would be expected and appropriate in a playroom setting can greatly hinder a specialized interview of this sort.

However, if the child is being seen in order to assess therapeutic needs, a limited range of other toys may well be needed, including a doll's house, domestic and zoo animals, and small doll's figures of the sort used in play therapy.

Otherwise, many investigative and therapeutic assessment interviews can be conducted quite comfortably using a set of anatomically correct dolls, including grandparent dolls, and teenage dolls, as well as a baby doll. It is helpful if these dolls can be matched to the ethnic identity of the family, whether they be Afro-Caribbean, Asian, or other. Plasticine or Play Dough is sometimes very useful for children who wish to express feelings of anger or frustration using the material, as well as for children who may wish to try and model, for instance, an erect penis, or something relevant to their sexual abuse. Finally, plenty of plain paper, crayons or felt-tip pens, should be available for the child on the low table provided. Children may often find it easier to start drawing straight away, in order to contain their anxiety, while the therapist makes preliminary opening comments. Such drawings may be tremendously useful in providing an opening for the discussion of possible sexual abuse.

Line drawings of adult male, female and children's bodies can also be used to help a silent child point out the location of the abuse on their own body, with the drawing. Similarly, glove puppets may be a way of engaging in playful interaction with the child, whereby he or she may 'talk to' a friendly gloved puppet about the abuse a little more easily than they may speak directly to the therapist.

Whatever the choice of equipment made by the therapist, it is important that he or she is comfortable with the available materials, and has them under control. These interviews are difficult to do and a novice interviewer might be well advised to keep the range of play materials to a minimum, until he or she feels comfortable in talking with children about the subject matter itself.

OBSERVATIONS

Reactions to the Dolls

The play of both non-abused children and of sexually abused children with the anatomical dolls has been described above. It is clear that sexually abused children can show a range of reactions to the dolls, and indeed to the whole process of making a disclosure. The interviewer should be prepared for children who demonstrate a fearful or even phobic reaction towards the dolls, refusing to touch them, or possibly refusing to undress them. These children will need to be dealt with sensitively, since they cannot be forced to engage in play which may be frightening to them. It may be that the interviewer will have to hold the Perpetrator Doll, while the child demonstrates abuse with the other dolls. Clarifying with the child who is to blame for the sexual abuse is an important part of reassuring such a fearful child, but if the anxiety levels are high enough such reassurance may still not be adequate to allow a child to spontaneously handle the dolls and engage in play. Under these circumstances, it may be more fruitful to check out with the child exactly why he or she is afraid of the dolls, and if it has anything to do with sexual abuse, for instance. For some children in this state of mind, drawing their experiences or indicating on line drawings of adult and child bodies where the abuse has occurred may be less traumatic than work with the dolls.

Similarly, very fearful and inhibited children may respond in a lively way to use of the glove puppets, for one of the puppets can be made by the therapist to ask questions of the child about the abuse. This may be particularly suitable for young children. By contrast, the sexually abused child who is wild, chaotic, and sexualized in the interview may present considerable management problems. As well as making sexualized approaches to the interviewer (without the child necessarily realizing that this is what they are doing: i.e., rubbing up against the interviewer, touching the interviewer's breast or genitals inadvertently, stroking the interviewer's hair or kissing the interviewer, etc.), these children may need to compulsively engage in sexual play with the dolls themselves. Naturally, this is all relevant information for the interviewer, but it is quite possible that such children may become very over-excited, possibly even sexually aroused, and masturbating, in a way which prevents progress of the interview itself. Under these circumstances it may be necessary to explain to the child that, first, the interviewer is going to believe what the child says, in words, about the abuse, and that therefore the child does not need to convince the interviewer by acting it out. Something simple, such as, 'You know, you can *tell* me about the abuse, you don't need to show me like this, because I will believe what you say'. It may be necessary to go on and explain to the child that he or she is behaving in a way which some grown-up has taught them, and that the interviewer would like to know more about this in order to help. Such simple clarifications or interpretations can often have a strikingly calming effect on the behaviour of a wild, sexualized and chaotic child. However, happily most children engage and play with the dolls quite readily, showing no fears, and finding the dolls quite 'friendly', as indeed they are. Nevertheless, at various points during the process of disclosure anxiety may overwhelm a child, leading to requests for the toilet, mummy, a drink, and so on. If the advice given above is followed, and if the interviewer can be fairly sure that this is not a genuine need to empty the child's bladder but is a result of anxiety, then kindly firm reassurance that the child will not be blamed for what he or she is going to say, coupled with a return of the focus of attention to the interview, will usually help the anxiety to quieten. If the child has to be taken out to the toilet this may be disruptive to the disclosure process, but the interviewer should accompany the child personally, keeping the contact going with the child until they both return to the room.

Fear of Disclosure

Without labouring the point, the majority of sexually abused children have been pressured into keeping the secret in a variety of ways, which include emotional blackmail and outright physical force. When a small child of four or five is told that 'this is our little secret, you must not tell anyone, if you do mummy will have a nervous breakdown and it will be your fault', then the fear of disclosing the secret is very intense. Similarly, older children may be threatened with very explicit physical assault, having their genitals mutilated, being drowned or burned by the perpetrator, and so on. While such threats may seem so grotesque as to be unrealistic to an adult, we must remember that the child's perceptions of these threats, coming as they do from a loved and trusted care-taker, is that disclosure will automatically be followed by a realization of the threat. Fear, therefore, often coupled with the sense of guilt, particularly in older children, about having kept the secret, is a very powerful inhibitor of disclosure, and must not be underestimated by the interviewer. With very frightened children it may be necessary for the interviewer to make a neutral statement, which is perhaps repeated at intervals throughout the interview. The statement should include the facts that very many children are threatened into silence, find it difficult to talk about abuse because they believe that something bad will happen to them, and that if this particular child has some of these worries, then the interviewer can understand how frightened he or she must be.

However, reassurance may simply be inadequate for certain children, and it should be borne in mind that another interview may be necessary, in order to build up a relationship with the child and to allow a disclosure at the child's pace, without a sense of pressure in any way coming from the interviewer. Even though it may be difficult to do this if there is a sense or urgency in relation to criminal or civil proceedings and evidence is needed, it should be remembered that the emotional well-being of the child comes first, and that an interview, no matter how skilfully conducted, which is overly pressurizing, and persistently enquiring about the abuse, may seem to a frightened child to be a repetition of the abuse itself. In other words, the interviewer should bear in mind that the child is actually emotionally re-experiencing the abuse, while describing it, sometimes in an extremely powerful way, which is brought home particularly clearly and concretely to the child through the use of dolls to re-enact the sexual act. Supervision in conducting such interviews, and adequate training before undertaking them, is absolutely essential, and even the most experienced interviewer can always benefit from supervision of technique to help refine his or her approach.

SPECIFIC STEPS TO PRACTISE WITH YOUNG CHILDREN

1. Free-play Period

Following suggestions from research workers, interested members of the legal profession and police colleagues currently working with sexually abused children, an initial period of free play and observation has now been included in the following interview format. This allows the child's spontaneous behaviour to be observed free from therapist intervention, and is therefore available as useful 'baseline' data, for both research and evidential purposes.

Once the child has settled into the room with the therapist, and after the purpose of the meeting has been explained to the child so that he or she can understand, the therapist should place a family of anatomically correct dolls (including Grandparents, Teenagers and Baby Dolls, if available) on a low table in front of the child. Next to the dolls, the therapist can lay out plain paper and a set of felt-tip pens, as described earlier.

At this stage in the interview the dolls should be *fully clothed*, and the therapist can introduce the free-play session to the child by saying something simple like 'Now I'm just going to sit here for a bit, so why don't you find something to play with?'—perhaps indicating the table with the dolls and drawing material.

Assuming that the child approaches the dolls and drawing materials, the therapist should observe silently, while the child either attempts a drawing or picks up the dolls. If the child prefers *to draw first of all*, the therapist should watch without offering a comment, and after 5–10 minutes at the most, the therapist should praise the child for the drawing and suggest that the child might now like to finish drawing. Should the child have drawn people, or made an unclear picture, the therapist should ask, in a neutral tone, if the child can say what is happening in the picture, and who the people are?

Should the child seem on the brink of making a disclosure of sexual abuse at this point, the therapist should *encourage* this to occur, particularly if the child can put the disclosure into words, describing the drawing. At the same time, the therapist should tell the child that he or she is being very *clear* (not good, bad, helpful or any other value-laden term which could be said to influence the child). The therapist should also explain to the child that when the drawing is finished, he or she will be able to play with the dolls, and to explain, with the dolls, what has happened.

Assuming the child has either finished the drawing, or gone straight to the clothed dolls, the therapist should allow 5–10 minutes of silent observation while the child plays with the dolls. The length of time may depend on the age of the child, for instance, 10 minutes may be a comfortable period for a confident nine-year-old to be allowed free play. However five minutes of free play for an anxious three-year-old, who blocks and looks to the therapist tearfully may be too long for that child. The free-play period should be ended at the therapist's discretion.

2. Undressing the Dolls and Naming Body Parts

At this point, the therapist should invite the child to undress the dolls. Older children of, say six years and upwards may be able to manage this task unaided, and if they can do so, the therapist should sit back and observe.

However, younger children under six and toddlers may well need help in holding and undressing the dolls. The therapist should offer help in a low-key manner, so that the *child* is in control of the play while the therapist merely facilitates this play, for example, by supporting the dolls or putting away clothes.

When the dolls are undressed, the therapist should then ask the child to name various parts of the dolls' bodies. If the child can spontaneously point out various body parts and name them, the therapist should respond positively, and encourage the child to continue to name body parts on all the family of dolls.

If the child appears anxious or unable to proceed, the therapist should point to parts of a doll's body, starting with the 'public' parts such as arms, legs, head, etc., and ask the child to name these parts. Although a positive response to the child's efforts should encourage the child to continue, the child may occasionally stop the play, looking embarrassed.

We have found it helpful first of all to *tell* children of all ages that every family has different names, perhaps slang names, for the private body parts. This is usually a great relief to young children, in that the therapist has now given them *permission* to share their family names for private body parts, without fear of ridicule or blame from the therapist. Now the therapist can point to the various private body parts on the dolls, and ask, in a friendly and relaxed fashion, 'What do you call that, in *your* family?' In this way, a picture can be built up of the child's level of awareness of sexual anatomy, while at the same time, and importantly, the therapist has established the *child's language* for talking about sexual matters. Hence, later in the interview, both therapist and child can be perfectly clear what is meant when certain slang words are used.

If the child is old enough to understand (i.e., five years old or more), the therapist can ask the child to point out which parts are *private* parts of the doll's body, and which parts are *not* private but public parts. If the child is doubtful about these concepts, the therapist can describe the 'public' parts as those areas of the body not covered by a swimming costume, for instance. This forms a good link to the next part of the interview, which involves checking the child's level of understanding about touching.

3. Types of Touching:

nice—appropriate
not nice—bad/inappropriate
icky—funny/confusing

The therapist can then explore with the child the difference between 'nice'/ordinary and 'not nice'/inappropriate touching by asking, for instance, if the child sometimes likes to sit on mother's lap for a cuddle. The child can be encouraged to demonstrate this, with the dolls, and in this way any possible fear of handling the dolls can start to be overcome gradually. At the same time, the therapist will start to hear the child's use of language, as well as start to get a sense of the child in the process of play. The child can then be asked if Mother kisses him or her, and how that happens; this gives the child the opportunity to demonstrate Mother's kisses using the dolls, and the therapist can ask if the child *likes* that kind of kissing?

The therapist can then ask the child if he or she sometimes has a cuddle with Father/Uncle Jim, or whoever else the suspected perpetrator may be, and the child should be asked to show the therapist this with the dolls. The therapist can then ask the child 'What sort of touching is *that*?' The therapist should allow *some time* for the child to respond to the question. If no reply is forthcoming, the therapist should continue 'Is that nice touching, or not nice touching, or icky touching?', and should observe the child's responses to the questions.

Time will now be moving on, and the therapist should by the end of the third stage in the interview have established a rapport with the child, if this is possible. Similarly, the therapist should have become aware of potential inhibitions and blocks to communication within the child. This awareness allows the therapist to introduce variations in his or her questioning technique (*see* later) in order to overcome such blocks.

4. Naming the Dolls

At this point, prior to a re-enactment of the abuse with the dolls, the therapist should allow the child the opportunity to *name* the alleged perpetrator, if this has not already occurred.

Perhaps it should be emphasized here that the stages in the interview described are *suggested* areas of work through which the therapist may move systematically in order to clarify issues of abuse. Not only will many practitioners perhaps wish to vary these suggested stages in the process from personal preference, but the responses of different children may suggest that the therapist should introduce a certain piece of play earlier in the interview for instance, or postpone clarification of certain issues until the child is ready and able to cooperate.

This capacity to be flexible within a framework is important, since it allows for a creative use of the technique and also allows the therapist to work with the child on issues introduced by the child, in a natural and easy way. Hence by Stage 4—Naming the Dolls (and in particular the alleged perpetrator/s doll)—some children may *already* have shared this information about the identity of the perpetrator with the therapist at an earlier stage.

Structured interview formats cannot and obviously should not inhibit certain desperate or very extroverted children from coming into the room, picking up the dolls and spontaneously naming the alleged perpetrator, for instance by saying 'Did you know my Uncle Jimmy did this (shows child sexual abuse with dolls) to me?' Naturally the therapist should take this as a disclosure of child sexual abuse and as a clear identification of the alleged perpetrator. This can then be referred to later on in Stage 4 with a fairly straightforward question to such a child, for instance, 'Just remind me of the name of the person who did that rude thing to you?' Then if the same reply, 'Uncle Jimmy', is forthcoming, the therapist can say, 'Show me which doll is Uncle Jimmy doll', hence allowing the child another chance to identify the alleged Perpetrator dolls.

Similarly, children who become relaxed quickly in the room may start to talk about the identity of the alleged perpetrator in Stages 2 and 3, when the level of awareness of sexual matters is being clarified and the child's language for body parts is being established. When types of touching are being discussed, such a child may suddenly say 'Uncle Jimmy touched my foofee (vagina) and it *hurt*'. The therapist can then take up the fact that this was not nice touch with the child, *as well as* using the opportunity to check this identification of the alleged perpetrator, by saying, for instance, 'What was the name of the person who hurt your foofee/Show me which doll that is?' In this situation, with this type of child, the therapist is now able to move into Stage 5— Re-enactment of the Abuse—by asking the child to use the named dolls to demonstrate what has happened. If the child names an alleged perpetrator and the appropriate doll is named, this is not necessarily the end of the matter. Specific enquiry should be made of the child as to whether any *other* people have touched him/her on private parts of the body, etc. If the child confirms abuse by others, the therapist should repeat the names of the others and ask the child to pick out and name the appropriate dolls as described above.

Working with conflicted, anxious children

However, clinical practice indicates that many children referred for specialist assessment of child sexual abuse may be conflicted, anxious children, terrified of the consequences of disclosure. Such children may need help to name an alleged perpetrator, and although the very process of helping the child in this way raises evidential issues, nevertheless from a clinical viewpoint, helping the child to break barriers of secrecy (often maintained through coercion and blackmail) must be seen as a first step in allowing therapeutic relief for the child.

This can be achieved as follows—The therapist picks up the Child Doll, and says to the child, 'This is going to be Jane/John Dolly, who is like *you*'. The therapist should now say to the child, '*Which* dolly shall we use to see if anyone has touched you in a rude way?' When the child has pointed to, say, a Man Dolly, the therapist should say to the child, 'What shall we *call* this Dolly? What is his name?'

By this stage in the interview it will be clear whether or not the child is able to engage in the process and, if possible, the therapist should allow a few moments for the child to pick out the alleged Perpetrator Doll, and to name it, *without* a sense of rush being conveyed. When the doll is named by the child, say, 'Uncle Jimmy', the therapist should then check this out with the child by saying, 'So this Man Doll, is Uncle Jimmy Doll, is that right?', and obtain agreement from the child. At this point, very anxious children may become aware of what is to follow, and may suddenly shake their heads to a direct question or say 'No', contradicting the identification of the alleged Perpetrator Doll. (See later for discussion of how to manage this situation.)

However, it is also possible that a child may be so anxious or conflicted about the disclosure that no matter *how* long the therapist allows for the child to name the alleged perpetrator, this will simply not happen. Under these circumstances, the therapist can, briefly and pleasantly, *reassure* the child that *if* something rude/sexual *has* happened, then it is *not* the child's fault, while at the same time acknowledging to the child that it is perhaps hard to say if someone has done a rude thing. The therapist should now firmly pick up a Grown-up Doll (or a Teenage or Child Doll if sexual acts are suspected between child and peers) and present this to the child, saying, 'Shall we call this Dolly, X person?' (i.e., applying the identity of the suspected abuser or the first abuser, if there are several people who are suspected). The child now has the opportunity to indicate 'Yes' or 'No', and if the response is 'No', the therapist should ask again, 'What *shall* we call this Dolly, then?' A persistent 'No' response from the child *may* indicate that the therapist has selected the wrong perpetrator. However, experience has indicated that if a simple mistake about identity has been made, then the child has few inhibitions about saying so. This, in fact, may be a relief for the child, since the flow of play towards disclosure may be broken with a *reduction* in anxiety, and therefore, it may be easy to say 'No, it's *not* X', or to shake his or her head.

The worrying possibility that children may *wrongly* identify an alleged perpetrator has been raised. Furthermore, the possibility that a technique which helps children in the naming process may inadvertently encourage *false-positive* diagnoses has been pointed out, and is part of the argument against using this clinical model for evidential purposes. The issue of false-positive diagnoses is discussed in detail at the beginning of the chapter, but it is important to say that great *caution* should be exercised in making a firm diagnosis of sexual abuse, including the name of an alleged perpetrator, when the child himself or herself has had difficulty in the naming process.

It is vitally important to stress here the major role played by *denial* in the dynamics of child sexual abuse and incest (*see* Chapters 3 and 8 for detail). Such denial is enacted by all family members, particularly perpetrator and victim, and from the victim's point of view is usually based on a terrifying fear of the consequences of disclosure. Many sexually abused children have been emotionally blackmailed and physically abused by the perpetrator.

Therefore, when the child, seeming frozen and anxious, and perhaps unwilling to *touch* the Perpetrator Doll (see section on Reactions to the dolls, p. 109), seems to deny the identity of a known or strongly suspected abuser, the therapist should *continue* the interview, using an amended technique, on the basis that the child will be *unable* to make a spontaneous disclosure without such help from the therapist. In practice, this may mean the therapist saying, for instance, 'Well, I can see it's difficult for you, right now, but I think we *will* call this X Dolly, because we know from your social worker/GP/other professional, that X has/may have done something rude to you'. The interview should now continue to the next stage.

5. Re-enactment of the Abuse

Moving on now to the actual scene of the abuse, with the dolls identified as described, the therapist should set the scene for the allegation of abuse by asking the child where Jane Dolly would be in the house at the time the alleged sexual abuse happened—the living room, the kitchen, the bedroom etc.? The child then needs to take hold of the dolls, and to show the therapist what the two individual dolls were doing at this time—were they standing up, sitting, lying down or what? The therapist can build up a *picture around the events,* for example, by getting the child to describe what he or she was wearing at the time, the decor of the room, and any other details which may provide circumstantial evidence of help to police colleagues, as well as being of therapeutic value in bringing the scene well and truly to life for the child and the therapist.

Helping the child to move on, therefore, the therapist should ask if he or she can show with the dolls what were the rude or sexual things which the Perpetrator Dolly did with the Child Dolly? By this stage, most children are relaxed enough to be able to hold the dolls and demonstrate what has happened.

At this point, it may be helpful to point out that the therapist should always try to start with simple, *open* questions, in helping the child to disclose, and should only move on to other questioning types when the child appears blocked or too frightened to answer (*see* p. 121).

The therapist may then first establish that X *touched* the child around the genitals, with the child demonstrating this using the dolls. Thus the therapist may say, 'Tell me or show me what happened?' (an open question). If this does not help, the therapist can say, 'Did X touch you?' (a closed question). Again if this produces no response the therapist may move on to present the child with alternatives saying, for instance, 'Did X touch you there or there?' (a multi-choice question), and if the child responds positively to this question the therapist can then say, 'Tell me about it/show me with the dolls' (an open question). In this way the therapist is following a sequence of questioning which becomes progressively more leading, as the child becomes more stuck, but when the questioning facilitates a response, as described, the therapist can then return to a non-leading, open-questioning mode. Because the child's resistance to answering may vary, depending on the emotional loading of the questions, the therapist should be prepared to work through a *range* of questions with the child, bearing in mind that open questions should be used preferentially, and that only as a final resort (which may occur in a short space of time with some children), should extensive use be made of hypothetical questioning (*see* p. 122).

The therapist may continue to question the child, asking for instance, 'Would X touch you on the outside of your minnie etc. or the inside' (a multi-choice question). Which fingers would he use?' (the therapist may hold up his or her hand, and ask the child to point out which fingers were used, since the anatomically correct dolls do not have separate fingers). The therapist may continue—'Would he like you to touch his body? Which part of his body? Can you show me? Having, for instance, established mutual sexual touching, the therapist may proceed to ask, 'Would X touch your minnie, etc. with any *other* part of his body? Can you show me on the doll?'. The child may then point to the penis on the Perpetrator Doll, and the therapist may ask, 'Could you show me *how* he would do that?'.

If the child is attempting to show, for instance, sexual intercourse, then the therapist needs to be aware that it is not adequate for the child to simply lie one doll on top of the other. If intercourse has occurred, the child can then position the genitals of the two dolls, as for intercourse. For instance, in discussing penile penetration of an orifice (the vagina, mouth or anus), the therapist may ask, 'Would X put his Willie in a long way, or a little way? Would that be a nice feeling or a yucky one?', or simply, 'Would you like it when X did that?'

It is important also for the therapist to remember that *one* re-enactment of a sexual act does not preclude a whole range of additional sexual contacts between the child and adult. Therefore, the child who has paused after disclosing one act may need to be specifically asked whether *other* rude or sexual games had been played, and if so to be helped to demonstrate what they were.

Moving on, therefore, the therapist may ask, 'Did X put his Willie somewhere else? Would he put it below the waist or above the waist?' (a multi-choice question). 'Can you point out on the Child Doll?' (a closed question). At this point the child *may* hold back, seeming fearful or unable to proceed. Again, and particularly with younger children, he or she should be reassured that *if* another sexual act has happened, then it is not the child's fault. If the child becomes totally blocked at this, or any other point in the interview, then it is particularly important for the therapist to help the child overcome the block by maintaining a flow and ascertain *intensity* in the play. For instance, the therapist may pick up the Perpetrator Doll and position it in a more unlikely way, such as lying at right angles across the Child Doll's knees, the therapist can then ask (using a multi-choice question), 'Would X touch you with his willie *here*, or *here*?' (another unlikely site), and so on, until hopefully the child will pick up the doll and indicate where the willie touched the Child Doll's body. If the child remains blocked, the therapist can put the willie of the Perpetrator Doll in the mouth of the Child Doll and ask, 'Did X do this to you?'

It should be remembered, for instance, that anal intercourse, buggery, also happens to little *girls*, and may leave few signs of penetration on medical examination. However, it should also be remembered that the most frequent types of sexual assault on young children are fondling of genitals, masturbation and oral–genital contact, none of which activities necessarily leave traces for a medical examination. Nevertheless, these assaults need to be systematically enquired for with a small child, using the dolls, drawings or other play materials.

6. Recapping, Reassurance and Relief

Once a child has shown with the dolls or with drawings what has or has not happened, the therapist should help the child to *recap* in words what has been demonstrated or refuted—to say in clear words what has or has not been done to them, and to confirm that this is the same as the play which has just been witnessed.

For instance, the therapist may say, 'With all those sex games you showed me with the dolls, which was the one you disliked most? And which next? and next', etc. Also the therapist can ask the child, 'Can you remind me *who* did these things to you, which you didn't like/liked a bit? Finally, the therapist should remember to enquire whether anyone *else* has touched the child in a sexual way, and if the answer to this is 'Yes', the therapist can take the child through the sort of questions described above.

In concluding the interview, it is important to reassure the child that the adult concerned behaved *wrongly* in doing such sexual things, because the child was too *young* for that, and the adult should have known better. The therapist may need to repeat, several times during the interview, that the child is *never* to blame, even if the child enjoyed aspects of the abuse, and even if the adult gets into trouble.

At this point in the interview, if a disclosure has occurred, and sometimes even if this has not been possible, it is helpful to ask the child, 'If X were here, what would you like to say to him, or do to him? Show me with the dolls'. This gives the child an opportunity for further therapeutic relief, as described earlier, and the chance to verbalize or ventilate angry feelings. For instance, an angry small boy who has disclosed buggery may take the opportunity to shout at the Perpetrator Doll, to hit the doll, and even to attack its genitals. Children who have also been physically abused and coerced into sexual acts may find this a very helpful way of showing their upset and angry feelings about the abuse, and this may be the *first* opportunity for the child to express such feelings in a *safe* context. Again, the therapist should reassure the child that he or she has done the right thing to tell this 'bad secret', and that from now on, grown-ups are going to make sure that the child is kept safe from bad secrets.

In 'winding down', it is important to stress four things:

a. It is *never* the child's fault that the adult has sexually abused him or her. The adult always takes responsibility for this.

b. That the *therapist* believes the child in the disclosures which have been made.

c. That the therapist will try to *help* the child and the perpetrator, since it is important to emphasize that the perpetrator needs help for this problem.

d. If *no* abuse has been demonstrated, the therapist should praise the child for being helpful, and for clarifying matters.

As the interview comes to an end the therapist should help the child to redress the dolls, and make it clear that these have stopped being Jane Dolly, etc., and are going back to being ordinary little girl and family dolls. Discussion should be taken up with the care-taker about future work, for instance group work for the child and follow-up at a later date, in such a way that the child is aware that his or her needs are being dealt with, and that the interview is part of an ongoing process of therapeutic assessment.

Clinical example

An example of *therapeutic relief* gained *after* having made a disclosure of sexual abuse with the dolls in the Interview was seen in the case of Anthony, aged seven years. Anthony had lived all his life with a single-parent mother who was known to have a pathologically overclose relationship with him. Anthony had been in intensive individual therapy (three sessions per week) for four years in order to help with his conflicts. Anthony's middle-class mother was felt by all the many professionals involved in the case to be a borderline personality type, with major difficulties in perceiving her son as a separate person.

At the point of disclosure, it emerged that Anthony had for years been sent to one of his mother's boyfriends at weekends, where he had stayed unsupervised in what turned out to be an extremely dirty, poorly-cared for flat. Police investigation showed that the boyfriend had a long list of convictions of indecent assault on young boys, and on being questioned by the police he admitted to minor, indecent assault of Anthony, and was arrested and charged, and eventually imprisoned.

When seen in the diagnostic interview, Anthony had already been removed from his school under a Place of Safety Order, and had an immediate medical examination which confirmed anal interference and showed lax anal tone. Anthony told the doctor that he had been buggered, and in the psychiatric interview demonstrated this very clearly indeed, by putting the penis of the Boyfriend Doll into the anus of the Anthony Doll, and confirming that it went in and out, as in intercourse.

However, it also emerged that this child had been physically beaten by the boyfriend and coerced into a variety of unpleasant oral–anal foreplay games, as well as being forced to crawl around the room, with his lower body unclothed and his bottom in the air, in order to 'turn on' the boyfriend. Added to this was the complication that Anthony had developed a strong attachment to the boyfriend, whom he saw as his 'friend' and to whom he also felt lovingly.

During the doll play, Anthony was asked by the therapist if the real boyfriend had put *his* penis into Anthony, just like the Boyfriend Doll had done to Anthony Doll? Anthony put the hand of the Anthony Doll over its mouth, and with the other Doll's hand, wiped its eyes, indicating that the doll was crying and sad. When the therapist interpreted this as Anthony not wanting to say in words about the abuse, because then the boyfriend would get into *more* trouble, he nodded sadly, and made the two dolls hug and kiss each other.

At the end of this interview, and after the disclosures, however, Anthony's mood had changed to one of anger. He made the Boyfriend Doll hit the Anthony Doll very hard, and said that Anthony would never get better. Following this the Anthony Doll was beaten up against the wall and trodden on the floor by the Boyfriend Doll, and Anthony himself tried in a sad tired voice to shout abuse at the Boyfriend Doll. Then Anthony made the Boy Doll take revenge on the Boyfriend Doll. After this the Anthony Doll cried and the play stopped. Anthony then drew a picture of the boyfriend in prison, with bars on the window, and when the therapist asked whose *fault* it all was that Anthony had been sexually abused, he pointed to the drawing and said *'Him, he's a bad lot really'*.

As the dolls were packed away, Anthony asked if he could take Anthony Doll with him. The therapist explained that all the dolls had gone back to being ordinary hospital dolls, so that they were going to have a little rest now, but that Anthony could see them next time. In a sad voice, Anthony said that it was good to talk, and that he wanted to see the therapist again.

QUESTIONING TECHNIQUES

We have found it helpful to use a *mixture* of open-ended, closed multi-choice, and hypothetical questions, in talking with young, suspected abused children. As described earlier, the notion of starting with simple, non-leading questions, and working towards complex leading questions, only if necessary, is the suggested model for this questioning technique.

Type of question	*Example*
Open	Did anything happen?
Closed	Did anyone touch you?
Multi-choice	Did X or Y (person) touch you?
Hypothetical	Suppose you *had* been touched, (like the doctor told us), *who* would have touched you?

It is clear, looking at this model, that if the interview is being conducted partly, or primarily, for investigative and evidential reasons in relation to court proceedings, then the therapist would be well advised to use simple open or closed questions wherever possible. This help to avoid the possibility, in cross-examination of the therapist's evidence, of criticisms being made about the value of a child's responses to hypothetical and multi-choice questions. For example, it may be said that the answer is often suggested within such questions, and of course this point has a certain validity. Another way of expressing this point is to say that the therapist is 'leading' the child, and that the child's responses are therefore evidentially useless or very suspect.

One of the major problems here is that a wide conceptual gulf still exists between the strict legal view of an 'ideal' interview, where a compliant, verbally fluent, spontaneously responding child will simply 'tell his/her story', to an objective, non-leading interviewer. This issue has been discussed elsewhere (*see* Chapter 5), but it is important to say that even if a purely research/evidential approach is used during the interview, it is still unhelpful to think in terms of establishing 'the truth' about the abuse, 'beyond all reasonable doubt', as might be expected in criminal proceedings. Because of the frequent lack of corroboration available in such cases, it is probably more appropriate to think in terms of using non-leading questions to establish the facts, 'on the balance of probabilities', as is expected within the civil courts. For various legal reasons, it is probably true to say that only a very tiny number of cases of sexual abuse cannot be diagnosed with certainty.

However, returning to the model of questioning techniques described, and moving from simple open and closed questions to multi-choice questions, it is important here to vary the *set* of one's questions and the order in which possibilities are presented, so that the child is not presented with a series of *similar* questions, where a positive 'yes' response, might be chosen to, for instance, every second possibility presented to the child. If possible answers are suggested predictably, it could be argued that the child is *learning* correct responses to the interviewer's questioning sequence; varying the set of questions will, therefore minimize 'leading' the child towards the 'correct' answer, which young, fearful, abused children may be only too eager to supply.

In using this approach, the child's *response* to each question must be carefully gauged before moving on to the next question. Therefore, the therapist is following the *child's* responses in disclosure (as described earlier), rather than applying a fixed formula of questioning to a passive recipient.

For instance, the therapist may ask (hypothetically) 'If X did put his willie somewhere else, would he put it below the waist or above the waist? Supposing he *had* gone and put it above the waist, where would he have put it? Would he have put it in the ear, or nose, where? Would it be put outside the Child Doll's mouth, or inside? (multi-choice question). If he put it inside the mouth, would he make the mouth wet sometimes?' This latter question is testing for an experience of ejaculation and the therapist may then ask, 'Did it taste sweet or sour? Did you spit it out or swallow it?' (multi-choice questions). 'What colour was it?' (closed question).

With a child who is totally *denying* sexual abuse in the face of contrary referring information the therapist may find the use of hypothetical questioning very helpful, particularly in Stages 4–5.

Hence, the use of a *variety* of questioning techniques—open-ended, multi-choice and hypothetical questions may help to overcome blocking and psychological resistance on the part of the child.

However, the thrust of our suggested format for interviewing sexually abused children is to create a structure within which a child will be able to communicate *freely,* and in which the therapist has a range of technical options, to aid the overall process.

(*See* Appendix 1 for a further case example.)

CONCLUSION

In conclusion, helping young children to describe experiences of child sexual abuse is a complicated and time-consuming process, and ample time should be set aside for this work. Susanne Sgroi has made the point that the child's sense of time, as it relates to his or her developmental level, will restrict most interviews with young children to one and a half hours, or less. However, the mechanics of setting up the interview may mean that two hours or more are necessary to avoid rushing.

Adjuncts and aids, such as anatomically correct dolls, drawings and other play instruments may be useful in this context. However, the diagnostician in the room is the *therapist* not the anatomically correct dolls.

It is important to remember that technique does *not* evolve solely around the use of these aids, but relies primarily on the empathic clinical skills and training of the therapists, as with most psychiatric interviews involving young children.

THERAPISTS' RESPONSES TO INTERVIEWING SEXUALLY ABUSED CHILDREN

Becoming aware that a child has been sexually abused has a number of effects on the interviewer, personal distress for the child, anger with the possible perpetrator, anxiety over the consequences of disclosure in terms of action to be taken. Maintaining appropriate support for the child is essential to help the child reveal and to elaborate his experiences, exaggerated sympathy may distort descriptions.

Having a co-therapist or a supervising team helps the therapist maintain an appropriate stance, and minimizes therapist responses which may lead to false-positive diagnosis, or a failure to observe cues due to a wish *not* to see. Solo interviewing seems to lead to more difficulties in making a diagnosis, and joint work seems to be essential to make an accurate assessment of a child's statements and descriptions.

Finally, it is important to stress that both the practice guide and the questioning techniques discussed are suggestions for clinicians, based on our experience to date in working with sexually abused children. We hope and expect that colleagues will be able to amend, refine and develop these techniques, in time, and also that our suggestions can be used *flexibly,* in order to facilitate disclosure by the child and work by the therapist.

STRUCTURED INTERVIEW WITH ADOLESCENTS OR OLDER CHILDREN

Use of the anatomical dolls has been found to be helpful with children as old as 11, 12 or 13. The therapist may well acknowledge to the child the fact that they are unlikely to still play with dolls but suggest that the dolls might assist the child in talking about things which are difficult to put into words. The therapist can then invite the child to point to the dolls or indicate sexual activities using the dolls if the child is too frozen to speak or has difficulty in verbalizing his/her experiences.

The therapist can be guided by the child's response as to whether or not the dolls are necessary, for example, the child who can use words to describe his/her experience quite freely and is old enough to conceptualize and understand sexual activities will not usually need recourse to the dolls.

The Presence of Others at the Interview

In interviewing the older child if a disclosure has already been made to someone else the child may find it easier to repeat his or her previous account during the interview. Alternatively, if a social worker or teacher is present to whom the child has already disclosed, the therapist may ask the child's permission for the teacher or social worker to remind him or her what it was the child told them originally so that the child is spared the need to repeat it. Alternatively, if a child has made a statement to the police, but seems to be blocking in recapping on this to the therapist, the therapist may ask the child 'if the police lady you spoke to were here what would she tell me was in your statement; would she tell me that someone had touched you in a way which you did not like? Would she say that person was someone you knew, perhaps a member of your family? Which member of your family was it? Would the policewoman have said you had been touched in a private part of your body, for example, around your vagina/anus? Would she have said the adult X or Y wanted you to touch them on a private part of their body? Would she have said they also wanted to put a private part of their body near a private part of your body? Would the policewoman have said they attempted to have sexual intercourse with you, you know what that means don't you? That is when an adult puts his penis into your vagina/anus.'

Using Hypothetical Questions to Reduce Distress

It should be remembered that some older children and teenagers are acutely distressed when recounting their experiences, and the therapist may have to employ methods of indirect or circular questioning or use hypothetical questions in order to facilitate a disclosure. Some children who have been threatened or subjected to perverse and cruel sexual acts are particularly vulnerable and the therapist may have to conduct most of the interview in the hypothetical tense—'If someone had touched you in a way that you did not like do you think it would be someone you know/do not know? Do you think you would have liked that? Do you think that the person who did that to you would have thought you liked it, or would they have known that you did not like it? Do you think they may have gone further and attempted intercourse? If that had happened to you do you think you would have told someone? Who would you have told? Or would you have kept it to yourself? What would you have thought might have happened if you had told someone? Do you think you would have been believed for example, by your mother or do you think they may have thought you were lying? If you had told your mother, for example, and she had believed you what do you think she would have done? Do you think she may have confronted your father? And what would have happened then? Might that have led to an argument and what would have been the result of it?'

Remembering the points made earlier (p. 121) about *mixing* the question types and varying the questioning 'set', the therapist will probably move from open to multi-choice questions, depending on the response of the child.

The child may often indicate her fear that confrontation between her parents would have led to a row, possibly violent, and more importantly to the breakdown of the marital relationship with possibly the father leaving the family home, and the child being deeply concerned lest the mother be unable to cope with the care of the home and children on her own. Fear of family breakdown is often paramount in the child's mind and is the feared disaster.

Acknowledgement of the child's dilemma to the child can often give some therapeutic relief. Positively connoting the child's sacrifice in having kept a sexual relationship with an abusing parent secret, sometimes for years, in order to prevent the feared consequence of the family breaking up can be helpful. The therapist can ask the child, 'do you think your parents know how grateful they should be to you for having kept this secret for so long, so that they could be helped to stay together?'

It is important to acknowledge fears that adolescents may have, for example, the fear of perhaps becoming pregnant after the onset of menstruation. This is often a precipitating factor to them making a disclosure. Concern about father's jealousy about boyfriends, concern about whether they should tell boyfriends, concerns about how far they should let a boyfriend go with them sexually are all preoccupations of this age-group. Again it is important to confirm for young people that they were right to disclose, but also to acknowledge their profoundly ambivalent feelings about having caused trouble in the family, got fathers into trouble, incurred their mothers' wrath, jealousy or feelings of anger and frustration at their own failure to protect their daughters, etc. Many of these issues need to be taken up during the context of ongoing therapeutic work.

INTERVIEWING BOY VICTIMS

Although the largest proportion of victims of sexual abuse are girls, a significant number of boys of all ages are also abused, most frequently by male perpetrators but sometimes by females.

Interviews with boys for diagnostic purposes should follow the same guidelines as for girls, but some special points need to be considered. Boys abused by male perpetrators often reveal at interview considerable confusion about being of the same sex and many express fears about homosexuality—either that *they* must have manifested some particular traits which the perpetrator interpreted as an invitation to commit homosexual acts, or that having been so abused they may identify themselves subsequently as homosexuals, perhaps with a tendency in their sexual orientation towards becoming a passive participant.

The fact that a number of male perpetrators of sexual abuse reveal a history of having been abused themselves as children suggests rather a tendency for male victims to identify with the abuser and to subsequently perpetrate abuse on others younger than themselves. Boys as young as nine years old have been seen to develop sexual activities with younger children.

Of those boys abused by females there is sometimes a tendency for them to form a passive sexual orientation subsequently and male homosexual prostitution has been thought to result in some cases. Boys often perceive themselves to have initiated or been responsible in some way for a sexual relationship with an adult female, who may actually have seduced them.

It is important to acknowledge to boy victims at interview their possible fears about their own sexuality. They need to be reassured that a homosexual, a passive, sexual orientation is not necessarily the result of abuse, and that many other factors play a part. Maximizing their options at this stage is often one of the goals of therapeutic intervention.

GENDER OF THE INTERVIEWER

Care should be taken *not* to recreate a quasi-abusive experience for the child victim by placing him/her in the room with a single therapist of the same sex as the alleged perpetrator. Children sometimes express strong averse reactions to such a situation, and their fear and anxiety can make it even more difficult for them to disclose what inappropriate sexual experience they may have had.

Thus, in the majority of cases where a child has been abused by a male, the interviewer should be female. However, there can be two therapists, male and female, working together, provided that there is flexibility between them which allows the child to engage primarily with one or the other. A child who has been abused by a female can talk to the male therapist if preferred.

Generally speaking, sexually abused children should not be interviewed by a single male therapist and a female colleague should be asked to join him (this can be the social worker, who knows the child well or has accompanied him/her to interview).

In ongoing therapeutic work there are thought to be several advantages in using male/female co-therapy pairs, normally that this can provide an important alternative model of 'parenting' or 'caring' with appropriate boundaries maintained between the therapists and the children. For older girls and boy victims it often provides a valuable experience of learning to trust a man again who can be relied upon *not* to abuse or take advantage of her/him.

CHAPTER 7

The Professional Network and the Management of Disclosure

Marianne Tranter and Eileen Vizard

THE PROFESSIONAL NETWORK

Any of the following professionals may become alerted by the signs and symptoms we have mentioned in the previous chapter indicating the possibility that a child is being sexually abused:

Teachers
Social workers
Health visitors
General practitioners
Day nursery staff
Police
School health doctors
Paediatricians
Play group leaders
Education welfare officers
Youth and community workers

Which professional first becomes concerned will largely depend on the context in which the child presents. Thus if a child has a medical problem, for example, vaginal discharge, urinary tract infection or abdominal pain, it is likely that the family's GP will be the first to be consulted or alternatively the school health doctor or school nurse. A referral may be made by the GP to a paediatrician for further investigation or examination.

In a young child under the age of five, presentation might be of, for example, soreness around the vagina, bruises around the perineum or thighs or signs of tearing or bleeding as seen for instance by day nursery staff when involved in routine care-taking including nappy changing. Day nursery staff may also observe some of the alerting behavioural or emotional symptoms we have mentioned, such as a child who masturbates a good deal, or who plays in a sexually explicit way with toys or with other children, etc. A mother may have discussed various concerns about a small child with her health visitor, whether these be to do with medical problems or the child's sexually precocious behaviour, the reason for which the mother does not understand.

In a school-age child, a teacher may have observed or become concerned about worrying behaviours and may have discussed these with his/her head teacher, who in turn may have consulted either the educational welfare officers or the social services department. Alternatively, if the child's behaviour was giving concern, a referral may have been made through the child guidance or school psychological service to a child guidance clinic or child psychiatric department for further investigation.

In the older child or teenager, teachers may have become concerned about the child's behaviour or emotional state. In some cases, the children themselves will have talked to someone, for example, a friend or teacher or social worker, about being sexually abused.

It is important to remember that child sexual abuse is usually disclosed through either:

1. *Direct presentation*—more likely in older children. Where the child or young person tells someone of the abuse, for example, social worker, teacher, GP, police, family friend or relative. The police is the agency which receives the greatest proportion of direct disclosures of sexual abuse. Sometimes a young person or friend or professional acting on their behalf might approach a voluntary organization such as 'Child Line', the Incest Crisis Line (phone-in services), the Rape Crisis Centres, or the Incest Survivors Group (a group of women victims who give counselling support to one another).
2. *Indirect presentation*—more likely in younger children. Many children do not speak about their experience of being sexually abused but present through a variety of signs and symptoms in the ways previously described. It is clearly this group who are much more dependent therefore on professionals recognizing these alerting signs and symptoms and acting upon them in the child's interest.

It should be remembered that usually it is the older postpubertal child who is more likely to be able to make a direct disclosure of sexual abuse by telling someone. Younger children often do not even have the language to describe their experience or the developmental capacity to conceptualize it in adult terms. They may attempt to make reference to it in terms of familiar experiences, and it is not uncommon for small children to demonstrate through play or verbally an experience of being abused using metaphor. A child may describe its father 'having a monster which is kept in bed' or 'a snake which bites them in the night', and one small child aged three who had been raped told her therapist the reason she had had blood in her knickers and had a sore bottom was because she had been 'stung by a stinging nettle'.

THE MANAGEMENT OF DISCLOSURE

Increasingly in the past five years sexual abuse has been included as a category of child abuse within the guidelines to local authorities and health and education departments recommended by the Area Review Committees and recently recommended by the DHSS.[1] Thus existing non-accidental injury guidelines are to be followed in cases of suspected or reported child sexual abuse.

The DHSS stipulated the need for a high level of interagency co-operation and support at each stage in the management of child sexual abuse:

1. *Recognition.* "Agency staff and independent practitioners need to be alert to behavioural factors indicating possible sexual abuse as physical indicators are not always present."[1]
2. *Investigation.* Professionals from social services departments, the NSPCC, the police and medical practitioners need to work closely together to effect a proper assessment and to gather 'evidence' where possible. The 1986 DHSS guidelines emphasize the need to *believe* the child pending further investigation.
3. *Support and protection for the child.* Following disclosure of sexual abuse, services must be available to provide support and protection for the child. "Care away from the family must be provided if safety at home cannot be assured."[1]

Thus suspicion or allegation of child sexual abuse to one professional should be communicated first within that professional's own agency, for example, with his or her line manager or consultant, and secondly should be communicated with all other relevant agencies, following the existing NAI guidelines. This recommendation was made by the Beckford enquiry, 'A Child in Trust',[2] and by the British Association of Social Workers in reaction to child abuse.

A case conference system is the formal setting in which professionals communicate concern, information and knowledge about an individual child and family, and this will usually be convened once an assessment of sexual abuse has been made. Many areas or district social services departments employ a child abuse coordinator whose work it is to collate information about suspected abuse, attend case conferences and record the decisions of those professionals in terms of whether or not a child's name is to be placed on the non-accidental injury register, which is held centrally in each social services department.

Each area also has an area review committee or equivalent consisting of senior staff from departments of health, social services, education and the police. Its function is to review and monitor children whose names are on the NAI register and to coordinate information, training and resources in respect to child abuse in its area.

Systems for managing child abuse may vary widely throughout the UK as each area and district review committee has a degree of autonomy and responsibility for laying down and monitoring the NAI procedures.

It is to be hoped that the recent DHSS guidelines[1] will assist the development of good practice on a national scale. Area and District Committee members meet on a regular basis. The safety and welfare of the child is the first priority and they should act accordingly. A child-centred policy is vital in the management of sexual abuse, and painful issues which arise from family separations can and should be dealt with during subsequent therapy.

Again the DHSS guidelines stress the importance of believing the child when he or she has alleged sexual abuse, and correctly point out that it is extremely rare for children to lie about such matters, although it is of course much more common for them to retract an allegation through fear of the consequences.[1]

If the abuse has occurred very recently there may need to be a speedy medical interview of the child by an experienced medical practitioner, either a paediatrician or police surgeon, who will need to investigate not only the presence of physical symptoms but also forensic evidence, for example, presence of blood, semen, hairs, etc., on the child. Police, social workers and doctors should coordinate their roles in talking to the child and work together in order to obviate the necessity to conduct repeated interviews of the child, which may be experienced by the child as an additional source of abuse.

Once sexual abuse has been diagnosed, it is the duty of the professionals concerned to protect the child as a matter of priority and to block further abuse. This may well require conducting a family assessment and deciding, for example, whether the child could be adequately protected by remaining at home with the mother, providing of course that the mother believes the child's allegations and is prepared to stick by him/her. In cases where a mother disbelieves a child or stands by the alleged perpetrator, the professionals may feel that the mother is unable to give adequate protection to the child, who may then have to be moved from the home for his or her own safety.

Management Model

Disclosure of sexual abuse may be made in the following ways:

1. Through *direct reporting* by the victim or another family member or friend to the police or another professional.
2. *Indirect presentation* of alerting signs and symptoms in the child. The recognition of these by a concerned professional leads to initial suspicion of child sexual abuse.

If the child presents with relevant physical symptoms, there should be a sensitive medical examination of the child. If there are emotional or behavioural symptoms, a concerned professional should talk to the child to elicit any relevant information and the child should then be assessed by an experienced interviewer.

If a professional has a suspicion of child sexual abuse, he should not keep that to himself but should think and consult with colleagues about the best ways of investigating that suspicion or concern further (*see* Chapter 4). At this point the professional network should be activated informally, with professionals seeking further information from other professionals about the child and family in order to assist the assessment process. The existing child abuse guidelines should be followed. Although in Great Britain professionals do not have a system of mandatory reporting, there is a strong ethical requirement of professionals to communicate their concerns about children at risk. However, the area of discretion in reporting can lead to a decision not to, through fear of the consequences for the child and the family.

If there is a direct report or allegation of child sexual abuse by the child, that professional should believe the child and should then activate the professional network by calling a case conference within the NAI guidelines. Action to protect the child is of paramount importance.

The following two cases examples illustrate ways in which disclosure might be made:

Medical setting—Case example
Rebecca, age five was referred by her GP to a paediatrician for further investigation of recurrent urinary tract infections and perineal soreness. The paediatrician could find no physical abnormality, but the possibility of sexual abuse was raised. She contacted the social work department at the hospital and she and the social worker saw the child on her own for individual assessment. Using a set of anatomically correct dolls, the social worker, who was experienced and trained in conducting such interviews, encouraged the child to talk about various forms of touching including inappropriate touching. The child was able to make a clear disclosure of having been subjected to digital penetration and attempted intercourse, both vaginally and anally, and had

also been subjected to oral intercourse. The amount of detailed information about sexual activity that Rebecca revealed was consistent with her having been sexually abused and, furthermore, she demonstrated negative reactions to what had happened to her.

A nurse from the outpatient department kept Rebecca company for a while on her own while the paediatrician and social worker had a chance to discuss their assessment. Both were in agreement that in their opinion Rebecca had been seriously sexually abused. Rebecca's mother was then called in and told that it was possible that Rebecca had been sexually interfered with and that this was a serious matter which the hospital was bound to report to the 'authorities', including the local social services department in the area where the family lived and the police. Rebecca's mother was also told that a medical examination by a specialist would need to be carried out by a doctor who was particularly experienced in conducting such examinations, i.e., a police surgeon.

The social worker telephoned the local social services department to liaise with them about what action needed to be taken. The social services department's policy was to inform their local police so that the matter could be fully investigated, and it seemed likely that a joint social work and police visit to the family would be made on the family's return from the hospital, incorporating an assessment of whether or not it would be safe for Rebecca to remain in the family home. The person she had named in connection with her abuse was in fact her father and the issue of whether or not he would leave the family home would need to be discussed.

A local police surgeon together with a woman detective constable from the local police came to the hospital and a physical examination of Rebecca, including cultures for venereal disease, was carried out by the police surgeon, in the presence of the paediatrician. The social worker asked Rebecca to repeat to them what had happened to her, again using the anatomical dolls helped by the woman detective constable who participated in this interview.

The social worker in the area where the family lived would investigate with the police officer conducting the enquiry whether or not Rebecca's father would be remanded in custody for questioning, in which case it would be safe for Rebecca to remain at home; or if the father would agree to leave the family home for the time being pending further investigation or a possible court hearing. If he were to be remanded on bail, application can be made for certain conditions that prevent him from living in the family home or making contact with his daughter until legal proceedings are complete. It is important to establish the mother's attitude to the child's disclosure of sexual abuse, for example, if she believes Rebecca and agrees with her husband leaving the home, she may well be able to take a sufficiently protective stance for Rebecca to remain at home. By contrast, if she did not believe Rebecca or blamed her in some way, then the social workers may consider the need to remove her on a Place of Safety Order and place her in a safe setting. Alternatively she could be admitted to the ward for a day or two until the situation could be sorted out.

In this particular case, Rebecca's father agreed to leave the family home and she remained there with her mother. Rebecca very helpfully told the hospital staff before she left that her father had also been doing rude things to her brother Jonathan, aged seven. When he was seen within a few days for individual assessment, the clinicians learned that he too had been subjected to severe sexual abuse by his father, including buggery. This highlights the importance of assessing siblings of the abused child because it is possible that they too have been subjected to some form of abuse.

The social services department arranged a case conference within the non-accidental injury procedures, at which were discussed the children's future care, their legal status, and their needs for treatment. The police completed their investigations but there was insufficient evidence to prosecute the children's father and they were subsequently made subjects of Care Orders but remained at home in the care of their mother. The father denied the children's allegations and said they were lying, but the children's mother believed them and she and her husband decided to separate and subsequently divorced. The mother and children joined the sexual abuse treatment programme where they made good progress. The children's access to their father was temporarily suspended and, in light of his persistent denial of responsibility for the abuse, it was difficult to see how contact between him and the children could be seen to be in their best interests. Given the pressure on them of being with their father against whom they had made serious allegations and knowing that he denied them would thus disconfirm a major part of their reality. In time, access may be reintroduced within a therapeutic context, but only if it is strictly supervised.

Community setting—Case example
A member of staff from a children's day nursery telephoned a local social worker to report the following incident: Sally, aged two and a half, who had had a persistent rash around her vagina and who was seen to masturbate a good deal uncovered a little boy at rest time, pulled down his pants and inserted her finger in his anus. The nursery worker was concerned about this behaviour and the social worker thought it important to investigate the matter further. She visited the girl's parents and said that they would like to have Sally medically examined in connection with her persistent vaginal rash. The social worker then took Sally with her mother to the family's GP who noted some redness around the vagina but saw no evidence of sexual interference. The social worker in consultation with her senior decided to seek a second opinion and approached another GP in the area who also had experience in her work as a police surgeon. On examination, Sally's anal sphincter was found to be loose and there was some evidence of a healing tear of the anal opening. The hymen was still intact, although the vaginal opening was larger than normal. Her opinion was that there could well have been some sexual interference.

The social worker thought it important that someone should talk to Sally, and she approached a local child psychiatrist who had experience of conducting individual assessment interviews where sexual abuse was suspected. Using a set of dolls, the psychiatrist and his social work colleague attempted to talk to Sally about parts of the body and touching, but unfortunately her level of comprehension and verbal expression was immature for her age and the interview was abortive.

A professionals' consultation meeting was held immediately after the interview, attended by the social worker, senior social worker, child psychiatrist, psychiatric social worker and Juvenile Services Bureau representative (police). Important information was provided by the police about Sally's father—that is that he had previously spend four years in prison for a serious sex offence against a young child aged four.

Although it had not been possible to interview Sally, medical findings, together with concern during several weeks about her sexualized behaviour at the day nursery, were sufficiently worrying for the professionals to consider that she might have been sexually abused and might be at risk of further abuse. When the parents were told of the concerns they denied that such abuse was a possibility and the mother was adamant that her husband could not, or would not, have touched Sally in a sexual way. The possibility that Sally had been abused but her mother had not seen it or known about it and had been unable to protect her, led the professionals to think that Sally's safety could not be ensured if she returned home, therefore, a Place of Safety Order was obtained through a local magistrate and Sally was placed temporarily with foster parents.

While with her foster mother, Sally revealed gradually more information about inappropriate sexual activity, and when her parents visited her there, she appeared to be very fearful of her father and would not go near him. Similarly, she would not go near the foster father for some time and was clearly apprehensive in the company of men.

Police investigations were carried out and completed and there was thought to be insufficient evidence to link Sally's symptoms with her father and thus there was insufficient evidence to institute criminal proceedings. However, Sally was made a ward of court, and after a lengthy hearing a judge decided that, on the balance of probability, Sally probably had been sexually abused by her father and that it was not safe for her to return home, especially as her mother did not believe this had happened and took her husband's side. Unfortunately, the parents, persistent denial meant that therapeutic help for them was not possible, since as far as they were concerned there were no problems which needed remediation. The prospect of Sally being able to rejoin her family may therefore be rather remote, since an assumption must be made that, without therapeutic change, the risk of Sally being reabused in the future remains unacceptably high.

THE PROFESSIONALS' RESPONSE

From Kempe's work[3] on the recognition of sexual abuse, it is known that there may be a long period of time during which sexual abuse is seen but not really perceived or understood by professionals, and this is really indicative of our need to deny the existence of such a distressing problem.

Some child psychotherapists, psychiatrists and social workers may interpret their young patients' revelations through play and drawings of a sexual relationship with a parent as fantasy and not as a description of a real event. There may be considerable reluctance to believe that the child may have been sexually abused and a wish on the part of the therapist that that is not the case. This may deter the therapist from pursuing a suspicion that what the child produces through sexualized play and drawings may indicate a re-enactment of an *actual* experience of sexual abuse.

The Issue of Denial of Sexual Abuse

To understand the issue of 'denial' in both family and professional systems, it is of interest to look at the way denial as a concept has developed.

Denial as a psychoanalytical concept

In the psychoanalytical literature[4] denial is seen as a defence mechanism, e.g. the 'denial' of painful experiences, or alternatively the 'denial' of an 'impulse or aspect of the self'. Freud described the denial of painful perceptions as a manifestation of the workings of the pleasure principle. Individuals, in the face of painful realities, deny them because they wish for happier experiences which they may then try to create through hallucinatory wish fulfilments. Painful perceptions thus have to overcome this resistance in order to reach conscious awareness.

In this sense it is important to distinguish between the mechanism of 'suppression', which is a conscious mechanism, versus the 'unconscious' mechanism of denial. Freud[4] came to view the child's description of sexual experiences as being the hallucinatory wish fulfilment against the pain of becoming aware of the parents' sexuality and relationship. This in turn has become a 'wish fulfilment' which has helped professionals *not* see that the child's statement may represent a painful reality, not necessarily a fantasy.

The second meaning of denial—the denial of aspects of self—has arisen from the description of defence mechanisms, of splitting of the self and projection of parts of the self.[1] Projective and introjective identification are the processes by which unwanted painful aspects of the self are split off and put into, or projected into another person. In this way, the unwanted feelings can be disowned, and pain avoided. The person on the 'receiving end' of these feelings may either reject them or, become 'identified' with them, so-called introjective identification. When this happens the person identifying with the unwanted painful feelings may start to behave like the person who has got rid of the feelings, and to act, perhaps, out of character.

It is now recognized that this type of identification process can and does occur in professionals, particularly by those working with difficult cases, such as child abuse. Professionals may identify with, or take on, the characteristics of certain members of the abusing family and may even go so far as to 'act out' these roles in case conferences. This is known as 'mirroring' the family pathology and a common example would be when one member of the professional network becomes over-identified with the child, starts to behave like a passive victim, and eventually ends up being blamed (scapegoated) by other professionals for management problems. Insight into this process can help to defuse many difficult work situations, in practice.

Denial—the professional network

Professionals' discomfort with certain children and families may be dealt with by a process of rationalization. Once it is accepted that abuse can occur, the signals which children and adults have been giving can be deciphered and their true meaning perceived.

Because families may use 'silencing' as a way of avoiding painful events,[5] the child has to be talked to individually in order to make a diagnosis, and the therapeutic task is to counter the silencing and blaming processes which deny that a child has been hurt by an adult.

The professional who speaks for the child who has been hurt, can also expect that the 'family' of professionals may well also trivialize, disbelieve, attribute false meanings or just ignore the implication of what has been stated or perceived, and even make the professional who has spoken to the child doubt what has been told. Again, this could be seen as an example of the rest of the professional network becoming over-identified with the family, leaving the interviewer disbelieved, just like the child.

Investigations of Professional Attitudes

In order to investigate the attitudes of professionals to sexual abuse, Bentovim and Okell-Jones[6] carried out a survey of attitudes through a questionnaire study. This was based on an approach described by Finkelhor.[7] In reviewing the American professional context, he described a sudden increase in reporting problems between 1976 and 1979 with the tripling of official reports of child sexual abuse during a brief period. He described the powerful emotional responses in both public and professionals alike. Treatment was often carried out in a panicky atmosphere of emergency; there was often inadequate consultation before action and, in addition, actions were not fully thought through and resulted in destructive unhelpful conflict with families and between professionals.

Finkelhor noted that sexual abuse was a problem which fell into competing professional and institutional domains. On the one hand, he saw it as a serious crime, particularly when it involved very young children, or on the other hand it was seen as a major and worrying mental health problem and issue in relationship to child care. He noted that the professionals who needed to deal with the problem had a very considerable degree of mistrust of each other.

To examine the approaches of professionals in the UK, a survey similar to Finkelhor's[6,7] was carried out between 1983 and 1984. This was at a time when professionals were being made aware of the facts of sexual abuse through large conferences and there was a mass of information in the medical and psychiatric literature about work in the USA. Such conferences were usually organized by the area review committee with a responsibility for child abuse, so that there were representatives of the law, including the criminal justice group, as well as those from the medical and social work professions.

The survey indicated that those professionals representing the criminal justice group—the police and probation service—saw the most victims and offenders, far more than did social workers or paediatric or psychiatric professionals. This finding confirmed the observations of Mrazek et al.[8]

Professionals were asked in the study to describe how they would manage a hypothetical case of child sexual abuse. Various possibilities were suggested, which included interviewing the child, making a family assessment, referring for psychiatric assessment, and the possibility of removing either the child or the perpetrator. There was a considerable discrepancy in terms of the different professionals' wishes to use criminal charges or family separation in response to sexual abuse disclosure. The police and probation group did not see referral to other professionals as a particularly appropriate response, but were more concerned with bringing criminal charges and obtaining custodial sentence, and they saw probation orders as a rather poor second-best alternative. The child guidance, hospital, community health and social work professionals tended towards seeing the possibility of families being able to stay together and becoming involved in various treatment approaches. The social work professionals tended to be much more neutral about the issue of bringing criminal charges and convictions. The polarity between treatment and punishment thus remains a powerful view among different professionals.

PERSONAL RESPONSES OF PROFESSIONALS

Anger, Distress and Pain

Giaretto[9] has described the sequence of responses which will be familiar to many professionals working closely in the field of sexual abuse. Feelings can range from intense rage with the man who abuses, coupled with a sense of disgust and outrage and murderousness, to possibly even excitement and titillation. There can be fury and anger with the partner who did not see, yet who must have seen, or who was there, but misread the signs. There can even be a sense of anger mixed with distress and pain for the victim, that he or she was not able to speak about the abuse earlier.

In becoming aware of a long-standing traumatic experience suffered by the child, the professional will often empathize with the child's distress, pain, anger, hurt and outrage. At the same time the professional may also identify with the child's sense of guilt and feeling of personal responsibility and shame, thinking that he or she is in some way responsible for the abuse. The professional is often also aware of the child's fear that following disclosure either his parents or the family will collapse in separation, with the child feeling responsible for the emotional pain and distress that ensues.

Professionals also struggle with a sense of dirtiness and contagion that can make them not want to see or hear or to avoid knowing what they know, or trying to resolve matters by projecting their anger on to one or other of the participants as a way of dealing with profound pain and distress.

Resolution by Proxy

Furniss[10] has described the process of what he calls "resolution of conflict by proxy". Here, the intensity of feelings and conflicts which are avoided by the family seems to be reflected by the professionals, who then find themselves in conflict with each other, rather than the family. The family projects different aspects of their fear onto different professionals—fear of loss, fear of suicide, fears of abandonment are transformed into anger and frustration with those same professionals. The professionals may become identified with different family members, one fearing a child will not be protected, another that a family will not recover from separation, and so on. Each professional fears the other will be incompetent or have the wrong idea and each wishes to show that a particular viewpoint is the correct one. There are many ways in which family conflict can be reflected by the professionals' own difficulties, whether this is in terms of the secrecy, denial of damage or hurt, scapegoating of particular family members, distancing between professionals, conflict within the professional hierarchy and between people with line-management responsibility.

Thus, as described earlier, a mirroring of the family pathology within the professional network can often be seen. There may be identification of one professional with the secrecy system in the family, who although suspicious of the abuse or even told by the victim decides to keep that information confidential and 'secret' from other professional colleagues, or even the professionals may deny the possibility of sexual abuse of a child known to them, thinking that the problem may go away and rationalizing this by convincing themselves that they are mistaken in their concern about possible abuse. Some professionals may see the victim but doubt the validity or the truth of the allegations, especially if the victim later retracts them through fear of the consequences. Sometimes, a professional who raises concern about the possibility of sexual abuse may be scapegoated by other professionals and considered to be making a fuss about nothing or to be simply mistaken, and that professional can sometimes be on the receiving end of considerable anger and suspicion within the professional network and accused of being destructive, especially if recognition of sexual abuse may lead to family breakdown.

Conflicts within Professional Role

Therefore, the professional may fear the effect of disclosure on the child and family and be concerned that the effect of intervention may be worse than taking no action at all: for example, GPs, social workers, etc., who perceive the whole family as their patients or clients may struggle with conflicting loyalties to all family members and think that family breakdown would be the worst outcome for all of them. Not taking action at this point may mean that the family stays together, but is must be remembered that the abuse is likely to continue and the abused child's future emotional and psychosexual development may become irreparably impaired as a consequence.

Professionals often find it difficult to acknowledge the reality base of their suspicion of sexual abuse and wonder whether they are really imagining it and think that perhaps their colleagues will think they have a prurient or salacious interest in the subject. That which is thus too uncomfortable to contemplate is often denied and ignored in the hope that one's suspicions were groundless. Professionals need to be aware that strong feelings aroused in themselves of sexual excitement may arise from two factors:

a. either from their own feelings or attitudes towards sexuality.
   or
b. from a process of identification with the feelings and attitudes in the

child or in the family. This process underlines the need for professionals to have adequate training and supervision in working with sexuality so that feelings aroused in themselves do not become defensively blocked and inhibit sensitive work, or become projected (negatively) onto the child or perpetrator in an overly protective or punitive way.

THE LEGAL CONTEXT

Discussion of sexuality in our society is not for the most part conducted openly and there is an enduring societal and cultural belief in the right of individuals to privacy in sexual matters. Indeed, the belief that men's sexual proclivities and means of sexual gratification are largely their own concern, extends to a tacit acknowledgement of the use of prostitutes, wives and even children to these ends. There is a surprisingly high level of tolerance for the accommodation of men's perverse and even sadomasochistic sexual desires, provided their sexual activities are conducted in a relatively unobtrusive or secret way. It is only comparatively recently that women and children have been viewed as relatively autonomous persons with individual rights, rather than being merely the property of husbands or fathers. Feminists would indeed argue that abuse of children is but an extension of men's abuse of women and as such is an extension of that unequal power relationship.

It was not until 1908 in England that incest and other forms of sexual abuse were included in definitions of criminal behaviour and so punishable by the courts. Prior to that time, they were viewed as aspects of immoral behaviour and so were the province of the Church and were dealt with by the eccesiastical courts.

Incest and other forms of sexual abuse are laid down as serious offences within the Sexual Offences Act 1956.[11] The *legal definition of sexual offences* is as follows:

Rape. Sexual intercourse without consent or by force. Consent by a child to intercourse is immaterial and penetration to any degree is sufficient within a definition of intercourse. (Sexual Offences Act 1976.)

Maximum penalty is life imprisonment or seven years for attempted rape.

Incest. Sexual intercourse between consanguinous relatives. By a woman over 16 to have intercourse with a man she knows to be her father, grandfather, son, brother or half-brother. By a man to have intercourse with a woman he knows to be his daughter, grand-daughter, mother or sister or half-sister. Consent is immaterial. (Sections 10 and 11 of the Sexual Offences Act 1956.)

Maximum penalty is seven years' imprisonment.

It is an offence for a man to incite a girl under 16 to have incestuous sexual intercourse with him. (Section 54 of the Criminal Law Act 1977.)

Maximum penalty two years' imprisonment.

Incest by a man is imprisonment if the victim is under 13, otherwise seven years; incest by a woman, maximum penalty seven years.

Unlawful sexual intercourse. It is an offence for a man to have intercourse with a girl under 16 to whom he is not married. Penetration to any degree is sufficient. There may be a defence offered in respect of girls aged 14–16 where (*a*) there is a marriage invalid under English law or (*b*) the man is under 24, has not previously been charged with a similar offence and reasonably believes the girl to be over 16. (Sections 5 and 6 of the Sexual Offences Act 1956.)

Where a girl is under 13, consent of the victim is no defence, not even if the man believed she was older.

For sexual intercourse by a man with a girl of 13 but under 16, two years' imprisonment.

Maximum penalty for sexual intercourse by a man with a girl under 13 is life imprisonment and five years for attempting this.

Buggery. Unlawful sexual intercourse by penetration of the anus. Penetration to any degree is sufficient, regardless of the sex of the victim. There will be no prosecution if two males over the age of 21 consent to the act. (Section 12 of the Sexual Offences Act 1956.)

Maximum penalty if victim, male or female, is under 16, life imprisonment; if boy is over 16 where there is attempt only, 10 years' imprisonment.

Assault with intent to commit buggery. Where the act falls short of buggery or penetration cannot be proved. (Section 16 of the Sexual Offences Act 1956.)

Maximum penalty is 10 years' imprisonment.

Gross indecency. Acts of indecency between males, including mutual masturbation or genital contact. (Section 13 of the Sexual Offences Act 1956.)

Indecent assault. An assault or touching where there has been the application of force, or hostile act or gesture accompanied by circumstances of indecency. (Sections 14 and 15 of the Sexual Offences Act 1956.)

Maximum penalty for indecent assault on a woman where the victim is under 13, five years' imprisonment, otherwise two years. Indecent assault on a man under 16, ten years.

Indecent conduct with or towards a child. This can be done by any person who commits an act of indecency towards a child under 14 or who incites a child under 14 to commit such an act. For example adults who ask children to touch them or who incite two children to commit an indecent act with each other, providing one of them is under 14 (Section 1 of the Indecency with Children Act 1960.)

Maximum penalty is two years' imprisonment.

Causing or encouraging prostitution of a girl under 16. Where a girl is allowed to consort with or be employed by a prostitute or person of low moral character and where the person who has responsibility for her has knowledge of or allowed the action to continue. (Sections 25, 26 and 28 of the Sexual Offences Act 1956.)

Maximum penalty is two years' imprisonment.

For permitting a girl under 13 to use premises for intercourse (Section 25 of the Sexual Offences Act 1956) the maximum penalty is life imprisonment, and for permitting a girl over 13 but under 16 to use the premises for intercourse (Section 26 of the Sexual Offences Act 1956) the maximum penalty is two years' imprisonment.

Indecent photographs of children. It is an offence for a person to take or allow indecent photographs of a child to be taken, or to distribute or show such photographs or to have indecent photographs for view for distributional publications. Indecent photographs of children under 16 may include films and copies of films and photographs or video recordings. (Section 1 of the Protection of Children Act 1978).

CRIMINAL PROCEEDINGS

Investigations

If an alleged sexual offence is reported to the police or to another professional agency who in turn report it to the police, there is an obligation to pursue investigations into the allegations. There will be a focus on gathering evidence, since if the matter is to proceed to court the test will be whether an offence was committed 'beyond all reasonable doubt'. In the UK the police may well send details of their investigation to the Director of Public Prosecutions or more recently to the Child Prosecution Service for advice about whether to proceed to court, but in a substantial number of cases there is insufficient evidence to take the matter before the courts.

Medical evidence is often of crucial importance in establishing that a sexual offence has been committed against a child, and when present can be used as corroborating evidence. However, there is a wide variation in the process of collecting medical evidence and its interpretation. If a child or young person is examined by a police surgeon and found, for example, to have a ruptured hymen, genital bruising or trauma, loose anal tone or tearing, the police surgeon may well state that the medical presentation is consistent with sexual abuse. On the other hand, there may well be a contradictory medical opinion which states that the injuries could have been caused in a variety of other ways, for example, through sport, rough play, falling on a hard object, etc. The court must then decide which of the medical opinions it will accept and it may well be useful for a second medical opinion to be sought, although it should be remembered that the child should *not* be subjected to repeated examinations. However, it is vital that professionals do not *over-emphasize* the importance of the medical examination itself (*see* Chapter 4), and that the results of this examination are seen in a full psychosocial context.

In some cases there is forensic evidence such as the presence of the perpetrator's blood or semen or hairs on the victim, and this can then be used to confirm that the alleged perpetrator was responsible for the abuse. However, in most cases there is no forensic evidence, especially if the offence was last committed several days previously and the child had been bathed since then, or in the case of oral–genital contact or acts of gross indecency, including masturbation, etc., there is no medical evidence.

Child as Witness

In the case of a child over the age of 10, who is deemed to be legally responsible and can understand the meaning of telling the truth, that child may with the assistance of the police make a statement about their experiences, naming the perpetrator. If the matter proceeds to court within the UK, it is the right of the alleged perpetrator, as with any other offence of which he is accused, to have his accuser cross-examined. Therefore, children may well have to go to court to give evidence against someone they know well, very possibly a member of their family. Within an adversarial system the word of the perpetrator, if he denies the offence, is judged alongside the word of the child, who may be subjected to the same kind of pressure as are adult witnesses testifying in court. There is often a basic assumption that children are unreliable witnesses and courts are often cautious in sentencing a man on the basis of a child's testimony. It may be said that children are placed in a similar position as female victims are in rape cases, the defence counsel often seeks to discredit the victim in an attempt to invalidate her evidence.

If the child is under the age of 10, the 'corroboration rule' requires that there be some external form of corroborative evidence in addition to the word of the child, since the word of a young child on its own is not deemed to be reliable and there is an assumption that young children may not understand the meaning of telling the truth, may imagine things, or may lie. However, the court may exercise its discretion in deciding whether or not a child is capable of understanding the meaning of 'swearing the oath' and may then proceed to give sworn evidence which has significant status.

Young children under the age of seven or eight would be placed in an invidious position were they to be expected to go to court to be cross-examined in respect of their allegations, in that they are dependent on either another adult witness who has seen the act testifying to its validity or on the alleged perpetrator acknowledging guilt or responsibility for the abuse. Again, there may be highly suggestive medical evidence to confirm sexual abuse of a young child, but without forensic evidence linking the injuries to a particular perpetrator, the word of the child alone linking the symptoms to a particular person is insufficient evidence to prosecute the alleged offender. It is of interest to remember that within our legal system the alleged perpetrator is regarded as innocent until proved guilty whereas the child victim may be assumed to lie until proved otherwise. However, the DHSS in its guidelines to professionals stipulates that the child's allegations of sexual abuse should be believed until proved otherwise.

Videotape Evidence

Where a young child victim has been interviewed by police in conjunction with a social worker or child psychiatric professional and that interview has been videotaped, if the child has been able to disclose an account of sexual abuse there is then a record of the child's statement. Although some interest has been expressed in this country about the possibility of using videotaped clinical interviews in criminal proceedings, and therefore avoid having the child testify in court, there has been a good deal of opposition to this idea. As defence counsel point out, this would remove from the accused the right to cross-examination, and therefore to a fair trial. Thus videotape recordings of such interviews currently have no place in criminal proceedings, although in some states in the USA, for example, Texas, they have been used as part of the child's evidence. Sometimes an alleged perpetrator may be shown part of the videotaped interview of the child by the police and asked, usually in the company of his legal representative, whether he can explain the material contained in it. Where this practice has been adopted, as in the London Borough of Bexley, a higher rate of confessions has been noted.

However, even in the face of what might appear to be a very clear statement by a young child, defence counsel often advise their clients to plead not guilty, knowing that the task of the prosecution to obtain a conviction in such cases is indeed difficult.

CIVIL PROCEEDINGS

In cases where there is insufficient evidence to press charges against an alleged perpetrator in the criminal courts, professionals who are primarily concerned following the disclosure of sexual abuse, with the protection and welfare of the child, have recourse through civil proceedings to take action within the children's legislation in the UK in either the juvenile court, the county court, or the High Court.

Care Proceedings

The Children and Young Person's Act 1969 provides the opportunity to apply to a magistrates court for a Place of Safety Order for a period of up to 28 days, to enable the social services department to remove the child to a place of safety for his or her protection. Similarly, the NSPCC or the police can also apply for a Place of Safety Order. Within the time granted by that order, application may be made to a juvenile court for the matter to be put before the magistrates, who will then decide whether or not to grant an Interim Care Order. Further application may be made before the court for a full Care Order, giving the social services department full legal responsibility for the child thereafter until the child reaches the age of majority—18. Sometimes cases will be heard in the county courts as part of matrimonial proceedings in instances where, for example, a child has alleged sexual abuse by a parent or step-parent, who has subsequently left the family home and in respect of whom divorce or separation proceedings are pending. The child's allegations might well be heard within the context of making decisions about future care and custody and access to the child. Alternatively, county court judges may be asked to hear cases appealed in the juvenile court, where there is opposition, for example, to the making of a Care Order.

1980 CHILDREN'S ACT

Section 2 of the 1980 Children's Act provides for *voluntary* reception into care of children. However, this is often insufficient to protect the child especially in cases where, for example, the mother does not believe the child's allegations, since she retains the right to discharge a child from care within the first six months, unless after a period of time the Local Authority had assumed Parental Rights and Duties under Section 3 of the 1980 Children's Act. The decision to return a child to a home in which he or she has been sexually abused is a difficult one and usually needs to be taken in full consultation with the professional network, including the social services department who have a statutory duty to protect the interests of the child. Under Section 2 of the 1980 Children's Act the parents can act autonomously to discharge a child from care, but this may not be in the best interests of the child at that particular point in time and thus this section of the 1980 Children's Act clearly has severe limitations in being able to afford the necessary protection.

Wardship

Professionals also have the right to take the case to the High Court in the UK, where application may be made to have the child made a ward of court within the Family Law Reform Act 1969. In an emergency, immediately following disclosure of sexual abuse, an *ex parte* application may be made on behalf of the child before a judge or registrar so that immediate protection can be given to the child in a safe place. The local authority social services department often applies for interim care and control of the child within the wardship proceedings, pending a full court hearing when a final decision about the child's future placement and care may be made.

The Test of Evidence

In civil proceedings, the test of proof that sexual abuse has occurred is 'on the balance of probability'. Again medical evidence will be presented where applicable, circumstantial evidence may be provided about the child's context within his or her family and professional or expert witnesses may be called to recount what the child has said to them during interview. Again, because the adversarial system applies to civil proceedings too, the views of professionals can and often are challenged, both by defending solicitors or counsel and sometimes by other professionals appointed by the courts or by the parents to give a second opinion. Videotape recordings of diagnostic or assessment interviews with children have been used in civil court proceedings, either by being made available to independent professionals or the family's legal representative, or in some cases have been subpoenaed into court proceedings to be viewed as part of the evidence. Although in the High Court the principle of what is in the best interest of the child is paramount, judges have been at pains to permit as full a hearing as possible of the 'evidence' and circumstances in which abuse has occurred; this includes ensuring the accused the right to have his legal representatives cross-examine the medical and psychiatric and social work witnesses to ensure that serious allegations are adequately challenged, and the evidence examined, without recourse to the full adversarial system and the chance to defend against allegations. On the other hand, the court must address the safety and protection of the child and balance the rights of the child against the rights of the parent.

The Need for Family Courts

If child sexual abuse is viewed as a phenomenon which indicates family pathology and stress, there is a view which would favour hearing such cases in family courts, where the interest and safety of the child could be seen in the context of addressing the family's problems and thera-peutic and protective strategies for alleviating them. This would obviously suggest a conciliatory system, rather than an adversarial system such as is used in Scottish family hearings. But even in Scotland there can be no family hearing unless there is an acceptance of responsibility by the perpetrator.

Certainly, the fear of the legal consequences of admitting responsi-bility for sexual abuse of a child is often a powerful deterrent to the perpetrator, who knows that he may well, if convicted, go to prison where he may be victimized by other prisoners or spend his sentence in solitary confinement. Thus, there is sometimes a polarization between society's need to punish child sex offenders and an interest in offering them therapeutic help, such as can be provided for instance within a probation order which stipulates a condition of treatment. Similarly, the fear of family consequences of admitting responsibility exists. There may be fear of abandonment by a wife or family member, or even of being able to live with himself.

Linking Statutory and Treatment Processes

Where an alleged perpetrator continues to deny culpability through fear of the consequences, this is often antitherapeutic in that he cannot then perceive the need for change or for therapeutic intervention. In the long run, the prospect of child-care professionals thinking that the child could be safe again in the care of the perpetrator is remote, since an assumption must be made that without intensive therapeutic help, risk factors for future of re-abuse will remain high.

In the Santa Clara Community, USA, in a treatment project pioneered by Henry Giaretto and colleagues[9] that combines the use of legal sanctions stipulating the need to engage in a therapeutic programme, results have been encouraging and claims of long-term risk of recividism have been low—around 1 per cent of offenders in treatment subsequently reoffending. This observation needs replicating in other settings.

In the UK, a considerable amount of work has been done at the Hospital for Sick Children with families where either (a) there is a treatment condition in respect of the perpetrator through a Probation Order, or (b) where the child or children in the family are subject to Care Orders or Wardship orders affording them necessary protection, but giving their families the opportunity, provided they accept the terms of the therapeutic programme, to work towards family rehabilitation, where that is possible.

However, a legal process whereby perpetrators are encouraged to deny a charge of sexual abuse may mean, unfortunately, that denial of responsibility becomes an intractable state for the abuser (who fears the consequences of acknowledging responsibility in the future) and this can seriously mitigate the possibility of therapeutic change. A change in sentencing policy aimed at combining legal sanction with treatment may alleviate the problems. Treatment Orders stipulating that the perpetrator live separately from the victim while engaging in a treatment programme may facilitate more effectively the rehabilitation of an offender to his family or to society with (hopefully) some reduced risk.

A further stage may be the development of a continuing system linked to Care Orders and treatment or a plea bargaining system. In this system a perpetrator could opt for treatment rather than face prosecution, but his children would be protected by Care Orders.

References

1. DHSS (1986) Working Together—Guidelines for Professionals. A Discussion Document. London: HMSO.

2. Blom-Cooper L. (1985) A Child in Trust. Report of the Inquiry into the Death of Jasmine Beckford. Brent Council.
3. Kempe C. H. (1979) Recent Developments in the field of child abuse. *Child Abuse and Neglect* **3**, 4–15.
4. Freud S. (1905) *Three Essays on Sexuality,* Standard Edition, 7th edition. London: J. Strachey, Hogarth.
5. Kingston W. and Bentovim A. (1980) Creating a focus for brief marital or family therapy. In: Buckman S.H. (ed.) *Forms of Brief Therapy.* New York: Guilford Press.
6. Bentovim A. and Okell-Jones C. (1984) Professionals' Attitude to Sexual Abuse. Presented to International Conference on Child Abuse and Neglect, Montreal.
7. Finkelhor D. (ed.) (1984) Professionals' responses to sexual abuse. In: *Child Sexual Abuse : New Theory and Research.* Glencoe: Free Press.
8. Mrazek P., Lynch M. and Bentovim A. (1983) Sexual abuse of children in the United Kingdom. In: Mrazek P. and Kempe H. (eds), *Sexually Abused Children: Abuse and their Families.* Oxford: Pergamon.
9. Giaretto H. (1982) *Integrated Treatment of Child Sexual Abuse.* Palo Alto: Science and Behaviour.
10. Furniss T. (1983) Mutual influence and interlocking professionals–family processes in the intervention of professionals in families of sexual abuse. *Child Abuse and Neglect* **8**, 210–223.
11. HMSO (1956)—Sexual Offences Act.

CHAPTER 8

Assessment of Families for Treatment

Anne Elton

INTRODUCTION

In the following two chapters we will describe the assessment of families and their subsequent treatment. In order to do this we would first wish to describe briefly the theoretical basis of our family work. In our conceptual model the assessment occurs before the treatment and informs it. With abusing families there is a clear time-demarcation between the activity of assessment, i.e., the interviews for that purpose, and the treatment sessions.

Basic Theoretical Background—Family Theory and Family Therapy

At the time when family therapy was first developed most professionals in the mental health field had been trained in an analytical or psychodynamic model. In their work they focused very much on the past, examining ways in which patterns and ideas from the families of origin influenced the families in treatment. Workers like Stierlin[1] and Boszormenyi-Nagi and Spark[2] examined the loyalties and earlier patterns of relationship which led to dysfunction in the present. Ferreira[3] and Byng-Hall[4,5] explored the 'myths' which persist through generations preventing change. For such workers the detailed assessment of the family, both present and past, was the treatment. Their theory of change was based on the notion that understanding of past patterns and beliefs would lead to alterations in the present. Although this is an over-simplification, the important feature from our point of view is that there was no possibility of separating assessment from treatment since the two occurred simultaneously.

In contrast, the systems theorists, Watslawik,[6] Haley[7] and Madanes,[8] developing their own ideas from the work of Bateson, focused very much on the 'here and now'. Their primary concern was to understand what prevented change and in particular to distinguish false 'first-order' change from real 'second-order' change. The former is an apparent structural or behavioural change which none the less may only represent a reversal of the original pattern. The latter requires changes in the system in a number of dimensions simultaneously.

In order to try and facilitate such change this group of workers made a brief initial assessment of the false solutions to the problem presented by the family, and then focused on the here and now work strategically using tasks and messages, often paradoxical, to help the family achieve real change. Although this group of workers make a brief assessment, treatment begins virtually immediately, that is, it is not separated in time from the assessment but begins in the first interview.

Minuchin[9,10] also does not separate brief assessment of the patterns of relationship, particularly concentrating on control and the boundaries between family members. Indeed, he may start work on restructuring patterns through enactment of change within minutes of the family entering the room. Although he might investigate the patterns and expectations in parents' families of origin at some stage in the treatment, this would be done briefly and linked to structural work on change in the here and now.

The Milan approach[11,12] has similarities to both the strategic and to the psychodynamic schools. It resembles the former in that there is a brief stage of hypothesizing before the initial interview. Like the latter they may engage in lengthy exploration of issues from the family of origin throughout the treatment process. They may continue to formulate pre-session hypotheses during the course of the treatment and these hypotheses may alter as further information is gained. In this way there is no clear separation of the assessment and treatment processes. In their approach the paradox may be manifest as a positive connotation of a piece of behaviour, seen as negative rather than an actual task-setting paradoxical behaviour. The Milan approach resembles the dynamic in that they may engage in lengthy explorations of family-of-origin issues throughout the treatment process, and also in that their pre-session hypotheses may alter through treatment in the light of further information gained. In this way there is no clear separation of assessment and treatment processes.

Great Ormond Street—Focal Approach

We[13,14] use the first one, or at most two, interviews to gain information about the family on a number of levels. These include past history, in particular stressful events, patterns of family relationships, and 'myths' which appear pervasive, as well as current patterns of relationships and interactions (control, boundaries and so on). We then make a focal formulation which seeks to explain the current patterns of behaviour in terms of the past. Using the ideas of Ezriel[15] we hypothesize that the presented dysfunctional patterns of family behaviour represent an attempt to avoid disaster which the family fear would occur with a different pattern of interaction. The nature of the disaster reflects a family myth which arises from some actual past experience.

Having made our formulation we then use it to assist the treatment process. In particular we would be looking for change both in the area of observable structure and interactions and also in the beliefs held by family members.

In order to make our assessment we employ a variety of interviewing techniques such as direct elicitation of information about the past and present, circular questioning, moves towards restructuring and detailed observations of patterns of interaction and behaviour. During the treatment process we may also use whichever approach seems most likely to help a given family achieve change, be it structural, strategic or predominantly reflective. We have applied this approach to abusing families in the past, exploring in particular the interactions and beliefs which lead to abuse and family breakdown in order to identify the specific changes which would need to occur in order to lessen significantly the risk of breakdown in the future.

Although we separate the activities conceptually and in time by having one or two assessment interviews followed by treatment, in our ordinary clinical practice, families may by no means always perceive two discrete activities. While we would usually hope to share with them our initial focal hypothesis by the end of treatment, we do not generally do this at the outset (*see* Appendix 2 for case example).

However, when we are working with abusing families we feel that there has to be a very strong contractual element in the treatment process. Indeed, this may often be built into the statutory or legal situation of the family—they must cooperate in treatment, and work towards certain specific aims in order to achieve any possibility of rehabilitation. Since it would clearly be unethical as well as inappropriate to expect either the family to commit itself to an unknown process or ourselves to take on such a family without some hope of conceivable change, we clearly distinguish between assessment and treatment stages. Our assessment of the necessary change is naturally derived from information provided by the other professionals concerned as well as that directly from the family. The specific treatment aims, as well as the respective tasks of the various workers, also have to be identified and shared.

Having made our assessment and formulation we then feel free to use a variety of therapeutic techniques during treatment. The particular approach selected will depend partly on therapist skills and partly on the area of family functioning which we are currently trying to help change. Therefore, when trying to alter patterns of interaction in the here and now we use structural techniques, or possibly strategic moves; when we are concentrating on the beliefs held by family members we may gain historical information either by straightforward questions or exploration using circular questioning. Some of these techniques will be described in more detail in Chapter 9.

THE ASSESSMENT PROCESS

Who Should be Present?

Before embarking on a family assessment meeting, it is first essential to identify who should be present. This decision has to include involved professionals as well as family members. If all family members are free (that is not in prison) it seems extremely important to have all of them present *provided* it is known that the perpetrator is able to acknowledge some degree of responsibility.

Perpetrator(s) who deny the allegations

If it is known that the perpetrator totally denies any responsibility, or if either parent denies that abuse has occurred, it seems counterproductive to have him present at a family meeting with the victim. There are two reasons for this. First, it puts the victim in a position of intolerable conflict to be with an adult who denies the allegations, or refuses to take any responsibility for his behaviours. Second, it may be misleading to the family to have a joint meeting since they may perceive it as meaning that we would consider rehabilitation as an active possibility.

In such situations it may be helpful to see the perpetrator alone, or with his key professional if he has one, to learn his point of view on the events in the family. In such a meeting it could also be appropriate to discover whether he believed that acknowledgement of responsibility would be more or less likely, open up a channel to future rehabilitation, or whether he perceives such an admission as having only negative consequences such as the break-up of the marriage, or his being attacked violently by the mother.

Perpetrators who accept responsibility

Assuming, however, that the adults are able to admit some responsibility, it seems essential that all members (except perhaps very small children) are present. Although an acknowledgement of responsibility is primarily intended to help the victim(s) by beginning to release them from their burden of guilt, it is equally important for them that their siblings hear what the parents have to say. Not surprisingly, siblings are often more likely to blame another child than to blame the parent, since it is very natural for children to criticize each other and much less likely for them to blame adults.

Inclusion of other family members

Apart from feeling that as a general principle a proper assessment of family patterns and interactions can only be made if all members, including infants, are present, it seems particularly important to include sibs since without their presence we would have no way of knowing how far the taboo of secrecy around sexual matters can be broken. Indeed, we would regard parental failure or refusal to bring other children as likely to be indicative of their deep reluctance to share both the fact of abuse and something of the emotions surrounding it. To this extent we would have reservations about the commitment of the family members present to treatment and to change.

The presence of key professionals

Although there are many times when family assessment interviews would appear to be heavily weighted with professionals, it seems essential that all key workers are there. At the assessment stage this may also include workers with a responsibility for planning and decision-making in terms of child care, such as senior social workers and *guardian ad litem*. We would invariably expect the key social worker to be present, and indeed this would hold for all subsequent treatment meetings. If children are living away from home they will have a key care-worker, or foster parent. Perpetrators are likely to have a probation officer. The views and knowledge of all these professionals are essential to assessment. So too are the family's views of their various professionals, their capacity to recognize their various roles and, most importantly, any evidence the family gives of trying to split the professionals and thus to manipulate the situation.

Interview Techniques and Approach

Information

Information has to be gained in a number of areas. These are:

Members of the household and family membership (including extended family).

Current care and custody arrangements, including access provisions.

Circumstances of disclosure (to whom, when and including previous attempts).

Reactions of both the victim and other family members following disclosure.

Views of the family also whether abuse occurred, why and whose responsibility.

Information regarding any criminal proceedings.

Salient information about the victim (i.e., previous traumatic history, relationships to parents, etc.).

Description of emotional relationships in family.

Description of marital relationship, history, shared interests, past problems.

Information about families of origin, in particular any history of abuse of either parent, patterns of sexuality and violence. Identification of change wished for, both by family members and by relevant professionals.

Noting any discrepancies in information given at interview to information previously given to other professionals.

Technique

Given that assessment interviews are very emotionally demanding on families, we might often help them start by asking them what they perceive to be the worries of the referring professional, and then perhaps of any other professionals who are present. In this way the family is helped to begin talking of painful issues through the eyes of someone not directly involved in the tortured emotions. This approach also helps to clarify that everyone has worries, including the professionals, and that the child's interest are the primary concern of the worker. It may allow the parents to express their agreement or disagreement with this. If there are siblings, it is important to join with them, perhaps by asking whether they understand why they are there. In doing this, we also discover how much they know about the abuse. While we would not ordinarily expect a victim to relate details of the abuse which she will already have confided to at least one person in the room, it is necessary to be sensitive to those children who want to retell many details. They may need to do this because they are preoccupied with its horror and are trying to work through their traumatic experiences. Alternatively, they may not be convinced that their mother has really heard, understood and appreciated their pain.

Case example—family 1
Wallace was a 15-year-old boy who had been systematically tortured physically and sexually by his stepfather. He talked in graphic detail of the 'torture sessions'. He described severe nightmares and also fantasies of doing to others what had been done to him. His mother had known that abuse was occurring but had told him to conceal the fact from the doctors who treated him.

Circular questioning involving people not actually present can be a helpful joining approach, particularly in getting the family to think about really painful and conflicted issues. For example, if a family is stuck in being able to describe the abuse at all, asking 'What would the police statements say?' frees the family to start speaking. This technique is particularly useful when discussing child-care plans. Asking parents, 'What would the court want to know was happening to feel sure that your child is safe?' or, 'What do you think the social worker's senior management would expect her to do?', allow the family to express points of view with which they may disagree emotionally because they feel angry or unhappy about the consequences but which they are able to understand cognitively as fairly natural in the circumstances. This process may reveal how much the family is able to stand back a little from their own pain and appreciate the stance of the agencies as arising from concerns for the children's welfare rather than a punitive desire to be avenged on the adults. A useful function of circular questioning is in identifying any capacity for empathy between family members. We may ask a mother of a silent and inhibited child, 'What would he say if he felt he dared to?', or a perpetrator of a confused and torn mother, 'What would she want you to do for her to feel able to trust you again?'

Denial/secrecy

If an area is being shrouded in denial and secrecy, in particular if the family reveal that there are important members who do not know about the abuse (e.g., grandparents), we can ask, 'What would they say if they knew?' 'Will it be easier/more difficult if they find out from someone else by accident?'

When we feel that there is *genuine warmth* between members but inhibition in showing it, we may employ a more direct structural approach: 'Ask her now', or, 'Can you explain to her now', or indeed 'Would she like a cuddle? Perhaps you can give her one'.

Although we obviously gain a great deal of information by straight-forward direct questioning, a very helpful way of hearing more about the patterns of behaviours and relationships in families of origin is to ask, 'If this, the abuse, had occurred this way in your family when you were a child, what do you think your mother would have done?'

Non-verbal behaviours

Finally, we have to make detailed observations of the non-verbal behaviours of the family. The affectionate looks given despite an apparently critical comment, the lack of eye contact, glances to a family member requesting permission to speak, warm or complicit non-verbal touching or smiles all reveal more than many words do. We also note which family member assumes control in which situation on both talking and in management of young children. Usually we have to remember which members are not allowed to take control, or are undermined when they attempt to do so.

EVALUATION OF PROCESS AND OUTCOME

In assessing the treatment prospects for families in which child sexual abuse has occurred, we find it helpful to think in terms of prediction of outcome. Thus we may have a hopeful, a doubtful or a hopeless prognosis. The prediction made about any particular family will naturally influence the recommendations we make to a social services department or to a court regarding the prospects of successful work with the family and the chances of rehabilitation. In order to make any formulation we have to evaluate the following factors:

1. Responsibility for the abuse.
2. Scapegoating.
3. Evidence of hostility.
4. Evidence of warmth.
5. Position of the victim.
6. Mother–daughter relationships.
7. Marital relationship.
8. General family patterns—rigidity, enmeshment, lack of boundaries.

1. Responsibility of the Abuse

The perpetrator

First, we assess the extent to which the adults take responsibility for the abuse. In considering this we note whether the perpetrator denies the offence completely, acknowledges it in part or totally. Where admissions are made it is important to assess whether the perpetrator really assumes full responsibility. When disclosures have only recently occurred it is not realistic to expect the perpetrator to show any genuine feelings of remorse, or indeed to have any real appreciation of the harm done to his victims. He is too likely to be preoccupied with his own and the family's immediate future to have sufficient emotional energy to devote to the abused child. He may well be facing court proceedings, or be in prison. He is certainly likely to be living away from his family with no immediate prospect or even guarantee of ever returning home. Therefore, the most that can be looked for in the perpetrator at this time is a cognitive acknowledgement of responsibility. Although in a specialist setting such as ours we can only observe the perpetrator in the interview situation, we can, and must, also take into account information from other professionals and from the family regarding his stance from the moment of disclosure. Those men who immediately and consistently acknowledge the offence are able to take responsibility in a way which probably indicates their own wish to have the abusive part of their relationship stopped. It is not so easy to make a prognosis about those who either fail to admit the abuse immediately or who make an admission which they subsequently retract.

Case example—Jacqueline's family
Mr T. came for a first session with his wife and his family. The family social worker and probation officer were also at the meeting, as well as their three daughters, Jacqueline 17, Christine 15 and Helen 13, each of whom Mr T. had abused. The mother leaned closely to her husband and gazed at him with adoration. Mr T. looked very tense and highly anxious.

Therapist: "Mr T. must have been waiting a long time for this meeting and thinking about it a great deal. I think it would be very helpful if you could tell the children what you want them to know, as a result of what has happened. We know that children and young people can become very confused when something sexual happens between a parent and a child. What would you like the children to know from you and your thinking about it all? What would you like each girl to know and understand?"

Mr T.: "So far as I am concerned it is a drink problem—lustfulness—I love my wife and my daughters so."

Therapist: "So you think it is a drink problem and lustfulness. Can you explain to them a little bit more how it works—when you say a drink problem what do you mean exactly?"

Mr T.: "It has become a habit—for years—just being idle, just being lazy—10 or 12 pints every weekend, routine."

Therapist: "What effect do you think that amount of drinking had on you?"

Mr T.: "Making me lazy, I did not take the family out at the weekends, did not do anything, being selfish."

Therapist: "So you think it is something to do with being selfish? Are you saying that although you and your wife had a sexual relationship, it did not seem enough?"

Mr T.: "There was not much time together."

Therapist turns to Christine who had been the family spokesman during the earlier part of the session and he checks with her whether she would agree with her Father about her parents not having much time together.

Christine: "Yes, I agree with that, there were so many of us. We were so young, going through different stages. During the day Mum would be with us, then Dad would come home and want to be with us and they just did not have time together."

Therapist (checking with Jacqueline, the girl who had spoken about the abusive relationship): "Do you agree with that? Do you see your parents perhaps not as Mum and Dad should be, together, but somehow separate?"

She nods in agreement.

Therapist (turning to father): "So can you help us understand how it was you came to find yourself having sexual feelings towards the girls rather than to your wife? Can you help us understand that?"

Mr T. (turning to his wife): "I would far rather it had been with my wife than the children." (Then hesitates.) "I have no idea why I found myself being sexual with the children." (Puts his arms across his chest and shoulders.)

Therapist: "So you have no idea what drove you to it?"

Mr T.: "If my wife had been there—I would have coaxed her—the wife has always been too tired—she has had no assistance in the home. There is always a bowl full of washing, a bowl full of ironing. I have always sat on my backside, whereas if I had helped we would have had time, we would have been able to make love."

Therapist (to mother who has been looking downwards at her knees): "Is that right? Do you think it got to the point where you could not respond to your husband because you were too tired?"

Mrs T.: "No, it is not quite like that. I loved just to hold him, to kiss and cuddle, but sometimes I just could not respond, even after one or two hours. I just could not relax. It was not all the time, only sometimes, sometimes it is wonderful, it still is." (Looks adoringly at her husband.)

Therapist: "Do you think all those things perhaps triggered your feelings, Mr T., towards your children?"

Mr T.: "It could be."

Therapist: "Tell me Mr T., we were discussing with the rest of the family before you were able to come from prison, how they saw things? The girls told me that they were confused and were wondering, was it something that they had done that made you do something sexual towards them? Who do you think is responsible?"

Mr T.: "We have always been a happy and jolly family. They have never made any advances to me."

Therapist: "So who is responsible?"

Mr T.: "I am the guilty one."

Therapist: "Do you think if Jacqueline feels terrible because you are in prison and wished she had never spoken about it, do you think she should think like that?"

Mr T.: "No, not at all."

Therapist: "Could you tell Jacqueline that she is not responsible but you are?"

Mr. T.: "Jacqueline, you are not at fault. I want you to be happy as you used to be; do not be sorry for me. I do not want you to worry about me, I want you to love me as a father, not in any other way."

Therapist: "So, although it is a terrible thing to be in prison, has it perhaps given you some time to think about these sorts of things much more deeply?"

Mr T.: "Not in prison, that's a terrible place for a man in my position to be, but it is a deterrent. I certainly will not do anything of this kind again."

Therapist: "But the problem is all three of the girls love you very much, they found it very hard to speak and they told us that they were very worried that may be your marriage might break down if they were to speak."

Helen began to cry and therapist noted that it is indeed very upsetting. Jacqueline moved to comfort her but mother dissuaded her. Helen curled up in a ball. Jacqueline sat back in her place and the therapist tried to indicate that her gesture towards comforting her sister was helpful.

Therapist: "I think the family miss you, and you miss the family very much."

Jacqueline handed out a handkerchief to her younger sister as father again clasped his head and said "my fault". Mother again looked down to her knees.

Therapist. "Yes, you are responsible, and it is helpful that you have indicated to the family that it was something between your wife and yourself that you had not sorted out. That you could not say to your wife, yes something is wrong and I am doing things to the children."

Mr T.: "I wish I could have done that."

This section shows the father in the family regretful, sad and taking some responsibility. But when his period in prison was discussed, although he said that no one should worry about him, he also said that that was not the right place for him to be. The distress and unhappiness that then spread around the family, leaving one of the children crying, revealed the underlying pattern of relationships. The father made a gesture of comfort towards the children; the mother blocked him, turned away from the children and quite harshly said that they should let the younger one, Helen, cry it out. There is something of a lip service here to the taking of responsibility, and an illustration that a man in prison finds it very hard to be in touch with full feelings of regret. The mother, although not explicitly blaming the children, at a crucial moment does not give emotional support. There is a marked absence of any sort of conflict between the parents and the total picture of togetherness and forgiveness, together with the obsequiousness and lack of any overt challenge between the father and the professionals, buries any ordinary anger towards a father who has betrayed his parental trust. Any possibility of anger on the young people's part for their own sense of hurt is swamped by the sense of guilt and responsibility the parents project, even by father's statement of saying that no one should worry about him. In this enmeshed extremely close family everyone has to subscribe to parental togetherness and to the total obliteration of a very real event and a betrayal within the family.

The mother's assumption of responsibility

It is equally important to assess the mother's capacity to assume some responsibility. In some families, albeit a minority, the mothers actively participate in the sexual abuse. In those situations it is essential that they acknowledge a similar degree of responsibility as the male perpetrators.

However, more commonly, the mother's responsibility is either an active collusion, in that they do have knowledge of the abuse and fail to take appropriate protective steps, or a more subtle denial or distancing state in which they are not available to the victims, who cannot, therefore, even attempt to confide in them. In both such situations, the mothers may react to the final disclosure with genuine shock and horror, since their denial mechanisms may have been so successful that they have really 'forgotten' any confidences made or behaviour observed. Having actually absorbed the fact that sexual abuse has occurred, mothers may take responsibility for their collusion or unavailability more or less fully.

Case example—Alice's family
Alice's mother openly expressed great guilt at having misinterpreted her daughter's increasingly negative behaviour to her family, in particular to her stepfather who was abusing her. She had thought that this behaviour arose either from jealousy of her siblings or from incipient adolescence, and therefore had tried to push her daughter more into her stepfather's company.

Although Alice's mother expressed some anger to Alice for not having confided in her directly, she recognized that they were both rather self-contained people and in that respect took responsibility also for her daughter resembling her.

Case example—Teresa's family
Teresa's mother showed much more ambivalence. She repeatedly recounted an incident when Teresa, aged five, had come home from her father's home with blood on her knickers and wrapped in tissues in a manner which the mother was convinced Teresa would have been unable to do herself. Although she questioned Teresa as to the cause of the injuries, receiving unsatisfactory

replies, despite her suspicions she failed to take Teresa to a doctor or, indeed, to act in any way. Once the disclosure was made the mother persistently justified her earlier failure to act on the grounds that she herself was recovering from an illness, which was indeed true. However, since she had not been able to conceive of any alternative courses open to her at the time she was able to feel less responsibility and guilt.

Case example—Wallace's family
In this family the mother had explicitly known of the abuse at the time of occurrence. However, she was unable to demonstrate any real feelings of responsibility. Wallace's arm had been broken by his stepfather during sadistic and sexualized tortures. When the mother realized the arm was broken she immediately took Wallace to hospital, but although she knew the cause, she gave the hospital a false account and told Wallace to do the same. Her explanation was that she feared that Wallace would be more severely hurt by the stepfather if she told the truth. In holding this belief and fear she was implicitly denying that she could have any potent responsibility as a parent. She subsequently showed a consistent denial of her own individual authority in ignoring a disclosure of abuse made to her by Wallace's sister.

In assessing the mother's position it is important to distinguish between those who really did know what was happening, like Wallace's mother, and those who were not emotionally available to the child, like Alice's. We would emphasize that the mother's guilt at the lack of closeness between herself and the victim child is not to be equated with collusion in the abuse. Collusion implies a degree of conscious knowledge about what is going on; it is probably more common for mothers of sexually abused children to cut themselves off from the signs available to them, not to let their minds know what their eyes could notice or their ears hear. To label such mothers as colluding is to attribute an unfair degree of responsibility, perceived by them as blaming. In doing so, we would risk losing not only their own cooperation in treatment but very likely the victim's cooperation since she/he would be sensitive to the difference.

There is a group of mothers who assume almost total responsibility themselves. In so doing they deny that responsibility lies with the perpetrator, even if he genuinely appears to be taking it. This attitude may reflect either their very ambivalent feelings towards the victim or it may indicate that the mother cannot bear the pain of believing that sexual abuse had in fact occurred at all. In attempting to deny the responsibility of the perpetrator she may be struggling to preserve the marriage, but can only do so if she absolves the perpetrator, even at the cost of assuming the responsibility herself.

Case example—Veronica's family
On hearing of the abuse Veronica's mother became extremely disturbed and was unable to see Veronica. However, she never really denied that sexual

abuse had occurred. This may well have been because Veronica's father admitted it immediately. Since her mother could not face her, Veronica was taken into care. The mother did not throw Veronica's father out of the home, but within 24 hours went round to his workplace and begged him to return. She described herself as prostrate and on the verge of suicide during the day when her husband was away. Her eldest son bore this out, saying that both he and a neighbour had to watch over her during the whole time. Subsequently, Veronica's mother assumed the major responsibility for the abuse, blaming herself for the sexual (and other) problems in the marriage. She believed she would not be able to survive without her husband (he expressed the same feeling about her), and was well aware that in choosing him she was sacrificing Veronica. It is probably significant that the marriage had always been fraught with problems but that the interaction was one of intense mutual dependency. Indeed, the father's explanation of his turning to Veronica as a sexual object was that he could never possibly have turned to another woman, even momentarily, since his wife virtually never let him out of her sight. She often either worked with him, or visited his place of work. He could never have arrived home even minutes late without arousing great suspicion. He would not have been able to "hurt her" in that way.

2. The Degree of Scapegoating

The most typical pattern of interaction observed in these families is one which includes some scapegoating, particularly of the victim. Most commonly she occupies a somewhat isolated and distant position, having little direct and spontaneous interaction with the rest of the family, and with little or no concern shown by other members about her distress. The victim herself may of course play quite an active part in maintaining such a distance, usually because she blames herself and fears rejection. In the assessment, it is, therefore, very important to see if this isolation and distance can be shifted to any degree (*see* Case example below). While it is common for the victim to be actively scapegoated, it is also important to assess whether this is being done more subtly.

Case example—Kathryn's family
Kathryn's stepfather readily acknowledged that he as the adult was responsible for the abuse and her mother assumed some appropriate responsibility for not having taken adequate steps to protect Kathryn. However, it was noted that neither expressed any warmth or sympathy with Kathryn, who throughout the meeting appeared deeply depressed and received no spontaneous attention from either parent. When the parents were asked why they thought the abuse had happened, both adults immediately attributed it to Kathryn being "too cuddly" and Kathryn herself explicitly took the blame. The whole family, including Kathryn, described the mother as being the member who had suffered most from the abuse because she was having to cope with her husband. In all this Kathryn's needs were almost completely overlooked.

Another common way of scapegoating the victim is to censure her for not having disclosed the abuse earlier. The fact that such children often have described previous attempts to confide is ignored.

Obviously scapegoating of the perpetrator is also not uncommon. Where this happens the mother is likely to institute divorce proceedings, to talk with considerable fury of his general inadequacies, as well as the sexual abuse. It is perhaps most usual for such scapegoating to occur in families where there are other major problems, often associated with high conflict and poor organization; behaviours such as alcoholism, marital violence and so on. Not surprisingly, such scapegoating of the perpetrators is also likely to be associated with a low degree of maternal assumption of responsibility. It is also noteworthy that when the perpetrator becomes 'free' again the couples frequently get back together; in doing so they are likely to need to find an alternative scapegoat unless real changes in family interactions have occurred.

It is important to assess how much scapegoating appears to be an integral part of the family pattern. It may occur not only over the abuse (or indeed not over the abuse at all), but also over ensuing events such as the involvement of social service departments, the statutory sanctions and, above all, the separation of the family. Although victims may feel very anxious and guilty at involving perpetrators in criminal proceedings and therefore punishment, there often appears to be less scapegoating of them for this than for any subsequent separation of the perpetrator from the family. This is perhaps not surprising to the family therapist since punishment is an event which occurs to an individual and need not affect the system in any long-term way, whereas the subsequent separation either presents a permanent change or demands that the family change in order to achieve rehabilitation. As one family said with anxiety and rage, "If we change we will never be the same again". It is not surprising that fear of such a leap into the unknown leads to scapegoating of someone.

Blaming oneself may be construed as another form of scapegoating. There are many victims who fall into this category. In evaluating this we have to note a far greater degree of guilt than is common, an actual belief that the victim is responsible. Such belief must be held tenaciously, even when the other members of the family actually deny it, at least overtly. Such children may be among those who subsequently seem bent on self-destructive courses of action.

3. Evidence of Hostility

While it is natural for family members to express and show anger towards the perpetrator, or to the mother, or to the victim, it is important to assess whether the emotion expressed is anger, which may be functional and productive, or unconstructive rage. The latter type of hostility is perhaps most often directed towards the professional network. The family may rage that the statutory measures are punitive, that not enough treatment is available or that too much is. In expending their energies on a prolonged battle with the professionals, the family are both closing ranks and avoiding facing the work which has to be done within.

Case example—Wallace's family
Mother continuously complained about the social services department who had taken the children into care. Although she acknowledged that their actual lives might have been endangered if they had remained at home with the stepfather, and although she herself admitted that she had found it very hard to throw him out since she perceived him as depending on her for his sanity, she blamed the authorities for causing more distress to the family than the stepfather—this despite the fact that both children clearly expressed terror of him. Mother's constant criticism was that the authorities should have taken the responsibility for removing the stepfather and so resolved her conflict by removing it. Her need to blame the agencies prevented the children, as well herself, from using treatment and avoided facing intrafamilial issues, in particular any disappointment the children may have felt at her prolonged covering up of the abuse.

The chilly ignoring of the victim mentioned above is often blatantly hostile and indicative of scapegoating. Mothers who rage most furiously at the perpetrators may be trying to escape their own feelings of self-blame. Similarly, perpetrators who bitterly blame the mothers for not providing adequate protection, or a good enough marriage, are likely to be avoiding their full share of responsibility rather than productively working on dysfunctional family patterns.

Case example—Frances' family
Frances' father volunteered to make a statement to the police acknowledging abuse. Although he undoubtedly made a very full confession, during the course of so doing he implicated the mother by highlighting her failure to protect adequately, on at least half a dozen occasions. This was so marked that the police officer asked if he was trying to wreak some kind of vengeance on her. Significantly, some months later the mother's new cohabitee, who was also a man with a record of sexual offences against children, also criticized the mother strongly in a family interview where the focus was on trying to help both the mother and the cohabitee take appropriate responsibility for inappropriate secrecy in their own relationship.

4. Evidence of Warmth

In evaluating families it is important to note any signs of genuinely warm interactions and feelings, either from parents to victims, between partners, or between siblings. During stressful initial interviews families are clearly unlikely to act in a relaxed manner; they are also usually in crisis. Therefore, there may be far less overt warmth shown than is actually available. None the less, it is important to see whether it is possible to help the family show any warmth, particularly from the mother to the victim.

Case example—Alice's family
Alice's mother complained that Alice has never talked to her about the abuse; all that mother knew she had learnt from the perpetrator and from reading Alice's affidavit. The referring professionals were concerned about the emotional distance between mother and daughter and feared that more active negative feelings were developing because of their lack of closeness, and the mother's anger at being excluded. In the initial meeting, the mother actually left the room when the abuse was first discussed. However, she returned a few minutes later apologizing and explaining that she did not want the children to see her break down. Once the professionals were able to recognize and acknowledge her distress, the tension decreased. Her mood became warm, albeit very sad; her irritability indicated her unhappiness.

Following this explosion she was able to approach her daughter in a more openly caring way to help her talk about the abuse. Although Alice was not able to respond verbally, she could respond to her mother's physical care and comforting.

5. Position of the Victim

It is essential to assess the state of the victim. Is she able to speak with any confidence of being heard and believed? Is she very tentative and inhibited, or is she quite frozen? If and when she does speak, do the rest of the family hear what she says and acknowledge it, or do they ignore it, or actively undermine it? How much opportunity to speak is offered by the family to the child? If space is only made when the worker intervenes can the child respond, and if so do the family then allow it or do they quickly again interpose their concerns? In many families the greatest amount of active discussion may be between the parents and workers. If this is the case, it is important to note whether such discussions are relating to the child's needs or to the parents. In Alice's family almost the entire discussion related to the children's needs, although Alice could not actively participate at all. In Kathryn's it was impossible for the parents to tolerate more than a few minutes of discussion of Kathryn's and her sister's needs; the whole family emphasis, shared by her daughter, was on the mother's needs.

Noting which areas the family elects to discuss and which they try to avoid can give some indication as to why a child is frozen. In Kathryn's case it seemed clear that her silence, withdrawal and depression reflected scapegoating, hostility and attempted denial in her family. In

Alice's situation it seemed much more likely that her frozenness reflected her own personal feelings of guilt (which were particularly strong since her stepfather explicitly avowed he was "in love" with her) and her sense of having supplanted her mother however unwillingly. There was a real and genuine wish on the mother's part to reach out to her daughter and cherish her.

6. Mother–daughter Relationship

In sexually abusing families there are commonly problems in the relationship between mother and daughters. In particular, there is likely to be a lack of closeness. There are often more active tensions and negative interaction patterns. It is important to get a picture of the quality of the relationship throughout the child's life and in particular prior to the abuse. In doing so, we can begin to assess how much work may have to be done to improve the relationship, or even whether this is unlikely to be successful. In some cases mothers may make it clear that they have never been able to feel properly loving and bonded to this particular child—perhaps for reasons of birth trauma, or because of handicap in the daughter or crisis in the mother's life at that stage.

Case example—Frances' family
Frances' mother was able to acknowledge that she had never felt closely bonded to Frances, who was her first child. She had always felt rather anxious and uncertain towards this child, although she had not appreciated just how distant she felt until the birth of Frances' brother two and a half years later. When he was born, the mother made an immediate and warm attachment. Unfortunately this only served to make her feel even less close to Frances, since she now perceived the failure in their relationship and so felt less adequate as a parent; she also attributed some blame to Frances. Because of her distance from Frances, the father had always been over-involved in her care. Once the brother was born, mother became absorbed in him and so two very strong generational pairings developed. The increasing closeness between Frances and her father inevitably resulted in an increasingly distant and tense relationship between Frances and her mother.

This pattern, with variations, is commonly found in abusing families. It is not unusual for over-close father–daughter relationships to develop in response to the father being the primary emotional carer, and also to his attempting to compensate for the implicit (or at times even explicit) emotional rejection of his daughter by his wife. Clearly, in such situations the daughter has never developed trust in her mother.

In other families, the mother–daughter relationship may initially and essentially have been reasonably close and warm. Life-events may intervene to create a new distance, with possibly some feeling of loss and rejection in the daughter. In Alice's family, the mother had four younger children in quick succession. Between the births of the third and fourth children, the stepfather had an accident which disabled him. The mother was preoccupied with the babies and increasingly relied on Alice, the eldest child, for help in tending the father.

A common pattern is the latest reversal of caring roles; it is the mother who is perceived as needing the most care and cherishing, the children who give. Kathryn's family illustrated this very blatantly; the whole family agreed in expressly stating that mother was most hurt and in need. Wallace's family also showed this pattern, although less overtly. There the mother perceived the sick stepfather as the most needy, but out of loyalty to her the children absolved her of most responsibility for ignoring their needs because they recognized her need to be 'nurse' to a fragile partner.

7. Marital Relationships

Actual and potential strengths

In evaluating the marital relationship we try to assess the actual and potential strengths in the marriage. The most important factor to assess at the outset is the degree of mutual dependency, regardless of the quality of the relationship. As we have seen above, the 'bad' marriages may sometimes be the strongest since mutual dependency makes the partners cling to each other at all costs.

Therefore, the first question we have to ask is, 'Is the mother likely to be able to stand a prolonged period of separation from her husband?' That is, can she function as a single parent? Second we must ask, 'Is this mother likely to be able to withstand a period of separation when her husband is legally available to her (i.e., not imprisoned)? Can she make that choice and stick to it until the necessary therapeutic work has been done?' Obviously this is not a question to which anyone can give a definite answer, including the woman herself. But we have to ask it, if only to help the mother begin to appreciate how long she may be torn between loyalty to husband and loyalty to child. Sometimes we can gain clues as to how warmly she may be able to relate to the child whose presence keeps the husband absent. Alternatively, we may see a degree of resentment and ambivalence which seems unlikely to decrease significantly. In such cases we may question whether it is in anyone's interests, including the child's, for the mother to attempt to put the child's needs first, rather than to recognize the situation and allow her own needs to become paramount sooner rather than later. Veronica's family was one where the mother clearly made that decision herself from the outset.

'Sticking to' separation

Third, we ask if a mother can stick to her chosen separation in the face of pressure from the father and the children for his return. There are many families where the perpetrator has also abused the mother physically or sexually; this is particularly so where there are problems of alcoholism, or psychiatric illness. The mother may express real relief at his absence, they may have tried to escape by going to refuges, etc., but as in so many relationships of this kind, they quickly succumb to fresh advances from the man, either from fear or from other needs in their relationship. Wallace, referred to above, begged his mother to write to his sadistic stepfather breaking off the relationship. However, two months later when talking of the future, he mentioned in a matter of fact way the possibility that his mother would again elect to live with his stepfather. No one in the family really imagined that the mother, even armed with an injunction forbidding him to come to the house, would be the first to call for help. Indeed, all feared that she would open the door and let him in, to try and 'save' him from his own illness. The children had imaginary escape routes worked out over the garden wall, via the neighbours and so on; they had no confidence that their mother could climb those walls, either literally or, more importantly, metaphorically.

The observation of non-verbal behaviour

Although some wives may give quite definite answers to these questions at the assessment stage, it is vital to observe their non-verbal behaviour as well (as for example in Jacqueline's case). A woman may say emphatically that she would not let her husband back home until treated, while giving him warm and protective glances and coldly ignoring the abused child. Discrepancies between the verbal and non-verbal responses provide important information. In our experience most mothers are confused and uncertain at this point; perhaps what is most important in prognostic terms is that they recognize their own ambivalence and confusion, and despite it make enough positive moves towards the child.

The only response which is unlikely to alter is that made in Veronica's family; namely that the parents clearly decide to remain together from the outset. This decision means that the social services department has to find alternative care for the child immediately. Unless the parents change their decision very quickly, the degree of rejection of the child in favour of the marriage is such that it is not likely to be in the child's interest to return her home in the foreseeable future (indeed probably never), and therefore alternative long-term care has to be sought. However, in cases where there is confusion and doubt we have noted a range of responses. These are—mothers who initially indicate more pull to the husband actually deciding to manage on their own and coping well; mothers who not only reject the husband but actually divorce him joining up with him again as soon as he is free, either then cooperating in work with professionals or else refusing to do so; parents who agree to separate but never take any active steps towards doing so; mothers who manage well while the man is in prison but quickly succumb to pressure from him in the first crisis following his release, for example when he is homeless or ill.

8. General Family Patterns

While there is naturally a range of interactive patterns in abusing families, several occur with great frequency (*see* Chapter 3). First, there are the *enmeshed, conflict-avoiding* families—members may say, 'We are a very close family'. Underlying this supposed closeness is a marked lack of communication about real feelings and in particular differences of opinion and experience. The unspoken addendum is, 'We do not need to talk to each other because we all think alike'. There is an actual denial of difference; if it cannot be ignored it is not tolerated kindly, let alone with pleasure. Katherine's family illustrated this (*see* p. 177); their criticism of her cuddliness arose because she was unlike her mother and sister in having this quality.

Case example—Hannah's family
This family provided an extreme example of denial of individuality. Hannah was brought up by her father and paternal grandparents, in a household which also contained a number of paternal uncles. The grandmother made it clear she could not bear any real disagreement, even going to the lengths of denying it when she heard it. The grandparents were actually divorced, but following their divorce had continued to live under the same roof, separately but amicably. Hannah's father said depressedly that he would never try to argue with his mother as it would be fruitless. Hannah, living away from home, began to feel some anger at her family, but was distressed at not being able to 'feel enough'.

Associated with such patterns, are *very rigid families*. This group may tolerate conflict but will label family members with roles which seem unalterable, or at least prevent the family perceiving any deviation from the fixed role. So a child may be described as provocative, or sexy, compliant or unfeeling; one parent as caring and the other as indifferent. Certain relationships will be defined as good and others as poor; despite evidence of potential for the opposite in the family's framing, the need to have certainty in such matters acts as a self-fulfilling prophecy. These families often perceive the authorities as necessarily and inevitably ranged against them. In consequence, it is extremely difficult to form a constructive therapeutic alliance with them.

Secondly, there are families who are *disorganized* and apparently also *demand conflict* in order to function at all. Obviously some of the apparently unsatisfactory, but deeply mutually dependent marriages fall into this category. In these cases, the conflict may well be contained within the family, usually between the parents. Sometimes the only thing which allows the parents to stop fighting each other is to join in a battle with the professionals. Children are initially triangulated in such conflicts. Sadly it is all too often the case that the only way of freeing them is to remove them permanently from their families.

THE ASSESSMENT OF OUTCOME

Having considered the above factors we then have to decide whether the outcome is likely to be hopeful, doubtful or hopeless for a specific family.

Hopeful Outcome

There are seven characteristics of the family and their relationships with professionals which help make for a hopeful outcome:

1. We can predict a hopeful outcome when the adults in the family take responsibility for the abuse and for their lack of appropriate child care. We would expect this group to accept the need for treatment, including separation of the abuser from the child, and to recognize that they themselves need to change in order to create a different and safer environment for the child.
2. We would expect both parents to take responsibility rather than one blaming the other entirely and the latter taking full responsibility.
3. Although we would emphasize the need for there to be a real acceptance of responsibility by the adults, at the outset we do not expect to see any genuinely felt grief and shame at the hurt caused to the child. In our view this is unrealistic at this initial stage when the family is still in crises, facing prolonged breakdown, and, for the perpetrator, possible imprisonment.
4. We can expect a hopeful outcome where the childrens' needs are acknowledged as being primary and where the parents' behaviour

confirms this acknowledgement; for example, living separately so that the abusing parent is at least temporarily removed from the child. In addition, there should be a lack of scapegoating or blame of any particular child, regardless of any actual problems presented by that child.

5. If no other family member, for example, siblings or grandparents, expressed blame or scapegoating at the visit, we would regard it as hopeful.
6. We can predict a hopeful outcome if we observe some possibility of change in the communication patterns within the family system as well as a potential for change in terms of boundaries. We would also look for indications of attitudinal changes.
7. Where there is the potential for secure attachment between parents and child we can be optimistic. However, we must qualify this by noting where attachment between victim and perpetrator is very strong and not necessarily ambivalent. This very strength may constitute a negative indication, particularly in a family where there is only a single parent—the perpetrator.

Case example—Margaret's family

Margaret aged 12 told her mother that her father had sexually abused her, involving her in oral sex. The mother confronted the father and told him to seek psychiatric treatment. When two months later he again abused Margaret she told her mother, who immediately took the matter to the police.

At our first meeting the family showed many hopeful signs. The father acknowledged that he was totally responsible for the abuse and even showed some real distress. The mother also acknowledged responsibility, both because she had distanced herself from her husband, being burdened with child care, and because she had somewhat undermined him after he become unemployed. She recognized that she had expected Margaret to be too responsible. Both parents recognized some marital difficulties. They also saw that the generation boundaries were rather confused, in that they alternatively made considerable demands on Margaret and her 11-year-old brother to be substitute parents to the younger children, and in other ways had real problems in being firm enough with them. There was a marked lack of scapegoating in the family, indeed quite open communication and considerable affective warmth was present between all members. The parents accepted without question the need for the father to live away for a period, indeed the mother made it clear that she would insist on this even if the law did not; she herself continued for many months to feel that it was not yet time for her husband to return home, although she missed him in sharing care of the children. She maintained this view despite the fact that she became pregnant by him during his absence. The pregnancy itself constituted evidence of improvement in the marital relationship and a reestablishment of appropriate generation boundaries.

Despite very real and practical problems the whole family, led by the parents, cooperated actively in the treatment. Although there were worrying and difficult moments during the treatment, the family repeatedly demonstrated the strengths which were noted in the original assessment. The first was an openness in communication of worries within the family and to the professionals involved. Margaret immediately told her mother that she was worried about her father watching her after school when this was not allowed. The second was that even when the family ran into difficulties when trying to establish the best living and child-care arrangements, they never scapegoated any member; rather, the difficulties arose from each trying too hard to help the others.

Doubtful Outcome

In our experience this is by far the largest group. Indeed, it is so large that it might almost be subdivided into:

a. Doubtful but with some real optimism.
b. Very doubtful indeed but without strong enough grounds to justify hopelessness.

The predictive factors are as follows:

1. There is uncertainty about the parents taking full responsibility for the state of the child or the particular form of abuse, for example, statements such as, 'Of course it was my fault, but she was so cuddly'. Parental acceptance of the need for treatment is at best ambivalent; they may strongly oppose some of the necessary conditions, such as temporary separation of child from abuser, or regular treatment sessions. They may not recognize that there is a primary need for the parents themselves to change in some way. Their opposition to statutory action may be bitter and intense beyond the normal opposition based on a need to hold on to parenting rights.
2. There is a lack of recognition that both parents share responsibility; instead partners may blame one another or, alternatively, they may scapegoat the victimized child.
3. Children's needs are not easily recognized as primary. The adults may periodically, or even continually, assert their own needs, overlooking the childrens'. For example, 'I don't believe that it is a family without a man in it, I couldn't bear that. If that is the case then the children will have to go elsewhere.'
4. Children remain unsure. Attachments are ambivalent and continue to be anxious. The quotation above illustrates one way in which attachment is bound to remain insecure. There may be evidence of the main attachment figures providing inadequate care on a long-standing basis, or even a history of active parental neglect.
5. There is apparently limited potential change in communication, boundaries, alliances and attitudes. That is to say, family patterns

appear rigid rather than reasonably flexible. Scapegoating is a commonly observed response and likely to be part of a pernicious pattern. Even if the parents do not actively scapegoat the child there is a risk that other family members may do so.

6. Relationships with the helping professionals may reflect the family's ambivalence, mirroring the swing between clinging and rejection which is evident in the parent–child relationship. Access is not likely to be very well used (either missed on occasion or unnecessarily curtailed). Similarly, the families may be unreliably accessible to professionals.

Case example—Katherine's family

Katherine, aged 13, told a teacher that her stepfather had been abusing her, fondling her and attempting genital contact. When social services department became involved it transpired that he had attempted sexual interference five years earlier (before his marriage to the mother) and again three years earlier. He had also tried to molest Katherine's elder sister, Jenny. At the time of the assessment interview he had been given a suspended sentence and was living away from home. Although he readily acknowledged that he had sexually abused Katherine, he and the mother attributed the cause as "Katherine being so cuddly". She herself saw this as the reason and clearly blamed herself. The parents did not volunteer a full account of the history of the abuse, concentrating on the incident three years earlier, which mother referred to as "the serious one". In so doing, they implicitly tried to deny the first incidents which occurred before mother married the perpetrator; it was clear that mother found her degree of responsibility for choosing to live with him following these incidents almost intolerable. They explicitly denied any recent incidents, i.e., those which had caused Katherine to talk to her teacher (those had been fondling). On both the earlier occasions Katherine had confided in her mother. The girls' view of the events subsequent to disclosure was that they had been sent to stay with their natural father for a few days (outside their normal regular visits to him) while the crisis in the family subsided; on their return all was 'as normal' and nothing was said again about the abuse. The mother's view was that she had had a very anxiety-making three years during which she had tried very quietly to monitor contact between Katherine and her stepfather, and had also stopped the girl's wandering around the house in a state of undress or half-undress. However, she had not shared her actions with either her husband or her daughters. Both adults were clear that their marital relationship had suffered considerably in those years.

There were three very worrying aspects to the family presentation. First, Katherine was implicitly scapegoated by all as the cause, because of her 'cuddliness'. There was no single sympathetic move to her from any member of her family, despite her evident misery; indeed there was evidence of chilly hostility. Her mother showed no concern about her real depression.

In marked contrast, the family, including Katherine, tried to comfort mother when she broke down talking of the misery she was suffering without her husband. They all agreed that she had suffered most. She expressed the very clear, indeed rigid, view that she could not live without her husband; she had been a single parent for a few years between marriages and could not repeat the experience. She talked of sending the girls to live with their father instead of her living without her husband. By the end of the meeting both the family and the professionals believed that it was most likely that she would do that.

Related to this both adults expressed considerable hostility to the professionals. Although it was clear, and indeed half acknowledged by the mother, that her genuine attempts to protect her daughter had been ineffective, they were angry at the professionals' intervention. Not only were they opposing statutory child-care actions, they also complained that treatment would be too time-consuming or too distressing. They related that three years earlier they had asked the GP in an oblique way about referral of the stepfather to an adult psychiatrist and had not pursued this for fear that his work prospects might be adversely affected by him being a 'psychiatric patient'. Perhaps most worrying of all, the stepfather threateningly suggested that plans which involved keeping him living away from his wife might lead to his abusing other (stranger) children. Since he was not able to say that a court might regard a man who offended periodically but repeatedly at intervals over years as one with a high risk of recidivism, we wondered if he were indicating to us his own awareness of many so far undetected offences and if his resistance to treatment reflected his terror of 'being found out'.

A family with a very doubtful prognosis was the following.

Case example—Frances' family
Frances was aged 10 when her mother learned from a neighbour that the father had been involved in sexual activities with both Frances and the neighbour's daughter. When challenged the father admitted some considerable sexual involvement with Frances, of a mutual masturbatory nature. The mother ejected him from the home, assured social workers that she would never let him see Frances unsupervised again, and the father agreed to comply. However, at an initial assessment session the parents walked out, ostensibly because they did not feel that Frances' younger brother John, aged eight should know anything at all of what had gone on. No statutory child-care action had been taken, but the social worker eventually persuaded the mother to allow Frances to attend a treatment group; in this, she presented as a highly sexualized little girl, very devoted to her father and, extraordinarily, lacking any anger to him. The mother agreed to attend a few family sessions of a group for mothers, in the course of which she made it clear that the marriage had been fraught with problems for years and that she herself had never felt that she bonded closely to Frances, although she did attach closely to John. Two years later the family again appeared in a major crisis. The social services department discovered through father's charges to the police that mother had recently acquired a new cohabitee who had a known history of convinction for sexual offences against children. At about the same time the cohabitee discovered from Frances that her father had started to reabuse her some time earlier.

At reassessment it was clear that the mother had totally failed to adhere to her agreement to supervise Frances' access to the father, leaving them alone frequently and even allowing Frances to spend nights alone with her father.

Also she had failed to establish either from friends or from her cohabitee what his history was, although she was warned about him. She had allowed him to sleep with John. He for his part denied having committed the offence for which he had been convicted, but at the same time said that he had received treatment for it. The mother made it clear that she would not really be able to tolerate a separation from the new partner; she also insisted that he was innocent. In this situation the children were removed from home.

Although the family did attend for treatment, the patterns of denial persisted with only temporary modifications. The distant relationship between mother and Frances improved a little, but the mother openly felt very uncertain of her power to prevent Frances seeing her father. Frances for her part was never able to hear her father's acknowledgement of responsibility but explicitly blamed herself; and it was clear that this view was shared implicitly by both her mother and brother. Given the long-standing poor relationship between mother and Frances and the correspondingly devoted relationship between her and her father, it seemed extremely likely that if she returned home she would, sooner or later, seek him out for comfort. John on the other hand was very closely identified with his mother's needs, to the extent that none of the professionals could feel confident that he could possibly disclose any advance made to him by the new partner, should that ever occur. He was too sensitive to his mother's needs to risk the consequent separation.

Hopeless Outcome

1. In this group, the parents deny any significant responsibility for the child's stress. Instead the child is blamed or rejected outright. In addition, the professionals who are attempting to help are also blamed and their offers of work are refused or seriously undermined.
2. There is no sense that the children's needs are recognized at all by the parents. Even if the parents do express a wish to maintain an active relationship with the children, the wish can clearly be seen as an expression of parental need rather than an attempt to meet the children's.
3. Attachment is either extremely ambivalent or more likely avoidant. Access is poorly taken up, contact is perfunctory and there is no response to help offered towards changing their attitudes.
4. The parents have failed to acknowledge long-standing family problems such as drug addiction, alcoholism, promiscuity or severe psychiatric illness. Treatment had, therefore, not been sought.
5. On the various paradigms of family relationship, such as communication, affective status and boundaries, there is evidence of major confusion, disorganization and severe dysfunction. In addition, relationships with the professional system remain at break-down point throughout the history of contact.

Case example—Holly and Aileen's family
Holly and Aileen were sisters of 15 and 11. They were taken into care following a disclosure of sexual abuse by their uncle towards one of their schoolfriends. During this investigation it was discovered that this uncle, a man with a known long history of serious sexual offences, was living with the mother and the girls despite an injunction that he should not do so. Although the parents were at that point living apart they, together with the uncle and other men, had been known to engage in various group sexual practices. The two girls, especially Holly, were noted to be showing worrying sexual provocativeness themselves. The mother was in fact rejecting Holly, scapegoating her, but clinging to the younger girl Aileen, who initially presented as a frozen little girl, unable to speak for herself and highly aware of her mother's needs and distress. At the point of assessment the parents were engaged in a bitter marital battle, part of which was fighting for custody of the girls. However, it was also known that at times they joined together to fight for joint custody against the social services department, since this was the only way in which they related amicably. Both parents acknowledged the risk the uncle presented to the girls. Ostensibly the mother had denied to the professionals that she was continuing to live with him, but during the assessment she made it clear that she would break down without him. Her daughters were able to hear this. In acknowledging her own paramount need for the uncle she allowed the professionals to make alternative permanent arrangements for the girls. Holly was subsequently able to disclose that she had been sexually abused and made it clear that she herself did not wish to have any further contact with her family. The younger, Aileen, was sad that her mother had chosen her uncle rather than her, but was able to begin separating emotionally from her mother. After several months she too was wishing to be found a new family.

References

1. Stierlin H. (1977) *Psychoanalysis and Family Therapy.* New York: Aaronson.
2. Boszormenyi-Nagi I. and Spark G. (1973) *Invisible Loyalties.* New York: Harper & Row.
3. Ferreira A. J. (1963) Family myths and homeostasis. *Archives of General Psychiatry* **9**, 457–463.
4. Byng-Hall J. (1973) Family myths used as defence in conjoint family therapy. *British Journal of Medical Psychology* **46**, 239–250.
5. Byng-Hall J. (1979) Re-editing family mythology during family therapy. *Journal of Family Therapy* **1**, 103–116.
6. Watslawik P. (1978) *The Language of Change: Elements of Therapeutic Communication.* New York: Basic Books.
7. Haley J. (1977) *Problem Solving Therapy.* California: Jossey Bass.

8. Madanes C. (1981) *Strategic Family Therapy*. California: Jossey Bass.
9. Minuchin S. (1974) *Families and Family Therapy*. Harvard, Mass.: Harvard University Press.
10. Minuchin S. and Fishman C. (1981) *Family Therapy Techniques*. Harvard Mass.: Harvard University Press.
11. Palazzoli S., Boscolo L., Cecchin, G. F. et al. (1978) *Paradox and Counter-paradox*. New York: Aaronson.
12. Palazzoli S., Boscolo L., Cecchin, G. F. et al. (1980) Hypothesising, circularity, neutrality: three guidelines. *Family Process* **19**, 3–12.
13. Kinston W. and Bentovim A. (1981) Creating a focus for brief marital and family therapy. In: Budman S. H. (ed.), *Forms of Brief Therapy*. New York: Guilford Press.
14. Glaser D., Furniss T. and Bingley L. (1984) Focal family therapy: the assessment stage. *Journal of Family Therapy* **66**, 265–274.
15. Ezriel H. (1956) Experimentation within the psychoanalytic session. *British Journal of Philosophical Science*, **7**, 24–41.
16. Furniss T. (1983) Family process in the treatment of intrafamilial child sexual abuse. *Journal of Family Therapy* **4**, 263–279.

CHAPTER 9

Family Treatment—Treatment Methods and Techniques

Anne Elton

FAMILY TREATMENT IN CONTEXT

While this chapter is concentrating on family treatment, we would emphasize that in our experience treatment of sexually abusing families has to be multifaceted. Indeed, we have adopted much from Giaretto's model[1] in our own programme. We would not regard family work alone as sufficient to meet all the needs evinced by various family members. Work may have to be done with certain individuals, either victim, perpetrator or mother. Each of these may also benefit greatly from work done in groups of peers. These groups are described more fully in Chapter 10.

We are not describing individual work in detail since in our programme most of this is actually done by the social worker in the community who has the statutory authority. While this is perhaps most intensively done with those children who are in care and living away from their natural families, there are also children at home and mothers who receive much individual casework and counselling from their social workers. A few children and adolescents receive more intensive individual psychotherapy in a hospital or clinic setting. In our experience this is most often helpful to the particular child after he or she has received some group treatment. However, since we are actually involved in the individual treatment of so few children we are not devoting a chapter to that area.

Marital work may often be necessary. Much of the ongoing work with the families, or with subsystems of the family, is done by social workers in the community with the responsibility for child care. If children are living away from home they may also be involved in individual or group work in their residential setting. Consequently, there needs to be a considerable emphasis on networking—the various professionals involved both sharing information and working out which aspects of treatment each is responsible for.

While ideally we might hope that some families are able to achieve real systemic change, we also have to remember that we are always working with abusing families who are not ordinarily living together during all stages of treatment. Although it may be possible, and indeed therapeutically helpful, not to force the pace of change in many families, there are genuine time restrictions for these particular families. If a child is living away from home and able to make some individual advances faster than the rest of the family can, then it may be that that child can never return home. Such decisions do have to be made. Similarly, we have to remember that the child is, and remains, our primary client, *not* the family; if their interests are in conflict, then we have to consider the former as paramount. Therefore, although we would very much hope to be able to facilitate change in the whole family, we can have no hesitation in helping the child achieve change alone. Obviously, viewed from a systemic perspective this may in itself militate against change in the rest of the family. However, if we can only help an individual victim change and develop at the cost of the rest of the family, we have to choose that option.

A wide variety of techniques of family intervention seem to be helpful. These are:

1. Use of contracts.
2. Educational approaches.
3. Structural/behavioural techniques.
4. Exploration of family histories.
5. Use of a position of neutrality
6. Networking; the open sharing between professionals.

Use of Contracts

As already described in the previous chapter, a number of families may have a specific agreement made in the courts to participate in treatment. A perpetrator may be given probation, with a condition of attending treatment. If the local authority has parental rights and powers, they may make clear their expectation that parents as well as children attend for family sessions if the family wishes to work towards rehabilitation.

Contracts are frequently made around access of the perpetrator to the victim, and indeed to other children in the family. Again these may be made by the professionals directly involved with the family, or by the courts. One of the clearest of these was laid down by a High Court

Judge. In deciding that a suspected perpetrator should return to live at home, he explicity directed that the parents should sleep on a different floor to the abused child, and that the father should not be involved in any intimate care of the child (bathing, etc.) and should never, at any time of day, go into her bedroom.

Although such directions cannot actually be enforced in practice, we would ordinarily discuss similar specific 'agreements' during an active rehabilitation phase. The monitoring has to be done by the mother, and the children of course may and should feel free to disclose breaches (see the case example of Margaret's family in Chapter 8). The reasons for such arrangements are two-fold. First, it keeps alive in the family's mind the genuine risk of reabuse, a particularly important reminder at a stage when they would wish to 'forget' or deny it in order to cope with their own anxieties. Secondly, the victims are very confused about any physical contact with men, particularly the perpetrators. Their previous experience leads them to perceive any demonstration of affection as a prelude to sexual activity, even when it is not. They are often helped by knowing not only that there are safeguards against worrying contexts, such as being in the bathroom or bedroom together, but also that for a period their mother will always be present when their father is. In her presence they can both learn to renegotiate the relationship so that it can include, without anxiety on either side, normal physical demonstrativeness. If a child feels any anxiety about the nature of a father's approach, she can immediately convey her feelings to her mother, who in turn may be able to reassure her or, if necessary, protect her. It should be noted that many perpetrators themselves have similar anxieties about recommencing any physical demonstrativeness and value their wives' presence.

2. Educational Approaches

Many, if not most, abusing families are uncertain or confused about various aspects of sexuality. In particular they are ignorant of the process of sexualization and the risk to the child that it entails. Understandably, it is very painful for parents, particularly perpetrators, to hear and acknowledge these dangers. Parents tend to blame their children for provocative sexual behaviour and still often have a view, current in society, that children do not naturally have sexual feelings. They expect their child to be able to 'forget' any awakened sexuality and to act as if it did not exist. They need educating about the naturalness of sexual feelings in children. Some parents are helped by being asked 'How easy would you find it never to have sex again?' Siblings (or parents who deny any problem in giving up sex) can be helped to understand by finding analogies to other practices that they recognize as hard to stop, such as giving up sweets or smoking.

Parents may also need help to appreciate that their child not only has to unlearn some behaviours, with clear but unblaming guidance, but in addition have to be helped to find others to replace them. Masturbation is the only safe way in which children can cope with untimely awakened sexual feelings. While many parents accept that the practice of masturbation exists, relatively few are able to discuss it with their children without some prior work.

3. Structural Techniques

Structural techniques are often used in helping the family change patterns of interaction, here and now, in the interview. A capacity to change provides valuable information as to prognosis; if the family succeeds in doing it in front of the worker the family's own sense of self-esteem is likely to be the greater, since they can demonstrate to outsiders their ability to behave differently. We would, therefore, use such behaviours predominantly to help family members show warm, caring and empathic feelings to each other. This is most likely to occur when the family shows frozenness and inhibition of warmth, although it might also be used to see if a disagreement could be resolved.

Case example—Sheila's family
Sheila and her mother showed a striking separateness in the initial interview, not looking at or touching each other. The mother began by describing her feelings of exclusion from the close father–daughter relationship and showed warm and loving feelings to her husband as well as anger at the abuse. She agreed that she had been mixed in her feelings to him, until she had read his police statement.

Mrs L.: "Sexual intercourse, anal intercourse, oral sex and he has the cheek to ask me to bring him some tobacco and a photograph of Sheila. Then he writes to say will I forgive him and can we begin again when all this is over."
Therapist: "Had you known then that there was sexual intercourse between Sheila and your husband?."
Mrs L.: "It was in her statement so I believed her (spoken much more quietly and reluctantly), but when I heard it read out in court it was different."
Therapist: "So it was when you heard it spoken out loud that you really heard?" (Then notices Sheila has hand to her eyes, blinking away tears. This is the first response she has shown.)
Therapist to Sheila: "You are crying, Sheila, what has made you unhappy?" And gesturing to mother: "Can you find out why Sheila is so upset?."

Mother turns to Sheila, puts her arms out and Sheila collapses into them.

Sheila: "I have dreams about it."
Mrs L.: "What did you say love?."
Sheila: "I have dreams about it."
Therapist: "Mrs L., can you find out what sort of dreams Sheila has?"
Mrs L.: "What sort of dreams do you have love?"
Sheila: "I dream he pushes me down stairs."
Mrs L.: "Oh God."

The therapist then helped the mother to find out whether Sheila also dreams of the sexual experiences, which was the worst and so on. In doing this he used structural techniques to help the mother and daughter communicate directly, both in words and non-verbally.

Behavioural techniques are often used to set tasks. These are most likely to arise in a rehabilitation stage and the kind of contractual arrangements, monitoring the access between perpetrator and victim, may fall into this category.

4. Exploration of Family Histories

Examination of family histories is another essential therapeutic technique in our view. Only by understanding the previous experiences of the adults can there be any hope of helping them identify the causes of the abuse and the changes they need to make, particularly in their own adult relationship. It is also an approach which may assist the perpetrators to regain a little self-esteem, since in unravelling the threads of their own previous experiences they may appreciate (as may their wives also) that they were themselves often victimized in the past, either overtly or more subtly. If this realization helps them feel a little less self-punitive guilt as well as increasing their empathy for their own child victim, it may considerably assist in preventing further abusive behaviour.

Case example—Tony
Tony was a man in his mid-forties, who had served a prison sentence for abuse of his stepdaughter. There was an unanswered question about whether he had also abused his own daughters by a previous marriage. Tony, in order to try and resolve this, had consulted a hypnotherapist, without success; he had made a serious suicidal attempt related to his lack of recall and anxieties about the past. In a family session he began to talk about his own childhood, describing numerous sexual encounters and approaches he had received from men when he was a boy. He was not worried by intrafamilial behaviour. He described overhearing larking about and shrieking upstairs, followed by a massive explosion between the parents and subsequent silence. He was certain that his father had been involved in a sexual relationship with his sisters, although he had never been able to talk to his sisters about it.

He then described the very stressful period of his father's death for which he felt responsible. He had refused to go and help his father at work (they worked together) one night when his father requested help, because he was very tired. When he went to work the following morning he found his father critically ill, and he died a few hours later. Tony felt exhausted and lay down on the bed where his father had been. He suddenly found himself praying that all the father's sins would be taken on his head. After this he felt that all the life had gone out of his marriage, he had turned to a younger woman and had never resolved the conflict with his first wife, and later abused his stepdaughter.

5. Use of Neutrality

Neutrality is used to describe a therapeutic stance whereby the therapist does not get drawn into aligning himself more with any one family member than with others, and perhaps equally importantly it means the therapist does not appear to take sides against any member. It therefore presupposes an independent view.

Neutrality is often difficult to achieve in family therapy since the various members of families in conflict will naturally try and persuade the therapist to 'take their side'. In families of abused children it may be particularly difficult to achieve because abuse is in fact *not* condoned by society, or professionals, or indeed families themselves. The latter naturally anticipate a judgemental stance and side-taking. If treatment is to be successful it is essential to convey a real neutrality. Various techniques help to achieve this position.

We have already described in some detail (*see* Chapter 8)[2] the kind of circular questioning used in the assessment process in particular. It continues to be helpful at any point in treatment when the family is struggling with painful decisions in which some member's interests are inevitably going to take second place. Circular questioning means that individuals are not asked directly what they themselves would do or feel, but are asked what they imagine some other person would feel. Questions may present possible alternative answers. For example, 'Do you think that your mother would be more likely now to ask X what they did, or less likely or the same?' Interestingly, although at times it is hard to suppose that the family cannot perceive what would be the most desirable answer (from their point of view), it is far easier to indicate an attitude truthfully in response to a circular question than to a direct question. If a father is wishing to return home prematurely he might be asked, 'What do you think your wife would do if you asked to stay at home?' (either suggesting a number of specific alternatives or not). If he believes that she would let him do so without hesitation it is easier for him to say that in response to the above question than to say 'Yes' in response to the direct question. Equally, if the wife shares his view she is more likely to agree if he suggests it as an option. If the worker puts it directly, the family are more likely to pick up on the lack of neutrality in the framing of the question, and either try and fit in with it or react angrily, complaining that the worker does not trust them, etc.

6. Positive Connotation

Positive connotation is a technique whereby the therapist positively reframes behaviour which the family perceives as negative. It therefore often implies an apparently paradoxical statement by the therapist, for example 'John is being very helpful to his parents by having tempers because he takes up so much of their time that they haven't a moment to relax and think about Y.' (i.e., the father's obsessional symptoms). More or less complex messages may be given to the family to explain the possible value of the behaviour complained of—but the important implicit and often explicit statement to the family is 'don't change'. Used in this paradoxical way it can effectively decrease the family's resistance to change by mobilizing them to consider alternatives.

Positive connotation of a paradoxical nature has a limited use with abusing families. Their denial mechanisms are so strong and their investment in achieving *their* aims so high that they are likely to be confused and to hear the message as a straight statement. Thus it is not, in our view, normally likely to be helpful to connote positively the trustworthiness of parents whom none of the professionals in fact can rely on to be appropriately protective, open and so on, or to connote the sexual abuse as positive in its function of keeping the family together.

Positive connotation in a direct sense has, on the contrary, an important place. When people are struggling against almost over-whelming natural inhibition and a practice of secrecy, we can genuinely praise all moves made towards more openness. At times with a very resistant family parental choice (such as reluctance to cooperate with professionals) may be positively connoted with advantage. It can be used too to help children understand very painful facts, such as why their parents need to choose each other rather than the child, or why they deny the abuse.

Case example—Brown family
This was a family of four children, aged 3–15, all of whom had been horrifically and multiply abused by both parents and the parents' lovers. All the adults persisted in total denial of the abuse. While all the males received prison sentences, the mother was freed on a technical legal point and subsequently came to one family session. The purpose of this meeting was to see if she could

then, being free of fear of imprisonment, admit any abuse; if not this would be a meeting terminating access. She was totally unable to admit to abusing her children, although she knew that if she did she might have access.

Therapist: "What would you imagine a mother who had done the things described to her children would do?"
Mother: "She wouldn't be able to live with herself; she couldn't."
Therapist: "Do you mean she might kill herself?"
Children: "Yes, she would."
Therapist (to the children): "I think that your mum is being very helpful. She is saying that she couldn't be a mum to you if she admitted to the abuse because then she would be dead, she'd kill herself. So she is letting the social workers find other homes for you, giving up the possibility of seeing you, because she would be better off still alive."

7. Networking

We have already described the importance of keeping close working relationships with the other professionals engaged in work. One important aspect of this, not already touched on, is our view that there can only be a limited degree of confidentiality. Since the interests of the child are always regarded as paramount, we have to be free to inform other agencies of any serious concerns we develop during the course of treatment. Therefore, if a girl reveals in a group meeting (normally confidential) that she has had a further episode of abuse, we have to report to the social services department. Similarly, a number of families have treatment as well as assessment sessions before the final child-care decisions are made. It has to be understood that we cannot withhold information which we believe would be in the child's interests for the court to hear.

An aspect of the open system between professionals is that we may participate in case planning sessions, reviews and other important meetings with other workers. Obviously the decisions made at such meetings are always subsequently shared with the families, but they are not always present themselves at such meetings.

SPECIFIC TREATMENT AIMS

Our primary aim in treatment is to ensure the protection of the children from further abuse (either from within or outside the family). In order to achieve this we would hope to help the family operate in less dysfunctional ways. However, these are very broad and perhaps self-evident aims. Therefore, it seems helpful to identify some more specific working targets. We have identified four which constitute the most important and persistently occurring problems:

1. Breaking the taboo of secrecy around sexual matters.
2. Enhancing self-esteem, and increasing self-assertiveness.
3. Working on rigid and enmeshed family patterns.
4. Helping offenders with their deviant sexual drives.

In discussing each section we will comment on and illustrate the techniques which seem most helpful in promoting change in that area of the family's life.

1. Taboo of Secrecy around Sexual Matters

Breaking this taboo is a primary aim and one which has to be actively dealt with at various points during the treatment, *not* just at the disclosure stage. It is clear from work not only with child victims but also with adult victims (often the parents) that this taboo is profound and persevering. Indeed, it may in a sense have been essential for the continuing sanity of the victims who could not disclose (or were ignored when they did so), since the only way in which to survive may have been to deny, even to themselves, a full appreciation of the abuse. The opening pages of *The Colour Purple*[3] illustrate this confusion, and partial denial:

> I am fourteen years old I have always been a good girl. Maybe you can give me a sign letting me know what is happening to me ---- Then he push his thing inside my pussy. When that hurt I cry. ---- She ask me bout the first one. Whose is it? I say God's. I don't know no other man or what else to say. When I start to hurt and then my stomach start moving and then that little baby came out of my pussy chewing on it's fist you could have knocked me over with a feather."

Anything else could have led to experiencing even more overwhelmingly painful emotions, with attendant risks of suicide. We can postulate that once the need for secrecy is learnt it becomes almost impossible to unlearn. This effective learning may explain why so many victims become in their turn mothers of victims. They have had to shut their eyes and minds to anything sexual. In order to start breaking down this taboo it is vital to be able to talk about the details of the abuse in a family context. By family context we mean one including any siblings, as well as both parents (if both are available). Parents (and indeed professionals) are often very reluctant to do this, expressing the fear that it will in some way hurt the siblings, or indeed cause unnecessary pain to the victim to have to repeat details which have already been disclosed to police, social workers and perhaps non-perpetrating parent. It is not easy to explain the rationale to families at this point, namely that the *secrecy within the family* has been a central factor in allowing the abuse and that this model may perpetuate throughout the life of the victim if the pattern is not breached. At this moment (the first family interview) the family is in a state of crisis; its emotional energies are concentrated on anxieties about the immediate future and not in any way available to contemplate long-term effects. Insisting on some description of the abuse can, therefore, be a difficult task to achieve in a therapeutic way, as understandably it is often only seen by all family members as inflicting unnecessary pain. None the less, if this is not done there is a risk that the professionals may be perceived as having joined the conspiracy.

The task can be made easier by dealing with the whole issue in a *very low-key matter-of-fact way*, certainly not commenting on any painful emotions at length, and *keeping a very unemotional stance* as a worker if the perpetrator is present as well as the victim. Given the horrific nature of some abuse this is not always easy to achieve. While we do not dwell on or explore the feelings of the victims at this stage, we can of course make empathic comments. We do ask whether the victim experienced physical pain, or say, 'that would probably hurt someone of your size', if we had any indication that this might have been the case. We might then say, 'I wonder if you cried?', partly to discover what response the child had made and partly to help siblings appreciate that the victim had been hurt. All children are aware of physical pain and so are more likely to be able to comprehend that their sib has suffered that, although they may not be able to imagine the sexual interaction. For similar reasons we ask if the victim asked the perpetrator to stop and what the response was. In doing this we can join with the victim, conveying our concern for her/him and can also hope that the siblings may be able to start doing the same thing.

Obviously it is important to do all this in language which is meaningful to the family; so that we have to discover the family words for genitals and sexual functions. Not to talk in the language of the family, but in proper names, could be another way of maintaining a taboo. (*See* Appendices 2 and 3.)

If siblings are aged over nine or so, we may often ask them first of all if they know what has happened. Margaret aged 12 was referred, her next sib being David aged 11.

Therapist: "David, do you know what has happened in your family?"
David (hesitantly): "Dad did something rude with Margaret?"
Therapist: "Oh, do you know what?"
David: "No"
Therapist: "What would you imagine he might have done. I mean what is rude?"
David (Still hesitant, looking to sister Margaret who indicates a willingness to talk.)

Therapist: "Margaret, can you help David?"

Margaret (Giggles and we acknowledge natural embarrassment): "He made me suck his cock".

Following this David tells us that he had known because he had overheard the details from his parents when they were quarrelling.

We would usually ask a family member other than the victim to describe the nature of the abuse. In so doing the victim is both relieved of having to repeat details and also knows that her experiences have been heard. If the family member can show empathy to the victim that is additionally helpful. In Alice's family on p. 197 one of the mother's complaints was that Alice had never talked to her at all about the abuse. Alice did agree that she might be able to if alone with her mother and using the anatomical dolls; however, she tried but again froze. Since the mother had read Alice's statement to the police she was then asked to use the dolls to describe to Alice what she understood had happened. The mother was able to do this, and in so doing to show her own distress about her daughter's suffering and Alice could respond by agreeing or disagreeing with the mother's descriptions.

Essentially *structural methods* are used; this approach seems important in this area since there is a fundamental necessity to name the sexual activity explicitly and to share factual information. The feelings of the victim and her family about the facts are also part of the factual information.

In naming the range of feelings about the sexual relationship it is essential to recognize that an appreciable number of children obtain some feelings of pleasure from at least a part of the abuse. In doing this they natually feel particularly guilty, since they assume that if they enjoyed it they were responsible. The nature of physical, including sexual, pleasure is frequently not understood by the adults in the families, let alone by the children, and families often need some fairly direct education on this. It is understandably painful for the parents to realize that their child is at risk of further abuse, including stranger abuse, because of her sexualization; that her provocative behaviour represents an active learning of sexualized responses to her father and is naturally transferred to other men and that preadolescent children may have genuine sexual impulses and feelings stimulated at an age when they cannot do much about it, except masturbate. *Education* is necessary for parents and children.

Case example—Alice

Alice, aged 15, was a child whose mother worried agitatedly about her inappropriately uninhibited behaviour with male family friends. Although the reasons for this had been described to her she remained puzzled as to why. She did say that Alice and one other of her sisters were the children in the family whom she'd had always been aware of masturbating most often. The therapist who had known Alice well because she had also been in a group with her, asked Alice in a very matter-of-fact way if it felt better getting herself excited or having someone else do it. Alice was clearly relieved by this open discussion; she could admit to her mother and sisters that she had enjoyed some of the abuse at first, but soon didn't and thought that she probably preferred stimulating herself. The whole discussion really allowed the mother to appreciate the way in which her daughter had been so over-stimulated; being currently sexually deprived herself since Alice's father was in prison, she could then have some empathy with her daughter which allowed her to then help Alice in a more sympathetic way to alter her public provocative behaviour. The mother *learnt* something about sexual eroticism.

While preadolescent children are not expected to participate in sex with peers, adolescents are in a different position. Many may normally choose to have full sexual relationships even before 16. There is clearly a risk that adolescents who have already been sexualized operate on the assumption that boys will only be interested in them if they have full intercourse, although in fact heavy petting may be at least as normal if not more so. Consequently victimized adolescents may get into difficulties with their peers, either because the boys are in a sense frightened off, or because they get known as 'an easy lay' and so in effect get abused by a number of transient peers. The fact that they themselves have had their own sexuality aroused inevitably makes it harder for them to resist such overtures. Sally was a case in point; at 15 she became pregnant by a 13-year-old whom she didn't really like, and who was not a close friend. After a lot of discussion she told her social worker that she wanted a termination. What emerged in the ensuing discussion of this event was Sally's recognition that she did 'like sex' and could not yet say 'no' to boys who were available but not wanted by her for any other reason. Her father on hearing this was able to express some sense of genuine remorse, believing that he might have taught Sally to enjoy what she could not yet control.

Discussion of sexuality is not of course confined to the victim's sexuality. The parents have to be able to discuss and reveal something of their own, either in parental groups (described below) or in marital sessions. Mothers may have to help their daughters by sharing with them the ways in which they played with boys or got sexually interested. In Alice's family the children were asked when they each imagined their mum began to like playing with boys; their guesses ranged from age twenty to five and the mother, highly amused, was able to then tell them about herself.

In particular the men have to explore their own sexual confusions, but that will be described more fully in a later section.

2. Self-esteem and Self-assertion

A second aim is to help the victims and their parents gain some greater self-esteem. Only if this occurs will they have a chance to make genuine choices about their lives and relationships. Without a greater sense of their own worth they are likely to be doomed to subsequent abusive relationships; the women since they have learned that that is what they are wanted and valued for, the men because they can only identify with aggressive abusers if they are to escape the victim role again. If the victims are stuck with feelings of guilt for the original abuse they may also select self-destructive paths in other ways too, for example, alcohol and drug abuse, suicidal acts and so on.

In treatment of the family we would hope that all family members may make some gains in self-esteem. Brothers, particularly perhaps adolescent brothers of girls abused by their fathers, are a group who may be particularly at risk of a major crisis of identity on discovering the father's activities. Many of these boys are extremely angry and reject their fathers, but are also not easily accessible to or actively participant in family treatment. Their mothers and victimized sisters may collude with their absences from treatment sessions, ostensibly protecting the boys' right to independence. However, in some families such protection makes for a strong underlying feeling of hostility to all males. The fathers may equally collude with the absence because they find it too painful to experience the son's anger and feeling of let-down directly. The self-esteem of these youngsters is not likely to flourish in such circumstances.

While we may feel that the most active therapeutic work done towards building self-esteem is carried out in the various treatment groups, it is obviously essential that the family confirms this. A fundamental necessity in furthering self-esteem is for any individuals to have their views and feelings heard and acknowledged as legitimate, even if their wishes may not, for whatever reason, be met. *Structural approaches* are most likely to achieve this end, in that they push for *clarity of communication* and *clear responses*.

Case example—Hannah's family
Hannah's family illustrates such a move. Hannah aged 13 had been abused by her father over a period of years; her mother had died when she was little and since that time she and her father had lived in the paternal grandparents' home. The father was one of four brothers, all of whom either still lived in this home or had returned to it from broken marriages. During the course of treatment it had become apparent that the paternal grandmother was not ever able to set limits on any of her children but also could not tolerate open conflict. Significantly the paternal grandparents were said to have separated in their marriage although they continued to live under the same roof. Hannah had been placed first in a residential setting and then in a foster home, since she had become school-phobic while living only with her grandmother, who had

been unable to get her to school. The grandmother had always made it clear that she could not "make" her sons do anything, and when the father was released from prison the question arose as to whether she would be able to ask the father to go away if he happened to turn up during a visit of Hannah's. Hannah had already been able to say that she herself didn't want to spend the night at her grandparents' home, although they were complaining that she was not allowed to. She was then able to say quite clearly to her grandmother that "I would like you to tell him (Father) to go away", to which the grandmother responded "No you wouldn't". Further discussion followed in which the grandmother was totally unable to shift her position, and the father visibly withdrew from the discussion in a depressed way. In response to the social worker asking him if he ever felt angry with his mother, he said that there was no point and that his mother denied the mere possibility. Hannah herself had previously been able to share both with her social worker and in the group some angry feelings towards her father; following this family meeting she became distressed and shared with her social worker the difficulty she had in feeling angry although she herself couldn't understand why; the social worker could use the information gained from family meetings to help Hannah understand why. In particular, Hannah was helped to realize that her own anger was real and valid, and that being able to express her own feelings, even if they were not allowed by her family, was a step towards real individuation. Hannah's father also recognized that his daughter needed another family in which to develop her own self, that his family was not able to change enough to allow her to grow. Hannah herself in her own developing wishes to live away and have decreasing contact with her grandparents was able to learn to assert herself and identify her personal wishes and feelings.

Her self esteem was so much greater that she could not only enjoy school and use it freely (both educationally and socially) but could also directly challenge her powerful grandmother, assert her own wishes and talk of realistic hopes for her own future.

Exploring family of origin relations can often be of some assistance in building up the self-esteem of either parent. As they come to realize how much they may be carrying on patterns learned in their own families they may gradually become more able to free themselves and elect to jettison certain parts at least as 'not belonging to me'. Hannah's father, in the excerpt described above, was clearly at that point depressed and hopeless about the possibility for change; he actually said that "he had given up, wouldn't try to argue with his mother". However, he welcomed the notion that his daughter might have some resemblance to her (dead) natural mother and that he himself had chosen his wife partly on the basis of her *difference* of personality: "she was up-front, could blow easily". In response to our gaining this description of his long dead wife, a suspected suicide, and *positively connoting* her differences as strengths, the father gained in liveliness and clearly agreed that he would be happy if Hannah might also manifest some personality traits inherited from her mother.

Although we could not be sure, it might also be the case that he himself might conceivably value his wife more retrospectively than he had done, and in doing so have a better respect for himself for choosing a partner who had had real strengths as well as undoubted problems.

3. Working on Rigid and Enmeshed Family Patterns

While one obviously sees a wide variety of dysfunctional family patterns in sexually abusing families, certain characteristics, described more fully in Chapter 8, are most commonly observed—a lack of openness of communication of feelings held by individuals, with a concomitant denial of feelings and differences. At the extreme some families appear to operate on a mechanism of total denial, which means a total uncertainty about the truth of anything. More ordinarily, the denial and communication problems are a function of the painful distance between mothers and victimized children.

Parental authority and responsibility are often very uneasily shared between the adults. Perhaps the most common feature is that one parent maintains the limiting disciplinary part of parental responsibility and the other the caring part, with each adult undermining the other's role. However, it may also be the case that one parent takes an extremely passive role overall. Another pattern commonly emerging and shared with many child-abuse families is that of reversal of child–adult roles where the child is expected to take on a caring role towards the parent. While this can and does arise in intact families (e.g. Katherine's family referred to in Chapter 8), it is understandably a most common feature in families where there is one parent present. The rigidity of expectation that a parent needs caring for is, however, most likely to arise in relation to mothers. In all families there is a confusion and reversal of ordinary and appropriate generational boundaries.

There are families who maintain relationships through the medium of intense and continuous conflict, frequently leading to actual physical violence. The adult partners in such situations may separate only to return to each other. It is in this type of family that one is most likely to find patterns of alcoholism, substance abuse and promiscuity, as well as sexual practices between the adults which would normally be regarded as perverted.

Finally, it should be noted that in all abusing families there is a problem in conveying convincingly deeply caring feelings, although these feelings may undoubtedly exist.

In therapeutic work we find that the whole gamut of techniques of family work may have their place. As discussed above, structural

approaches are likely to be most effective in trying to alter dysfunctional communication patterns.

The issue of parental difficulty in setting appropriate limits frequently emerges, both as a long-standing problem and also as a specific
and new one in a family made 'one-parent' by the absence of the father
following disclosure of abuse.

Case example—Alice's family
Alice's family illustrates this; she was the eldest of six daughters. Alice's
stepfather (who was father to the four younger children) had always been the
parent who disciplined most and he had become more fiercely strict following
an illness of his own about four years previously. It was around this time that
the abuse began and the births of the two youngest children occurred. Because
of the burden of caring for so many young children, the mother had always
placed great reliance on Alice's natural helpfulness and this had increased
markedly following the father's illness. In a family session about six months
after the stepfather's imprisonment, she reported that the four oldest girls
bickered inordinately. Alice was a particular focus on this squabbling,
although her mother was clear that Alice herself did not, in her view, always
provoke it either actively or even implicitly. The sisters then complained that
Alice was "bossy" and the mother agreed that at times she herself was irritated
with Alice for assuming control when she herself wanted to. However, on
further discussion it emerged that all four older children recognized that
mother did not always carry through her intentions. All were supposed to help
with certain household chores, but all, including mother, recognized that the
younger ones, particularly the third, was adept at wriggling out of her share.
Alice was the only family member who commented on this, hence much of the
wrangling. All the children expressed clearly the wish that mother would take
on very clearly the monitoring of the chores, and the reprimanding of any child
who got out of her share. The mother agreed to draw up a clear rota, with
herself as the final and only arbiter, and to discuss this with the social worker if
she needed any help. In this way the real problems of being a single parent
were recognized. The social worker's availability for support was emphasized
in order to help Alice relax from her nanny role, since she was told her mother
had an adult whom she could consult about parenting.

Through exploration of previous family interactions, Alice's
position of 'natural helper' was identified and was *positively connoted*
both by the workers and the mother. This freed all the children to
express a wish for their mother to be 'tougher', which she herself could
respond to with the help of a *behavioural structural task*. At the
following session a month later the mother recorded a decrease in the
siblings' arguing to a level she would regard as natural. This same
family also demonstrated a tendency to scapegoat Alice and in so
doing to protect the parents. This was most openly done by Alice's
sisters who were understandably very sad at losing their father and
unable to communicate any anger in their occasional visits to him in

prison, blaming Alice. The following abstract shows an approach to this aspect of the family interaction.

In this family the mother had also felt that some of the children's arguing arose from the sadness and depression suffered by the nine and eight-year-olds, who were grieving for their father. The nine-year-old was asked whom at this point she regarded as being responsible for the father's absence, and she replied "I know it's Daddy", (mother nodding firmly at this) "but really I think that it is Alice". On this being pursued she said "I think that she should have stopped it, told sooner", thus indicating that she did believe that the father had instigated the abuse. It was clear that in part the children's blaming of Alice reflected their mother's ambivalence since she was not able to understand any possible enjoyment Alice might have felt (*see* p. 197); that was helped by the mother's dawning appreciation of children's eroticism as natural. However, in this session when the sisters were then asked to imagine how they (or each other) would have stopped Daddy doing something they didn't like they found it very hard to come up with any picture; to that extent they then gained some understanding of the problem Alice had faced.

4. Helping Offenders with their Deviant Sexual Patterns

Although many of the men who abuse in the family have not, so far as we know, abused more than one victim, a very considerable number have, or have attempted to, make sexual advances to several children, either within or without the family. While most of the direct work on sexuality needs to be done with these men individually or in parent or adult groups, it can be therapeutically important to do some within the family. Gaining some understanding of the previous family patterns which led to the confusion over appropriate activity is essential for the whole family, not least because it aids the wives' understanding of their husbands' needs and also helps the victims appreciate that their father has a particular problem belonging to him—a problem for which hopefully he can receive some help in his own right. The identification of this problem again confirms for the victim that the responsibility for the abuse lies at the father's door (and perhaps further back to earlier generations). A primary therapeutic technique for gaining some understanding of the perpetrators' sexuality is an exploration of family patterns and expectations. In doing this the therapist may learn of specific early experiences which may have contributed to later abusing behaviour; for example, that the man was victimized himself, either explicitly or by suffering cruelty and severe neglect.

Case example—Sally's family
Sally's family presented a very different picture. Sally aged 14 referred to

above was abused from age 11–13 by her father, mostly in a manner involving mutual masturbation. The father received a relatively short prison sentence, and was able to attend family meetings even from prison. About five months after his release he said in a meeting "I know what I did was wrong, because I was sent to prison, but I don't really understand why it was wrong". He went on to describe his arousal by seeing his daughter's physical development: "Aren't all fathers excited by seeing their little breasts?" The therapeutic exploration of why he had not been able to resist temptation then ensued.

In exploring the family of origin a circular questioning was initially employed, partly in order to get another view on the father's family and partly to ensure that the focus of work was on both parents at least. The mother was asked how she thought her mother-in-law would have reacted to hearing of the abuse and then to speculate on how the mother-in-law had taught the father what is and is not permissible. This discussion then generalized to how the mother had been taught. Her response was that her mother had said "Don't go with men until you are married", but she then realized that her mother had never said to her "don't go with your father", and that indeed such a statement would have been unthinkable in most families. From this the parents were able to begin to identify the non-verbal messages given by the paternal grandmother. The father described an intensely close and infantalizing degree of physical care which had persisted throughout his childhood. Indeed at the time when he married he expected his wife to continue to do for him certain things such as wash his hair and massage him as had always been done for him. She, not surprisingly, refused to do most of this, although later sessions indicated that she had probably done more than would be common. Further history elicited that the father had become quite depressed following the death of his mother, which occurred around the time of Sally's birth (she was the younger of two daughters by six years). There was clearly a marital crisis, with the father first having an extramarital affair. When that was discovered the mother became depressed and phobic and the father began abusing Sally.

This father continued to struggle with his own sexual feelings and in particular his difficulty in understanding why they were wrong for many months. About five months after the meeting described above he confided in the social worker that he did not know "How to love his daughter if he couldn't do it sexually". This gave the social worker an opening to meet the older, now married daughter to establish her position and whether she too had been abused. It seemed clear that this had not been the case, but that she had in fact felt loved by her father. Therefore, subsequent family work concentrated on trying to help the parents recollect how the father had been able to convey his love to the oldest daughter. In the midst of this there was also a marital session with the parents explicitly on their own current and past sexual difficulties. It was only after Sally became pregnant that the father suddenly began to show some appreciation of *why* it was 'wrong' for a father and daughter to have sexualized contact. He said spontaneously that he had wondered if she had allowed the sexual relationship with the boy because of anything she had learnt from him, and Sally in effect confirmed that she had learnt that sexual contact was enjoyable. The father began to demonstrate both some real understanding of the harmfulness of his previous activity and with this some genuine remorse. While considerably more work needed to be done, it now appeared that he himself would have some deeper reasons for really avoiding inappropriate contact with Sally. She would no longer have to take primary responsibility herself (which had been her stance) or rely totally on the mother's monitoring.

In a truly 'incestuous' family the style of nurturing has always gone over the boundary of normal physical closeness and engendered a pattern of intrusiveness and no notion of privacy.

STAGES OF TREATMENT

While it is important to bear in mind all the above aims throughout the course of treatment, we have found that for many families treatment falls into certain stages and that certain aspects will predominate at each stage. It is important to recognize that there is considerable overlap between stages, and of course to acknowledge that not all families go through each stage. Work done on any area at one stage has to be repeated or at least actively confirmed at the next, since one common feature is for families to retreat from changes which they had apparently made and revert to familiar patterns. We have found it appropriate to identify four stages:

1. Disclosure period.
2. Period of temporary separation (either the father away or the victim).
3. Period of activity working towards rehabilitation.
4. Working towards permanent separation.

1. Disclosure

The primary therapeutic aim in the disclosure period is evaluative and the central purpose of the evaluation is assessing whether it will be possible for the child to remain with either one or both parents. The tasks of evaluation have already been described in detail.

2. Separation

During the period of family separation it should be recognized that most therapeutic work has to be done either with the individual family members (albeit in the context of a peer group rather than individually) or with dyads. *Building of self-esteem* is a central focus. It is not possible to work realistically on whole family patterns of functioning at a time when the family is not actually living together and so cannot try implementing new ways as a group. The most likely dyad to be available is the *mother–daughter dyad*, and work on strengthening that bond can be done. It may also often be possible to help mothers more generally with their parenting skills. This is particularly the case for those families where the previous pattern was of the father providing the controls over the children.

If the father is out of prison (for example, living in a bail hostel) it may also be possible to do some work on the marital relationship. In particular, such couples may have an opportunity to re-explore their own sexual and personal relationship before having to parent together again, albeit in a different way.

None the less, it is important to recognize that any gains apparently made and changes achieved in this period may immediately be reversed at the first crisis following the father's freedom to return home himself. At this point, a number of wives reverse their previous decision to separate (including at times actual divorces). A number not only change their minds, which may well be an appropriate and healthy decision, but immediately act on it; that is allow the husband to return without any preparatory rehabilitative work. Others, who may have always wished for rehabilitation but understood the need for a more prolonged period of work, may succumb to pressure from the husband. At this point, men often talk as if their prison sentence had been treatment (which sadly it rarely is); or perhaps more accurately they perceive the further separation period during which treatment can be done as a further punishment. It is in such situations that men may deny real responsibility for the abuse, or that they or the family may manifest considerable scapegoating of the victim who is blamed for the father's continuing absence.

Case example—Diane's family

Diane's family illustrates such a crisis. The father had served a prison sentence for abusing Diane's older sister sexually; there had always been a 'question mark' as to whether Diane had also been sexually abused; she had certainly been physically abused and was a very timid frozen little girl. During this period of separation the social worker had done a lot of work with Diane, both individually and together with her mother, in particular helping mother build up positive activities in a relationship with Diane. Both had also attended peer groups. When the father came out of prison there was a clear contract, both for marital and family work, and outlining times of access to the home, his access to Diane being monitored by the mother. Shortly after his release, the father felt under threat of becoming homeless, told the social worker and probation office but refused to give a guarantee that he would not return home should that occur. Significantly his wife also understood that he would return home if his accommodation problem reached a crisis, and was not able to decide that she would refuse to allow him to do so. The social worker took a Place of Safety Order and removed Diane, who was able to show some relief. In the end, the husband immediately returned home. The mother was able to appreciate how much he was then using his own confusing communications to focus anger on the professionals rather than look at his own considerable problems, and was able to insist that she herself would continue to attend a parents' group and that she would try to prevail on him to do so. Her ability to express a difference of opinion from her husband, however slight, was a change. The subsequent period of separation with Diane away was necessary to help her decide whom she would choose, husband or daughter, if there was necessity for a choice, and also help the couple to work on their own relationship.

The above example illustrates not only the enormous problems of achieving real change within the family, but also shows how necessary it is to have appropriate statutory sanctions regarding the children concerned. In our view, it is not reasonable to expect the adults to be able to foretell how they will feel at some unknown point in any future (i.e., when they are legally free to be together). Understandably, many will be driven by the strengths and needs in their own relationship to come together before enough therapeutic work has been done to ensure adequate protection for the children.

3. Rehabilitation

During the period of rehabilitation, the focus should be on the therapeutic aims described previously. Although there may be less direct work with the victim alone, her self-esteem can be observed from the way that she interacts with (and is attended to by) her family and from information about her independent peer relationships.

In working towards rehabilitation, it is important that the victim continues to feel adequately protected from further abuse (and the very real risks of further abuse should never be underestimated). To this end, it appears helpful to work towards something of an imbalance in the parenting relationship, making the mother explicitly responsible for the monitoring and direct access of the father and the victim. We have found (as have others in Seattle[4]) that girls value the presence of some specific rules about where their father does or does not go (such as never into their bedrooms if they are adolescent or near that age) and know that they could tell their mothers if they feel uncomfortable. A number of the fathers also appreciate this, particularly those fathers who recognize that they themselves are confused about normal physical contact with their daughters. We are aware that systemically we are therefore working towards a family structure which may be unequal in the opposite direction from that existing before disclosure. Whereas often the fathers were the apparently dominating parent, now we are advocating that the mothers have, at least for a significant period, some dominance.

Case example—Peter and Margaret
Peter and Margaret came for a meeting as a couple. Peter came from prison for the visit. Their position *vis-à-vis* the other was:

a. Wound around each other with no space between, or,
b. With Peter leaning back on his chair expounding his ideas, Margaret would be facing him but with eyes fixed on the ground, silenced.

She was trying to say that she was so desperate about money when Peter was in prison and that she wished a car would run her over. Peter was saying that she did not know what it was like to be in prison, she had always vowed she would visit him in prison whatever. He spoke in a bombastic, forceful, talking-down way. Each was appealing to the male and female therapist for support for their view about their plight.

The male therapist asked Peter to find out what *he* did that made Margaret so desperate, because clearly he wanted to convey his care, but she heard his anger. He asked her with considerable difficulty, "What do I do". Margaret said "The problem is Peter you are always asking me to bring things to prison when I am so short of money, yet when I bring you presents—drawings from the children—you don't want to know and pack them away".

Peter attempted to interrupt, with his justification that only certain things can be brought—again appealing to the therapist. The male therapist asks Peter to tell Margaret what he has heard her say that she finds difficult about him. He says, "I do understand". She replies, "What's the point".

The male therapist, pursuing a structured mode, again asks Peter to try to tell Margaret about what he has heard her say, he tries to re-engage the therapist, the female therapist indicates, "Talk to her—not to us". The therapists turn towards each other, and Margaret takes control of the situation, and they go over the issue of her visits to prison and his expectations and what is or is not possible.

We recognize that in doing this we may only be replacing one dysfunctional structure with another, but in the interests of the child's protection we have not found a better alternative. We have to take account not only of the victim, but often of younger siblings, and to recognize that in the present stage of psychiatric knowledge as well as the relative unavailability of services many men will not be 'cured' of their dysfunctional sexual tendencies, but at best can only be helped to 'manage and control' them. Family structures which assist them in that task are, therefore, likely to be helpful, at least in the short-term.

4. Working Towards Permanent Separation

If a permanent separation is the only solution available, the therapeutic aims will concentrate on helping the victim build up self-esteem, partly through the provision of an appropriately caring substitute family. In so far as the parents can help this transition caringly they should be given any assistance. In some situations, particularly those where the family consists only of a father and daughter, there can be no practical possibility of rehabilitation, yet there may well be good reason for considerable continued access and therefore family relationships do need to be given therapeutic attention. Hannah's case described above is one such family. Perpetrators who positively wish for help in their own right with their sexual problems should be referred to appropriate agencies since such help may well reduce the likelihood of further offending.

References

1. Giaretto H. (1981) A comprehensive child sexual abuse treatment programme. In: Mrazek P. B. and Kempe H. (eds), *Sexually Abused Children and their Families*. Oxford: Pergamon, Chap. 14.
2. Tomm K. (1985) Circular interviewing—a multifaced clinical tool. In: Campbell D. and Draper R. (eds) *Applications of Systemic Therapy*. London: Grune & Stratton.
3. Walker A. (1983) *The Colour Purple*. New York: Harcourt Brace Jovanovitch.
4. Berliner L. and Stevens D. (1982) Clinical issues in child sexual abuse. In: Conte J.R. and Shope D. (eds), *Social Work and Sexual Abuse*. New York: Hawarth.

CHAPTER 10

The Use of Groupwork in Treating Child Sexual Abuse

Judy Hildebrand

INTRODUCTION

Groupwork is increasingly being used as an economic and highly relevant treatment method with families in which sexual abuse has occurred.[1,2] It is all the more important, therefore, to continue to monitor this approach and to establish clinical impressions through research programmes. If our experience is to be of practical use and interest to others, it is essential that we emphasize the unresolved issues which still concern us, as well as noting our progress. This chapter will therefore describe the rationale and design of the groupwork programme, provide examples of the work itself and raise controversial issues.

Although the focus of this chapter is groupwork, it must be stressed that this approach is a complementary, integrated aspect of a treatment programme and is not in competition with other approaches. Since we know of no single exclusively successful way of working with families in which sexual abuse has occurred, there is room for individual psychotherapy, group and family work, play therapy and behavioural management advice.

Attendance in a peer group should, however, be a forerunner to individual therapy, since being in a group reduces the sense of isolation and 'badness' which most family members feel. Groupwork 'normalizes' the experience but does not condone it and it does offer peer support to rebuild on existing strengths. On the other hand, immediate engagement in individual work could reinforce 'being and feeling different' and could reinforce notions of pathology. In this respect, it is perhaps also unfortunate that the treatment programme described is based in a psychiatric department in a hospital, since this inevitably carries an implication of illness and pathology. This could lead to an association in people's minds between the aetiology of sexual abuse and medical and genetic factors, rather than to emotional and sociological factors. A roomy and confortable family setting would be more suitable than a hospital context.

Establishing the Programme

The initiative to treat sexually abused children and their families in group settings was taken by Dr Arnon Bentovim and his team at the Hospital for Sick Children in London. This approach was largely based on the work of Giaretto[2] and Berliner[1] in the USA. They used a group as a forum in which peers with similar traumatic experience could share these in discussion and play, could feel accepted despite them and could receive help to clarify their misconceptions about issues of blame, responsibility and guilt around the abuse. The team applied many of the ideas suggested by Berliner in her practical approach to education and support of children, in age-appropriate group activities. Given the team's view that children should be viewed in the context of their family system (*see* Chapter 9), this model was expanded to include groupwork for parents as well as victims and to hold regular meetings for the whole family.

Once families have been assessed and a disclosure made, the feasibility of their inclusion in a groupwork programme is assessed. This will depend on their willingness to attend, the distance to be travelled, the availability both of a place in our groups and of escorts if required. This planning must be done in conjunction with the local authority social worker who carries the brunt of long-term professional responsibility for the family. In addition to this weekly commitment, which may vary between six weeks and five months, family meetings are held every six to eight weeks in order to integrate and monitor progress. Due to concern to prevent abuse and in response to the referrers' requests for prompt assistance for the victims, more weight has been given to the needs of the parents and recognized victims, and less to the siblings and the extended family. It is not yet clear whether groups for siblings of abused children should be organized or whether their needs for understanding and support are already adequately dealt with in the family meetings described in Chapter 9. A model has developed so that all group and family work takes place in parallel over a six-month period. During the same period assessments are being carried out in readiness for the next six-month group phase.

Rationale

1. Taking a systems' perspective and encouraging children and adults to talk in peer groups about their experiences and feelings prepares

the way for more open communication in the whole family; this in turn mitigates against keeping inappropriate 'secrets' and lessens the likelihood of further abuse. Even where the abuse is per-petrated by a stranger, groupwork and family meetings can make a powerful impact on the whole family. However, there is a considerable problem for the group leader if a group includes both abusing parents and those whose children were abused by a stranger, since the family dynamics and the degree of adult responsibility for the abuse are not of the same order.

2. We have learned from clinical experience that poor self-esteem is a highly significant characteristic of abusers, their victims and other family members. Given research findings which indicate that an improvement in self-esteem has been the most frequently reported outcome from groupwork,[3,4] it seems logical to consider groupwork as a viable and valuable choice of approach in our treatment programme.

3. We consider the advantages of groupwork to far outweigh an individual approach in the vast majority of cases, although we appreciate that a sequential combination of the two can be helpful. We advocate groupwork not only on the grounds of economy or professional availability, but also because of the accelerated learning which we believe occurs through peers sharing information, exploring feelings and confronting each other.

"In an homogeneous group, 'patients' get early comfort and support from others with whom they have much in common. This along with the reassurance that they are not alone in their predicament can speed the early phases of a group's development and may also lead to more enduring understanding and intimacy which will promote the therapeutic process; on the other hand, such a group may lack variety, difference in perspective and therefore new information. Homogeneous groups may share common blind spots and will have only the therapist to challenge them."[5]

GROUPWORK MODEL

It is difficult to assign a precise label to the brand of groupwork practised by the team since the model has been drawn from so many sources. The term groupwork denotes different things to different people; we hold the view that the main emphasis of groupwork is sharing feelings and facts through the disclosure of one's private thoughts to others. This baseline at least is consistent with that held by most psychotherapists working with groups.[6] Where the team approach differs, however, is that we also consider we have a duty to effect change in a particular direction since all the groups have been convened because sexual abuse has occurred. The agreed premise is, therefore, the need to change attitudes, in order to ensure that:

a. parents protect their children from further abuse;
b. that children learn to protect themselves,
c. make their worries known, and
d. are freed from any sense of responsibility for the abuse.

In a relatively short period, therefore, the work is geared towards quite radical changes in behaviour, cognition and emotional responses. Hence, these are not just 'sharing' groups but are strongly task-oriented and aim to reach specific goals through focusing on certain issues such as where responsibility does lie for the abuse and how unclear generational boundaries may be conducive to abuse. Certainly, the groups are also intended to be therapeutic in the healing sense and curative. The model is undoubtedly a hybrid, reflecting strands from the major trends in small groupwork, teaching and other forms of therapy, especially family therapy. Straightforward information is provided using a training group or teaching model; for example, the children are taught what is acceptable touching. Training in social skills gives the children opportunities to role play and practice how to assert themselves appropriately and respond to others, as is done in intermediate treatment groups organized by social services for difficult adolescents.

Group leaders generally respond to their groups as a whole and in terms of their shared experience, in a model more consistent with classic group psychotherapy, for example:

"Lisa seems very upset today, I guess you all feel sad when you think about what went wrong in your family."

In addition, however, the leaders may also focus on an individual in a group or on couples as in the parents' group.[7] Indeed, some of the techniques used to help couples to work on their own relationship can tend to reinforce the space between one couple and another rather than induce interaction between all the group members, as would be aimed for in a pure psychotherapy group. For example, to encourage more open communication between a couple we ask each pair:

a. to guess what their partner likes and
b. dislikes about their sexual language when they are having sex;
c. to discuss this with each other and then
d. to check out the accuracy of their assumptions with each other.

Although we subsequently encourage the whole group to think about how little they had previously shared with their partners about sexual matters, we would not expect a couple to discuss the content of their private conversation with the others in the group.

While division into small groups can be a useful technique to encourage member participation and contact in the early stages, it should be used sparingly to avoid the establishment of subgroups, which in turn can lead to rivalry, a less cohesive large group and to avoidance of the joint tasks.

The group members' communications to each other or to the group leaders are perceived as an important part of the therapeutic process, although the transferences issues are not worked on.

Example
One man verbally abused and threatened a female group leader when the male cotherapist left the room. This was not taken up in individual or group transference terms, but in relation to the likelihood of reabuse, the subject under discussion which appeared to have triggered off the outburst.

To some degree, play and activity are used as means of communication and learning in groups. This hybrid model therefore contains aspects of group psychotherapy, group counselling, the task-centred approach, teaching, acting techniques including role-play[8] and play; all these aspects aim to promote a degree of personal change and increased awareness of what has brought them into the programme. Perhaps the team members function most like group counsellors, concerned with relieving particular problems and with modifying specific relationships but not expecting a fundamental change in personality as in group psychotherapy.

Because of the lack of adherence to any particular groupwork model, the team is able to modify its approach over time, adapting it to the needs of the family.

GOALS OF GROUPWORK

Essentially, the treatment programme aims to prevent further abuse and to minimize the long-term negative effects of abuse on the victim and family. Where the groupwork process produces a positive therapeutic impact, the assumption is that this results from the sharing process and an improvement in the participant's self-esteem. However, groupwork associated with sexual abuse programmes must effect more than therapeutic change, as mentioned previously. It has also to address issues of responsibility, education and management and to bear in mind that group attendance is generally only one aspect of a much wider professional involvement. In order to achieve its wider brief, the following goals are specified:

1. Clarifying responsibility for the abuse. Within a group setting,

individuals can more freely express their understanding and confusion, their agreement or disagreement about who is responsible
for the abuse and who should protect the children. The children are
helped to understand that there *are* grown ups who believe them:

"We *do* believe what you have told us and we think you have been very
brave to tell us."

2. Education as to appropriate and inappropriate sexual contact
   between adults and children (*see* Chapter 9).

   "It is always the grown-up's fault if they touch you in a bad way, even if
   sometimes it makes you feel nice or special."

3. Education in self-protection, appropriate assertion. For example,
   a four-year-old girl to a 10-year-old boy who bumps into her while
   running past:

   "Don't do that—it's *my* body!"

4. Education in getting help and making further disclosures. This is
   dealt with in both adult's and children's groups.
5. Encouraging parents to consider the quality of their own relationship and the way in which each of them communicated and related
   to their children. The purpose here is to help them gain a greater
   understanding of the links between their poor marital relationship
   and the distorted parent-child contact; to learn to understand how
   this can lead to abuse and to children not being 'heard' when they
   attempt 'to tell'.
6. Helping adults to understand that the way in which family life was
   structured could have been conducive to the abuse. In many cases,
   the father has been completely dominant in all aspects of family life,
   controlling activity and communication to such an extent that
   'secrets' could not be safely shared.

Case examples
One eldest daughter of 14 years was expected to take over all her mother's
duties while the latter was in hospital having a baby—this included all the
household jobs and sexual activity with the father.
Mr C. expected his wife to scrub his back and wash his hair as well as shave
him; when after many years she refused to carry on, his 12-year-old daughter
then took over, and during one of these activities he abused her.

7. Helping perpetrators and their families to work with professional
   agencies. It is evident from this list that the overall goal of the
   groupwork programme is *change*, but change in a specific direction,
   namely towards child protection. To that extent we could be
   described as benign agents of social control. Although many
   parents do wish to join the groups to get help for their children or

themselves, others are required to by the court, or strongly encouraged to do so by social workers and probation officers, who have considerable power in relation to the family.

ESTABLISHING THE GROUPWORK PROGRAMME

The groupwork programme includes groups for children of different ages, ranging from 3 to 16. The youngest age-groups include both boys and girls, while there are generally separate sex groups from then onwards. Since many of these children are not living with their natural parents, they may have to be escorted by their foster parent, a residential or field social worker. A group is also provided with these escorts and care-takers. In addition, there are groups for mothers, for male perpetrators and for parents. A detailed description of each group in the programme is provided in Appendix 4.

All the arrangements for groupwork attendance are made in family meetings, these are arranged by the case manager on the team in conjunction with the family's social worker and probation officer. The presence of 'the authorities' must surely affect the chances of a family attending. Parents are quite overt about their fury towards authority in general and the social services in particular, while anger and frustration with the group leaders is only minimally better disguised:

> "It's always those bloody social workers interfering; they get a real kick out of it if they can put you down."

> One excited 12-year-old deliberately moved her cup as the group leader poured her drink; as a result she was actually 'soiled' by him and she felt 'set up', frustrated and angry.

Since the families are naturally anxious about the groupwork, considerable efforts are made to convey as much information as possible in the family meetings about the purpose and process of the groups. Unfortunately, their anxiety is exacerbated as it is rare to include a family without a substantial wait; there are often long waiting lists for group places. Even when there are more agencies offering a comprehensive treatment approach to sexual abuse, there is still likely to be a practical problem of having insufficient staff and insufficient numbers of abused children of the same age needing help in the same geographical area at the same time. Delays can be untherapeutic, especially for children too young to have a concept of time; they may feel that promised help is not going to be given and so they feel further humiliated and abandoned. When these delays occur, family meetings and local social work involvement 'holds the fort'.

To establish a programme requires the active support of senior colleagues, equally excited and challenged by groupwork and un-frightened by the subject matter. They will have to allocate time for discussion of the groups' progress and for supervision. These arrangements should be timetabled in working hours to ensure that they take place and to demonstrate that the seriousness of the work is appreciated and sanctioned. The introduction of any new way of working can lead to rivalry or competition between staff, which may get displaced into competition for resources such as room usage. Controversies may arise over the need for extra equipment for children's activities or for additional time for groupwork planning and integration with the other agency tasks. It is worth remembering too that groupwork does affect the work of colleagues because large numbers of people arrive simultaneously; there is often a lot of noise and excitement before and after group meetings and there is likely to be more mess. A wise group leader shows consideration for colleagues and reinforces their tolerance! One practical way of demonstrating your concern would be to discuss groupwork plans in a full staff meeting prior to the start of the groups; also to arrange an agreed method of feedback from colleagues at a later stage.

Training Group Leaders

The team has discovered that group leaders are made, not born! They need to capitalize on their professional training, experiences presently available in their agencies, as well as being prepared to do some homework. In the treatment programme, each group is led by one experienced and one trainee leader; the latter may be of a different discipline or senior to the leader. Working in a multidisciplinary fashion has minimized issues of seniority and encouraged a genuine willingness on the part of team members to learn from each other. There are other reasons for adapting the co-leadership model described. At times, because of staff shortage, groups have occasionally had to be run single-handed. This proved to be less enjoyable and more stressful. In the children's groups, this was mainly due to the difficulty of establishing and keeping control as well as maintaining the focus of work. Not dissimilarly, in the adult groups, it was harder for one leader to resist the covert pressure of the group to avoid talking about controversial or painful issues particularly, since much of the material was also disquieting for the leader. Whether there are one or two leaders present, groups almost invariably avoid discussion of the serious issues around abuse; without direction they simply chat socially. One group leader adopted a short reminder using humour and repetition to counter group avoidance tactics: "Here we go again", was all that was needed to be said laughingly to stop the group sidestepping a difficult issue.

Group leaders openly comment on this process, acknowledging the difficulties but persisting with the task:

Towards the end of one group, the leader pointed out that there were only two more sessions to go; this was completely ignored and the group started talking about the colour of someone's boots!

"It really is very hard for us all to think about meetings finishing. It's easier to talk about the boots rather than the fact that they are also made for walking away!"

Co-leadership Model—Male–female Issues

Clearly the rationale for male–female leadership in most groups was to demonstrate that men and women can discuss, disagree and work together, and respect each other, whether or not they are sexual partners. As a 'parental' model they are often the targets of flirtation, and the focus of fantasies and projections. They represent either the idealized mothers and denigrated fathers or the reverse.[9] Issues like these are dealt with by making generalized comments to the group, rather than by individual interpretations. Since both male and female victims are generally abused by men, they need the opportunity of seeing a man who is not an aggressor, who can resist their often provocative demands for attention, and who can be a positive source of help.[10]

A male leader in the 15–16-year-old girls' group reported difficulties when his female co-leader was absent through illness; the girls became overly flirtatious, competitive for his attention and protective.

Many children equally need the experience of a mother-like figure who can be firm, protective and maintain appropriate generational boundaries. Working together as leaders can be extremely supportive but also has its potential problems. The leaders need to resolve and discuss their own sexual attitudes, any sense of competition they may feel and they need to respect each other as competent and willing to listen, otherwise they present their group with yet another inappropriate adult model of parenting and authority.

Some parents try to 'split' the leaders, either to have one for themselves 'on their side' or to avoid seeing a couple working well together.

Generally, two leaders mitigate against getting caught in a flow of denial and avoidance. However, in the male perpetrators' group where it was decided to use two male leaders to encourage more open communication, this induced an atmosphere of 'male camaraderie'. This is an example of a homogeneous group into which it was sometimes hard to introduce new information from a mother's, wife's or female victim's point of view. Similarly, in the mothers' group led by two women, there was a very strong tendency to assume that as 'we are all women together' we share the same views. It was quite difficult for a mother to suggest that she actually liked or respected a man. In the first few meetings, a major preoccupation was how best to emasculate men and there was little reticence about discussing their graphic methods either:

"I'd cut *it* off"—"no I'd cut *them* off"—"no, I'd cut the whole lot off—that's all they deserve!"

To introduce a male co-leader into the mother's group would prove, initially at least, a barrier for women still at a stage when they are unable to relate, other than extremely negatively, to any male. It would be extremely difficult for most male leaders not to succumb at some level to the transference and competitive demands of a very needy group of mothers. A dual male leadership would clearly exacerbate these difficulties, making any form of therapeutic empathy very difficult indeed and potentially a massive focus for women's anger. Because of the authority vested in the group leader there would be a strong likelihood that the anger would not get ventilated openly, thus reinforcing a passive position. Given that many of the women had experienced considerable sexual difficulties in their relationships prior to the abuse, they might be even more inhibited from discussing this issue with one or two male group leaders. On the other hand, omitting a male leader or co-leader in the mother's group is not consistent with our practice of providing a 'good or 'safe' model of both sexes.

Knowledge Base

Group leaders should have a basic understanding of groupwork theory[11] in order to understand the process and avoid focusing on an individual person or problem, without seeing the relevance of the content and his response for the rest of the group.

The curative mechanisms referred to by Yallom[12] when writing about group psychotherapy seemed to be equally relevant for our groups:

1. The installation of hope.
2. Universality: "In the therapy group, especially in the early stages, the disconfirmation of their feelings of uniqueness is a powerful source of relief".

3. Imparting of information.
4. Altruism: ". . . . . . patients help one another, suggestions, reassurance, insights or share similar problems with other members".
5. Corrective recapitulation of the primary family group: "Taking part in groupwork may provide an opportunity to deal with early past experiences since those experiences will influence the group members' current behaviour towards the leaders and other group members and in turn will be commented on".
6. Development of socializing techniques.
7. Imitative behaviour.
8. Interpersonal learning.
9. Group cohesiveness.
10. Catharsis: "In this process the person learns to express negative and positive feelings openly".
11. Existential factors. "Issues of personal responsibility are faced together with implications of behaviour".

Aside from a specialist knowledge of sexual abuse itself, group leaders need to be able to talk freely about sexual abuse, masturbation, physiology and reproduction. They need to be able to explain the likely sequelae to abuse, in terms of the individual, his or her family and in relation to the legal context. They should also have a clear idea of the developmental stages children pass through, what capacity they have at any given age to conceptualize, what kind of language they use, how long they can be expected to concentrate, how children in a particular age-group learn best, what sort of games they play, and how they would normally be expected to demonstrate their feelings. It is the group leader's task to find an appropriate level of communication as well as a suitable format for engaging them.

While there are clear tasks for each group, it should not be forgotten that each group really does have its own character and atmosphere and it is important that group leaders are flexible enough to use this difference constructively. No two groups are the same. One mother's group was characterized by laughter, tears and a cohesive spirit, while in another several mothers were clinically depressed, emotionally impoverished with little self-esteem and found it hard to consider other people's feelings. In one parent's group, several of the perpetrators appeared 'to go along with the system' rather than actually work on their difficulties. In another, the couples were far more inclined to share their private thoughts and discuss intimate matters. In many ways, such differences affect the way in which a group proceeds, focusing more or less on one aspect of the task. Also, group leaders themselves respond differently to different groups.

Style

Leadership style is inevitably idiosyncratic, reflecting the personality, professional expertise and life experience of the leader. As no two groups are ever the same, neither are any two group leaders. Although the reason for our groupwork is extremely serious, this does not preclude us from enjoying some aspects of the work. If leaders feel confident enough to use themselves positively in group work, by bringing in humour and a variety of activities, in turn this will create an atmosphere more conducive to facing facts and looking at painful situations.

Whether trying to encourage insightful discussions with the adults or introducing a variety of activities in the children's group, leaders need to be active, in control and task-centred. If given the opportunity, many of the adults would otherwise spend most of their time haranguing the authorities.

Children also need clearly defined rules and to be aware of what the adult leaders expect of them; given the issue of abuse and their own anxiety about being in a group, they can become over-excited and difficult to manage.

Interestingly, a group of girls aged 10–13 years found it impossible to wait outside the group room without constantly interrupting if they knew that both male and female leaders were in there alone together. This would have been a good opportunity to demonstrate:

a. firm and clear adult control—about where they were expected to wait;
b. the need to explain what is happening to children, so that they can see the sense of behaving as requested;
c. the links between their curiosity and 'fantasies' about what was going on and the abuse which led them to be in the group.

Boys aged 12–14 years present particular problems for group leaders; they are restless, extremely noisy, exhibit raucous and inappropriate behaviour, rush around and generally severely test the leaders' capacity to control them. Many of them want to obliterate their experience and resent talking about it. Often when they leave, they tear up the private books they have written in for the group leaders. The leaders of this group are often sandwiched between the buffeting they get from many of the boys and the criticism from other leaders whose groups cause less disturbance.

Group leaders should constantly bear in mind the extreme ambivalence that many people feel about group attendance and professional intervention, however benign. One way of managing these mixed feelings is to be quite open about how mixed the leader sometimes feels about working in this field with people he/she likes, knowing that they have committed offences which are illegal and unacceptable. Group members may demonstrate their views overtly aggressively, by non-cooperation, by constant acquiesence or by moving from an admission of inappropriate behaviour to a denial of responsibility. It is very important for group leaders to help people express their misgivings and mixed motives for attendance, even if this means being the target of the group's anger, for example:

One angry, highly qualified and articulate perpetrator in the parents' group normally behaved in an overly acquiescent manner towards the male group leader, who was also his case manager and the team consultant. He finally gave vent to his fury by talking about stuck-up professional do-gooders with all their power, sitting on their fat bottoms, etc. On another occasion this most articulate and well-educated man bent over the tea table and managed to stick his bottom up in front of the male group leader's face for several moments.

THE GROUPS

Structure, Themes, Activities and Goals

Table 10.1 delineates the different groups in the treatment programme, citing the major themes, activities and goals. A comprehensive resumé of each group is given in Appendix 4; it includes comments on structure, on the problems which generally arise in each group, and the methods used by the group leaders.

Issues Arising in Groups and Techniques In Response

Working in the groups can at times be both exciting and enjoyable, although extremely frustrating and sad at other times. On groupwork days, there is a notable rise in tension, for however effective the groupleaders, they are likely to have a struggle to both maintain control and keep the focus on the more painful and controversial issues. As previously mentioned, each group is quite distinct from any other, but in each we are dealing with predominantly similar issues, albeit at different levels. These will now be considered in turn, giving examples of the techniques employed:

1. Communication.
2. Self-esteem.
3. Sharing feelings of anger, pain and good things too.
4. Issues of responsibility.
5. Self-protection and assertion.

Table 10.1. Groups: constitution and themes, activities and goals

Age (years)	Numbers	Duration No of groups (length of group)	Leaders	Assertiveness training		
				Major themes	Major activities	Goals
3–6 girls and boys	6–8	6 (1 hour)	Male and female	Adults are responsible for abuse Self-protection What is inappropriate touching	Teaching, stories, discussion, role-play, video feedback, use of books	To educate To learn to say no To tell someone
7–10 girls and boys	6–8	8–10 (1 hour)	Male and female	As above	As above Personal books	As above To locate blame and educate To share with peers
10–12 girls and 12–14 girls	7–8	12 (1 hour)	Male and female	As above, also shared experiences, their view of themselves, low self-esteem	As above, also practising responding to various stressful life incidents. Topics discussed include contraception, boyfriends, abortion, etc.	As above, also to boost self-confidence, to consider how the future could be affected by the abuse, to lessen preoccupation with abuse by provision of regular discussion group
15–16 girls	8	16–20 (1 hour)	Male and female	As above, also ambivalence to perpetrators' concern re-future sex relationships, living arrangements	As above. Discussion self-assertion, video feedback	As above
12–14 boys	6–8	12 (1 hour)	Male and female	Feelings aroused by sexual abuse, issue of choice, responsibility as abuser, fears of homosexuality and becoming 'abuser'	As above and personal books	As above

...comes	8	20 (1¼ hours)	2 females	isolation, guilt, management problems, sexually abused mothers, families in the future, low self-esteem	Discussion, role-play, task-setting	As above
Perpetrators	8–10	11–15 (1 hour)	2 Males	Sexuality/poor marital relationships, prison and its effect, early experience of deprivation, violence and sexual abuse	Sharing their current news and histories Encouraging a sense of empathy with the abused	Taking clear responsibility for the abuse, recognizing family patterns over three generations, looking at marital relationships. How to deal with sexual feelings, how to cope with professionals
Parents	16–20	15–20 (1¼ hours)	Male and female and trainee	To consider above and parenting issues	As above Role-play, sculpting, couples work, task-setting	As above
*Care-takers including social workers, foster parents and escorts	6–8	6–15 (1 hour)	Female and trainee	How to handle children who have been abused	Discussion	Clarification of purpose of tasks of groups Support with professional colleagues

* The care-taker's group was a late addition. The escorts needed a forum for discussion and clarification about the purpose of the groups. Escorts also frequently requested advice about why the children behaved as they did and how they should respond. Specific information requested included the topic of sexual abuse, causation, incidence and current approaches in terms of therapy and the courts. Once this group was established and the 'escorts' became more comfortable with *their* tasks, we noted greater consistency in the childrens' attendance.

1. Communication

Communication via language

The idea of open communication was unfamiliar, and no doubt contributed to the abuse in the majority of families attending groups.[13] It is particularly important, therefore, that the leaders present a model of open-speaking and that they adapt their communication and language to a level appropriate to each group:

> "The important thing is to make the discussion as open, ordinary and educating as possible."

> "Language can offer an escape from assault."[14]

A particularly sensitive and emotive topic is the parents' sexual relationship and how that could link with the abuse. In the second or third parents group meeting, we routinely explain our need to find a common language in order to discuss sexual issues. We ask them to think of all the words they used as children to describe:

a. women's private parts;
b. men's private parts;
c. sexual activity itself.

This tends to create an embarrassed silence until the leaders suggest a few words, and group momentum takes off; adult terms are quickly added to the glossary. The list is written up on a blackboard for all to see—and it usually raises a lot of laughter and helps the group to coalesce.

Breasts	*Penis*	*Vagina*	*Sex*	*Anus*
headlights	willie	Mary	having it away	bum
titless wonder	tassle	cunt	having it off	bottom
boobs	knob	little man in the boat	having a bang	arse
tits of England	eccles		fuck	
Bristols	cock		grand slam	
tits	dick	tuppence	bit of the other	
breast plates	meat and two veg	fanny	nookie	
twin towers	pencil	pencil sharpener	bit of what you fancy	
mild and bitter			slap and sickle	
tweedle dee and tweedle dum	car	garage	a night on the tiles	
		crack	shag	
	sausages	mash	making love	
		vagina	a leg over	
			flat out	
			on the nest	

In various forms this exercise is used in most groups. Instead of shouting out the words, which might have proved too inhibiting, the 15–16-year-old girls in one group each wrote each word they could think of on a piece of paper—these were folded over and put into a hat. In turn, each girl and the two leaders pulled a paper out and read the words out aloud. In this way, they did not have to take responsibility for the words they read out, or for what they did or did not know about the subject.

It is essential to clarify both *common* and *idiosyncratic* vocabulary to avoid confused communication:

A five-year-old girl was asked what she called the area between the doll's legs and she replied "Her middle". The interviewer said, "Yes, but what is your special name for that in your family?" She repeated, "Middle". Again the question, "What do you call that bit of the dolly just there?" (pointing). At this point, the child got absolutely fed up, went up to the one-way screen, splayed her legs and pointed to her vagina and shouted "Middle".

Less obvious examples of language used by younger children have included nun/minis/tuppence/moneybox/Blackwall Tunnel—for vagina; hanging bum—for penis; back, dirty hole—for anus.

Unfortunately, sharing verbal knowledge does not always meet with parental approval, as in the case of the irate mother who heard her four-year-old daughter declare: "No one is allowed to touch my pussy!".

Although the anatomical dolls are successfully used to teach the younger children, the older girls of 10–16 years communicated their feelings on the subject by revulsion and a refusal to touch them, or vulgarly handling them and showing no gentleness at all.

Communication via private books

In several of the children's groups, each child has a notebook in which he or she can write private messages to the group leader and be given a reply in the book. Although not consistent with the idea of opening communication more widely, and sharing secrets with the group, it does offer an alternative to the more withdrawn or less articulate child to communicate their feelings. However, sometimes the 'follow my leader' phenomenon takes over whereby one child says defiantly: "I'm not going to write in my book", and therefore no-one else does either!

The following message and drawing was written by an 11-year-old boy in his notebook:

"I think that today's lesson was quiet interesting. It was good really to bring up sexual abuse because we have all gone through it, and I think that the how thing is an interesting idea comeing to a meeting saying all your problems, 'cause if you don't tell no one, you dont ever forget, lot of people have had bad experiences like we have but we just have to exsept it."

Some group members use the books as a method of communication with each other as well as with the leaders, these comments are generally not made openly.

10-year-old girls:
A. "Did you like any of the things your dad did to you?"
B. "A little bit at first, but then it got horrible."

Boys in particular often use their personal notebooks as an outlet for further aggression. They write abusive notes to the group leaders and often tear the books up when the group comes to an end. On the other hand they can also say: "I get fed up when others try to spoil the group."

Communication via group stories

Another method of encouraging communication is the group story. Each child writes a bit of the story and then passes it on to the next; halfway through they are asked to consider two possible endings and then complete the story. This story was written in a 10–12-year-old girls' group:

> Once upon a time there was a little girl who was eight years old. She lived with her mum and dad, her little brother who was five and her sister who was two. One day when her mum was out shopping with her brother and sister, her dad came in to her bedroom and started doing something upsetting. He made her cry very loudly. Her mum heard her when she came in and her father ran out of the room. They met halfway up the stairs. Mum asked why her little girl was crying. Dad said it was because she had been naughty and he had slapped her. The girl was too upset to tell her mum, she was too shocked. After she had calmed down she finally told her mum what her dad had done to her. Her mum was very upset and a bit torn because she loved her husband but she also loved her little girl. She found it very difficult to know what to do next, so she did nothing. The little girl thought that her mum didn't believe her, or may be hadn't even heard her. Next week when the mum went shopping, the same thing happened again and this time the girl didn't tell her mum. It went on for several years, until the girl was 15. By this time the girl had a boyfriend of her own and she told him what had happened to her. Her boyfriend was very upset and went to tell the girl's mum. At first, the mum didn't believe it until one day she came home and caught him 'in action'. This upset the mum very much and she went to the social services department and told her social worker. The social worker went with mum to the police station to explain fully what had happened. They accompanied them to the house by a policeman who asked to see the girl's dad. The dad was very frightened because he knew the policeman would take him away, but he couldn't say that he hadn't done it because his daughter had said he had and his wife had seen him doing it. He also said he was pleased in a funny sort of way because he didn't know how to stop. After several months the dad came to court and was fined £200. The dad said he was pleased that his daughter had told her mum and that the mum had heard her. A lot of hard work had to be done by all the family because of all the upsetting things that had happened. Mum had to really start listening to her children and dad had to learn what was the right kind of relationship to be having with both of his daughters. A few years later the mum found out that the same thing had happened to Anne's younger sister. This time, the mum ran away with her children to her own mum who lived in Scotland. The gran took them all to a women's group where there were women who had had similar experiences. The difficulty in this family was learning to live without the dad, who was now in prison, because although they all knew what he had done was very wrong, they still missed him because sometimes he had been nice. The girls sometimes felt that it was their fault that their dad was in prison. Their mum and their social worker explained that it wasn't their fault and they soon grew up happily.

The alternative ending suggested was that the girl runs away from home, never intending to return and taking positive pleasure from the fact that her father goes to prison!

The group then talked about what would have been most helpful. They suggested:

1. "her mum could have tackled her dad when the girl first told her what had happened."
2. "the girl could have told her mum when the same thing happened the following week."

Communication via genograms[15]

As a form of communication, genograms have proved useful both in eliciting information and helping group members to uncover family patterns through the generations.

In small adult groups, individuals have presented their own family tree to the group together with their observations about what they noted when they drew it:

Mrs L: "I hadn't realized how all the men in my family were away most of the time, either at sea, or as missionaries, or working away from home."

Mrs R. broke down in tears after being questioned about the gap in her genogram. There was no information about her father, as though he had never existed. When this was commented on, she then admitted for the first time in 24 years that she had been sexually abused by her father for several years.

2. Self-esteem

The whole of the groupwork process is predicated on sharing feelings and information; members of families in which sexual abuse has occurred are generally loath to do this because they feel so 'different' and generally have such low opinions of themselves and their abilities. A variety of methods are used to encourage individuals, at whatever point in the life-cycle stage, to become more open, autonomous, appropriately assertive to build on their strengths. These are basic prerequisites for an increased sense of self-worth and an awareness that individuals can effect some change in their own lives. Families are helped to realize that what has happened to them has also happened to others, and therefore does not mean that they need remain isolated and hopeless. One mother said, "I always knew I was plain and no one would fancy me". One perpetrator commented that he'd always been the black sheep of the family and didn't expect anything. Several 14–16-year-old girls were worried that if they got into a relationship in the future, the men would leave them, or they would dirty the men.

Except for the three to six-year-old children, each group member is asked to share some part of their personal story of abuse. Everyone is also asked to bring their news each week. In this way each person comes to realize that he or she is worth listening to and that they may all be able to contribute something useful to others.

One of the most spontaneously helpful boosts to morale in the group arose when a psychiatrically disturbed mother, Mrs O., regaled the group with horrific stories. These were about her own childhood abuse and her recent self-mutilation following the discovery that her cohabitee had abused her daughter. Although initially shocked, most of the group members tried to be supportive. Mrs O. decided to leave after three weeks; she kept getting lost, arriving late because she would forget which room we were in. She felt utterly hopeless about her relationship with her daughter and her own future. The group attempted to dissuade her to no avail, until finally one mother said; "You can't leave; I won't have it; I need you to be here!" and Mrs O. stayed! She subsequently even offered to go to court with another mother who was feeling very anxious.

One technique used specifically to encourage self-esteem and an awareness of others is the 'Brag' and 'Compliment' game. Each person is asked to say something nice about the person next to them. It is quite clear that many adults and children feel very uncomfortable about *being* complimented, but also very pleased and surprised. It appears to be an exceedingly rare experience for most of them.

a. The compliment

One couple to another: "We often talk about you two and when you said you have to talk openly to each other about everything, even the scratch on your hand, that helped us".

One 16-year-old girl to another: "I like the way you do your hair".

One mother to another: "I like the way you always stand up for yourself—whoever it is".

b. Accepting the compliment

This often appears to be more difficult to cope with than the compliment itself. This reflection of self-esteem frequently changes during the course of group life.

One six-year-old to another: "I like your jumper."
"Thank you, I like it too."

Sometimes the Brag or Compliment game can be used to reinforce learning. At the end of a session of a group discussion on sexy and modest behaviour a 10-year-old girl said to her neighbour, "I like your blue knickers". Amid laughter, the girl immediately sat more modestly.

Thus, this activity, designed for one specific purpose, often managed to serve a number of unexpected aims.

One ex-councillor's wife derived a great deal of satisfaction from helping others in the group and being acknowledged for her abilities. On one occasion, she wrote to the council on behalf of another mother needing better accommodation. She also offered to take minutes of our group meetings so that she could remind us each week of what we had talked about when we last met. The following is an example of her 'Minutes':

Mother's group: 'minutes' of the last meeting:
Present: 7
Absent: 1
Discussed:
> M. told us of an accident she had witnessed and helped with.
> Mrs P. witnessed someone being pushed under a train.
> We all spoke about having to say goodbye. Mostly about husbands and children. But also of friends.
> Being lonely.
> Shutting ourselves away.
> Not wanting to face others, feeling shamed, embarrassed and persecuted.
> Feeling no positive solution since this trouble happened.
> Losing friends.
> Receiving abusive phone calls.
> Relaying bad feelings about our husbands onto our children.
> We were asked to try and remember, and say something nice about our husbands.

Since the groups are task-centered and have an agenda which must be covered during the life of a group, there are relatively few opportunities for the members to spontaneously initiate activities, although the example above was one occasion where this did occur. It proved fruitful: the group felt what they had to say was important, the Minutes reminded them of issues which might otherwise have been 'pushed under the carpet', and they were given a model of a group member who could be innovative and effective.

Regardless of financial constraints, there was generally a discernible improvement in the mothers' appearance during the life of a group. They took far more care about their clothes, hair and make-up, and compliments from group members or leaders reinforced their growing self-esteem. This was often reflected in their finding new interests and work outside the home. For example, Mrs T. managed to get a part-time job in a launderette and was very excited to be earning her own money. Mrs R. who weighed at least 16 stone, started swimming regularly.

It is not clear whether positive reinforcement from the group leaders is more or less significant than from other group members. Our assumption is that young children, because of their developmental stage and natural dependency, look more towards the adults for confirmation and encouragement, whereas the adolescents will be most likely to trust in their peers, but covertly hear the adults also.

In the adult groups, the leaders' approval is more likely to be sought that that of their peers, since the leaders are rightly associated with having some power to make recommendations which could affect life outside the group.

To date, the use of a self-esteem questionnaire to test changes in this area, following groupwork, has been very limited, but this is an area which should be further investigated. A significant improvement was noted in several mothers' groups which used questionnaires, but as only a small number of members were involved, it is not certain if these results are generally correct.

On the whole, it is the mothers who arrange to meet when groups end rather than the parents, presumably because the mothers are the more isolated, and need the reinforcement and friendship of peers to continue to boost their self-esteem.

3. Sharing feelings

It is not quite clear the extent to which self-esteem, that is the value put on oneself by oneself, is dependent on reinforcement from others, but there can be little doubt that affirmation from others which is perceived as such has a part to play. This inevitably involves a process of sharing information and techniques and opening up of communication. The example given below demonstrates the different ways in which feelings can be shared:

A 12-year-old girl became very distressed, broke down and cried in the group. The other girls and the group leader encouraged her to explain why: some used words, some used touch and one wrote her a note. Eventually she was able to say that her stepfather had abused her best friend and she felt responsible for this because she hadn't immediately told an adult. Now her friend won't talk to her. The group told her to tell her mother how unhappy she was. The following week she told them she had in fact been able to talk to her mother about it and felt a bit better. Several of the other girls spontaneously commented that they had been helpful the previous week.

During one parents' group, Mrs L. had been crying throughout, but adamantly refused to speak. She and her friend, Mr P. were both divorced and had children of their own. They longed to live altogether but it took some time before the social services agreed to this because of allegations that Mr P. had sexually abused children on two occasions. The couple were furious with the authorities, feeling that all would be well if only they were together. In fact, when they were it turned out to be a great disappointment and she told the group how it was all his son's fault that everyone was this unhappy and arguing.

The group (*a*) pointed out that Mr P. should allow Mrs L. to cope with his son without him interfering or being overprotective, and (*b*) suggested that it was up to her and not the child to make some positive moves, in order to make things better (she was refusing to talk to the 10-year-old unless he started the conversation). She refused to comment on their advice and continued to weep. Later we learnt that on the way home at least six members of the group had met the couple down the road to try and comfort Mrs L.

The leaders had responded to this session by using a paradoxical approach derived from family therapy

> "We don't think that Mrs L. should try to love Mr P's sons, it is far too soon and he would know it is not for real. It is fine that it remains as she says: being pleased but not from the heart."

4. Issues of responsibility

Responsibility is a major theme in child sexual abuse and refers primarily to who is 'to blame' for the abuse. This is a more linear explanation, although perpetrators are seen in the context of their family system and understood in relation to the dynamics and structure of family life. However, to relieve the children of unwarranted guilt, the message that it is not their fault is made quite clear.

In the parents' group, we have used a particularly useful exercise which stems from a strategic type of questioning used in family therapy. The aim here is for both parents to acknowledge their part in what led up to the abuse. The following examples have been edited from a final group meeting:

Leader: "What would have to happen for the abuse to start all over again? We know it won't, but what were the circumstances that made it possible? What would you have to do to make it like that again?"

Mrs N. "Basically, it would happen if I didn't show enough affection to Steve (husband) or Catherine (daughter)."

Mr N.: "She (Catherine) clung to me, she was all over me. She's an adult now. She's a young lady. That can't happen anymore."

Mrs N.: "They need a lot of affection; if I hold back they'll go for each other again. We have always been quite good at communicating, but then came a black spot. The one we kept away from when we were trying to make a future from the past, if you see what I mean, we knew what had happened, and tried to live with it."

Leader: "I remember when we talked before, you said you became a bit like a mum to Steve. Do you feel you would have to do that again?"

Mrs N.: "No, I don't think so because he's changed. So many things have changed. He's working for himself . . . Whatever he did in life I had to help him with. Well, now his job is nothing to do with me. I'm really pleased. I mean, I'm interested, but . . . ."
Leader: "So you'd have to stop mothering him again to make it as a wife?"
Mrs N.: "Oh, yes."
Mr N.: "So many things have changed. We're talking about it . . . even what happens in the home. Wow!" (He laughs.)
Leader: "So you'd have to start mothering him again to make it possible for the abuse to happen again?"
Mrs N.: "No, I wouldn't. I'd kick him out!"

(In this example, it appears that the mother has gained greater awareness of the family dynamics and her role in the system. The husband doesn't acknowledge his contribution verbally but his behaviour in becoming employed and his improved communication with his wife implies that some changes have now occurred.)

Even among acknowledged perpetrators who have served prison sentences for their offences, there may be enormous resistance to discussing their own responsibility for the abuse:

One professional man frequently referred to his wife's brief infidelity as a causal explanation for his subsequent abuse of nine children. He perceived the actions of the social services as totally inept and responsible for the maintenance of his family break-up and the exacerbation of their problems. He was furiously angry at the power other professionals were now able to wield and could not connect his abusive behaviour with what he considered their interference and bungling. Whenever possible, he would rally the other parents in the group to criticize the authorities and to place responsibility for their family's misery onto them.

While the perpetrators are required to take responsibility for their actions and to consider what led up to it, mothers are also helped to look at the nature of their relationship with their daughters and to consider how they are going to cope with them knowing that they have been a rival. The responsibility clearly rests with the mother to initiate the new approach, but many find this both painful and infuriating. Some mothers were brave enough to use role-play to experiment with alternative approaches they could use with a daughter who refused to help in the house or was rude. Group members contributed ideas and learned from each other. They took great pride in having their ideas taken up by other mothers or approved by the leaders.

Consistent with our view that the adults have to take responsibility for the abuse and the effects on the family, we also made it clear that within the first two weeks both the mothers' group and the parents' group were expected to draw up a list of issues they wanted to cover. Clearly the message was that the group was theirs and they had to take

some responsibility for how it progressed. The following characteristically shows a difference of emphasis in each group:

Mothers' group A

1. Children to open up and talk openly about their experience.
2. Talking about your own feelings about yourselves.
3. Rebuilding your lives and coping with all the bits of the situation.
4. Getting your child/children to open up and speak out if anything
   should occur again.
5. Being able to find the right way to approach your child/children
   to talk about themselves.
6. Being able to trust your own children.
7. Being worried about your children when they grow up, and how
   they will be affected in later years; to be sure they don't get
   abused again.
8. Worrying about the children's future lives, in later life will the
   abuse put people off marrying them.
9. Your own feelings if you were abused as a child.
10. Your feelings towards the person/people who committed the
    abuse.

Mothers' group B

1. Getting children to school.
2. Social services—interference or help.
3. How to recognize signs of sexual abuse and avoiding it happening
   again.
4. Children—how to get them to talk.
5. What behaviour problems should we expect.
6. Finances—what's available.
7. Effects on rest of family.

5. Self-protection and assertion

Self-protection via appropriate self-assertion is a major focus in all the
children's groups; clearly it is essential for all the children to know
what to do if they feel worried or further threatened. We encourage
them to take an active part in age-appropriate activities designed to
reinforce their group learning and to help them deal with dangerous
situations which could lead to further inappropriate sexual contact.

With the youngest group of three to six-year-olds, group methods
include direct teaching, role-play, video, music and story-telling.

The following picture and brief 'story' were the focus of the group exercise given below:

Saying 'go away'[14]

This boy was just playing in the street, when a man came up to him.
The man asked him to come a bit closer, since he wanted to talk to him.
The man tries to touch the boy.
The boy feels '*icky*' and scared.
He stands tall, looks in the man's eyes, and says '*Go away!*'
He pushes the man's hand off, and runs to tell his Mum.
Did he do the right thing?

Exercise

Children seated in circle: male and female group leaders.

Group leader: "Here we've got a picture, now what do you think is happening in this picture? What's happening and what do you think this man could be saying to this boy? What do you think Sharon? There's no right answer to this: it's just what you think. Well, do you think the boy is pleased the man is talking to him?[11]

Sharon: "No".

Group leader: "No, he doesn't look pleased does he? In fact he looks quite angry. How can you tell he's quite angry Hugh?"

Hugh: "He's punching."

Group leader: "Yes, he looks as if he might be punching as he has got his fist clenched. That's quite right. What else is he doing?"

Group: "He's got his hand behind his back."

Group leader: "He's got his hand behind his back, and he looks very business-like, doesn't he?"

Cheryl: "And his face."

Group leader: "And his face, that's very good. What is it about his face?"

Cheryl: "He looks sad."

Group leader: "He does look sad, but do you think he looks strong? Is he looking the man in the eye? He is, isn't he? He's looking him right into the eye, do you see that Charlotte?"

(Children concentrating the while on the picture book held up by the group. They are also eating biscuits at the same time.)

Leader: ". . . and he's standing very tall and straight isn't he? Now what happens is that this man bent down and suggested that the little boy go home with him and see his kittens. What do you think the little boy could say to him Caroline?"

Caroline: "He'd say 'No'."

Group leader: "You are absolutely right, he was saying 'No' because it wouldn't be a good idea to go with that man and see his kittens, would it?"

Caroline: "No."

Group leader: "So what else could the boy say to the man?"

Caroline: "Go away."

Group leader: "That's very good—right. So do you think it matters how he says it? That's right, he stands up very straight and looks the man straight in the eye."

'Indirect questioning' is also often used to help older children express a view without feeling 'put on the spot'. Children enjoy guessing games, so many respond more readily to this indirect approach, for example:

"Jane, what do you think Anne should say to someone who tries to touch her in an 'icky' way?"

"Shawn, why do you think Paul got so angry when we were talking about what his father did to him?"

We also educate the older children about how their bodies function sexually, and how to talk about 'embarrassing subjects', ranging from their feelings about the other sex, from conception to abortion and contraception. Included in addition are issues about how, when and where to get help. We feel that increased knowledge can lead to greater personal confidence and ability to manage inappropriate sexual approaches. We stress the importance of getting help when they have been abused since they may otherwise find their future relationships affected.[16]

So all the children are 'taught' to be more self-assertive, responsible and how to look after themselves. However, it can be very disappointing when girls respond well when with their peers but are immediately put back into their victim role by a parent, for example:

One perpetrator greeted his 10-year-old daughter, who interrupted a parents' group, not with an explanation that the group hadn't finished yet, or that she would have to wait outside, but with a loud, "Hi, thunder-thighs!".

The technique of role-playing has been frequently referred to and it is one of the most popular and effective ways for children and adolescents to acquire skills in self-protection and in sharing their worries. If the groups have been *videotaped*, it also allows an opportunity for the group members to observe themselves in action. As with other group activities, the therapeutic benefit of role-playing is not confined to the acquisition of confidence and skills but may also be cathartic in allowing the expression of extremely painful and negative feelings. For example:

In one group of 10–12-year-old girls, the task was to act telling parents about an inappropriate advance by a stranger. It was always clear that the children always preferred to role-play others who didn't act very effectively, perhaps because they could more easily identify with such a situation. The victim in a role-play pleaded with her mother and father to listen and then became furious and angry when they only told her off. She started shouting "You're the parents, you're supposed to look after me". The leaders did not make explicit the link between her response and the victim's own personal experience but felt that she had been able to make use of the role-play to express her deep-down pain and anger.

Role-playing also stimulates empathy and the understanding of other people in the professionals' as well as the family network:

In one parents' group, couple A constantly berated the social worker, which encouraged the majority of the group to rally around them and against the authorities. Couple A was asked to act the parts of their social worker and probation officer and another two people offered to play the couple being as angry as possible.

This led to a greater awareness of the professionals' mixed feelings and difficulties and to a more reasonable form of communication between them and their clients.

CONCLUSION

We have found the groupwork programme hard work but in many instances also enjoyable and stimulating. Those leaders who have worked with different age-groups are probably less likely to identify with any one member of the family system and therefore to retain a more neutral attitude in their work. The problem is that the subject matter is highly emotive and touches on a complex web of relationships; groupwork *per se* is not a solution, but has to be seen as part of a comprehensive treatment programme involving all the family.

Our clinical impression is of considerable improvement in many of the families, and indeed the recidivism rate in terms of reabuse of those on our programme is currently 15 per cent. The self-esteem questionnaire used in some of the mothers' groups also indicated an improved self-image, which we take to be a positive outcome. As yet, it is not clear which combination of interventions in the programme, or changes at home or in prison, are responsible for any improvement. While there are similar characteristics in many of the families who attend groups, namely poor marital relationships, low self-esteem and frequency of sexual or other abuse in the previous generations, those who attend are not a homogeneous group. They come from a variety of backgrounds and have very different attitudes. Many report the groups to have been extremely helpful, while a few give the impression of not having been really touched or affected by the experience, rather that they went along with the system.

As yet we have no clear understanding of why adults leave the groups precipitately; approximately 1 in 12 leave, and they generally drop out in the early stages of group life, possibly because they have not felt safe enough to share their anxiety or fury or because they fear implicating themselves in further disclosures or allegations. We do know, however, that some mothers stop attendance once their child has completed his or her shorter group. Others who want to return to their husbands may find the group pressure to reject all men too hard to tolerate. It may be that by having a greater understanding of why people leave the groups we could improve our techniques to help those who may be the most vulnerable or likely to reabuse.

Paradoxically, we have come to realize that the more extensive a programme we offer, the more need we discover. Because of our limited resources we have not been able to offer groups for the adolescents over 16. We also recognize the need for multifamily groups in which many children have been abused by the same person, and for groups for parents whose children have been abused by a stranger. We would also like to introduce the idea of an initial large-group session for all the families and professionals who will be involved in attending a group or acting as an escort. There is inevitably a great deal of anxiety and some envy about what the children do in groups—

"My daughter says that they have biscuits and talk about clothes". Clearly, we do need to keep the boundaries and confidentiality between the group, but it may be that meeting other parents and professionals would start the sharing process and more clearly clarify the aims of the groups, although this is discussed in family meetings.

Several controversial issues have arisen during the course of our work and they continue to warrant consideration.

We have been perturbed by the effects in the adolescent boys' groups of a perpetrator 'victim' recounting his exploits in an excitable, detailed and lurid fashion. This raised the issue of whether such graphic accounts weren't in themselves a form of abuse. We subsequently decided that the need of victims were less well met in such mixed groups and the perpetrators are now seen separately. Fifteen to 16-year girls, who had been minimally abused, became reticent in the face of the severse abuse described by others. It was also harder for others to contribute if the group norm was abuse by a father or co-habitee and they themselves had been abused in a sex ring or their mothers had been active participants. This raises the issue of whether we should treat all the group members in the same way despite major discrepancies in their experiences.

Much of our programme is designed to help children behave more assertively in their own defence, and this may involve confrontation with adults in charge; this seems completely appropriate in the context of abuse but is also quite contradictory to the previous experience or training the average child has received. The issue raised therefore, is whether a child is able to differentiate between a benign and an inappropriate use of power; in other words will our training encourage them to generalize their assertiveness to irrelevant situations. Equally, it may be beyond the cognitive capacity of a three- to four-year-old to be able to adapt specific learning acquired in one context to another.

Straightforward factual information is given to the children in the groups, especially about physiology and sexual matters. As in schools, education in this area has been strongly resisted for years on the grounds that children should learn about such matters at home, if at all. Abused children and those at risk must be better protected but we do have to acknowledge that this may involve interfering with parents' rights to keep their children ignorant of sexual matters.

With the increase in public awareness and media coverage of sexual abuse, there is a greater demand for professional services but resources are limited. One of the difficulties experienced by team members is having to act both as case managers and group leaders. This can lead to much confusion; a case manager has a great deal of knowledge of certain families and is seen to have the power to affect decisions made by outside professionals working with these families. As a result, when the case manager is also acting as a group leader, he or she may become invested with additional 'authority' and treated with caution. The leadership partnerships may then become unbalanced and there is a danger that the case manager/leader becomes more identified with the family members already known to him/her. In addition, other group members may feel that their interests are being less well served.

To establish a truly comprehensive groupwork programme would be beyond the scope of any existing agency but it would be possible to have a network of coordinated agencies around the country dovetailing their resources. They would have to carefully consider issues such as who is responsible for working with the X. family, who has ultimate responsibility, how will decisions regarding treatment be made, who will carry out which administrative and coordinating function. It would be difficult, but it is possible.

References

1. Berliner L. and Stevens D. L. (1982) Clinical issues in child sexual abuse. In: Conte J. R. and Shope D. (eds), *Social Work and Child Sexual Abuse*. New York: Hawarth.
2. Giaretto H. (1981) A comprehensive child sexual abuse treatment programme. In: Mrazek P. and Kempe H. (eds), *Sexually Abused Children and their Families*. Oxford: Pergamon, Chap. 14.
3. Smith P.B. (1980) *Group Processes and Personal Change*. London: Harper & Row.
4. Smith P. B. (1980) *Personal Small Groups and Change*. London: Methuen.
5. Blackwell R. D. (1986) Group work. In: Maxwell H. (ed.), *An Outline of Psychotherapy for Medical Students and Practitioners*. Bristol: John Wright.
6. Oatley K. (1984) *Selves in Relation. An Introduction to Psychotherapy and Groups*. London: New Essential Psychotherapy.
7. Caillé P. (1985) Couples in Difficulties or the the Cruel Face of Janua. Presented at the Institute for Family Therapy, London.
8. Moreno J. L. (1946) *Psychodrama*. New York: Beacon House.
9. Zuelzer M. S. and Reposa R. E. (1985) Mothers in incestuous families. *International Journal of Family Therapy* 2, 93–109.
10. Gottlieb B. and Dean J. (1982) Childrens groups. In: Mrazek P.B. and Kempe H. (eds), *Sexually Abused Children and their Families*. Oxford: Pergamon.
11. Bion, W. (1961) *Experiences in Groups*. London: Tavistock.
12. Yallom I. D. (1970) *The Theory and Practice of Psychotherapy*. New York: Basic Books.

13. Alexander P. (1985) A systems theory conceptualization of incest. *Family Process* **24**, 79–88.
14. Vizard E. (1986) *Self-Esteem and Personal Safety*. London: Tavistock.
15. Lieberman S. (1979) Transgenerational analysis: the genogram as a technique in family therapy. *Journal of Family Therapy* **1**, 51–65.
16. Bentovim A. and Okell-Jones C. (1986) Sexual abuse of children: fleeting trauma or lasting disaster. In: Anthony E. J. (ed.), *Year Book of International Association of Child Psychiatry*. London: Wiley.

CHAPTER 11

Working with Substitute Carers

Anne Elton

Unfortunately, many parents of sexually abused children are unable to acknowledge appropriate responsibility for the abuse or for their failure to protect adequately. Consequently fostering, and for young children subsequent adoption, is becoming a necessary choice for many abused children. An even greater number may have to spend short-term periods in either a residential setting or in foster homes. There are, therefore, several practical issues to consider in relation to substitute carers:

1. How much information do substitute carers need about the abuse and what should they do if the child makes further disclosures?
2. *a.* What kind of contact is it helpful to make with the child? In particular, how can a contact be established which decreases the risk of subsequent abuse in (i) foster families and (ii) residential settings.
   b. How can the risk of subsequent abuse be forestalled?
3. What kind of relationship do the new carers have to the original abusive family?
4. What is a helpful relationship between the carers and other professionals?

INFORMATION NEEDED AND THE POSSIBILITY OF FURTHER DISCLOSURE

Older Children

It is never an easy task to decide on how much information about the abuse should be shared with substitute carers. In particular, it is difficult to decide on how much explicit detail of the nature of the

238

sexual abuse would be helpful. The age of the child being placed clearly makes a difference. Older children and adolescents may themselves express views on how much they would like a foster parent to be told and how much they wish left omitted. This group does have the language with which to convey further details of their new parents, should they wish to do so. Indeed, we hope that older children, once in a permanent placement, may be able to confide some details and also, equally importantly, some of their own feelings about the abuse to at least one member of the new family, probably the parent of the same sex. In general, it would seem appropriate to tell the new carers something of the nature of the abuse—whether it involved intercourse, whether it was done in the context of a gentle relationship or committed in a far more aggressive or perverse way.

Younger Children

With younger children, it may be helpful to tell the substitute carers more details since the child is less likely to be able to do so herself. It also may be important for the carers, who may, if not given reasonably full information, worry and imagine a whole range of experiences occurred although they did not. Alternatively, they may never consider one which did, for example, involvement of the child in pornographic photography, and so through ignorance fail to be appropriately sensitive to subsequent events which might trigger off memories for the child.

Obviously the reason for the new carers having specific information is so that they may be sensitized to the areas which the child or young person may subsequently find worrying, as well as facilitating any possible discussion of worries about the past which the child might wish to make. It is also important for the carer to know how much sexual experience the child has had, in order to be able to help her/him with the feelings in the same way as needs to be done in families (*see* Chapter 9).

Foster parents and substitute carers are often very uncertain about whether it is in the child's interests to allow discussion of the sexual abuse. Some may feel that it is important for any emotive issue to be fully discussed in order to avoid unhealthy inhibitions and so may feel that they ought to encourage the child to talk by consciously providing openings. Yet their own anxieties about appearing to show a prurient interest can make such encouragement awkward. Even if this is not so the child can feel under pressure, in some way a 'failure', if he or she does not wish to talk. Other carers may feel that the less said the better, that talk will only keep the abuse alive in the child's mind and they somehow cherish the hope that if there is no discussion the child may 'forget all about it'. Such feelings are likely to reflect the under-standable reluctance of the carers to hear about very painful and horrifying experiences, and are certainly likely to be communicated to the children inhibiting stress from any disclosures they might *need* to make.

Making Further Disclosures

It is not uncommon for children and young people placed in a new and caring environment to make further disclosures. This probably arises from the fact that the child feels safe, which allows him or her to reveal more of what happened in a previous home. He may of course be able to talk of his feelings about the abuse. Details of the abuse may be mentioned casually, without the child necessarily recognizing that she or he is revealing new information. This would be similar to the process in the therapeutic groups, where children may casually share the information that the abuse started when they were much younger than the age previously disclosed. Alternatively, children and young people may actually confide intentionally about a whole new area of abuse. For example, it was known that Hannah had been abused by her father but, once she settled in her foster home, she revealed that an uncle had also abused her on one occasion. Despite the fact that this possibility had been raised both individually and in family sessions, she was not able to disclose the fact until she felt settled in her new home.

Carers have to be very sensitive to new disclosures, accepting them without shock or horror, not probing anxiously and yet facilitating further discussion by saying, for example, 'Oh, did it hurt when daddy did that', while continuing to bath the child, and so indicating to the child that the adult is ready to listen to anything the child wishes to say, including things which may be upsetting or difficult. In order to allow discussion it is clearly essential that carers have an age-appropriate language for body parts and functions which they can use comfortably in non-emotive situations, therefore the child can feel confident of sharing further information if he/she wishes.

Talking about Past Experiences

Children do have very varied needs to talk about past experiences. Some, perhaps the majority, do it in occasional comments, referring to their distress or confusion. Those who feel considerable conscious anger with their original parents may often express that most forcibly and frequently, perhaps needing continuous reassurance that to feel anger does not necessarily mean being in some way unlikeable or naughty. Some younger children who have experienced the abuse as particularly traumatic may go through a phase of having to tell anyone they meet about it, often to the embarrassment and concern of their carers. While this phase may hopefully be short-lived, and while some of the more public telling, i.e., to the shop assistant, may be gently deflected or discouraged, the child may in fact be working through his pain by the retelling in the same way as children who have experienced painful medical procedures often gain relief be replaying the procedure over and over again.

In the early stages of getting to know a child it is obviously very difficult for any carer to know just what is helpful and appropriate for that particular child. In general, it seems best for the carer to be receptive to the child's spontaneous communications. This includes being sensitive to non-verbal communications as well as to explicit statements. The carer therefore has to convey to the child a genuine willingness to hear anything that this child may wish to say without intruding on the child's own needs for privacy.

DEVELOPING A STYLE OF APPROPRIATE CONTACT

Carers of abused children often need some professional guidance or opportunity to discuss physical caring. We have heard of foster fathers who are so worried about the children's possible responses that they totally refuse to participate in any physical care at all. At the other extreme there are foster or adoptive parents who deny any anxieties and in so doing may be denying the possible reality of the child having genuine anxieties and confusions. Some may be over-inhibited about ordinary rough and tumble and avoid such situations, thus depriving the child, albeit with good intention, of an important experience. Others, aware of the child's deprivation of physical contact and play, may try to compensate by a too-frequent initiation of horseplay, etc. More commonly, foster parents may be over-inhibited about ordinary physical 'fun-play' tickling, and so on.

Once aware of sexual abuse there is a tendency to experience a degree of discomfort about physical contact of any sort. What sort of contact is appropriate, what is inappropriate? We know that deprived and rejected children need affection and warmth, but what sort of contact is appropriate when these children have also been sexually abused? It is only by being aware of the traumatic nature of the betrayal of trust that it becomes possible to see that caresses which may appear to be affectionate and caring in one context, can feel like a repetition of abuse in another. Indeed, some abused children consciously avoid any physical contact, even incidental, for a long time.

Substitute parents should be aware of the issue of sexualization and recognize that inhibited provocative behaviour is a response to past traumas and not a sexual invitation. It is necessary to monitor a particular child's responses, and to be aware of what is a genuine need for comforting, and what is enacting a pattern of traumatic sexualized behaviour. These issues can only be sorted out through discussion and mutual support. It is a difficult task to remain aware of oneself, yet at the same time to maintain spontaneity. As Minuchin and Fishman[1] have described, techniques of professional actions and responses have to be practised before they become a spontaneous part of oneself.

Being able to gently discourage close physical contact and tactfully to model more modest behaviour is an important aspect of helping develop a child's social skills. Perhaps the only fairly general precept would be to suggest that male substitute carers move in to physical contact very gradually, and that initially they do so in the presence of the female carer so that the child can feel protected by being able to express any confusions they experience to the 'mother' who has actually been present during the bathing, cuddling, horseplay and so on.

Foster Families

This means that foster or adoptive fathers in the early period of contact should maintain the same rules as perpetrators do when they first return home. That is, the 'father' be prepared to take a role which is basically controlled by the mother, avoiding being alone with a child for any significant period. Thus if they are together in a room with the child the 'father' may need to withdraw or ensure that mother comes in, or that the child joins the mother. In some situations a direct statement to the child/young person is helpful. The foster father of a 14-year-old girl, recognizing her anxieties the first time they washed the dishes together, said 'Look, I'm not the sort of bloke who touches kids privates'.

This is not to imply that there is any specific risk as such, or that the foster father or adoptive father will indeed make any approach. But the problem is that a child who has been abused becomes extremely confused about issues of closeness and distance. Given the traumatic nature of the experience an ordinary approach or contact can be experienced as an abuse, even when there is no actual abuse or no inappropriate contact intended. If a foster or adoptive mother is physically present, she can reassure an anxious child that what occurred was an ordinary contact not a sexualized one. Clearly, in the early stages, foster and adoptive parents and residential staff require the protection of another adult as much as the child does.

Risk of subsequent abuse

Understandably some abuse does occur in foster and adoptive placements for complex reasons. These may relate to the sexualization of the child, to the activation of latent sexual problems within the family, or to an individual carer being sexually aroused by the child's sexualization. In such situations the carers perceive the child's behaviour as a sexual invitation rather than a learnt response to past traumas. Their own personal needs or desires then impel them to relate sexaully to the child.

A child may initiate a great deal of horseplay because he or she is accustomed to it and enjoys it. However, she/he may also see it as a prelude to more specific sexual contact. The child may be confused with both kinds of touch or be confused about which is really desired. Therefore, the assessment of families who are going to foster or adopt should focus specifically on areas which are known to be associated with sexual abuse; for instance, previous family histories of sexual abuse, major sexual difficulties in the marriage, severe inhibition in talking of sexual matters, or couples who avoid conflict and use outsiders or their children in order to maintain a united front.

There will inevitably be periods of testing out, including around the new carers expectations and responses to sexualized behaviour. Foster and adoptive parents and residential workers have to be able to develop clear rules in terms of being able to say no, to maintain appropriate distances and to be aware that sexualization has to do with confusion about who is responsible—the child or the adult. If an adult responds appropriately to sexual action of the child, it confirms for the child that it is the *adult's* responsibility to define limits, not her's. But if reabuse occurs, traumatic responses are maintained. Foster or adoptive parents need to expect approaches from children, to be aware of their true nature, and to be prepared to deal firmly and to have rules so that no one is put at risk. The relief for the child or young person whose inappropriate sexual role is not confirmed is considerable, and the sense of freedom and ability to be able to grow, gratifying. Sexualized behaviour can diminish and modesty grow with appropriate encouragement.

Dealing with childrens' sexual responses to other children, helping 'normal' sexuality to develop during adolescence, coping with mixed feelings towards the natural parents, developing compassionate and not only critical attitudes, are all part of the fostering and adoption task.

Case example

The foster parents of Tanya and Mary, aged nine and seven, observed how the children would put their minimal nightdresses on early, then dance around displaying their naked genital areas. They had been afraid of saying anything for fear of making the children feel an inappropriate degree of guilt. The foster father had dealt with the situation by leaving the room, the foster mother by silence. They discussed how they thought they would have dealt with a similar situation with their own children (now grown up). They were able to develop a very matter of fact style of comment, e.g. simply telling the girls not to 'play like that now you are undressed or down here where there are people about'.

Foster parents may also have to deal with markedly over-anxious, inhibited behaviour which may not match their family style. Young children may be extremely anxious about any physical contact after bathing, although this might be normal for a child of that age. The foster parent may have to stand back in a 'let me see how well you can do it for yourself stance' only moving in if there is a need related to an important matter of hygiene. Older children are able to be more self-centred and private.

Case example
Ely aged 12 always did all her undressing/dressing in the privacy of the bathroom to the surprise of her 11- and 8-year-old foster sisters, although they shared a room with her. The foster mother had to explain her sensitivity to them without giving away any confidences.

There are times when foster parents have to intervene such as when a child makes remarks about the abuse.

Case example
Jane aged four became extremely upset during a game of 'sleeping lions' at a childrens' party; the game obviously reactivated memories of an abusive incident. Her foster mother not only had to calm Jane down but also give some kind of explanation to the host adult who had heard some of Jane's comments.

Mary aged three years six months, told a foster brother that her father had done rude things to her, touching her private parts with his willy. The boy was puzzled and went to his mother saying, "it isn't true that Mary's daddy did that, is it?" The foster mother had to deal with both children's distress.

Perhaps one of the greatest fears which foster parents have is that a sexually abused child will talk a lot in detail to their own children, not only upsetting them but also making them fearful of their own fathers, or of other men. Even worse is the fear, unfortunately not always unfounded, that the abused child will induct their children into unusual and inappropriate sexual play.

Case example
Barbara aged eight was first found to have been sexually as well as physically abused when her foster mother found her trying to suck the foster brother's penis in the bath. It then transpired that various male friends of the natural

mother had abused Barbara. Unfortunately the foster mother was unable to tolerate her anxieties about Barbara's possible future behaviour and a new placement had to be found.

Residential Settings

Sexual abuse is now being acknowledged as a major problem of a betrayal of trust, not just in families but also in settings providing care, education and recreation for children. A series of disclosures involving teachers, youth workers or residential workers indicates that children can be at risk of abuse in the very context which is supposed to be caring, protecting or educating them. This is of even greater concern when children have already been abused in their own family context, with a danger of reabuse through sexualization.

It is not surprising that some people choosing to work with children, albeit a small majority, have latent sexual difficulties. These may lead to abusive responses being triggered by the work itself. Children who are vulnerable and needy may well demonstrate their need for closeness. This in turn is misinterpreted as the responses of a sexually sophisticated child and the sexually abusive pattern is continued as in a family context. The problems of disclosure in residential settings are the same as in families. There may well be very high degrees of secrecy, knowing yet denying a fear of the explosion and damage to a career if the fact is revealed or if there is a suspicion.

Education for residental staff

The need for a thorough educational programme for people in residential work is essential to understand the way patterns of sexual abuse can be recreated in any residential context, whatever its origin. Staff support groups are needed to be able to discuss such issues. There can be considerable confusion about the issue of sexuality within residential contexts, especially where sexually active adolescents and young people are living. In some settings the age difference between the young staff and older residents may be very little. This contributes an added confusion and stress for staff, working with clients who could, in another situation, be perceived as possible legitimate sexual partners.

Young people may have found sexual activity to be a way of dealing with their own loneliness or isolation. A permissive or restrictive view of sexuality by staff members can affect the atmosphere of residential settings in the same way that such views affect families. These may represent a combination of philosophical ideas as well as the personal views of the individuals in control.

A child or young person who has been sexually abused needs a setting which provides safety, security and protection, and not a confirmation of a sexualization which can only maintain traumatic responses. He or she will test the responses of both adults and children. As in families, there is a need to follow similar rules in terms of establishing the boundaries of physical proximity and closeness for male workers, and for them to avoid being alone with the child without the presence of protective others. The choice of staff to be key workers, especially the gender, needs to be made carefully in relationship to the particular child, and may depend on whether he or she is showing a promiscuous pattern of responses, or a frozen angry response.

Allegations against staff members

If allegations are made against staff members, they have to be investigated fully, and a sexual abuse therapeutic team linked with police and social workers may be able to look at the whole context and understand what has contributed to the allegation and how to help. If the allegations are founded then the staff member concerned has to be treated as any other perpetrator. Allegations, however, may also be made without definite foundations.

When allegations are made it is easy for staff to fall into the trap of secrecy, protection and avoidance of conflict between members by focusing anger on the external world, on authority—the hierarchy or management. However, the crucial issue is that a child has experienced trauma, even if there has been no abusive intention or abusive action shown. It becomes essential for a worker against whom an allegation has been made to be able to acknowledge clearly to the person who has felt abused, and that this is an authentic feeling. If the worker created this feeling, this is his responsibility even if he had no abusive intention. However, these issues need to be talked about since if the child is confused about what constitutes appropriate ordinary physical contact and affection, and what is sexual contact which is abusive, then he needs some help. The role of groups for staff in helping members to talk about what is appropriate or inappropriate, how to manage physical relationships, how to adopt a role which is not unconsciously sexualizing and provoking, is essential in these situations as part of a general educational approach. Similarly, the workers need to be able to think about their own sexuality and to become aware of the sort of contacts that are made both consciously and unconsciously.

RELATIONSHIP WITH ORIGINAL FAMILIES

There are problems for residential staff and foster families in relating to the parents of the abused child. Feelings of anger, disgust and hostility described previously can be even more profound in residential staff and foster parents who live with the children. It is easy to become identified with their pain and distress. Carers can feel enraged with the parent who abuses, and equally so with the parent who was not aware that the abuse was taking place. The abusing parents themselves may maintain their denial of responsibility by undermining and attacking residential workers and foster families. They may even allege that children are being abused in their new homes. Secret coalitions may be made with residential staff against social workers or therapeutic teams, and attempts made to separate children from their new parental figures. This may be a repeat of family patterns inducting new people into the familiar game.

Even when new families overcome their strong negative feelings towards the original parents, they do have to absorb something of the original family patterns as all fostering families have to do. They may have to be involved in joint work with the professionals and the natural family and they should look for positives within that family and find ways of accepting very different styles of family life without necessarily being critical. When a child has clearly been hurt by a particular pattern of family behaviour, it is all too easy for a new family to assume that their style must be in some way be 'better', especially as it has not led to abuse.

Maintaining Original Dysfunctional Patterns

Even when there is no conceivable chance of the child or young person being reabused sexually within the new family, there are risks of the child maintaining ways of relating which are dysfunctional. Those children who have had a protective role in their own families—they have been used to defuse parental conflict, or have had to provide care for their parents—bring such roles with them into their new family. If they are not given any opportunity to protect they may feel a total loss of identity; yet the new carers have to achieve a delicate balance between allowing for the child to give some care, while also providing them with the appropriate opportunity to be dependent.

We have already discussed the various problems that abused children and young people have with individuation. In some ways, placement in a new family of itself may exacerbate this difficulty, since the child is not really in a position to make a choice. More significantly the new family may have—indeed ideally should have—some very different interactive patterns from the original abusive family. Most notably these families are likely to be selected because of their openness, in distinction to their secrecy. Since children are likely to want to please care-takers to whom they become attached, (e.g., Lindsay[2]) they may struggle to fit into family patterns which are unfamiliar and which are not natural to them; if they cannot do this 'in exactly the right way' they may again feel failures, even if their new family does not make that judgement. Whatever the situation, the child may be trying to fit in with someone else's pattern rather than feeling free to discover their own.

Case example
Hannah found a conflict over expression of anger and distress in her new family. In her own family, all feelings of anger were rigorously denied open expression. In her foster family there was a fairly volatile style of interchange and of sharing of feelings, including negative ones. Following a family meeting including the original family and the foster mother when the natural family's total incapacity to admit anger became apparent, Hannah became quite distressed for several days and confided in her foster mother that she "didn't know why she couldn't feel angry with her father". At the next meeting her foster mother, genuinely trying to help kept telling Hannah to share her feelings openly with her at home saying "Mary and Charlotte (the foster sisters) do it".

It became clear to the professionals that she was unwittingly putting pressure on Hannah "to be like us" and so not allowing for Hannah's individual needs. This became even clearer when the workers suggested some compromise: "Do you think that it might be helpful for Hannah to tell you privately first what she is upset about, when that happens".
Foster mother: "But that is not the way it happens in our family, that's asking our family to change. I'd be doing something different for Hannah to what I do for my own girls."
Therapist: "You haven't had Hannah in your family till now." and to Hannah: "I have a feeling that it's very difficult for you to find out what is your personal way of dealing with anger, and you don't know whether to be an X. (original family) or a Y.?"

Following this, the foster mother was able to appreciate the pressure that Hannah was feeling and to acknowledge the need to compromise. In doing that, she also discovered that Hannah was able to express her anger, albeit in a manner which the foster mother disliked, but at least this enlightenment meant she no longer needed to worry that it was 'all bottled up inside'.

RELATIONSHIP TO PROFESSIONALS, THERAPEUTIC WORK

While many foster and adoptive families may value and wish for some continued professional input to try and ensure a smooth and satisfactory placement, there are others, in particular adoptive families, who may not want professionals to remain involved. It is natural for families who have reared their own children satisfactorily to wish to retain a similar degree of independence in relation to an adopted child. Foster families do expect, and usually wish for, continued social work contact, but may not be keen on involving their own children in family meetings. Yet there are times when it is very much in the interests of the abused child, and of the placement going well, to have some joint discussion, or at least for the new family to have some direct knowledge of the personnel or agencies other than the key social worker who have been meaningful in the fostered child's recent life. The child/young person may make it clear that they so wish.

Linking Therapeutic Work with Care-taking

One way of doing this is to have a fairly neutral meeting in the thera-peutic agency with the professionals whom the child wants her new family to meet. This would not be with the purpose of sharing any very personal information with the new family, but more as a way of allowing the child or young person to introduce new family members to professionals who have had a part to play in her other life. In doing this, the door is opened to the natural possibility of the child or young person subsequently sharing with new family members something of her past experiences and also facilitating any possible new referral should such an event be felt helpful.

Case example
Hannah at 13 wanted her family group worker to meet her new family; this comprised a foster mother and three daughters, aged 18, 15 and 12. Hannah knew that her foster mother knew about the sexual abuse, but that no one else in the family did, although she thought that she would like the girls, especially the 18-year-old, to know sometime. A meeting was arranged with the family group worker, with the explicit understanding that there was no intention on the worker's part of breaching confidence and sharing any information at all; the girls already knew that Hannah attended the hospital. Before the day of the meeting Hannah herself chose to confide in the 18-year-old the reason for her removal from home, although the worker did not actually know this until later.

Attendance at a therapeutic group may place a particular strain on substitute carers. The aim of the group is to help the child or young person to be in touch with the traumatic experiences that they have had and to work through them. The distress and anger often released in a group session may inevitably spill over beyond the group. It may, therefore, often seem a burden to have to escort a child to a group and to contain his or her feelings afterwards. There may be some acting out subsequently at home, and the foster parents or professional bringing the child may not be aware of the details of the group activity which sparked off the distress. They may be aware in principle of the need to express painful feelings about the abusing family and the value of this in terms of working through the traumatic experiences, but they actually have to contain the child and cope with the behaviour. At times this can produce real conflicts between the therapeutic team and the caring parent; these need resolution and expression of healthy differences of opinion. It can help the child or young person considerably if such conflicts can be aired openly in family and professional network meetings rather than being hidden. In this way, the child experiences open conflict resolution rather than a collusive pattern of denying differences.

Case example
Doreen's residential worker and social worker were rather worried at Doreen's sexualized advances to boys in her home. These increased in the early stages of the group. Discussion of the activities in the group, in particular exercises around self-assertion, helped them to see that Doreen was probably actually testing out in 'safe' situations, i.e., with little boys. The care workers continued helping Doreen achieve appropriate peer group behaviour. Towards the end of the group they reported that Doreen was behaving much less provocatively. Although they were still concerned at her occasional 'corridor cuddling', they were also aware that overall she was now disinclined to spend any significant time alone with a 15-year-old boy who made appropriate overtures to her. In this she was demonstrating her anxiety about any potentially close heterosexual relationship.

Although foster parents may find the child's responses to the groups distressing or puzzling at times, they do also frequently feel the benefits. Foster parents, residential carers and escorting social workers may often report a considerable increase of openness in the child's communications to them, which they feel amply reward them for the difficult task.

Case example
Jane's foster mother was very puzzled by reports of 'screaming' in the group. However, when this was explained she was able to link it very particularly to a comment from her Jane: "If I saw him (her abusing stepfather) in the street and he spoke to me I'd tell him he was a pig and cross the road". The foster mother perceived this as a much more adult response from Jane than her previous half-frozen but angry fear.

If children/young people in new families or residential settings are to gain the fullest possible benefit from attending groups, it is essential that there are reasonably regular meetings between their carers, social workers and some member of the treatment team. In these meetings issues about the treatment can be raised, as well as any other concerns from carers or child about new or old relationships, contact with the family, and so on.

It may also be very helpful if the foster parents and workers can attend a group for carers parallel to the group for the child victims. In this way they are made more acquainted with the work going on with the children. More importantly, however, they should participate in self-help groups for themselves, sharing issues and concerns arising from their own experience with the children in their care. Such self-help groups also exist in some local areas, quite independently of treatment groups for the children.

References

1. Minuchin S. and Fishman C. (1984) *Techniques of Family Therapy*. Harvard: Harvard University Press.
2. Lindsay C. (1985) Consultations with professional and family systems in the context of residential and fostering services. In: Campbell D. and Draper R. (eds), *Applications of Systemic Family Therapy*. London: Grune & Stratton.

CHAPTER 12

The Results of Treatment

Arnon Bentovim, Annemarie van Elburg
and Paula Boston

INTRODUCTION

The aims of treatment can be summarized as follows:

1. To limit the physical/emotional damage to the child and improve the child's emotional functioning. This goal is accomplished by helping children understand what has happened to them and teaching them skills to prevent recurrence, and also work to assist the child to deal with traumatic experiences.
2. To ensure that children are living in a context where they are protected from further abuse. This is achieved by ascertaining the family's capacity for child care within a legal framework, strengthening their abilities to protect and providing alternative care if necessary.
3. To make significant changes in the family structure which contributed to the sexual abuse of a child, by working on marital and family relationships to improve the functioning of all members of the family, so that the child can be fully integrated into the family if possible.

EFFECTS OF INTERVENTION

Literature Survey

There are many questions which remain unanswered about the effect of intervention in child sexual abuse. Our approach is in accord with the CIBA Foundation's report[1]—once a professional has made a diagnosis of child sexual abuse, then a child-care issue is involved and perpetrator and victim should be separated. This can either be achieved voluntarily or the arrangement may need to be enforced legally. The assumption is also made that sexual abuse predisposes the victim to psychological damage which can only be remedied by the provision of a different environment with some form of psychological treatment.

The assumption that psychological damage itself occurs has been a contentious issue. However, a review of the literature[1,2] has indicated that when different studies are reviewed, deleterious effects are noted. This is particularly the case if sexual abuse is extensive, lasts over a significant period of time, and is a highly secret act which occurs at significant phases of a child's development.

There are consequences of professional intervention. It is unclear which interventions are most helpful and least damaging. For instance, it is not known whether imprisonment of an incestuous father is the best course to prevent recurrence of incest and provide psychological relief for mother and daughter. Alternatively, as a result of the father's imprisonment, the victim may experience further anguish and guilt over the loss of a parental figure and the family suffer loss and impoverishment. In addition, we do not know whether the economic consequences of losing one parent are likely to produce even greater distress for the remaining parent. Do households reorganize with the rapid incorporation of another adult? Are professionals needed to fill a void with supervision, therapy and financial support? If a child has experienced incest, is the best response to search for an alternative family or other residential placement, or should an intensive effort be made to rehabilitate the original family? Thus fundamental questions need to be asked.

1. Can incest be stopped?
2. Can the family survive in a helpful way?
3. What are the long-term helpful or detrimental effects on both the victim and other family members of rehabilitation or of a child having to be placed in a new family?

Kroth[3] has stated that there is currently no scientific basis to decide whether any one approach is better than any other in dealing with incest offenders, victims and their families.

Review of Specific Issues—Stopping Sexual Abuse

Kroth has commented on the generally low rate of reoffending reported in most studies. An alternative explanation is that incest offenders are unreliable in reporting data and that the true statistics would be higher. Soothill and Gibbons,[4] and Gibbons and Prince,[5] long-term follow-up of incest cases showed 13 per cent of fathers had committed sexual offences before conviction for incest and few (3 per cent) were convicted of sexual offences following. Other sexual offenders i.e., other sexual offences within the family and outside resulted in a 10 per cent reconviction over 16 years, 29 per cent over 25 years.

One explanation for this data is that perpetrators may become more skilful at manipulating the system from previous experience. However, one can assume that in cases where the family break up and perpetrator and victim are not living together, the chance of re-enactment is substantially reduced. However, in our own clinical experience there is the possibility that the perpetrator persuades his family to allow him to return or he may find a new family with similar needs to the old family. Abuse will then recur. This seems more likely when there is a failure to provide adequate treatment. De Francis[6] reported that in 51 out of 68 cases the offender left the household subsequent to the disclosure. Professionals may well feel that with the separation of the family or a period of imprisonment or separation, the child will be helped. This ignores the fact that in a population with a very high divorce rate, there are many single people, both men and women, looking for partners. One of the main dynamic factors related to sexual abuse is then brought into play, the adult's need for a partner, over and above the parental need to protect children.

Break-up of the Family and the Effect of Treatment

Maisch[7] reported on 96 cases of incest in which the offender and the non-offending parent were married. Following disclosure, 47 per cent chose to keep the marriage together. Many thus choose to separate or divorce, since the experience of betrayal and let down is powerful and consequent distrust very high.

Kroth[3] carried out an interesting review of the Giaretto project in Santa Clara County, California. Instead of following a population through the treatment cycle, he examined people in the early, middle and later phases of treatment. The Giaretto project, which has provided us with a helpful model, relies on a mixture of individual and marital counselling in the context of a variety of different self-help groups which gradually attempt to deal with the various major inter-actional problems described. Kroth reported that only 30 per cent of the clients were sure about staying together when they started treatment. At the end of treatment, 71 per cent were quite sure about staying together. Kroth's research points to a very major change in attitude within the families over the period of work, with a far greater commitment to protection of children. Giaretto[8] claims that 90 per cent of the families who had been in treatment for a minimum of 10 hours of therapy were reunited, with extremely low rates of recurrence.

These findings are startlingly different to other treatment projects (e.g., that of Sgroi[9]), and need replicating. It may well be that other treatment approaches are not so far-ranging; there is also the possibility that perpetrators choose diversions, such as treatment, instead of prosecution and prison. Other workers, for example, Berliner and Stevens,[10] have not been so optimistic about the effects of treatment. They have advocated a separation of as long as two years for the perpetrator, with a demand that he become involved in intensive treatment in his own right while the children and mother have group help. When fewer fathers are treated directly[9] there was a far higher degree of marital breakdown and family separation than reported by the Giaretto project.

Emotional Cost to the Victim of Sexual Abuse

The Kroth[3] study indicates that a marked improvement in family functioning and attitude to abuse occurs, but does not report on individual follow-up and observation of children's and young people's emotional responses. There are a variety of studies of the effects of sexual abuse. Kilpatrick et al.[11] reported that immediately following the event there was a profound distortion of mood and disruption of general psychological functioning, but these problems settled within six months, although some earlier studies found no adjustment problems a year after disclosure[5,12,13] the work reviewed by Finkelhor[2] indicates the accumulating evidence of short-term and longer effects. Such responses depend on the extent and length of abuse, and factors connected with the abuse, for example, use of violence, secrecy and threat.

Is there any evidence about which treatment would be useful to the victim? Katan[14] found that even non-incestuous rape led victims to retain intensely ambivalent feelings towards their parents in adulthood. This supports the idea that the resolution of feelings with family members may be even more important in incest. Reports of cases indicate that group therapy may be helpful, and the Giaretto project[8] does appear to indicate that self-help groups guided by professionals are successful.[3] We were interested to follow up our own approach, which combines family and groupwork, to test these issues about the effectiveness of intervention further.

THE EFFECTIVENESS OF THE
GREAT ORMOND STREET PROJECT

To assess fully the impact of treatment requires systematic prospective examination of children and families and their responses to a standardized treatment process. The clinical experience reported in this book is based on the development of a treatment project which incorporated a number of elements found to be helpful in other approaches, for example, the Giaretto model of working with children and parents' groups, and also a number of elements of standard family therapeutic approaches to treatment of children and families.

Information Gathered

We were able to obtain systematic information on aspects of individual and family functioning (*see* Chapter 2), and so could review outcome of our approach to some extent. As the treatment programme was being established a full range of treatment was not available for all families, and legal and child-care approaches varied from family to family as there were so many different referral agencies.

To give some indication of the effects of intervention we carried out a follow-up study on 120 families. They were referred between 1981 and 1984 and followed up in 1986. In the 120 families there were 180 victims and 226 siblings. The majority of referral agencies were concerned to get help so as to reduce further risk to the child and to know how best to plan the child's future—return to a family or a new family?

Because the treatment project has always taken the view that child protection was a primary issue, it was inevitable that the principal source of referral would be a social services department (78 per cent). In 40 per cent of cases a charge had been made against the suspected perpetrator(s). Request was then made for assessment and treatment of either children, parents or the whole family. About a fifth (22 per cent) of the cases were referred because of suspicion due to various symptoms, and a request was made for diagnostic services, there was then the issue of what sort of legal context was appropriate and what sort of action or treatment would be best.

The treatment project was able to offer 87 per cent of the families some form of treatment. A small percentage of cases were dealt with by offering ongoing consultation to professionals and a few families were referred elsewhere. Inevitably, in the early stages of the development of a treatment project, there is considerable enthusiam and a desire to test treatment processes by offering to work with a wide variety of families. After some years, it becomes possible after a fuller range of treatment to evaluate which families are more likely to respond to a particular treatment programme.

The follow-up study was carried out in 1986 on cases referred initially between 1981 (the beginning of the project) and 1984. It therefore represented a follow-up of between two and five years. Inevitably, this unevenness of follow-up means results have to be interpreted with much caution since they represent both short-term and some longer-term follow-up observations. The follow-up was carried out through examination of case notes, interviews with the social worker who had an ongoing commitment to the family and professionals who worked with the family in the treatment project. In addition, a questionnaire covering similar ground was given to family members to complete. Although analysis of this information is still not completed, there are some findings which are relevant and which can be reported.

We were interested to know what happened to children and families after treatment and whether any of the interventions were effective in terms of improvements in emotional health and prevention of reabuse in children and facilitation of family change. We were concerned also to know whether the intervention given in the hospital had helped the social worker and community agencies provide an effective service. The specific outcomes are outlined below:

1. Specific questions about reabuse and emotional status of both victims and sibs.
2. The perspectives of the outcome of the case for the treating professional, the social worker in the community and the family.
3. What happened to each household member, for example, where they lived, marital state, etc.
4. Changes in the family.

Treatments Offered

One of the difficulties in following up the early cases of the treatment project is that the treatment model itself was in the process of evolution, so that in the early phases there were limited numbers of treatment groups available for young people and their parents. Subsequently, a range of family meetings with professionals and groups for children of all ages and parents has evolved. Therefore, the follow-up is of families who have had a variable amount of intervention (but less intensive intervention than is presently available).

Specific courses of treatment completed

Just under half the 120 families (46 per cent) completed a course of treatment, and a further third (36 per cent) attended some sessions.

About half the victims completed children's groups (47 per cent) and a further quarter (27 per cent) attended some group meetings. Ten per cent had some form of individual treatment. Twelve (10 per cent) couples out of 120 attended parents' groups and 35 (29 per cent) attended mothers' and fathers' groups (23 mothers, 12 fathers). During the early developments of our clinical skills and treatment structures, a number of children and parents did not accept treatment or dropped out. The clinical impression gained during this period was that the stronger the mandate for treatment, with legal sanctions and care orders, the easier it was to persuade families to commit themselves and become involved with the treatment process. Although concern has been expressed about the value of treatment attended involuntarily, our clinical impression does not support this concern. Once families are embedded in the treatment process of group and family work they become well-motivated and loyal to others.

Changes achieved through intervention

When we asked the community professionals about their impressions on whether children and parents had benefited from treatment, they tended to be more enthusiastic than the therapists themselves. It may well be that those involved directly in the treatment find it more difficult to see the longer-term benefits, alternatively other professionals may be grateful that the burdens of these very difficult cases are shared and therefore see the process in a more positive light. These are issues which clearly need further exploration and systematic evaluation. When we asked the families' social workers to rate the overall situation of the victims and their siblings, they noted a significant amount of improvement in the victim's situation compared to siblings.

Table 12.1 shows the improvement rate as far as the overall situation was according to the social workers. We have already noted that siblings of victims were very often far less disturbed than the victims

Table 12.1. Overall situations of victims and siblings (according to social worker)

Situation	Victims		Siblings	
	No.	*%*	*No.*	*%*
Improved	110	61	57	25
Remained the same	43	24	133	59
Situation became worse	18	10	13	6
Not known	9	5	23	10
Total	180	100	226	100

themselves, so that the fact that 59 per cent remained the same does not in fact mean that they continued in an overall worse situation.

As a corollary of the social worker's assessment of the overall situation of the victims/siblings, we made an assessment of the involvement of the social services worker with the child and family.

Table 12.2 shows that for at least three-quarters of the cases, we felt that there was strong support and good communication between the professional network locally and with the treatment agency. A smaller

Table 12.2. Ratings of involvement of social services with sexually abused children at follow-up

	Children	
Involvement of social services	*No.*	*%*
No support/disagreement	3	3
Support not sufficient	16	13
Support sufficient	89	74
Communication failure with Great Ormond Street	6	5
Not applicable	6	5
Total	120	100

percentage of cases we rated as having insufficient support from social services, or no support. In 13 per cent of cases we found that local support seemed to be sufficient but there had been a communication failure between the treatment agency and the agencies locally. Communication issues are important to attend to, as the success of a treatment project depends on the support of community agencies.

It would be interesting to know whether participation in a treatment project helps victims directly, and because community professionals are seen as integral members of the treatment team, also helps to 'cement' the attachment between child, family and social worker.

Changes in the Family

Description of families at follow-up

Is the improvement perceived by social workers achieved through rehabilitation of children to their families, or to family separation, or to placement in a new family?

Tables 12.3–12.5 describe the family at follow-up. Again, it should be noted that the length of follow-up varies between two and six years, so that some of these families are still in the process of change. It is striking that only in 22 per cent of cases is the household the same as it was at the time of the referral. An examination of marital status shows that 47 per cent of families maintained the same status, but there is a considerable degree of separation and divorce in 50 per cent of families. However, it should be noted that a number of parents re-marry or get married when they had been cohabiting prior to the

Table 12.3. Household membership status since the time of intake

Household membership status	No.	%
Stayed the same	27	23
Changed	92	76
Not known	1	1
Total	120	100

Table 12.4. Marital status at follow-up

Marital status	No.	%
Stayed the same	56	47
Has changed*	60	50
Not known	4	3
Total	120	100

* Reflects only a change from intake. For example, a divorced parent who had not remarried would have been categorized as staying the same.

Table 12.5. Marital status after intake

Marital status change	No.	%
Separated	22	18
Filed for divorce	5	4
Divorced	31	26
Married to perpetrator	4	3
Not applicable	58	47
Total	120	100

abusive event, as an expression of solidarity. It was shown earlier in Chapter 2 that these households had been together for quite con-siderable periods of time in many cases. Further analysis would be necessary to know whether discovery of the abusive event, management (e.g., imprisonment, care proceedings or treatment) or earlier factors played a part in decisions about staying together or separating. In about a quarter of families either one or both partners have made a new relationship.

An examination of what happened to the children (*Table* 12.6) shows that although a third of the siblings are with both their parents,

Table 12.6.   What happened to the children?

Fate of children	Victims		Siblings	
	No.	%	No.	%
With both parents	25	14	76	34
With mother only	59	33	74	33
With father only	9	5	11	5
With relatives only	2	1	2	1
With foster parents	18	10	14	6
Shared	31	17	7	3
Independent	36	20	42	18
Total	180	100	226	100

only 14 per cent of victims are with both their parents. Another third of both victims and siblings are with their mother only and a small percentage with father only. These are cases where abuse was by another family member. Ten per cent of the victims and 6 per cent of the siblings are with foster parents and another 17 per cent of victims and 3 per cent of siblings are placed in other contexts such as residential homes or other residential establishments. Twenty per cent of victims and 19 per cent of siblings are now independent. This reflects the age structure of the population of children and the length of follow-up.

Of the perpetrators, the largest number were at home, 43 per cent (27 per cent had remained at home and 15 per cent had spent time in prison before returning home; *Table 12.7*).

Table 12.7.   What happened to the perpetrator?

Fate of perpetrator	No.	%
Remained at home	32	27
Left home	21	18
Has been imprisoned	5	4
In prison—returned home	18	15
In prison—not returned home	22	19
In other institution	4	3
Not applicable	17	14
Not known	1	1
Total	120	100

Household Consensus on whether Abuse had Occurred

One interesting issue which we wished to explore was whether the household had believed that abuse had occurred (*Table* 12.8). When we looked at the situation at intake (274 families, *see* Chapter 2), we noted that in less than half of the families referred (43 per cent) was

Table 12.8. Household consensus about the issue of child sexual abuse

Consensus on occurrence of CSA	At referral		At follow-up	
	No.	%	No.	%
CSA occurred	117	43	76	63
CSA has not occurred	32	12	19	16
The household is divided on the incident	74	27	24	20
Not known	51	19	1	1
Total	274	100	120	100

there a consensus between all family members that abuse had occurred. A smaller percentage (12 per cent) had a consensus that abuse had not occurred and there was division between family members in a quarter of the cases. Unfortunately, there were a large number of cases not known (19 per cent), so that it is hard to be firm about interpreting these figures. However, clinically the issue of acceptance of abuse and the occurrence of abuse is one of the key issues in knowing whether to offer families treatment. On follow-up of 120 families there seemed to be a change in that 63 per cent of the household held a consensus that abuse had occurred, whereas 16 per cent had a consensus that abuse had not occurred and 20 per cent were divided.

Therefore, one of the effects of the joint work between community agencies and the treatment team is to ensure that the child is in a context where he is believed and where there is a consistent view held by all members of the household. It would also mean that where the perpetrator is a household member he is agreeing and has accepted the fact that abuse has occurred. Perhaps to explore this it is necessary to ask the question—does the perpetrator himself admit that abuse had occurred? At follow-up it appeared that only 29 per cent of the perpetrators admitted abuse and 69 per cent denied (2 per cent unknown). This contrast between household consensus that abuse had occurred and denial by perpetrators may well account for the pattern of the relatively large number of perpetrators at home (43 per cent), and the small number of children (14 per cent) rehabilitated to both parents. This factor also affects who is offered and accepts treatment, which families can be rehabilitated, which parents remain together and which children need new families.

It may well be that in a system which requires legal action, together with a child-care focus, denial by perpetrators and parents putting their own relationships before their childrens' needs, may well act as obstructions to the possibilities of treatment. In the USA where plea-bargaining is possible (e.g., the Giaretto project), it would be interesting to know whether treatment is chosen rather than prosecution and thus more families can be included in treatment, and more families can achieve rehabilitation. There may be great fears of the consequences of being 'open' and acknowledging abuse, strong denials may be made to avoid prosecution, subsequent imprisonment or the removal of children.

What Happens to the Perpetrator?

Table 12.9 shows that despite the fact that there was such a low rate of admission of abuse in the early phases of our project from 1981 to 1983,

Table 12.9.   Perpetrator response at follow-up

	Raw	%
Had abuse been admitted		
Yes	35	29
No	83	69
Not known	2	2
Total	120	100
Was there a trial		
Yes	73	61
Waiting	2	2
Not applicable	44	37
Total	120	100
Outcome of trial		
(73 perpetrators who were sent for trial)		
Acquitted	6	8
Probation	7	10
Suspended sentence	10	14
Treatment ordered	1	1
Prison sentence	48	66
Not known	1	1
Total	73	100
Prison sentence		
(48 perpetrators who received a sentence)		
Less than 1 year	4	8
1–2 years	20	42
3–5 years	15	31
Greater than 5 years	4	8
Not known	5	10
Total	48	100

61 per cent of perpetrators did go on trial, and of these 66 per cent received a prison sentence. There was a far lower percentage of probation orders and suspended sentences, and only 1 per cent had some form of treatment order. Thus during the early phase of the treatment project, a therapeutic option—probation orders with treatment—was not used very much. Our figures however may well reflect the degree of failure by the perpetrators to take responsibility for abuse, resulting in a more negative response by the courts; it will be noted that 8 per cent were acquitted. Prison sentences ranged between one and five years. It would be interesting to repeat this follow-up on a more recently referred population, to determine whether the percentage remains the same as for this earlier referred group; our impression is that there is even more denial currently.

Children's Responses at Follow-up

We were interested to find out whether there had been any change in the sexualization and the problems of children. *Table 12.10* shows the degree of sexualization and emotional problems for the group seen at

Table 12.10. Problems with children at follow-up

Problem	Victims		Siblings	
	No.	*%*	*No.*	*%*
Sexualized behaviour				
No evidence	131	73	196	87
Moderate evidence	34	19	—	—
Marked evidence	4	2	1	—
Not known	11	6	29	13
Total	180	100	226	100
Other emotional disturbance				
No evidence	78	43	132	58
Moderate evidence	72	40	45	20
Marked evidence	16	9	17	8
Not known	14	8	32	14
Total	180	100	226	100

follow-up, comparing victims and siblings. It will be noted that only 20 per cent of the abused children showed sexualized behaviour compared to 36 per cent of the children at intake (*see* Chapter 2), and that 48 per cent showed other emotional problems compared to 69 per cent at intake (*see* Chapter 2). This does represent a continuing degree of disturbance, and further work would be necessary to determine whether there has been significant amelioration or whether the level of disturbance remaining is to be expected in relation to other social and family factors. Siblings are less disturbed and show less sexualized behaviour at follow-up, but the contrast is not as great as at referral (*see* Chapter 2).

Recurrence of Sexual Abuse

An important issue is the question of recurrence of child sexual abuse (*Table 12.11*) At follow-up we had evidence of recurrence in 16 per cent of children, the possibility of abuse in a further 15 per cent and no

Table 12.11. Has sexual abuse recurred on follow-up?

Occurrence of sexual abuse	No.	%
Yes	19	16
Not clear	18	15
No	83	69
Total	120	100

recurrence in about 69 per cent. It is of course difficult to know how to interpret these recurrence rates, since professional awareness of any reabuse is itself an important goal. We have a clinical impression that a number of children were able to be absolutely explicit and clear in speaking to a professional when abuse recurred and did not allow abuse to continue.

Further analysis and research is necessary to show which factors prevent reabuse, for example, treatment and imprisonment, and which factors influence the possibility of reabuse.

At follow-up professionals considered the risk for more abuse to be high for 7 per cent of the victims, and moderate for about 25 per cent. Therefore, although intervention of various kind can ameliorate the situation it certainly cannot remove the risks, and certain of the children were felt to be at risk not just within their own families but in new family contexts because of sexualized behaviour which had become part of their repertoire when relating to others. The assessment of particular approaches to reducing these risks is a further important task.

Family Change

To assess family change systematically would require the use of a standardized instrument of assessment. We were interested, however, to find out in a clinical sense whether the family context in which the children were living had changed. We hoped to find out, for example, whether other children had been abused in the family, whether the relationships had improved or worsened, whether there were depressive states or illness, whether there were changes that were perhaps 'structural' in the sense of parents separating, the presence of a new partner, or new family for the child which would ensure that the child was no longer at risk. Was there some degree of genuine change in the family itself if it remained unchanged in constellation, for example, changes in marital relationships and ways in which children were related to in the family?

Our systematic information on these issues is limited, but *Table 12.12* indicates that the major changes that occurred were structural, that is some change in family arrangements which made for a safe

Table 12.12. Family change

Family change	No.	%
Worse—other children abused, abuse increased, suicide, mental illness	4	3
No change—could still be at risk, or more CSA	23	19
Structural change—e.g. perpetrator separated from child, mother protective	78	65
Structural change, and changes in family relationships, i.e., in marital, parental and parent–child relationships	6	5
Not applicable	6	5
Not known	3	3
Total	120	100

context for the child, or improved protectiveness on the part of the mother. Few families were rated as showing considerable relationship changes. When social workers were asked what they thought would make the most difference as far as prevention of abuse was concerned, they felt that practical family change would make the most difference. This seems to indicate that there may well be a degree of intractability seen within the patterns of the family which makes for difficulty in achieving more far-reaching changes with the therapeutic work offered. Alternatively, therapeutic work helped make it possible to create a protective context. It may well be that a family having to live with both legal and child-care interventions can only make a moderate degree of change as far as its own structure and organization is concerned. These issues clearly need further exploration, and the assessments described here are clinical and not tested for reliability.

In addition, it will be important to examine the sorts of family life that will be made by the young adults who are now living independently. Will they repeat patterns by choosing partners to compliment their own victimization or will they be able to create new patterns of relationships that are different from their own families? Our own impressions are that the devotion and commitment of families who believe their children, workers and alternative families in the community may well help to give a reasonable number of young people a different experience of parenting which, hopefully, they may well be able to use in future relationships.

References

1. CIBA Report (1984) *Sexual Abuse in the Family*. London: Tavistock.
2. Finkelhor D. (1984) *Child Sexual Abuse: New Theory and Research*. New York: Free Press.
3. Kroth J. V. (1979) *Child Sexual Abuse: Analysis of a Family Therapy Approach*. Springfield, Ill.: Thomas.
4. Soothill K. L. and Gibbons T. C. N. (1978) Recidivism of sexual offenders: a reappraisal. *British Journal of Criminology* **18**, 267–276.
5. Gibbons T. C. N. and Prince J. (1963) *Child Victims of Sex Offences*. London: Institute for the Study and Treatment of Delinquency.
6. De Francis V. (1969) *Protecting the Child Victims of Sex Crimes Committed by Adults*. Denver, Colorado: American Human Association. Children's Division.
7. Maisch H. (1972) *Incest*. New York: Stein and Day.
8. Giarretto H., Giarretto A. and Sgroi S. (1978) Co-ordinated community treatment of incest. In: Burgess A., Grath, A. and Holstron L. et al. (eds), *Sexual Assault of Children and Adolescents*. Lexington, Mass.: Lexington Books.
9. Sgroi S. M. (ed.) (1982) *Handbook of Clinical Intervention in Child Sexual Abuse*. Lexington, Mass.: Lexington Books.
10. Berliner L. and Stevens D. (1982) Clinical issues in child sexual abuse. In: Conte J. R. and Surpe D. (eds), *Social Work and Child Sexual Abuse*. New York: Hawarth.
11. Kilpatrick D. G., Veronen L. J. and Resick P. A. (1979) The aftermath of rape: recent empirical findings. *American Journal of Orthopsychiatry* **49**, 568–669.
12. Bender L. and Grugetti A. E. (1952) A follow up report on children who had atypical sexual experience. *American Journal of Orthopsychiatry*, **22**, 25.

13. Burton L. (1968) *Vulnerable Children*. London: Routledge & Kegan Paul.
14. Katan A. (1973) Children who were raped. *Psychoanalytic Study of the Child* **28**, 208.

Transcript of Interview with Sexually Abused Children

Marianne Tranter and Eileen Vizard

Jane, aged 5, was referred to a local Child Guidance Clinic for investigation of disturbed behaviour and bedwetting. The mother had told the GP that she thought Jane may have been sexually abused by her father.

Jane and her brother Anthony, aged 10, were both seen by the local psychiatrist and subsequently by a therapist experienced in working with sexually abused children, together with their social worker.

On that occasion the children settled to draw whilst we talked, and whilst establishing people's names and surnames Jane was reluctant to give her surname and her brother explained: "It's Jones but she wants to be Robertson, that is why she is confused."
The children knew that their surname was that of their real father, Anthony Jones, but that their mother, having remarried, was Mrs. Robertson. Anthony said he did not want his real dad to be his dad: "Because of what he did to Jane."

Initial contact with children and mother.

Spontaneous information volunteered by Anthony. Clarification of children's understanding of their parentage, etc.

First reference of father having done something to Jane.

I asked Jane if her brother knew why she wanted to be a Robertson and she thought he did and Anthony said: "Because of what dad did to Jane."

Anthony repeats it.

The children, although they did not know Mrs. Lowe previously, knew that her job

Clarification of the role of the social worker.

was to help children and she reminded them that she was a social worker. In clarifying the purpose of coming to the clinic Anthony suggested it was something to do with a statement, to write it down and go to court against their father. Jane thought similarly to her brother. I explained that we were going to be talking and drawing and then it would be time for them to go home. I suggested Mrs. Robertson and Jane went for a drink. I saw Anthony in the company of Mrs. Lowe.

> Therapist asks the children why they think they have come to the clinic and then explains what will happen.

> Children seen for individual assessment. Social worker present.

Individual interview with Anthony

I began by reminding Anthony that he had said something about his real dad, Anthony Jones, and not wanting him to be his real dad and I had wondered why. Anthony said:

> Therapist refers to something the child has already said and seeks further information.

"Well, two weeks before Christmas on a Sunday Jane was getting dressed and he was tickling her and he asked me to go and make some tea and so I went into the kitchen. I heard a noise in the front room and I looked and saw him moving his finger round Jane's private."

> Child gives spontaneous verbal account.

I asked "Did Jane have any clothes on?" Anthony said "Only her vest." With the anatomically correct dolls, choosing an adult male doll, I asked whether dad had clothes on. Anthony said: "Yes, his security clothes."

> Open question.

> Therapist uses dolls to assist child in giving description.

I asked "Was that something to do with his job?" Anthony said "Yes, he drives a van for his job." I asked "Did he have shirt and trousers on?" Anthony said "Trousers and jumper." I took a girl doll and asked: "What was Jane wearing?" and Anthony said "She had her vest on." I recapped "So you were in the kitchen and you heard, was it a scream?" Anthony nodded—"And Jane was bending down putting on her socks."

> Open question.

> Recap.

I asked "How was dad?" Anthony said "Near the TV." I asked "What was he doing?" Anthony said "Standing putting on his jumper."

I asked "and then what?" and Anthony said he saw his dad moving his finger around Jane's private. His dad had said "Be quiet" and had covered her mouth with his hand whilst he touched her private. Anthony said "Jane was screaming and I saw it and I felt horrible and went back to do the tea."

Child continues to describe what he has seen, in response to gentle, open-ended questions.

Child says how he felt.

He said "I saw him rubbing his willy round her private."

I asked "Did he have clothes on?" Anthony said "He pulled down his trousers and pants."

I asked "So you saw him?"

Anthony continued "Rubbing his willy on Jane's private."

Recap.

Anthony enacted this with the dolls showing how his father would place his hand over Jane's mouth whilst doing this.

Child shows the therapist what he saw.

I asked "What did dad's willy look like?" Anthony said "All fur and greyish and wrinkles and fattish and not that long."

I asked, looking at the male doll, "Was his willy hanging down or different?" Anthony indicated that the penis would be sticking up.

Therapist checking whether penis was erect or flaccid.

I asked "Was it soft or hard?" Anthony said "Soft, fat and lumpy."

I checked "and he put that near Jane's private where she does her wee?" Anthony said "Yes" and that they would be standing up and dad covering her mouth.

Recap.

I asked "and what was Jane doing?" and Anthony said "Screaming and trying to get away."

I asked "and then what?"

Anthony said "I felt all funny, and he turned Jane round, covered her mouth and put his finger in her bum, then I came in and he was doing up his trousers. Dad said 'You two sit down on the bed' and then he opened the drawer and had rude cards, men and ladies doing things and ladies putting willies in their mouths."

I asked Anthony "How did that make you

Child recounts how he felt seeing this.

feel?" Anthony said "All scarey. He tried
to do to me what he did to Jane but I
grabbed Jane and ran out into the garden
where there is a toilet and we locked
ourselves in for one to two hours. Then
we went upstairs. Jane was scared and
said "I'm going to the toilet" and then
Dad got a knife from the kitchen drawer
and put it to my throat and said "If you   Child describes the way in
tell what I've done you'll know about it."   which his father threatened
He held the knife across my neck."   him, and how that made him
I asked Anthony "How did that make you   feel.
feel?" and Anthony said "More scared."
I asked "and then?" Anthony said   Open question.
"He put the knife away and we went home,
we had to go on the bus and dad said
"I hope you remember what I said."
I asked "What do you think he meant,   Therapist checks child's
Anthony?" Anthony said "When he put   perception.
the knife across my throat and told
me not to tell."
I asked "So you had to keep it a secret?"
and Anthony said "Yes, until Jane was
talking to Mum about our Dad and she
was getting to the point of telling her
and then I came in and told. I couldn't   (Anthony kept the secret until
keep it a secret anymore. It was very   this point.)
upsetting. Jane would not sleep on her   He describes his own feelings
own. I sleep in there now and Jane sleeps   and Jane's reactions.
with Bryan, he is someone our mum looks
after because his mum can't cope with him."
I asked "When did you tell your mother,
was it before or after Christmas?" Anthony
said "It was after, in April." I asked
"So you had to keep it secret for quite a
few weeks. How did that make you feel?"
Anthony said "I was scared but I feel   Child relieved having disclosed
better now." I asked "What did your   the secret.
mother say?" He said "Mum was upset
and couldn't sleep." I asked "Did Jane
say anything to Mum?" and Anthony said
"Yes, Jane told me she was going to
tell Mum." I said "So you helped her.
You did the right thing. That was a very   Therapist reassures the child.
tough secret to have."

We told Anthony that he had been a good
brother for being able to tell quite clearly
what he had seen. Anthony told us that
Jane had told their mother that their Dad

had been doing it to her before without him knowing because she would sometimes go on her own to see him because he would come and get her.

I asked Anthony whether his dad had ever done anything similar to him. He said "No, he just tried to do what he did to Jane." I asked "What did dad try to do to you?" Anthony said "Grab me and pull down my trousers." I asked "What do you think he was going to do?" Anthony said "Bend me over and put his willy in my bottom." I asked Anthony how he knew that and he said "I could tell by the look on his face, it was the same as when he did it to Jane."
I asked "Did he ever try to do that to you before?" and Anthony said "No". I asked "How about when you were little?" and Anthony said "I don't know, I don't remember." I asked "Did he want you to touch his willy?" and Anthony said "No." I asked "Did dad ever touch his willy in front of you?" Anthony said "Yes, he pulled his trousers down and showed his willy and said 'I've got hairs round it', his willy was pointing downwards."
I asked "Did dad ever touch your willy?" and Anthony said "Yes, to wash it."
I asked if he touched it any other time and Anthony said "When I hurt my groin." I said "You mean to check whether or not you were hurt?" and he said "Yes". I asked "Has any other person done rude things to you?" and he said "No." I asked "What about your second dad?" He said "No, he never tried it, he made our lives better even though he had bills to pay he made it a good Christmas, made Jane and me happy." I asked "So he was kind was he?" and Anthony said "Yes, very kind."
I asked Anthony whether he ever dreamt about what had happened and he said "Yes quite a lot of dreams, about three times a week." I asked him what he dreamt about and he said "What I saw, then I could not get to sleep. I had the picture of it in my mind." I said "That must have been very scarey. Do you still dream

Open question section.

Child describes thinking he may be abused by father.

Therapist checks child's memory of any possible abuse in the past.

Spontaneous description by the child.

Therapist checks that the touching was in a 'normal' context.
Open question.

Therapist asks re child's response to what happened.

about it?" and he said "Not as much, not as scared as I was." Anthony said he did not like telling everyone about what had happened in case they passed it on and everyone would know and someone may tell his mother and then she may be upset. I told him I thought he was right to tell to stop something like this. Anthony added, "Yes, and I would not want it to happen to other children." He said he had been to a psychiatrist and had told her in the same way that he had told me about it. I told Anthony he had been very helpful in understanding what had happened. I asked him whether he knew other children did have similar things happen to them. Anthony said he had heard about this on the news but some of the children were dead so could not speak and not stop men who did this. I said "So you know some children are dead?" Anthony said "Yes, it is best to tell the police so he cannot do it to other children." We then concluded his interview.

Therapist reassures child.

Child mentions that he has told someone previously.

Demonstrates knowledge of phenomenon of abuse.

Demonstrates concept of social responsibility.

Individual assessment interview with Jane

I began by reminding Jane that when we had been talking previously with her brother he had said she wanted to be a Robertson and I wondered why he had said that. Jane initially could not remember and I continued that Anthony had said it was something to do with their first Dad and what he did to her, but again Jane could not remember. I asked Jane if she could remember what Anthony said their first Dad had done which was not nice but Jane made no response.

Therapist links to something which has already been said.

Jane appears to be 'blocking' memory of conversation which had taken place ¾ hour previously.

Taking the anatomical dolls, which we had dressed, we selected one to represent Jane, one to represent Anthony and one to represent Dad Jones and pursued the scene of Anthony's reference to her not wanting to be a Jones because of what their Dad did. I asked if she could tell me what it was and whether it was

Therapist uses dolls to assist her and refers again to what Anthony had said.

something not nice. I asked "Might he have done something that was not nice?" and Jane nodded.
I asked her "What does your brother know?" but Jane shook her head and denied that Anthony had seen. I asked again what it was that Dad Jones had done and was it something that hurt but Jane made no response. I repeated the question and asked whether it was something that scared her, but again she made no response. I asked if she could remember and she said "No." I asked if it was hard to say and I showed Jane the anatomically correct dolls. She was rather resistant to undressing the dolls so I helped her. I noted her word for vagina was 'private'. Looking at the girl doll Jane, I asked whether she thought her Dad Jones had hurt her and if she could point to the bit of herself on the doll which had got hurt. Jane pointed at the lower abdomen of the doll just above the vaginal region. She said she was pointing nearer to the tummy than the private. I asked if she could then point on the Dad doll (which Jane was resistant to undressing) whether there was a part of him that hurt her tummy and Jane pointed to the doll's hand and said "He scratched it." I asked "Sometimes did he scratch it near the private part?" and Jane said "Yes." I asked "Did he scratch it on the outside or inside?" and she said "the outside." I asked "Which bit of the hand did he touch it with?" and Jane indicated a finger. I asked if she could show with the dolls and she indicated the father doll's hand touching the vaginal area of the Jane doll. I asked "How would that feel?" and Jane said "Hurting." I asked "Would you want Dad to do that?" and she said "No." I asked "What would you say?" and Jane said "No." I asked "Why?" and Jane said "I don't want to." I asked "Where were you when this happened?" and Jane said "In his house." I asked "Which room?" and she said "Upstairs." I asked "Which room?" and she said "The second room." I asked "Was there anyone else there?" and she said "No, only me, my brother

Therapist makes tentative suggestion, given child's response to her father previously.
Open question.
Having previously indicated that her brother knew something, Jane now denies it.

Child frozen and unable to speak.

Therapist acknowledges child's difficulty and uses dolls to try to make it easier for her to speak.

Therapist asks Jane to point to where she may have been hurt.

(Resistance to undressing the dolls may be significant.)

Child responds and names part of father's body which hurt her.
Therapist checks for digital penetration.

Child is able to be quite precise and shows touching of her genital area.
Child identifies the *feelings* associated with experience, and her wish that Dad would not do it.
Open question re context of abuse.

Open question.
Child gives clear description.

and my Dad." I asked "What was Dad wearing?" and she said "Clothes" and I asked "and you?" and she said "Nightie."
I asked whether she had her knickers on or off and she said "On." I asked whether Dad would touch her with his hand on top of her knickers or underneath and she replied "Underneath." I asked "Was there another bit of Dad that he touched you on the private with?" and we undressed the father doll to look at him. She named the parts of the body and her word for penis was 'private' too. I said "Now we can see all of him can you see another bit that he would put near your private?" I reminded her that she had indicated he had put his finger there and asked "Was there anything bigger than a finger he would touch you with?" and Jane said "No." I asked "Was there a bit that would scare you?" and she said "No."

I asked Jane "*If* Dad touched you with something else, which bit of him might he touch you with?" but she did not know. I asked whether there was a bit that might be hard to remember and Jane said "No." I asked whether dad ever put his hand anywhere on the back of her and she said "No." I asked "Can you remember what hurt you most?" and Jane said "Hand." I asked "Was there something that hurt you more?" and she said "No." I asked "Which bit got hurt?" and Jane pointed to the 'private' of the Jane doll and named it. I asked "When that got hurt did you ever cry?" and Jane said "No." I asked "What did you do?" and Jane said "I ran to Lisa's." I asked if she shouted and she said "No." I asked if she thought her dad would think it was OK to shout if he would hurt her and she said "No." I asked "What would he say?" and Jane said he would say nothing. I asked "Would he ever try and stop you shouting?" and Jane said "Yes, he covers his hand over my mouth." She showed with the dolls how that would be. I checked "Did he do that when he hurt you so you could not shout? How did that make you

Open question.

Either/or question.

Either/or question.
Therapist checks for any other form of sexual contact.

Child denies further contact.

Hypothetical question to check validity of child's negative response (given Anthony's account).

Recap.
Child continues previous statement.
Therapist checks child's emotional response.

Open question.
Child volunteers further information.

Child identifies *feelings*

feel?" Jane said "Horrible." I asked "Would dad ever want to put his private near you?" and Jane said "Yes." I said "Could you show me, where would you be, which bit of you would he put his private near?" At this point Jane pointed to the vagina of the Jane doll. I asked "How would you be, lying down or standing up?" and Jane said "Lying down." I asked if she could show me with the dolls but she could not. I asked what sort of feeling that would be and she said "Scarey." I asked whether he would put his private on the outside or the inside of her private and she said "Outside." I asked if he would keep it still or move it and she said "Still." I asked "How did that feel?" and Jane said "Horrid." I asked if his private was hard or soft and she said "Soft." I asked if it was thin or fat and she said "Fat." I asked "How did that make your private feel?" and Jane said "Fizzy." I asked "What made it feel fizzy?" Jane pointed to the penis of the Daddy doll. I asked "What made it feel fizzy?" and Jane said "It feels wet, like when you drink some coke and it gets fizzy." I asked "What got wet?" Jane pointed to the vagina of the Jane doll. I asked "What made it wet?" Jane pointed to the penis of the father doll. I asked "What colour was that wet?" and Jane said "White." I repeated the question and she repeated the answer. I recapped "And it looked fizzy and it went here?" pointing to the vagina of the girl doll. I asked "What did you do, did someone wipe it?" and Jane said "Yes." I asked "Who?" and Jane said "Anne." I asked "Did dad try to put his private anywhere in the back of you?" and Jane said "No."

I pointed out that Jane's private, legs and feet were all below her tummy, and her chest and face were above, and wondered whether there was anywhere above that her Dad had put his private and Jane said "No." I asked if she could remind me where he put his private and she pointed to the doll's vagina. I asked

associated with the experience.
Direct question to check for other possible sexual contact.

Either/or question.

Child frozen and resistant to touching male doll.
Child describes feeling.
Either/or question.

Child describes feeling.
Either/or question.

Open question.
Child chooses own word to describe feeling.
Open question.
Therapist seeks clarification.
Child continues to use own words to describe (?) ejaculation.
Child seems clear that his penis made her vagina wet.

Child described the *colour* of emission.
Recap.

Therapist checks for any other abuse, e.g. anal contact.

Therapist explores possibility of oral genital contact.

Recap.

whether it hurt and she said "No." I asked "Did Dad ever want you to touch his private?" and Jane said "No." I recapped "But he touched your private" and Jane said "Yes." I asked "Did Anthony see that?" and Jane said "No." I said "Was it just when you were there?" and Jane said "Yes." I asked "How old were you when he first did that?" and she said "Five," I asked "Did he ever do anything when you were less than five?" and Jane said "No." I asked "Did he ever do anything rude to you when he lived at your house?" and Jane said "No." I asked "Did he say it was OK to talk about it?" and Jane said "No." I asked "What did he say?" Jane said "He said no, nothing else." I asked if he said she must not talk and Jane said "He said he would get his friends round to punch her mother and father up." I asked if she had to keep it a secret and Jane said yes. I asked "What sort of secret was it?" and Jane said "Special." I asked whether it was a nice kind of secret or a nasty one and Jane replied "Nasty." I asked "How did that make you feel?" and she said "Scared." I asked "Is it OK for Dad to do those things to you?" and Jane said "No."

Therapist checks for other forms of contact.

Therapist elicits factual information re context of abuse.

Therapist explores whether or not child was told to keep abuse secret.

Child describes her father's threat were she to divulge the abuse.

We asked Mrs. Lowe whether she thought it was OK for Jane's Dad to do those things to her and she said she thought not. We asked if Jane liked it and she said "No." I asked "Did Dad know you did not like it?" and Jane said "No." I said that he should have known better because he is grown up. I asked "Did he ever do anything to Anthony?" Jane said "Only put a knife to his neck. I was peeping through the door and I saw." I asked "Did Dad ever show you some pictures that were rude?" and Jane said "Yes, round his house." I asked "What was happening in them?" Jane said they were rude. I asked "Who was in them?" and Jane said "One grown up man and a little girl." I asked "What was happening in them?" but Jane did not know but said they were rude. I asked "Did they have clothes on?" and Jane said "Yes." I asked

Confirmation for the child that the abuse is wrong and that she was not to blame but the adult was responsible.

Jane confirms Anthony's statement.
Direct questioning following Anthony's statement.

Jane confirms it.

"Did you like the pictures?" and Jane
said "No." I asked "Did Dad do rude things
to you before or after he showed you the
pictures?" and Jane said "No." I asked
"Did mother believe you?" and Jane said
"Yes." I said I was glad and it was right
that mother believed her because girls
did not fib about these things. I also
said I thought she was right to tell other
grown-ups like ourselves to help make
sure her Dad did not do those things to
her again. I asked "Was there anyone
else who did anything rude to you?" and
Jane said "No." I asked "Who was the
only person?" and Jane pointed to the
father doll and said "Dad Jones."

Reassures that child is believed
and was right to tell re abuse.

Open question re other
possible abusers.
Open question.
Child confirms the name of
abuser.

Interpretation of interviews

Anthony was able to give a spontaneous and clear account of having
seen sexual activity between his father, Anthony Jones, and his sister
Jane whilst on visits to his father's house. He was clearly upset about
what he saw and had taken some protective action towards his sister.
He recounted with conviction how his father had held a knife to his
throat and threatened him should he ever tell about what he had seen.
This had clearly played on Anthony's mind and had been the subject of
subsequent nightmares.

Jane found it more difficult to talk spontaneously about her experiences but we were fairly peristent in our questioning given the clarity of
Anthony's account and in due course, Jane, as well as having indicated
digital contact between her father and herself, went on to describe
penile contact and quite spontaneously appears to have described
ejaculation, describing wetness or emission as being white and fizzy
(like Coca Cola). Both children also made mention of having seen
photographs depicting sexual acts.

The detailed account given by both these children of sexual activities, which have a high degree of consistency between them although
they were interviewed separately, is very suggestive of them having
been sexually abused, and the person they have named in connection
with this is their natural father.

The interview should be viewed alongside other factors, e.g. information about the children's behaviour and emotional state, any
medical signs and family factors, before assessment can be completed.

An Assessment Interview— The Cambell Family (Post-diagnosis)

Arnon Bentovim

The Cambell family was referred by the social worker and probation officer to assess what sort of ongoing therapeutic work was needed for the parents and for the girl of 12, Anne, who had been abused by her stepfather over a three-year-period. The family was a complex reconstituted family. Father had brought a daughter into the marriage, 14 at the time of referral, and mother brought Anne. Some 12 months previously there had been a breakdown between father's daughter and the family. With the help of the social services department she had been placed temporarily in a foster family. There were also three younger children of the current marriage, two had been born with serious metabolic conditions, necessitating a good deal of contact with the hospital, special diets being prescribed, and a family aide assisted mother in their care.

The abuse had been revealed by Anne to her mother, who had spoken to the social worker known through the fathers's daughter, thence to the social services department; they had in turn spoken to the police. Terry, the father, had been charged and was living separately in a probation hostel. He was spending the day in the family home to help look after the younger children. He was unemployed at the time of the referral. A probation officer had been appointed to help prepare a court report and the social worker and the probation officer had a number of meetings with Terry and Jean, the mother. Terry had made it clear that he was going to plead guilty to the offence. The court had given permission for the family assessment meeting, hoping that the ensuing reports would assist it to make a decision about an appropriate sentence to give Terry. There was agreement therefore that the parents and Anne would come to the meeting together with the probation officer, social worker and the family aide who had such an important role in supporting the parents with the younger children. It was decided at that stage not to see the younger children as they were all under five, and the older half-sister—Terry's daughter—was not invited as she was not living at home.

ESTABLISHING THE PURPOSE OF THE INTERVIEW

A helpful way of establishing the purpose of an interview is to ask each person what results they hope for from the interview. It is also often helpful to ask family members to say what they think the professionals really want to get from a meeting and try to distinguish between what family members think that professionals will ask in their presence, and what they think the professionals want to achieve. In doing this the parents may name really frightening issues, such as removal of the children from them forever. Once such disasters have been spoken about in this indirect way, the real possibilities can be discussed openly. The professionals can then be asked what their agenda is.

In the case of the Cambell family it was clear from preliminary discussions with the social worker and probation officer that there was an open and a reasonably good collaborative relationship between the professionals and the family and clear evidence of working together. Therefore, it could be hoped that it would be possible to have a straightforward open session about aims and objectives. The professionals were able to say that they wanted help in terms of formulating what work needed to be done with Anne and with the parents, and with the family as a whole.

A team of co-therapists met with the family together. A male and female team is often helpful in being able to link with all the members present, including both father and mother. It is often difficult for a woman to link with a male offender because of initial defensiveness and self-protection on the perpetrator's part. Similarly, it can be hard for a girl who has been abused to talk with a male therapist, although the presence of both men and women does give some sort of reassurance that it is possible to have non-abusive or threatening workers of both sexes and to have openness and sharing between the sexes. To establish a rule of openness it is important to have the family members and professionals present at the assessment. It is often very easy for an individual, a man, a woman or a child, to speak in great detail in a one-to-one situation, but far more difficult to speak in a group context. Therapeutic work has to find ways of speaking about the unspeakable, seeing the unseeable, and hearing the unhearable. Essentially the assessment marks the beginning of a therapeutic process which is to encourage openness and sharing, rather than closeness and maintenance of sameness. In the Cambell family there was a contrast between the parents. Jean, who had grown up in Australia, was somewhat taller than Terry. She had a somewhat harsh, masculine voice, tended to look in a fixed way without making eye contact and she sat next to Terry, who was sitting next to the social worker and then Anne. Terry was slighter in build, he talked in a softer more diffuse way. He had a mild handicap, one leg being shorter than the other from a childhood complaint. Anne, like her mother, was forthright, spoke clearly and was articulate. She had a concerned parental way of talking and it was easy for her to take a parental role in the family.

Dialogue
First therapist (male) to mother: "What do you hope to get out of this meeting?"
Jean:"To understand what has gone wrong and to do what we have to, so we can go on with the married life."
Therapist (to the father): "And what about you?"
Terry: "To understand why I did what I did, to get to the bottom of it."
Anne: "To know why dad did it—and to help him to be able to speak up properly so we can get together as a family sooner."

Comment
It was interesting to note that mother spoke about continuing the married life, the stepfather about understanding and the girl about being able to speak out. Issues of openness, the marriage and being responsible for oneself and one's actions are stated from the outset.

SPEAKING ABOUT THE SEXUAL ABUSE

It is essential that the sexual abuse is spoken about, in terms of the event itself, what happened, how long it went on for and what was its nature so that everybody knows what everybody else knows, both families and professionals. It may seem redundant to speak about what everybody in fact knows, and there are many families who wish to hide, push back events into secrecy and resist speaking with considerable vehemence and force. 'Why should we speak about it?', they might say, 'It's all over now, it's in the past, why bring it up now? You are bringing into the present what was in the past'.

In talking about sexual abuse, we are breaking the taboo of secrecy about sexuality from the outset, since treatment necessarily involves discussing sexual feelings and activities in various contexts. One way of doing this is not to talk about the event itself to begin with, but to track and trace exactly how it was that people came to know about the event, so that the interview would not focus so much on 'What did he do?', but, 'What did mum ask you about what he had done?'. The question might be 'What was in the police statement, how did she put it, what words would she or he use, what were the words she did use; what were the words that you have in your family to describe sexual parts, sexual activities'.

Discussion of the Sexual Abuse

Dialogue

First therapist (male): "I think it would be helpful at this point if we could begin to talk about what happened in the family that brought us here today. Your social worker in writing to us has been extremely careful not to give too much detail because of course this is a very highly confidential matter, so that I think it would be helpful for us to hear something about it."

Second therapist (female): "I think that your social worker has known you for quite a long time and one evening I gather that you, Jean, asked whether your social worker would come round and talk to you. Is that right?" (turning to mother). "We were wondering how did you first know that something had happened?"

Jean: "Anne told me."

Second therapist: "When was that, was it bedtime, teatime?"

Jean (turning to Anne): "It was at washing up time."

Anne nods in agreement and says in parallel with her mother: "At washing up time."

Jean: "She just said that her dad had been touching her up. I just enquired a bit more then it all came out. Terry wasn't there at the time, he'd just gone out for a quick drive in the car. I got a bit ratty with Anne and she told me then, didn't you?" (During this phase the mother was smiling, made eye contact with the therapists, eye contact with Terry who was making eye contact with Anne and there is an attempt at a light atmosphere, although covering a great deal of tension.)

Comment

The therapists started by tracking who said what to whom, and when it was said, rather than worrying too much at this stage about *what* was said.

Dialogue

Second therapist: "You were cross with her?"

Jean: "Oh, only temporarily, nothing serious."

Second therapist: "So Anne said wait a minute mum, this is what dad's been doing?"

Jean: "Yes, that's right, something like that."

First therapist turning to Anne: "What did you say to your mum exactly? Do you have special names in your family for parts of the body? What's the usual name for private parts, what about the penis, do you call it 'willie' or something like that?"

Anne (answering quite nervously): "Sometimes I call it bits and bobs."

First therapist: "I suppose it depends on what are the bobs and what are the bits." (Everybody laughed.)

First therapist (to Anne): "So what did you say?"

Anne: "I said to mum that dad touched me up" (and she agrees with the therapist that she thought her mum knew just what she meant).

First therapist: "What did your mum say to you, did she say what do you mean, what did she do?"

Anne: "No, she said 'What'! Then she told me to sit down and tell her about it."

Comments

The use of humour as a method of joining with all members of the family is a useful technique to use in a situation which is as fraught as this. The ability to be able to laugh about sexual matters, to be able to capitalize on the humour inherent in sexual jokes, is a powerful way of defusing anxieties and enabling people to find talking about such matters is *not* impossible.

In this description the therapists learn that once Anne has made her disclosures her mother immediately responded to her in a caring, believing, protective way.

After hearing further details of the abuse from the father and Anne, the therapist moved on to exploring why Anne had kept the secret.

Dialogue

Anne: "I really would have liked to have told my mum."

First therapist: "What stopped you, do you think?"

Anne: "The first time it happened I knew it was wrong but I did not know how to tell my mum. After that I could not tell her."

First therapist: "Why couldn't you?"

Anne: "Well, I was worried that the marriage was going to break up."

First therapist: "Did dad say to you this is something you should not talk about because there could be trouble, that sort of thing?"

Anne: "Well, one time when my mum was in hospital having a baby, dad said to me, don't tell mum, it will be the last straw."

First therapist (to father): "Do you think Anne realized what the consequences would be of speaking to police, social workers and so on?"

Terry: "I don't think she realized the full consequences of it, she knew about not upsetting her mum."

First therapist to Anne: "Is that right, did you know that the police might come in?"

Anne: "Well I knew it was wrong and that the police would come in if there was full intercourse, but if there wasn't full intercourse I didn't think the police would come in."

First therapist: "How did you know that the police might come in if there was full intercourse?"

Anne: "Well, on the news you hear things like that."

First therapist: "I wonder if you ever tried to say to dad I wish you would stop this, I don't like it, what do you think would have happened?"

Anne: "Well I did say that to dad once, please don't do it but he cried and said he was very sorry and he said he would not do it again."

First therapist: "But did he come back again?"

Anne nods and she and father make eye contact with each other.

Anne: "He did come back once or twice more after that."

First therapist to father: "Terry, what do you think made her decide that she was going to talk about it now rather than to continue to keep silent?"

Terry: "Well I think it was because Anne had seen quite a lot of rows, she had seen her mum dreadfully upset. There was something pretty wrong and there was something that I could not talk about, it was probably this."

First therapist (checks with mother): "Is that correct Jean?"

Jean: "Yes, I knew something was wrong, I could not put my finger on it, but I knew Terry was holding something back."

In this first part of the session the workers established that sexual abuse had occurred, and that the whole family saw it as the responsibility of the father. They also noticed an absence of scapegoating either of Anne or of Terry, and the openness and non-verbal contacts between the family illustrated some real warmth.

At this stage it was necessary to explore why a disclosure had occurred at the time it had. Perhaps Anne's self-sacrificial maintenance of silence was no longer serving a purpose. Her parents continued to be in conflict, and perhaps she needed to speak out as a way of getting others to deal with her parents, rather than having to cope alone.

To explore the family's response to the revelation of abuse it is helpful to ask the family what explanations they have for the fact that Terry, for instance, had found himself abusing his stepdaughter. In this case Terry's answer was to say that he was not quite sure what it was that started it, what he was feeling or thinking at that time. However, there were links with his childhood and non-communication in his marriage. He was about to say that everybody blames their parents when the therapists asked Jean if she could say what she has learnt from Terry about the connection between marital problems and personal experiences.

With some difficulty the mother then said that the way she understood it was that her husband could not speak to her, could not reach her, could not find a way of helping to heal her hurt and so tried to reach her through Anne. Jean also indicated that they had a problem of having inconclusive futile arguments. Terry grew up in a family where violent argument was banned as his mother had 'heart trouble'. He, therefore, backed away from argument with Jean, who was left frustrated and isolated as she had been in her own family. The children then came and helped by serving tea to them both.

Terry also said that when he was quite young an older cousin had tried something sexual on him. He then went on to say spontaneously that it was this fact the particularly horrified him—that he could do something to Anne which he so disliked having done to himself. He talked about having started work and somebody touching him up there, and this incident making him absolutely sick, and yet he could allow himself to do something like this to her. He showed some beginning of a feeling of remorse at this point, far more than during the earlier phase of the interview.

PROFESSIONAL WORKERS' CONTACT WITH THE COUPLE

The social worker who came to the session described the work that she and another female colleague had done with Jean and Terry. During these sessions Jean had been able to get extremely angry with both Terry and the social worker, while Terry burst into tears. The focus of the work was very much around how the family dealt with the problems of Terry's daughter who was placed outside the family because of behavioural difficulties. During this phase, the abusive contact with Anne was occurring, and she played the role of the 'good one', father's daughter the 'bad one'—all ways of avoiding mutual conflict between the parents which would have ended in disaster, it was feared. They reported that the situation was changing. Terry was now beginning to talk rather than bursting into tears or remaining silent. The secrecy system had seemed necessary to maintain the complimentariness of Jean's anger and Terry's distress.

The first therapist then asked Terry if he could give an example of something that indicated a change. Terry replied that since he had had to live away from the family, and had begun talking to his probation officer—a man—and his link-worker in the hostel, that he had begun to think about the role that he had been playing, perhaps going right back to his childhood. He felt that he had been taking the role of a peacemaker. His probation officer confirmed this, and added that perhaps Terry had been a sort of balance between his mother and his father. Terry added: 'It is only by seeing how I was with my family that I can see what I have been doing to Jean, and I can now take a more direct approach".

CONCLUSIONS

Understanding the Family

We thus saw that it was possible to see Terry's abuse of his stepdaughter as part of a family interactional pattern. It appeared to be a pattern which helped maintain an uneasy balance between the parents. The couple had a good many stresses to contend with, including their own children with metabolic problems needing hospitalizations and special dietary attention. Also, they have the difficulty of having their own children approaching adolescence in a reconstituted family. Each of the girls seemed to have their own unique role in relation to the long-standing pattern of parental differences, and fears of another marital breakdown. The cycle of mother's frustrated anger, father's inability to respond and the children's roles in comforting each of the parents and bringing them back together to begin the cycle all over again, is well described by the family.

As work with the family proceeded, other disasters would probably become evident, particularly connected with sexuality. These parents, through their own sexuality, had producd two of their three children with a metabolic condition, and one would certainly wonder about a deeply held notion that sexuality between adults was dangerous and that perhaps sexuality is less dangerous with a child. Factors from the father's family, such as possible avoidance of any emotions and sexuality between the parents because of some link with heart disease, and therefore again with death and disaster, are stressful experiences which would make sexuality dangerous.

Changes to be Achieved

Arising from these speculations and views of the family's processes and the meaning of their destructive actions is the question 'What change would need to be achieved to make for a family that could be functional and for a family that could be rehabilitated?' The distance between mother and daughter needed to be bridged and the marital situation to be rebalanced. The variety of fears and expectations which shaped the particular pattern of the parents' current interaction needed to be addressed. They needed to be able to take a far more equal role to each other, face the feared disaster of confrontation and anger without the use of children or professionals who were locked into the parental relationship as a way of avoiding the feared disaster. There needed to be resolution not only of the fact that one daughter had been abused, but also that another daughter had been excluded from the family.

Prognosis

In terms of categories of prognosis, this would seem to be a case with a hopeful prognosis. Terry took full responsibility and was accepting the necessity of living away, and pleading guilty in the court proceedings.

All family members have cooperated actively in the process of trying to sort out what could be done to create a change. Jean took responsibility for having dealt with family problems in an impatient way because of her own experiences. When Anne spoke to Jean she did then speak to social services. There was no obvious scapegoating, and there was a sense that everyone was putting the need of the family to get back together as primary. The presence of the younger children and their physical demands were an obvious spur, and there would be a risk of Anne's needs being ignored as she conveyed such an adult-coping ability. There was some acceptance and understanding of there having been long-standing patterns and problems which needed modification, and cooperation with professionals did seem to be reasonable. There was question of how much professionals were used to maintain family problems rather than necessarily resolve them.

Outcome

This was borne out in subsequent work with the family, as they attended for couples work. Terry was placed on probation rather than being imprisoned. Anne did come to a group and was a very articulate member. However, soon after her father returned to live in the family after about six or eight months' work, she made a suicidal attempt. She said that she thought her parents were beginning to row again. She felt hopeless and felt the whole thing had been a waste of time. She then lived separately from the family and began some individual counselling for herself, while work with the couple and family meetings continued until some more genuine change occurred between the parents in terms of their own ability to confront their differences.

Treatment Process—
Case Study of the Jones Family*

Arnon Bentovim

The process of work illustrated in this case study is a treatment team offering a joint assessment to a family with community agencies—social work and probation; treatment with the victim and ongoing consultation. The family was chaotic, high in conflict, with many problems, and family members had skills at organizing and drawing in many community agencies.

The daughter, Sharon, was 16 years old when the abuse came to light through her speaking to a teacher at school. The abuse, which had progressed to intercourse, had been occurring for three years approximately two to three times a week.

After matters had been disclosed, the father accepted responsibility, and was remanded in a bail hostel. During the adjournment for social enquiry reports, a referral was made to the sexual abuse team, and permission was given for a meeting of the family with the professionals.

THE FAMILY

This was a family with two very deprived parents; mother's own mother had died when she was quite small, and she was brought up by her father. Sharon's father had a very severe stepmother and frequent confrontations with his own father. The family was known to social

---

* This study is based on a paper 'Working with incest: an alternative to custody' by Jean Gadsby and by Ken Thompson with a comment by Arnon Bentovim (*Probation Journal* December, 1985, 143–145). Permission to quote from the original paper is gratefully acknowledged.

services because the mother was only barely managing to care for her four children. Support had been given by way of a family aide in an effort to model mothering for the mother. They were known to the probation service because in anger the father had thrown one of the babies into her cot and injured her. The family had therefore had a previous experience of a sanction, and support from the community.

SHARON

From the age of eight or so the eldest daughter felt herself responsible for keeping the family together. She felt that she had to keep the house clean and decorated, the children reprimanded and encouraged, and her father placated when angry. Mother, never having experienced mothering herself, saw this as quite appropriate and she went out to work.

A social worker new to the family became involved at the point when the incest had been exposed through Sharon speaking to a teacher at school. The father was away in a bail hostel, and Sharon was in care. The social worker referred the family to the child sexual abuse team. They were offered family interviews which Sharon and the social worker would join, and Sharon was offered a place in a group. Initially, while father was still living at the probation hostel, Sharon returned home. Meanwhile, the social worker and probation officer, who had been asked to complete a social enquiry report, decided to see the family together with the hospital team. This was not easy because the probation officer usually worked in a more traditional way with the offender, while the social worker did have some family therapy training. The probation officer felt it necessary to join the family interviews, in order to formulate a constructive treatment plan to incorporate in his social enquiry report.

All members of the family, both parents, Sharon, a younger sister Tracy (13) and brothers Darren (11) and Lee (9), were seen together with their social worker and probation officer. There were two therapists: a female therapist who had seen the family on the first occasion and was also the therapist for the group to which Sharon had been referred, also a male therapist who joined for this meeting. It was difficult for the therapist working with a young person in a group to be the sole therapist to the family, since it might well have been difficult for her to give an intervention which appeared to be at some variance with the work of the group and there could be a danger of alienating the young person. Sometimes it is necessary to take a different therapeutic direction strategically, and this is more easily taken by another therapist, allowing the young person's therapist to maintain an alliance with that person through the therapeutic process. The mother, in her late thirties, was a dumpy woman with a strong regional accent. She was brought up in the North of England, while the father, a large farm labourer, grew up in the South. Sharon was an attractive, tall, slim girl. Her younger sister who attended a school for children with learning difficulties looked more like her mother in appearance, while the two boys were slim. The mother's attitude and way of interacting gave an impression that she was one of the children, and there was a distinct impression that the father and Sharon were the parental couple.

The court hearing was in the next few days and this seemed the natural topic to explore with the family.

Dialogue
Mother: "I think the law is all wrong. They should go together."
First therapist (female): "How do you mean?"
Mother: "She was as guilty as her dad. She is older. If she was a child of eight or seven it would be different."
Second therapist (male) to the first therapist: "Has Mrs Jones said in previous meetings when she thinks the abuse began?"
First therapist: "We did talk about this last time. I don't know Mrs Jones whether you now think you knew when it did begin or not."
Mother: "I haven't got the foggiest" (one of the younger boys adds "idea").
First therapist: "Mrs Jones used to go to work in the evenings and this is when it used to occur." (Sharon is looking down at her hands, father is sitting back with his arms firmly folded.)
Second therapist: "If I was to ask now how old Sharon was when it began do you know what she would say?"
Sharon: "13 or 14 . . . 13."
Second therapist (to first therapist again): "Do you think that Mrs Jones would imagine that a girl of 13 or 14 would be as responsible as one of 16?"
First therapist: "I am not sure really."

Comment
Since the second therapist was new to the family, instead of 'taking over' in his way of questioning, he asked the initial questions of the first therapist since these matters may very well have been dealt with previously and a 'gossiping' technique can be a helpful way to talk about difficult areas indirectly. The whole family is listening in, but the technique of talking between the therapists prevents the family responding in its usual way.

Dialogue
Mother (interrupting): "Well, I do. She knows all about it, she's seen it on television."
Sharon: "I never saw the television."
Mother: "Well you told me Sharon that you'd seen it on the television."
Sharon: "What did I see on the television?"
Mother: "That thing that you've been doing, I wouldn't like to repeat."

Second therapist: "But what do you call it in your family, because you've got quite grown up children."

Mother: "Having sex with her dad—I didn't know anybody would have sex with their father. I didn't even know what the word meant, I didn't."

Second therapist: "If it had started when she was seven?"

Mother: "Then that would be wrong. She wouldn't know would she?"

Second therapist: "Would she deserve to be there with her father if she were 7?"

Mother: "No. I was there when she was 7, I was at home."

Second therapist: "What if she were 10?"

Mother: "She was a teenager, she was 13."

Second therapist: "And you think somebody of 13 would be responsible?"

Mother "Yes."

Second therapist: "Do you think the same as an adult or a little bit less or more?"

Mother: "Less, less than an adult."

Comment

At this point mother had perhaps reduced her attacking, angry response to Sharon compared to the earlier part of the session.

Dialogue

First therapist (picking up the theme of anger, addressed one of the boys and using a circular questioning mode asks): "Do you think your mum's more angry with Sharon or with your dad at the moment?"

Darren: "With both of them."

Mother (breaking in to his comment): "I am not angry with your dad."

Darren (responding to her): "I don't know."

Mother: "Of course I'm not, otherwise I would have left him wouldn't I?"

Second therapist (to father): "Do you know why it is that your wife isn't angry with you?"

Father: "I help her and I'm a good worker. The kids work with us. The kids understand the situation. From what I gather they don't want to lose me."

First therapist (to father): "We don't know whether you're going to have to go to prison or not, but say you did not have to go to prison, who do you think the family would choose to have, you in, or Sharon in, which way do you think they would choose?"

Father: "I don't know. I wouldn't want to influence them in any way."

First therapist: "But who do you think they would choose if you had to guess?"

Father: "Well, I think they would choose me. It's a solid foundation to bring them up as well. Because Sharon in two or three years time she's going to go off in any case."

Therapist (to Sharon): "What do you think?"

Sharon: "Yes, that's right."

Father and mother together; "Well, she doesn't want to come back in any case. We have given her the offer."

Father: "If I didn't go to prison I could get a four-bedroomed house, and there would be locks on every door. Everybody would abide by certain rules. All of us in agreement."

First therapist (to social worker): "Is that realistic? Would Sharon be able to decide to come home if there were locks on the doors?"

Social worker: "It would be Sharon's decision, but I do not think it would be influenced by locking doors. I've known the family for some time and they always leave their doors open, whether there are locks on them or not. It would be very difficult to imagine that they could become a very well regulated family."

First therapist: "So it's only going to affect the family very deeply if Mr Jones has to go to prison? If not things are going to go on exactly the same?"

Social worker (responding to first therapist): "Well at the moment it's very hard for Sharon to know what to do because she is really waiting to hear what the sentence will be."

Second therapist (to social worker): "Do you think that if her father did go to prison Sharon might think about going back home, or do you think even if she has the idea that everyone would be so cross with her that she would not wish to?"

Social worker: "I think she would probably get back into the same situation with her mother, that is to look after everybody and do all sorts of tasks for her, cooking, sewing and . . . ."

Father: "No she wouldn't. You're thinking the dead opposite to the way we're thinking."

Second therapist: "In what way?"

Father: "Well our general practitioner thinks if she came back home it would be a totally different situation. There would be house rules for all of us."

Second therapist: "But do you think that if you did have to go to prison Sharon would wish to return to the family, or would she just feel everybody would be so angry she could not bear to be there?"

Father: "It would make no difference to me. If I go inside my life is finished. I would commit suicide. Because when I came out I would lose everything. I wouldn't be able to fight for the little bit of home I've got at the moment."

Second therapist (to father, again using a circular modality of questioning): "What do you think the court would want to hear from you that would help them take a different line? For instance, instead of giving you a prison sentence, suspending a sentence or giving you a Probation Order?"

Father: "I'm not sure."

Second therapist: "But will the court expect you to say the same as your wife, or that you are more responsible, as you are the father?"

Father: "Well I would say we are equally responsible, otherwise it wouldn't have started in the first place."

Comment

In this family, both the parents were feeling that Sharon and father had an equal responsibility. He believed that locks would keep the situation in control. This is not really taking adult responsibility. Also, he is seeing quite clearly that the family would want him and not Sharon and that Sharon would be leaving the family in the next two to three years. Mother seemed to indicate along with the father that the relationship between the parents and the family was more important than the parental relationship with Sharon. Their notions of locked doors and organization are of course totally at variance with any experience of the family in the past.

After some further exploration of the issues the therapists withdrew and the family was given the following intervention.

INTERVENTION

Dialogue

Second therapist: "The thing which impressed me (and I am new to the situation so I see it afresh) is that, we see many families in our project and what impresses me is what a close family you are. In many families for instance, the wives would be in an absolute rage with their husbands."

Mother and father speaking simultaneously: Yes, that's right. I expected this. I expected to be thrown out."

Second therapist: "Many wives would have said to their husbands, I know that Sharon is lovely, but I'm supposed to be your wife. You could have told him just to get out." (Agreement nodding from members of the family.)

Second therapist: "But you know that the most important thing whatever happens, even if Mr Jones goes to prison, is that you have to stay together as parents to look after children. As you said Sharon will be going away in two to three years time. I mean in many families we would have seen mothers getting very close to their daughters, saying 'What on earth has this beast done to you, after all you were only 13 when all this began. After all, you would have said, you were only a child, of course you would be scared of him, of course you couldn't tell anybody.' But I think because of your love and care for the family you've been doing the exact reverse of that."

Mother: "You mean I haven't been showing this?"

Second therapist: "Yes, that's right. You've appeared to be hard with her. So you've been saying to Sharon you're the bad one, you're just the same as your husband. You might even find yourself going so far as to say you're more responsible than your husband, it's all your fault, it's all your responsibility. (To Sharon) And I think it's not the case that your mum really thinks that, I think she is trying to help you to grow up and to grow away from the family. You see your mum and your dad know that if something awful were to happen and your father were to go into prison that you'd want to help everybody, that you'd want to come into the house, that you'd want to wash up and do everything for them as you used to do. You might even find yourself literally throwing your life away in all that. I think your parents are making it easy for you to say 'Thank goodness I'm out of the family now'."

Mother: "Well I could have left home couldn't I? But I couldn't because my own father had heart trouble and I had to look after him after my mum had died. If my dad were alive today I would still be with him. I might have married somebody else at home."

First therapists (to Sharon): "You see I think this is what's happening, I think it's your parents' way of helping you grow up."

Mother: "It's still not the same without Sharon being there."

First therapist: "That's what everybody feels in their heart."

Second therapist: "But they just don't show it, and it's the same for you isn't it Mr Jones?"

This intervention, which gathered together the different elements of what the family had said, was an attempt to take what the family said and turn it into a positive reframing, and a positive connotation of the apparently negative and rejecting attitudes of the parents. It stated the couple were having to put their needs first, before the family, as a way of helping Sharon not to repeat what had happened in the family before in terms of her parental role. Hopefully this will block the family's attempt to tempt Sharon back into the family and to resume her role if father were to be away or if father were to receive a Probation Order. At the same time, hopefully, it also would maintain some sort of alliance between them, so that Sharon can see the parents as ambivalent rather than totally rejecting. Hopefully it would also reduce any possibility of her feeling intense guilt and responsibility, for she would have to do reparation by looking after the family and her father again. By naming the attitudes of anger with father and what her mother might do, it would give Sharon a view that she was not responsible, that it was due to the parents' inabilities rather than the realities of the situation.

This intervention together with other work did appear to help Sharon get placed in a foster family and enabled further work to go on between Sharon and the rest of the family following the court hearing and sentencing.

REPORTING TO THE COURT

Eventually the social enquiry report prescribed a plan based on sessions at Great Ormond Street—a Probation Order held by the probation officer, working alongside the social worker, with back-up from the child sexual abuse team. This was accepted by the judge as a matter of precedent rather than convention. The judge declared that he was satisfied that this was an offence against the family, and that it should be dealt with in a family way.

Had he not made a Probation Order the alternative was that Mr Jones would undoubtedly have been imprisoned for between two and seven years (the usual expectation for this type of offence—depending on the severity). Had this occurred it was believed that the family, which was already in disarray, would have totally disintegrated. Mother was threatening suicide; the elder son was contemplating running away. Tracey, Sharon's younger sister, was educationally subnormal and would have experienced profound difficulty in coping with a family in total distress. The youngest son Lee would have just become lost. Clearly father's presence was required at home to prevent all these possible occurrences, as well as to stem a tide of over-involvement by the neighbours.

The family all attended court, and during the hearing (while in the foyer) showed themselves to be under stress—the children shouting, clowning and kicking the weakest member, while mother remained uninvolved. The social worker, who had stayed with the family during the proceedings in court, felt, after this episode, that she could well understand why Sharon felt the need to try to take control.

WORKING WITH THE FAMILY

Following the court granting a Probation Order, the probation officer, social worker and the family have met once a fortnight at the probation office for one hour, and the leaders have attended Great Ormond Street about every six weeks for supervision. The family only failed to turn up once, when they heard that the probation officer was ill, and knew that the social worker did not have an Order for them to attend.

Meanwhile Sharon, now living in a community home, attended a group for female adolescent victims at Great Ormond Street. Father was offered a place in a group for fathers of incest victims by Great Ormond Street, but he refused. There was no joint parents' group available at that time which would have been more acceptable. Social services offered an adolescent group to the two older remaining children, and two hours of volunteer time to the girl who is slow learning; these were taken up. The social worker and probation officer decided on the following plan for work for themselves:

1. Interviews would take place in the probation office, as attendance would be easier to enforce there. Meetings were to be once fortnightly with the whole family.
2. Supervision of the workers would be by the Child Sexual Abuse Team at Great Ormond Street.
3. The social worker and probation officer would meet at lunchtime before the evening meeting, to work out a hypothesis and to catch up on the crises of the intervening fortnight.
4. Initially in the meetings the decision was that the social worker would take the lead, working mostly systematically, while the probation officer would work at not reassuring the family.
5. There would be a break of 10 minutes before the end of the meeting, when the leaders would withdraw to consider whether they wished to make a statement to the family.

During the family meetings, Sharon was gradually opening up in the children's home and becoming a more normal 16-year-old. The male staff, however, were finding her quite provocative. Her view of what had happened was that she had stopped her father getting into towering rages by placating him sexually and so protected the rest of the family, her mother included.

The issue for social services was whether they could leave Tracy, the other teenage daughter, in the family. The decision to leave Tracy was made because it was felt that she could not keep secrets, and they thought that she would let the workers know if there was cause for concern. She also was not in the same parental role as the girl who had been involved.

ANALYSING THE WORKERS' ROLE

In the initial sessions the workers aimed to assist the parents in taking control; for example, getting them to see that the children sat in their chairs, stopped them interrupting and playing up. As they joked, threatened, walked out and shouted each other down, the workers always asked the family for feedback on how each affected the other by their actions. They were particularly anxious to work at the mother–daughter relationship and to stop Sharon whenever she tried to take on mother's role. Sharon found this very frustrating.

In one session the family were asked to draw a family tree and every member of the family was involved. This led to the mother taking the boys up to Somerset House to try to trace their grandmother. On another occasion father was asked to help his son deal with people who bullied him. He said that he did not hit anyone while he was at work, but he took them outside to thump them, which was not exactly the sort of help being sought.

COPING WITH CRISES

Apart from the usual weekly crises of disputes with neighbours, schools or with each other, the problems were exacerbated by the housing department moving the family to a new area in order that their house could be modernized. The family were very pleased that they managed to carry out the move at very short notice with no apparent crises; however, they had not taken into account the effect on all the children, two of whom had to go to new schools. The parents thought that all they had to do was to go to the new school and say 'please have my son'.

It was at this stage that Darren came to the social services asking to come into care, saying that he was very afraid that he would really hurt his younger sister, perhaps a fear of identification with his own father. The workers were slow to accede to Darren's request, but he remained determined. Perhaps he could see that his elder sister was getting something better, and he felt that he should get a better chance too. He went to an assessment centre where he remained for six weeks. However, at the end of that time he was returned home, because it was felt that there was no more appropriate alternative to offer him, and that if he were taken into care it would further disrupt the family dynamics.

Sharon by now had moved to foster parents who had never fostered before, but who had had great experiences in bringing up their own six daughters and one son. They dealt with her in a very straightforward, no-nonsense way. The foster parents were very clear about discussing things together.

Sharon's early contacts with her parents took place at the family meetings, but when she started work she was no longer able to get to the meetings and on one occasion she engineered a meeting with her parents without her foster parents' permission. This led to an agreement to arrange contact with her parents. Her recent contacts with her mother have been by telephone and occasional visits home.

ON REFLECTION

A year later, both probation officer and social worker felt that there were some areas in which there had been very little influence on the family; it seemed unlikely the parents would be persuaded that the children should not be roaming wherever they liked in the town; it seemed unlikely that they would share the organization of their finances with each other; it seemed unlikely that they would ever stop having rows with their neighbours. However, the incest victim had been able to distance herself from the family and to experience a normal family life. The father was working for promotion in his work; mother's appearance had greatly improved, although she was still overweight; the children settled into their new schools. (The second daughter was not felt to be at any risk of abuse.)

All the family came regularly to meetings; they sat down and discussed the problems they saw and the workers were not bombarded with worries from school, housing authority, neighbours or police. Contact was reduced to once a month and sessions concentrated on the development of living skills. All the family were just a little better at looking at each other's needs and just a little better at supporting each other.

COMMENT

Sharon's spontaneous comment, that she stopped her father getting into towering rages by placating him sexually and so protecting the rest of the family, is a key statement in cases such as these. One sees that the family homeostasis, their togetherness, was helped by the way one of the children would take on the absent parental role, and a sexual role towards the other parent. In such a family one has to be very clear about the possible changes that can be achieved, given the level of dysfunction. Although workers may have been disappointed at the limited improvement, the facts were that for a family not to be constantly pulling in different agencies, as they had been previously, does represent some improvement.

It was helpful that both social worker and probation officer presented the judge with a clear view of the family, a clear therapeutic programme, and evidence of a coordinated plan between the agencies. The regularity of contact with this family was striking, and it would appear that the double hold through both the probation service and the social services was far more effective in motivating the family to attend than the social worker alone or the probation officer seeing one member of the family but not influencing the total system. Once the community agencies who have the relevant responsibility and statutory duty create a satisfactory working relationship, then the therapeutic work follows. In a sense all the family were on probation, and all the family were in care!

Detailed Group Programmes

Judy Hildebrand

Details of each group currently in the treatment programme:

> Goals
> Themes
> Activities
> Potential problems for group leaders
> References

In some instances, additional information is also provided.

This section should be of particular use to professionals wishing to establish groups.

CHILD SEXUAL ABUSE

LITTLE CHILDREN'S GROUP: AGES 3–6

Structure

Optimum no. 6–8
Co-therapists—male and female
Weekly meetings—1–1½ hours
6 Meetings
Refreshments

1. *Goals*
    i. to educate;
    ii. to teach self-protection; and
    iii. to inform on how to get help.

2. *Themes*
    i. Adults are always to blame in sexual abuse:
    (otherwise children tend to blame themselves).
    ii. What is appropriate/inappropriate touching:
    (to help children clarify the difference).
    iii. Which are private parts of the body:
    (to help children establish some discretion).
    iv. How to tell someone/get help/say 'no' to abuse:
    (in order to avoid the abuse).

3. *Activities*
    i. Direct teaching.
    ii. Group discussion.
    iii. Use of illustrations as basis for story-telling to teach preventative action.
    iv. Use of dolls to demonstrate 'public' and 'private' areas of the body and names for them.
    v. Use of role-play.
    vi. Making a film to emphasize appropriate responses to potential abusers.
    vii. Assertiveness training: children are taught how to give clear messages in response to inappropriate advances. This includes both *what* to say and *how* to say it; e.g., with a loud voice, look the person in the eye, stand straight.
    viii. Repetition, practice and reinforcement are used.

4. *Potential problem areas for group leaders*
    i. Given the age spread and difference in developmental achievement it can be difficult to involve the younger as well as the older members.
    Older children may contribute more verbally but can also be encouraged to help the younger ones. It might be more suitable to have a group for up to four and four- to six-year-olds.
    ii. Ensuring adequate balance of didactic and participatory involvement to achieve goals and avoid boredom.
    Whilst focussing on the story and picture, they are being taught appropriate responses and joining in the discussion.
    iii. Need to remember the need for variety of age-appropriate activities to sustain the interest of young children.
    They can't be expected to sit still or concentrate on one activity only in an hour.
    iv. Need for positive encouragement.
    v. Need to remember that group leaders are acting as models of grown-ups who *will* listen to the children. Clearly this

training may not be as effective with the children of determined reabusers or adults unwilling to take responsibility
for protecting children brave enough to speak out.

vi. Need to refer to good or bad *actions* of adults rather than
stereotyping the adults themselves as good or bad, given that
most perpetrators are members of the family circle.

References

Mrazek P. B. and Kempe C. H. (eds) (1981) Groupwork with young
children. In: *Sexually Abused Children and their Families*. Oxford:
Pergamon. Chap. 15, part IV.

Vizard E. (1986) *Self Esteem and Personal Safety*. London: Tavistock.
(A very full, step-by-step illustrated book and video-tape for
groupwork with young children.)

CHILD SEXUAL ABUSE
GROUPWORK FOR 7–10-YEAR-OLDS
Structure

Optimum no. 6–8
Co-therapists—male and female
Weekly meetings—1 hour
8–10 Meetings
Refreshments

Please refer to previous age-group for goals/themes/activities/problem
areas as well as the list given at the end of chapter.

Group leaders will naturally need to respond to the increased
intellectual and emotional sophistication of the group members in this
age bracket.

Private books are introduced at this stage, to encourage the less
articulate and withdrawn with an alternative form of communication.

This will both affect the pace of the work and require a less simpli-
fied use of language. Children will be encouraged and helped to
express their own views more and share experiences with each other.
Given their increased attention span they will need less physical
activities than the younger age-groups but still need active participation and variety.

They also enjoy role-play and the use of video. One group sang a
relevant song to the leader's guitar.

Potential problems:
1. These children will be aware of and possibly confused by the difference in what they learnt at home and the discrepant attitudes of the group leaders. Issues of loyalty need to be addressed, so it has to be repeated that it is people's behaviour which is 'bad', not the persons themselves.

2. They need to know if it is safe for them to disclose 'secrets' in the group; that is, will it create more difficulties for the family if they discuss secrets, or will the information not be shared with other grown-ups. Clearly, one cannot ignore what we learn but it is made clear why and when any information is to be shared.

3. They need to know how long the groups will last and what could happen afterwards if they have similar problems again.

References

see p. 302.

CHILD SEXUAL ABUSE
GROUPWORK FOR 10–14-YEAR-OLD GIRLS
Structure

Optimum no. 7–8
Co-therapists—male and female
Weekly meetings—1 hour
12–16 Meetings
Refreshments

(This group is helpfully divided into younger (10–12 years) and older (12–14 years) groups, but the approaches are similar and they are described together.)

1. *Goals*
    i. to increase self-esteem and self-confidence;
    ii. to locate 'blame' with perpetrator;
    iii. to inform child of possible options to cope with future risks; i.e., assertive style or response, who to tell, where to get help.

2. *Themes*
    i. Sharing of common experiences (in order to lessen isolation and guild).
   ii. Issues of low self-esteem.
  iii. Their right to say 'no' and to educate to avoid a recurrence of the abuse.

3. *Activities*
    i. Each group member in turn presents her *news*—often leading to points for general discussion.
   ii. Focus on one topic per week; e.g.:
       a. role-playing to practice complaining about inappropriate touching;
       b. watching video of TV programme on child sexual abuse as basis for discussion;
       c. education about bodies and how they function;
       d. sharing experiences of sexual abuse.
  iii. Each meeting ends with girls writing personal messages in their books which will be read by the group leaders and replied to before the next meeting.
   iv. Compliments—whereby each member says something nice about the person either side of them to boost their self-esteem: many of them are quite unused to being positively regarded and find it very hard to handle compliments.

4. *Potential problems for group leaders*
    i. How to incorporate and avoid scapegoating of group members intellectually unable to keep up with others. It may not always be an appropriate solution to put them with a lower age-group. It will be better to subdivide into 10–12-year-olds and 13–15-year-olds and minimize this likelihood.
   ii. Importance of keeping in contact with specific case manager responsible where there is a serious concern about the emotional state of a group member. One girl in a group was extremely depressed and a strong suicidal risk; it was an urgent matter to inform the responsible social worker and the team case manager.
  iii. Girls flirting with and competing for the attention of the male group leader.
   iv. The female co-leader could become an object of envy and scorn (like some mothers). Two female leaders would not provide a model of a concerned and capable man (father). Many of the girls are quite provocative in their dress and behaviour and, like others of their age, need firm rules.

The male leader needs to be very careful to avoid physical contact, since this could be open to misinterpretation.

Reference

Gottlieb and Dean (1981) The co-therapy relationship in group treatment of sexually mistreated adolescent girls. In: Mrazek P. B. and Kempe H. (eds), *Sexually Abused Children and their Families.* Oxford: Pergamon.

CHILD SEXUAL ABUSE
GROUPWORK FOR 15–16-YEAR-OLD GIRLS
Structure

Optimum no. 8
Co-therapists—male and female
Weekly meetings—1 hour
16–20 meetings
Refreshments

1. *Goals*
    i. To provide an opportunity for sexually abused girls to share their experiences and problems with peers.
    ii. To provide a therapeutic milieu once a week for such discussions and thus lessen the need to focus so much on the abuse at other times.
    iii. To help minimize the long-term negative effects of sexual abuse: a matter of concern in all the groups, but most likely to be discussed more fully here.

2. *Major themes*
    i. Low self-esteem—feelings of worthlessness, having been used, being made different, feeling dirty.
    ii. Their confusion about sexuality and concern about their own bodies, and about future sexual relationships.
    iii. Ambivalent feelings towards the perpetrators—love/hate, sympathy/anger, the breaking of trust, especially in connection with non-stranger abuse.
    iv. Ambivalent feelings towards mothers—anger because the girls felt they failed to protect their children, yet also a wish

to be close to them, triumph at being chosen as father's sexually favoured partner, but guilt at usurping the mother's role; confusion, guilt and resentment at being blamed for the abuse; and feeling both powerful and powerless.
v. Relationships with boyfriends and peers.
vi. Education about the facts of life, contraception and abortion.
vii. Emotional problems, resulting from being abused.
viii. Living arrangements—i.e., in care, with foster parents, at home with their family. This covers both their feelings and wishes and the practical issues.

3. *Activities in the group*
   i. Sharing, i.e., drinks/biscuits, group leaders' attention.
   ii. Talking on set themes: *a.* the group at large;
   b. in pairs.
   iii. Group exercise or game to name body parts and words for intercourse in their own colloquial language to overcome shyness and inhibition and find a shared language.
   iv. Learning to assert/defend/protect oneself from intrusive behaviour through discussion, repetition and the use of visual material—video, film and books.
   v. Education via visual material about sexual intercourse, conception, birth; also general discussion and information about contraception.
   vi. Discussions of how their abusive experience will affect their future.

4. *Potential problem for group leaders*
   i. Group resistance to sharing experiences.
   ii. Sometimes problems of control, that is girls can become very over-excited and be 'hard to contain'.
   iii. Projection of strong feelings from the girls on to the leaders —anger, resentment, sexual provocation.

5. *General points*
   i. Necessity for leaders to establish 'rules' for the meetings and maintain them; for example, no smoking and one person talking at a time.
   ii. Talking and structured games proved easier than group and role-play exercises.
   iii. Girls likely to be very curious and critical about the leaders.
   iv. Emotional problems may be of a very serious nature; for example, self-mutilation, suicide attempts, anorexia, pregnancy, promiscuity and drug-taking.

References

Berliner L. and MacQuivey K. (1982) A therapy group for female adolescent victims of sexual abuse. In: Rosenbaum M. A. (ed), *Varieties of Short-term Therapy Groups*. New York: MacGraw-Hill.

CHILD SEXUAL ABUSE

GROUPWORK FOR 12–14-YEAR-OLD BOYS

Structure

Optimum no. 6–8
Co-therapists—male and female (parental model)
Weekly meetings—1 hour
12 Meetings
Refreshments

1. *Goals*
    i. To provide weekly opportunity for boys to share experiences and problems related to sexual abuse.
    ii. To clarify confused feelings and ideas associated with the abuse.
    iii. To educate them in ways of preventing further risk situation.

2. *Major themes*
    i. How and why might an adult abuse a child?
    ii. Who is to blame for child sexual abuse?—always the adult.
    iii. Does a boy have a choice when an adult abuses him?
    iv. Feelings aroused by sexual abuse:
        a. towards perpetrators;
        b. towards other adults;
        c. towards making friends;
        d. towards the boy himself by his peer group.
    v. Fears for the future appear to be most strongly addressed in this group, especially becoming homosexual, abusing others, becoming promiscuous, and having problems in heterosexual relationships.
    Because of negative sexual attitudes towards homosexuality it is often difficult for confused boys to talk about it openly or positively.

3. *Activities*
    i. Getting to know each others' names and discussing their experiences.
    ii. News Game in turn to keep group aware of change in each boy's circumstances and helps them express present anxieties.
    iii. Use of personal books in which each group member writes privately each week and receives a reply from group leaders.
    iv. Ending with complimenting each other to boost self-esteem. Boys find this difficult as they see compliments as suggesting they might be homosexual.
    v. Specific themes are focused on each week, e.g., appropriate contact in families, being assertive, how to cope with sexual confrontation. Methods are—discussion and role-play.

4. *Potential problem areas for group leaders*
    i. Need to establish ground rules because of difficulties in maintaining control over very anxious or often over-excited boys:
        a. talk one at a time;
        b. no one leaves the room without leader's permission;
        c. no hitting out.
    ii. Difficulty of combining boys who have been perpetrators (as well as victims) of sexual abuse with those who have been victims only.
    Concern that some of the sexual activity reported by victim perpetrators could be abusive to other group members who are not perpetrators.

5. *General impression*
    Boys have mixed feelings about the groups, although meeting others and sharing their experiences without being rejected is considered helpful. It may be especially hard for boys to use this approach when at an age when they are being encouraged not to show feelings and 'be soft'.

References

Freeman-Lango R. E. (1986) The impact on sexual victims—males. *Child Abuse and Neglect* **10,** 411–414.

Nasjleti M. (1985) Suffering in silence: male incest victims. *Child Welfare* **LIX,** 260–275.

Pierce R. and Pierce L. H. (1985) The sexually abused child— a comparison of male–female victims. *Child Abuse and Neglect* **9,** 191–199.

CHILD SEXUAL ABUSE
MOTHER'S GROUP
Structure

Optimum no. 6 (if 1 therapist), 8 (if 2 therapists)
Group leaders—both female
Weekly meetings—1½ hours ideally
12 Meetings

1. *Goals*
   i. To share their experiences as parents of abused children.
   ii. To recognize and acknowledge how the marital relationship, family structure and organization may have contributed to sexual abuse.
   iii. To consider the nature of her own relationship with the abused child if the latter was unable to share this 'secret'.
   iv. To boost self-esteem, independence and assertiveness so that mothers take on an appropriate protective parenting role.
   v. To aid mothers to manage anger and ambivalent feelings towards the abused child, siblings and father/stepfather.
   vi. To further more open communication between mother and child and confirm the generational boundary between the two.
   vii. To encourage self-help.

2. *Major themes*
   i. The mother's sense of isolation and shame *vis-à-vis* the community.
   ii. Feelings of guilt, e.g.:
      a. Cohabitee violent yet mother lets him stay.
      b. Suspicion that something was wrong but she didn't confront the perpetrator.
      c. Failure to protect child.
   iii. Mother herself has been abused and had not previously disclosed it: effects in the past and present.
   iv. Fury versus men.
   v. Fury versus women who allow their husbands to return to the family often following prison sentences.
   vi. Difficulty in managing their child:
      a. Over-permissive as result of abuse.
      b. Punitive/rejecting because of abuse.
      c. Children 'won't listen'.
   vii. Increasing independence—i.e. most women had taken on financial responsibilities and were now making decisions and enjoying it!

    viii. Distress at the loss of their adult partner where their relationship had been 'good enough'; split loyalties to children and fathers/stepfathers.

3. *Activities*
   i. Initial introductions including telling their story about the sexual abuse. Expressing mixed feelings about group attendance.
   ii. Inviting mothers to draw up lists of issues to be covered during the life of the group. Leaders include theirs also if not covered.
   iii. Discussion.
   iv. Some role-play, but many mothers found it hard to imagine they were someone else, as they were so occupied with their own situation. It was most useful in looking at alternative ways to handle children—but no mother would role-play a perpetrator—possibly not wishing to because empathetic or fearing they would increase their own understanding of their part in the abuse.
   v. Coffee/tea/biscuits at the beginning of group to encourage sharing and our respect for their efforts to attend.
   vi. In one group, one member wanted to make notes of each meeting to remind us of main points at next meeting.
   vii. Task-setting/homework related to group discussion.
   viii. Video—to boost self-esteem—how they helped others.
   ix. Sculpting to demonstrate painful situations.
   x. Use of self-esteem questionnaires at the start and end of the group.

4. *Potential problems for the group leader*
   i. Individual needs frequently seem so great that it is hard for some mothers to heed other people's distress. Group leaders need to link individual *and* group themes.
   ii. The tendency to get drawn into an 'all women together' situation and avoid painful issues.
   iii. Difficulty for unsupported mothers to feel confident about the group ending. This highlighted the importance of liaison work with other professionals.
   iv. Envy of group leaders, their status, authority and apparent lack of problems.

5. *Variation in intensity*
   This is very often a very sad group, yet there is always the potential for some humour if the group leader is flexible enough to demonstrate sensitivity to a wide range of feelings.

THE STAGES IN GROUPWORK FOR MOTHERS OF SEXUALLY ABUSED CHILDREN

Stage	Objective	Content	Techniques used	General response

I. Creating the Environment	a. To establish safe context
	b. To ventilate intense feelings
	c. To share experiences and problems with peers
		Introductions
		  a. Staff
		  b. Others
		Hosting—welcome
		Refreshments
		Issues of confidentiality
		self-disclosures
		blaming others
			Self-esteem questionnaires acknowledging mixed feelings about group attendance
			List of aims drawn up
				Reluctant sharing followed by rapid relief and surprise at others' experiences of abuse
				Reduced anxiety
				Hostility towards perpetrator/professionals/child
				Shame—isolation
				Uncertainty about leaders being helpful/judgemental

II. Turbulence and Learning	a. Mothers to gain understanding of their role in abuse—linked with family dynamics and structure	Information about abuse Relationship with outside agencies Blaming self Discussion of individual	Task-setting—'homework' Intensificating and escalating use of humour Role-play Encouragement towards	Group cohesion Overt anger Increased self-awareness Guilt a. Mother allows

Phase	Objectives	Content	Techniques	Outcomes
	b. To give help with management of abused child	experiences in families of origin (mother's own abuse)	independence and assertion	partner to stay although violent
	c. To improve communication with professionals	Past difficulties in marital and sexual relationships	Acknowledgement of personal strengths	*b.* Mother allows partner to stay despite suspicion
		Relationships with children: emotional and management issues		*c.* Failure to protect child
				Expression of concern for others increases
				Awareness of increased anger/permissiveness towards abused child's management
				Distress at loss of partner
III. Consolidation and ending	*a.* To look ahead	Recap on what has been learnt/changed	Task-setting	Increased independence: coping well alone concern for others increased self-esteem sadness of ending
	b. To acknowledge what their own strengths are	Fears for the future	Role-play	Some personal contact continued beyond group life
	c. To prepare for group ending	Recognition of symptoms and ways to respond to prevent future abuse	Compliments	
			Coping strategies	

Reference

Hildebrand J. and Forbes C. (1987) Groupwork with mothers of sexually abused children. *British Journal of Social Work*, **17**, 285–304.

CHILD SEXUAL ABUSE
GROUPWORK FOR FATHERS
Structure

Optimum no. 8–10
Co-therapists—male
Weekly meetings—1 hour
10–15 meetings

1. *Purpose of groups*
   i. To further the process of fathers in taking responsibility for the sexual abuse; those fathers being 'further on' being helpful in encouraging others. Those men with group experience at special units such as Grendon can serve to induce others.
   ii. To consider common factors which lead to their sexual interest in children, namely:
      a. their experiences in their family of origin;
      b. their marital relationships.
   iii. To discuss ways of dealing with sexual feelings in the future.
   iv. Considering the use of violence and threats.
   v. Considering their need to communicate rather than act.
   vi. Attendance in a mens' group can also be seen as a precursor to attendance in a parents' group, where possible.

2. *Themes*
   i. Common experiences of violence, rejection, privation and sexual abuse in their own families of origin, in a context of secrecy.
   ii. Sexuality in media, TV, etc.
   iii. The negative attitudes of the professionals, particularly social workers, towards the fathers and families; the conflicts which arise between them.
   iv. How they choose partners. What can be expected from marriage, sex in marriage and current attitudes.
   v. Their experiences in prison; their treatment by officers and other prisoners; being special; the humiliation and pride; being on Rule 43 or 'toughing it out!.

3. *Activities*
   i. Having to 'tell story' to other fathers and new members.
   ii. Responses to TV programmes, media, etc.
   iii. Reporting 'what happened to you this week'—good things, bad things.

4. *Potential problem areas for group leaders*
   i. The 'old lags club' syndrome, breaking into 'prison' talk, anger with social workers, professionals, everyone else but themselves. 'Club' support against the world.
   ii. Difficulty in getting the fathers to challenge each other; occasionally one man will challenge the others' 'denial', but this is rare and generally an attack is mounted against social workers 'outside'; and they attempt to induct the group leaders into their world view!
   iii. Difficulty for group leaders to deal with their own anger and outrage at these men; yet a tendency to identify with them as *victims* in their own family, in prison, in society rather than facing them with *their* own abusive behaviour. It is hard to both like individuals and find their behaviour abhorrent.

5. *General points*
   Men's groups have a role especially when:
   a. they are living separately in institutions such as prison or a hostel;
   b. the family is doubtful about rehabilitation or where parents are in major conflict, or have decided to separate;
   c. the men want and need to work on their own attitudes. The group support is often experienced as helpful, meaningful and supportive. Generally, initially, most perpetrators require the pressure of mandatory attendance; they either feel they are already being pushed in prison or the groups have little to offer.

   It is essential that wherever possible the men move to a mixed group—they then have to face challenges from other wives as well as their own, and there is less likelihood of a 'men's club', or 'old lags' atmosphere—less 'male camaraderie' and they are forced to acknowledge the need for shared responsibility and care for their children. Changes in attitude, following on from joining the mixed group, is often quite startling.

CHILD SEXUAL ABUSE
PARENTS' GROUP
Structure

Optimum no. 12–16
Group leaders—male/female (plus 1 trainee)
Weekly meetings—1½ hours ideally
12 Meetings

1. *Goals and related themes*
   i. To help parents accept and share responsibility for sexual abuse.
   ii. To consider how the marital relationship and family organization may have contributed to the abuse.
   iii. To share experiences and help others in the group.
   iv. To focus on poor communication between family members.
   v. To deal with sexual issues.
   vi. To uncover incidence of parents' past experience of being sexually abused and consider how this might link with the present abuse.
   vii. To help face the future as intact families or face the family splitting up.
   viii. To ventilate feelings about agencies in order to improve the relationship between families and the professionals involved.

2. *Activities*
   i. Initial introductions combined with sharing of reasons for attendance.
   ii. Discussion in large and small groups.
   iii. At the first or second meeting parents raise the issues they wish to discuss.
   iv. Role-play to demonstrate interaction between mother–father, mother–daughter and family–professionals.
   v. Sculpting—used to emphasize feelings often difficult to articulate.
   vi. Each couple keeping the group up to date weekly with their news.
   vii. Doing genograms and explaining them to group—noting patterns through generations.
   viii. Setting 'homework' on related themes from the group—use of task-setting.
   ix. Group discussion on words for sexual organs and activity, couples privately disclosing what words they liked their partner to use. To encourage truthful communication between partners.

3. *Potential problems for group leaders*
   i. Need to include everyone in discussion.
   ii. It can be difficult to encourage interaction between group members and avoid acting as a 'switchboard' when it is essential to pursue a particular theme.
   iii. Mixing previous group members in a new group can prove both advantageous and difficult. While old members encourage the new to participate, demonstrating that change is possible, they tend also to become dominant, adopt a 'holier than thou' stance, and suggest alliances with the group leaders. Indeed the latter may well unintentionally prolong and reinforce their 'special' position.
   iv. Including anyone who has *not* acknowledged responsibility for abuse in a group can be extremely difficult to handle and lead to scapegoating of that person, or attack and undermining of the group.

4. *General points*
   i. Important to respect adults as such, their efforts to attend groups and the difficulties they are experiencing in the outside world.
   ii. Important to use humour and varity of intensity as appropriate to mood and theme—session on sexual vocabulary provided a hilarious 'ice-breaking' occasion.
   iii. With very large groups—exercises in small groups of four then feeding back to the large group helps people to get to know each other and feel more able to contribute.
   iv. Importance of generalizing issues and problems; i.e. not focusing too much on the individual perspective. Use group members to suggest alternative ways of coping with problems raised by individual couples.
   v. Sculpting is a very powerful technique to demonstrate how the couple saw their family situation before the abuse, how it is now and how they would like it to be.

Reference

Duhl F., Kantor L. and Duhl B. (1973) Learning space and action in family therapy: a primer of sculpture. In: Stock D. (ed.), *Techniques of Family Psychotherapy*. New York: Grune and Stratton.

CHILD SEXUAL ABUSE
CARE-TAKERS' GROUP
Structure

Optimum no. 6–8
Group leader—female
Weekly meetings—1 hour
6–15 weeks
Refreshments

We found it essential to provide a group for those foster parents, residential workers and others who brought the children to the groups.

1. They needed to be sure of the purpose of the children attending as well as the main themes the group would cover at each meeting.
2. The care-takers wanted an arena for expressing their own concerns about handling the children who might show anger, distress, withdrawal or excitement before and after the groups.
3. They also wanted specific guidance as to how to cope with quite sexualized behaviour.
4. Information requested about:
   a. Sexual abuse itself.
   b. The value of a group approach.

Problems for group leader
1. Ending is difficult as group members consider the number of meetings too short for them, and may be anxious about how they will cope with the child/family in the future. The group is a safe place for them to air their difficulties.
2. Difficulty in some groups which combine both professionals and parents.
3. Difficulty of consistent professional attendance due to leave rotas, residential shifts, etc.
4. It is not possible in the care-taker's group to adequately help parents who have themselves been sexually abused and want personal help.
5. When a male co-habitee brought a child along all the other group members were female and were very resentful of this 'intrusion' of a male although he was not a perpetrator.

General issues
1. We provided refreshments in acknowledgement of their efforts as a preliminary to the group.

2. If we require people to support the treatment of the children it is essential they are included in the early planning stages, and the practical issues such as travelling expenses and escorts are carefully organized.

The following issues are typical of those raised by members of the care-taker's group:

1. Melissa, aged 15, considers attendance at her own group a punishment as she is already receiving individual help locally.
2. How to cope with an abused child who tells everyone she meets what has happened to her.
3. Why should my child (client) be mixing with more sophisticated/worldly children?
4. Bringing children here makes it harder for us to manage them afterwards.
5. My foster child's therapist is dubious about her coming to a group because she believes she and the child are making progress that may be undone.
6. Why am I in a separate group from my (newly) adopted child? We talk about past events in our family and I want to know what she is experiencing in her group if I am going to keep communication open.

CHILD SEXUAL ABUSE : GROUP ACTIVITIES

Following is a list of ideas useful in several of the children's groups, making appropriate changes in content, pace, vocabulary and complexity to take account of the various developmental stages of the children.

In addition there is no doubt that food plays an extremely important part in all the groups. It can signal the beginning or end of a meeting; it gives the members an opportunity to receive something, to share with others, and 'to break the ice'. In the adult groups it afforded the opportunity to displace some negative feelings about the group leaders onto their admittedly poor tea-making skills and to demonstrate the group members' greater competence. A word of warning, however; it takes a wise group leader to know when to risk doughnuts, chocolate biscuits and crisps in a children's group.

Group activities
1. Describe your family through talk, drawing, family tree, etc.
2. Write down *all* the words you know for private parts of the body. (Papers then placed in a hat and everyone picks out one and reads it—this way no one has to own their words, it reduces embarrassment and guilt and provides amusement.)

3. Share something about your experience of sexual abuse.
4. Look at pictures of potentially dangerous abusive situations—discuss what is happening and what to do.
5. Discuss who you would tell if bad things happen and then practice role-playing telling a friend, mother, etc.
6. Practice role-playing telling friends why you have to go to groups, why you live in a foster family, etc.
7. Use books/dolls to explain reproduction and physiology.
8. Role-play fending off abusers including baby-sitters. Practice shouting for help.
9. Discuss what children of the same age-group might like to do together to see if this can be linked into group work.
10. Discussion of what constitutes 'good', 'bad' and 'icky' touching for a baby, five-year-old, 13-year-old and grown-up.
11. Sculpting family before and after disclosure of abuse to aid discussion and expression of feeling.
12. Use of film material.
13. Discussion of how group may have helped them, whether or not all parents/children always want to come.
14. Use of compliment game to boost self-esteem.
15. Use of personal books for older children with opportunity for private communication to and from child/therapist, e.g., where they will live.
16. Help children to bring good and bad news.
17. Use of Plasticine/anatomical dolls.
18. Trust games/exercises to encourage communications.

Index

Active meaning systems, 44
Adolescents,
    assessment of, 87
    running away, 70
    sexual activity of, 3, 193
    sexual development of, 5
    structured interviews with, 125
    effects of abuse on, 31
    signs and symptoms in, 69
Adoption, 238
    see also Substitute carers
Adults,
    effects of child abuse, 31
    rationalization of abuse, 8, 18
    responsibility of, 17, 62
    seduced by children, 62
Advertising, children in, 60
Alcohol abuse, 35, 71
Allegations,
    against residential staff, 246
    by family members, 75
    false, 97, 99
        by spouse, 75
Anorexia nervosa, 61, 70
Anus,
    damage to, 25, 26
    examination of, 79
    signs and symptoms in, 67
Assertion, as focus of groupwork, 230
Assessment of child abuse, 73–80
    in adolescence, 87
    confirmation of refutation, 77
    family context of allegation, 75
    of family for treatment, 153–181
        degree of scapegoating, 166
        evaluation of process and outcome,
            160
        evidence of hostility, 167
        focal approach, 154
        general family pattern, 173
        interview techniques, 158
        interviews, 155
        marital relationships in, 171
        mother–daughter relationship, 170

Assessment (*cont.*)
        position of victim, 169
        process of, 156
        professionals in, 157
        responsibility of the abuse, 161
        signs of warmth, 168
        when perpetrator denies abuse, 156
        see also under Treatment; Family
    interview, see Interview
    medical examination, see Medical
        examination
    need for information, 74
    of outcome of treatment, 174
    sequence of, 73
    status of concern, 73
    steps in, 76
Authority, hostility towards, 211

Behaviour,
    changes in, 208
    non-verbal,
        in assessment for treatment, 172
        observation of, 160
    over-sexualization, 69
    of victim, 29, 67, 68, 70
Buggery, legal definition, 144

Care, children in, 197
Care proceedings, 148
Case conferences, 132
Causation, family system view of, 41–58
Child sexual abuse,
    assessment of, see under Assessment
    basic issues, 16–39
    causation, see Causation
    concepts of, 10
    concern about, 1
    definitions, 1, 11, 16, 40, 61
    effects of, see Effects of sexual abuse
    factors contributing to, 35

Child sexual abuse (*cont.*)
  frequency of, 11
  historical aspects, 59, 60
  levels of, 10
  patterns of, 17, 18, 19
  physical abuse associated with, 71
  preconditions for, 32
  recognition and disclosure, *see*
    Recognition of abuse;
    Disclosure of abuse
  recurrence of, 265
  signs and symptoms, *see* Signs and
    symptoms
Child in court, 85, 92
  videotape evidence, 147, 150
  as witness, 146
Children,
  in advertising, 60
  communication with, 88
  giving consent to sexual activity, 6
  indecent photographs of, 145
  initiating sexual activity, 17
  in parental roles, 50, 53
  protection of, 256
  rights of, 9
  role play by, 233
  seducing adults, 62
  sexual activity of, 2, 3
  sexual development of, *see* Sexual
    development
  sexual feelings in, 184
  sexual impulses in, 63
  sexual knowledge of, 2
Children and Young Person's Act 1969,
  148
Children's Act 1980, 149
Chlamydia trachomatis, 64, 65
Cinderella syndrome, 27
Civil proceedings, 148
Colposcopy, 79, 80
Communication,
  encouragement of, 208
  in groupwork,
    language, 220
    genograms, 224
    private books, 221
    stories, 223
Confidentiality, 25
  in interview, 107
  therapist's responsibility, 42
Conflict, resolution by proxy, 141
Consent to sexual activity, 6
Contraception, 9
Court proceedings, 145
  child as witness, 85, 92, 146

Court proceedings (*cont.*)
  medical evidence, 146
  reporting to, 295
  test of evidence, 149
  use of leading questions, 101, 102
  videotape evidence, 147, 150
Criminal proceedings, 145, 146
Cultural patterns, 9

Denial of abuse, 46, 138
  as psychoanalytical concept, 139
Diagnosis of abuse, false-negative
    and false-positive, 100, 117
Disclosure of abuse, 76
  case reports, 134, 136
  by direct reporting, 134
  effects of, 55
  fear of, by victim, 111
  indirect presentation, 134
  in interview, 91
  legal context, 143
  management of, 130–152; *see also*
    under Treatment
  mother's attitude, 135
  professional's response, 137
  treatment following, 200
  ways of, 134
Divorce, 24, 173, 254
Dolls,
  behaviour of victim with, 96
  non-abused children's play with, 94
  use in interviews, 89, 108
    naming, 115
    reactions to, 109
    undressing and naming of parts, 113
Drug abuse, 34, 35

Eating disorders, 61, 69
Effects of sexual abuse, 18, 25, 255
  in adolescence, 31
  in adults, 31
  loss of self-esteem, 27
  physical, 25
  pregnancy, 26
  in preschool children, 31
  psychological, 26
  psychosomatic response, 28
  in relation to age and development, 31
  repetition of sexual activities, 28
  in school age children, 31
  sexual confusion of victim, 28

Emotional development, effect of
  abuse on, 31
Emotional problems of victims, 29, 30

Family,
  active meaning systems, 44
  assessment for treatment, 56, 153–181
    degree of scapegoating, 166
    doubtful outcome, 176
    evaluation of outcome, 160
    evidence of hostility, 167
    focal approach, 154
    general family pattern for, 173
    hopeless outcome, 179
    interviewing, 155
    interviewing techniques, 158
    marital relationships in, 171
    mother–daughter relationships, 170
    outcome of, 174
    position of victim, 169
    process of, 156
    professionals in, 157
    responsibility and, 161
    warmth in, 168
    when perpetrator accepts
      responsibility, 157
    when perpetrator denies abuse, 156
  breakdown of relationships, 24
  break-up of, 254
  building self-esteem, 194, 200
  change after treatment, 258, 265, 266
  changes in structure, 24, 252, 259
  characteristics of, 16
  children in parental roles in, 50, 53
  circumstances overcoming child's
    inhibitions, 34
  conflict-avoiding, 46, 173
    help for, 52
  conflict-regulating, 53
  confused roles in, 33
  consensus of abuse, 262
  contact with professional workers, 273
  in context of allegations, 75
  coping with crises, 297
  cycles of interaction in, 44
  description of, 23
  dimensions of life, 46
  disorganized, 43, 174
  effects of disclosure on, 55
  elements of interaction in, 43
  endogamic, 46
  exploration of history of, 186
  factors contributing to abuse in, 35

Family (cont.)
  father and daughter as couple, 51
  formulation of, 55
  generalities of life, 57
  hostility towards authority, 211
  issues to be examined, 56
  loss of self-esteem, 207
  mirroring, 139, 142
  modesty in, 5
  mothers as caretakers, 49
  number of victims in, 20
  occupational levels, 24
  overcoming inhibitions, 34
  patterns of relationships, 154
  permanent separation, 203
  potential for treatment, 56
  promiscuous pattern, 53
  recreation of abuse patterns, 45
  relating to substitute carers, 247
  recurrence of abuse patterns, 45
  reversal of patterns, 46
  secrecy about sexual matters, 190
  situation, 23
  social class of, 24, 25
  stability of, 24
  systems model of, 43
  taboos between members, 9
  theory and therapy, 153
  treatment of, see under Treatment
  understanding, 286
  using 'silencing', 139
  working with, 296
Family courts, need for, 150
Family Law Reform Act 1969, 149
Family systems view of causation, 41–58
Fantasy in interviewing, 89
Father and daughter as a couple, 51
Forensic evidence, 146
Foster parents, see Substitute carers
Frequency of abuse, 11

Gardnarella vaginalis, 64, 65
Gender identity, 2, 5
Genital damage, evidence of, 25, 61
Genograms, 224
Gonorrhoea, 64
Gross indecency, 144
Groupwork, 205–237
  adolescence, 218
  advantages of, 207
  aims, 300, 303, 305, 307, 309, 315
  assertion of, 230
  brag and compliment games, 225

Groupwork (*cont.*)
  building self-esteem in, 224
  care-takers, 219
  children's activities, 231, 318
  co-leadership, 213
  communication in,
    genograms, 224
    language, 220
    private books, 221
    stories, 223
  constitution and themes, 218, 219
  curative mechanisms, 214
  detailed programmes, 300–319
  education in self-protection in, 210
  establishing programme, 206
  fathers, 313
  goals of, 208, 209–211
  indirect questioning, 232
  issues arising in, 217
  issues of responsibility, 228
  keeping minutes, 226
  knowledge base, 214
  leaders, 236
  male–female issues in, 213
  model, 207
  mother–daughter relationships in, 229
  for mothers, 214, 219, 226, 229, 230,
      258, 309
    stages in, 311, 312
  parents, 219
  people's ambivalence towards, 216
  problems of leaders, 301, 303, 304,
      306, 308, 310, 314, 316, 317
  programmes, 300–319
    care-takers, 317
    establishment, 211
    7–10 year olds, 302
    10–14 year old girls, 303
    12–14 year old boys, 307
    15–16 year old girls, 305
    fathers, 313
    little children, 300
    mothers, 309
    parents, 315
  rationale, 206
  reasons for leaving, 234
  results of, 234, 255
  role-play in, 233
  rules, 216
  self-protection as focus of, 230
  shared feelings, 227
  style of leadership, 216
  substitute carers and, 250
  training leaders, 212
  with care-takers, 317

Groupwork (*cont.*)
  with perpetrators, 219
  young boys and girls, 218

Handicapped children, 71
Hospital, medical examination in, 80
Hostility,
  evidence of, 167
  to professional network, 178

Incest, 5, 16
  disclosure of, 69
  false allegations of, 98
  false retractions, 98
  legal aspects, 143
  pregnancy from, 70
  prevalence of, 12
  reoffenders, 253
Incest taboo, 9, 10
Indecent assault, 144, 145
Information, need for, 74, 99
Initiation rites, 6
Interactions in families, 43
Interviews, 77, 84–129
  of adolescents, 125
  aims of, 90
  approaches to, 92
  assessment for treatment, 158
  attitude of interviewer, 90
  bias of interviewer, 100
  boy victims, 127
  of children in care, 107
  clinical approach to, 86
  clinical example of, 123–124
  confidentiality in, 107
  developmental issues, 89
  disclosure during, 91
  effect of parent's presence, 106
  equipment needed, 108
  false allegations in, 97, 99
  false-negative and false-positive
      diagnoses, 100
  false retractions, 98
  fear of disclosure, 111
  free-play period, 112
  gender of interviewer, 128
  glove puppets in, 109, 110
  guide to practice, 105–129
  issue of fantasy, 89
  new approach to, 86
  of older children, 107

Interviews (*cont.*)
  practical procedures, 108
  questioning techniques, 118, 121, 167, 127
  range of questions, 93
  reassurance and relief, 120
  recapping, 120
  re-enactment of abuse, 177
  seeing child alone, 105
  siblings, 106
  sources of error, 97
  specific steps, 112
  therapist's response to, 124
  toys in, 108
  transcript of, 269–277
  types of touching described, 114
  use of dolls in, 89
    naming, 115
    reactions to, 109
    undressing and naming parts, 113
    victim's behaviour with, 96
  use of leading questions, 101, 102
  use of play, 88, 97
  who conducts it?, 92
  'winding down', 120
  working with anxious children, 116

Kiddie porn industry, 60

Latency period of sexual activity, 4
Legal context, 143

Management, 130–152
  case conferences, 132
  failures in, 85
  interagency co-operation in, 132
  professional network and, 130
Marital relationships,
  after treatment, 260
  role in assessment of treatment, 171
Masturbation, 185
  in adolescence, 6
  in children, 3
  compulsive, 66, 69
Medical evidence, 146
Medical examination, 77, 78–80, 133
  after disclosure, 134
  colposcopy in, 79, 80
  personnel, 78, 79
Modesty in family, 5

Mothers,
  accepting separation, 172
  assumption of responsibility, 164
  attitude towards disclosure, 135
  blaming, 168
  as care-takers, 49
  participation in abuse, 164
  rejection of, 51
Mother–daughter relationship, 170, 229

Neisseria gonorrhoeae, 64

Over-sexualization, 69

Parents,
  authority of, 196
  responsibility of, 196
Patterns of abuse, 17, 18, 19
Perpetrators,
  admitting responsibility, 229, 262
    assessment for treatment, 157
  age of, 23
  alcoholism in, 71
  beginning of abuse, 61
  blocking of sexual outlets, 33
  denial of abuse, 138
    assessment for treatment, 156
  with deviant sexual patterns, 198
  explanation of, 32
  factors contributing to action, 36
  factors in his family of origin, 36
  fate of, 261, 263
  helping to work with professional, 210
  internal inhibitions of, 34
  involvement of other individuals, 41
  known to victim, 22, 63
  motivation, 33
  preconditions of actions, 32
  punishment of, 151
  relationship to victim, 22
  reoffending, 253
  reproducing own abuse, 128
  response at follow-up, 263
  responsibility of, 62
  role in abuse, 32
  scapegoating, 167
  sex incidence, 23, 32
  social class, 25
  traumatic conditioning of, 33
Physical abuse with sexual abuse, 71

Place of Safety Orders, 148
Play,
  interpretation of, 97
  of non-abused children with dolls, 94
  sexualized, 95
  use in interview, 88
Police,
  investigations by, 145
  involvement of, 135
Pornography,
  children in, 60, 239
  effect on children, 95
Positive connotation, 188
Pregnancy, 26, 70
Prevalence of abuse, 11
Professionals,
  anger, distress and pain in, 141
  attitudes of, 139
  conflict of roles, 142
  contact with family, 286
  denial and, 139
  effect of intervention by, 253
  hostility to, 178
  mirroring of family pathology by,
    139, 142
  personal responses, 137, 141
  relationship with substitute carers, 248
  resolution of conflict by proxy, 141
  response to disclosure, 137
  working with family, 296
Prognosis of treatment, 56
Prostitution, 69, 145
Psychosomatic illness, 68
Puberty, sexual development at, 5
Punishment of offenders, 150, 151

Rape, 255
Recognition of abuse, 60–64
Residential homes,
  allegations against members of staff,
    246
  education of staff, 245
  relating to original families, 247
  sexual abuse in, 245
Responsibility,
  admission by perpetrators, 161, 229
  clarifying, 209
  as issue in groupwork, 228
  mother's assumption of, 164
  of parents, 196
Risk factors, 71
Role play, 209, 233

Scapegoating, 166–167, 285
School, abused child at, 131
School-age children, effects on, 31
Self-assertion, 194
Self damage, 69
Self-esteem, 194
  building, 200, 224
  loss of, 27, 99, 207
  questionnaires, 227, 234
Self-protection, as focus of groupwork,
  230
Sex incidence,
  of abused children, 12, 19
  of abusers, 32
  of siblings of victims, 20
Sex play, 3
Sexual abuse accommodation syndrome,
  27
Sexual activity,
  in adolescence, 3, 193
  of children, 2
    adult's responsibility, 17
    latency period, 4
  in residential homes, 245
  secrecy about, 59
  witness of, 3
Sexual development,
  adolescence, 5
  biological factors, 2
  children, 2
  puberty, 5
  stages, 29
  'testing out', 63
  views of, 6, 8
Sexual experience,
  age of, 7
  at various developmental stages, 29
Sexual feelings in children, 184
Sexual intercourse, unlawful, 144
Sexual knowledge, 2, 7
Sexual offences, legal definition, 143
Sexual Offences Act 1956, 143
Sexual relationships, regulatory
    function of, 54
Sexually transmitted diseases, 64, 68
Sexuality, 243, 244
Siblings,
  assessment of, 136
  fate of, 261
  sex of, 20
Signs and symptoms, 12, 61, 64–70
  alertness to, 130
  behavioural, 67
  five to twelve year olds, 68
  presentation of, 131

Signs and symptoms (*cont.*)
twelve to 18 year olds, 69
under five year olds, 67
Single parents, 72,
Social class of families, 24, 25
Step-parents as risk factor, 35, 72
Substitute carers, 238 253
developing style of contact, 241
family rules, 242, 243
groupwork and, 251
information needed by, 238
further disclosures and, 240
relating to original families, 247
relationship with professionals,
248, 249
risk of subsequent abuse, 243
victims making disclosures to, 240
Symptoms, *see* Signs and symptoms
Syphilis, 65

Taboos, 9, 190
Teenagers, *see* Adolescents
Television, violence on, 96
Therapist, responsibility of, 42
Touching, 114
Toys, use in interview, 108
Traumatic stress disorder, 26, 27, 98
Treatment, 25
aims of, 189, 252
analysis of worker's role, 297
assessment of family for, 153–181
degree of scapegoating, 166
evaluation of process and outcome,
160
evidence of hostility, 167
general family pattern and, 173
interviewing, 155
marital relationships in, 171
mother–daughter relationship, 170
position of victim, 169
process of, 156
professionals in, 157
responsibility and, 161
signs of warmth, 168
when perpetrator accepts
responsibility, 157
when perpetrator denies abuse, 156
assessment of outcome, 174
break-up of family and, 254
building self-esteem, 200, 224
case study of, 289–294
changes to be achieved, 287
characteristics of hopeful outcome, 174
children's response, 264

Treatment (*cont.*)
circular questioning in, 187
clarifying responsibility, 209
confidentiality and, 25, 42
contracts, use of, 183
courses completed, 257
curative mechanisms, 214
description of family after, 259
at disclosure, 200
discussion on sexuality, 192, 193
doubtful outcome, 176
educational approach, 184
effectiveness of Great Ormond Street
project, 256
effects of intervention, 252, 256
exploring family history, 186
exploring family of origin relations,
195, 199
family changes following, 259, 265, 266
during family separation, 200
fate of children after, 261
follow-up, 257
groupwork in, *see* Groupwork
hopeless outcome, 179
household consensus on abuse, 262
linked with care-taking, 249
linked with statutory processes, 151
methods and technique, 182–204
networking in, 189
neutrality, use of, 187
of perpetrators' deviant sexual
patterns, 198
positive connotation in, 188
potential for, 56
prognosis, 56
recurrence of abuse, 265
during rehabilitation period, 202
responsibility of therapist, 42, 43
results of, 252–268, 288, 289, 298
of rigid and enmeshed families, 196
role play in, 209
stages of, 200
structural techniques, 185
types offered, 257
understanding family, 283
of whole family, 41
working towards permanent
separation, 203
working with family, 293
Treatment orders, 151
Trichomonas vaginalis, 65

Unemployment, 35, 72
Urinary tract infection, 67

Vagina,
  foreign body insertion, 66
  trauma to, 25, 26
Victims,
  age of onset, 21
  assaulting other children, 69
  behavioural problems, 67, 68, 69, 70
  behaviour with dolls, 96
  building self-esteem, 194, 200
  case study of, 290
  characteristics of, 16
  commencement of abuse, 61
  conflicted and anxious, 116
  cross-examination of, 85, 92
  deleterious attitude towards, 84
  discussing past experiences, 240
  duration of abuse, 21
  effects on, 25, 26, 31, 255
  emotional cost to, 29, 30, 255
  fear of disclosure, 111
  frightened, 87
  interview with, see under Interview
  involvement with other individuals, 41
  loss of self-esteem, 27, 99
  number in the family, 20
  overcoming inhibitions, 34
  overcoming resistance of, 35
  over-sexualization, 69

Victims (cont.)
  physical effects on, 25
  protection for, 91, 92, 132, 133, 189,
    252, 256
  psychosomatic response of, 28, 68
  relationship to perpetrator, 22
  repetition of sexual activities, 28
  risk factors, 71
  scapegoating, 167
  self-blame, 167
  sex incidence, 12, 19
  sexual confusion of, 28
  sexualized approach of, 29, 110
  signs and symptoms, see Signs and
    symptoms
  transcript of interview with, 269
  traumatic stress disorder, 26
Videos,
  pornographic, 95, 96
  sex and violence on, 3
Videotape evidence, 147
Violence,
  in family, 35
  on television, 96
Vulvovaginitis, 64, 66

Wardship, 149